Daily
Life
in the
World
of
Charlemagne

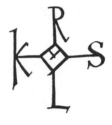

The Middle Ages
a
series
edited by
Edward Peters

Henry C. Lea Associate Professor of Medieval History
University of Pennsylvania

upp
University
of
Pennsylvania
Press

PIERRE RICHÉ

DAILY LIFE
IN THE
WORLD
OF
CHARLEMAGNE

WITH EXPANDED
FOOTNOTES

TRANSLATED, WITH AN
INTRODUCTION, BY
JO ANN MCNAMARA

Translated from Pierre Riché, *La Vie Quotidienne dans L'Empire Carolingien* (Paris: © Librairie Hachette, 1973), by arrangement with the publisher and author

Design by Tracy Baldwin

Library of Congress Cataloging in Publication Data

Riché, Pierre.
   Daily life in the world of Charlemagne.

   (The Middle Ages)
   Translation of La vie quotidienne dans l'Empire carolingien.
   Includes bibliographical references and index.
   1. France—Civilization—700-1000. I. Title. II Series.
DC33.2.R5413 944'.01 78-53330
ISBN 0-8122-1096-4

Printed in the United States of America

*Table
of
Contents*

In 732, Charles Martel defeated a Saracen army attempting to extend the power of Islam beyond the Pyrenees. His victory ensured that Frankland—the greater part of modern France and western Germany—would be transformed from an outpost of Mediterranean civilization to the center of a new Christian civilization. Twenty years later, the Roman Pope crossed the Alps to transfer the crown of Frankland from the fading Merovingian dynasty to Pepin, the son of Charles Martel. For roughly one hundred and fifty years, the new dynasty based its power on the theory that power should follow worth, not blood, and that the hierarchy of the Christian church should have a strong voice in defining worth and determining its possessor. Much was done in those years, and much was undone. On Christmas day, 800, in Rome, another Pope conferred yet another crown on Charlemagne, Pepin's greatest successor, and designated him Emperor of the Romans. Frankish rule extended beyond the core to the North Sea, beyond the Pyrenees into Spain, beyond the Alps into central Italy and far into the Germanic and Slavic forests of the east. A new world power had emerged, and succeeding years saw a cultural and economic resurgence which gave luster to the Carolingian achievement. But by 842, that power was broken. In a chaos of fratricidal strife, the competing nation states of early Europe were breaking the mold of Carolingian unity. While their leaders were thus engaged in internecine competition, the people were subjected to the persistent marauding of pirates from the north, who destroyed their prosperity and took many lives. Unable to sustain the power of his ancestors, the descendant of Charles in 911 conferred the duchy of Normandy on its Viking conqueror in exchange for his oath of homage. The Carolingian Empire—"the First Europe"—was at an end.*

As the historian Henri Pirenne perceived, early in our own century, the rise of the Carolingian Empire marked the end of the ancient world in Europe.† For the first time, an indigenous and non-Mediterranean civilization was be-

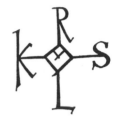

Translator's Preface

* To borrow the inspired title of C. Delisle Burns, *The First Europe*, London, 1948.
† Henri Pirenne, *Mohammed and Charlemagne*, New York, 1957.

ix

coming visible in the north. Knowing that great events cast their shadows before and behind, several generations of historians since Pirenne have devoted themselves to attacking, defending, amplifying, or correcting his theses with a view to determining the origins of later medieval institutions, social structures, and ideas as they sprang from the Carolingian world or its predecessor. This interest in long-term trends, valuable as it is, somewhat obscures the realities of the Carolingian world itself, as perceived by those men and women who lived in it. Thus the general reader for whom this book is principally intended and even the specialist will find unexpected pleasure and enlightenment in reading Pierre Riché's account of *Daily Life in the World of Charlemagne*. Here is a living society, given over not to theorizing about its place in the history of Europe but to the use, adaptation, invention, and abandonment of customs and institutions to serve immediate needs. The half-decayed features of an older world overlap, here in a particular moment in time, with the half-formed elements of the new.

As a contribution to the French publisher Hachette's extensive "Daily Life" series, this book was, from its inception, subject to the limitations imposed by the series. In his own Introduction, Riché has made modest excuses for his chronological boundaries. However, it is his close attention to the exact state of conditions at various points in the late eighth and through the ninth centuries that lends this book much of its fascination. Here is a world, theoretically shaped according to Christian principles, in which priests do not always know the formulae for performing the sacraments correctly. Here is an age in which much of Europe was still pagan and put forth militant resistance to conversion. Even in the heart of the Empire, participants in the great artistic resurgence of the period feared to express their impulses in sculpture because it might encourage a reversion to idolatry among the people. For the same reasons, bishops, who loved the bright murals on their own palace walls, doubted the propriety of even the most devotional art works in public churches.

This age, in which historians have subsequently detected evidence of the beginnings of new agricultural techniques which would allow for the eventual exploitation of

Europe's vast natural resources, looks rather different when viewed from the perspective of its own contemporaries. They saw a world of forest and wasteland, barely pierced in some areas by scattered villages and domains, where few peasants or even lords were rich enough or adventurous enough to take full advantage of the new discoveries. A lord might understand, for example, the advantages of marling (fertilizing fields with calcium-rich silt) but find himself hard put to make his tenants accept the added labor. The village smithy was a common enough sight, but it was a rare farmer who could substitute the more efficient but also more expensive iron implements for the wooden tools of his ancestors. That missionary was not being entirely facetious who told his flock that they would gain more prosperity from their old gods by turning their iron idols into ploughshares.

Full attention is given in this book to the growth of towns and the revival of commerce which meant so much to Pirenne and his followers as signaling the development of a bourgeois and capitalist Europe. But the reader is never allowed to forget the difficulties of transport or the danger from raiders and outlaws. And when the famous "Frisian cloth" arrived at its destination, the Emperor complained that it was too short to prevent his knees from freezing. Similarly, the broad changes in the social structure which marked the shift from the ancient to the medieval world are caught here in all the confusion of the ninth century. Though slavery was destined virtually to disappear in medieval Europe and though the conditions that resulted in that end have been traced to the ninth century, Riché's presentation shows us a rather different picture. As Carolingian writers noted, slavery was for them an increasing problem, not a declining phenomenon. Because of Charlemagne's conquests in the early part of the century, the number of slaves brought into European cities and offered for sale increased noticeably. At the end of the century, the unremitting activity of the Viking raiders resulted in the enslavement of growing numbers of Europeans. At another level, Riché depicts a Jewish population living under conditions markedly different from those found later in European society. They lived in this society with few of those restrictions which would later appear. Landowning Jews had Christian serfs. The freedom of social intercourse between Jews and Christians often enough led to the conversion of Christians, causing considerable anxiety among the anti-semitic minority of the ecclesiastical hierarchy.

Riché has also attended carefully to some of the false starts of the age—innovations which had no future in later ages. Drawing on his own extensive knowledge of the Carolingian intellectual milieu, he introduces us to such hopeful experiments as the development of a bilingual system in which the use of Latin was intended to parallel the development of the vernacular.* But the gap between Latin writers and Frankish speakers was never to be overcome. Even the Empire itself, in the form envisaged by its ninth-century supporters, was to have no future. The institutions and laws apparently designed by Charlemagne with a view to uniting his dominions broke down under his successors. A united Europe has, ever since, remained the impossible dream of the ruthless or the idealists among European statesmen. But the development of the famous feudal system which succeeded Charlemagne's rule is not traced here in the pattern of institutional investigation laid out by Ganshof and other scholars in our time.† Nor is this the kind of historical analysis of changing social relationships begun by Marc Bloch.** From contemporary sources, Riché has painted a vivid and deeply textured picture of the fear and insecurity which drove people, great and humble alike, to seek protection and sustenance from one another, from their stronger neighbors, and, in the last resort, from God and His saints.

Here are no dreaming rural idylls or vivid tapestries of a palace life of careless ease and high adventure. The pages of this book are peopled neither with the paladins who glitter in later medieval epics nor with "typical" peasants like Bodo and his wife in the pattern of Eileen Power's reconstruction.†† Short as it may have been in a history com-

---

* See P. Riché, *Education and Culture in the Barbarian West*, Columbia, South Carolina, 1976.
† F. L. Ganshof, *Feudalism*, New York, 1961.
** M. Bloch, *Feudal Society*, Chicago, 1961.
†† E. Power, *Medieval People*, New York, 1954.

prising many centuries, the Carolingian age absorbed the lives of several generations. Riché has not forgotten that to its people time went on and few days were typical. He has applied the techniques of modern social historians to the occurrence of birth, marriage, sickness, and death. Moreover, he reminds us that Carolingian castles and villages were outposts in a natural and human wilderness where nothing was more typical than the fierce struggle to live yet another day, another year, in spite of famine, disease, and violence.

The great events of political activity and military struggle were also a part of daily life for the people affected by them. Riché has re-read the sources familiar to students of the Carolingian period and mined them for evidence of this life. Thus he can show us peasants fulfilling their obligations, clerks writing out imperial orders, artisans building carts and making weapons, drunken soldiers hardly to be restrained from looting the Emperor's own cities—all those figures who contribute reality to the surface splendor of this age. Nor are the others neglected—the beggars, the dispossessed, the crippled, the fugitives, widows and orphans left behind in their progress.

In addition to the standard biographical, literary, and polemical sources, Riché has drawn upon the more unusual sources available from this age. Library catalogues, liturgical handbooks, manor censuses, and many other sources have contributed to this reconstruction of society. He has taken full advantages of the findings of archeologists and art historians and, of course, utilized his own extensive knowledge of schools and educators. The result is an imaginative book in the best sense of the word, wonderfully free of probabilistic phraseology. Rather than depending on what "could have been" or what people "must have thought" or what "surely resulted," he presents the facts recorded by Carolingians themselves. For example, the inventories of noble and ecclesiastical "treasures" tell us that they possessed quantities of gold, even though they preferred to shift to silver coinage. Catalogues from private libraries demonstrate that education was more widespread among the laity than is sometimes supposed. But other documents bring us up short on these generalizations. Education was a graduated phenomenon: Charlemagne and many like him could read but they could not write. At least one novice could read Latin but he could not tell his mentor what it meant.

Riché's reluctance to over-generalize is the foundation of this persuasive account of the diversity of the Empire. Nowhere in this book is it assumed that what was done in Italy was done also in Germany. Fashions in dress, like law and language, changed radically from one area of the Empire to another and from one class of people to another. Where one province could boast of a number of thriving schools, the next might have none. Though Charlemagne attempted to organize his own farms in a particularly regular, even bureaucratic pattern, the model cannot be extended to other domains. Nor does Riché assume that an order from the palace was always carried out in the field. In short, this is a book which has achieved a broad picture of an age through the technique of piecing together solid components of fact drawn precisely from the texts.

In making this translation, I have attempted to increase its appeal for the English-speaking reader by adding references to English translations of books mentioned in Riché's notes. Similarly, I have occasionally supplied notes to clarify terms which may not be familiar to the general reader. Consistency has been sacrificed to familiarity in the spelling of names of persons and places. Finally, I should like to take the opportunity provided by this Preface to make my thanks to a few of the people who have helped me in this pleasant work. Professor Riché himself read the manuscript, updated the footnotes, and saved me from more than one blunder, as have Professor Edward Peters and Robert Erwin on behalf of the University of Pennsylvania and its Press. For those that have escaped their attention, the responsibility naturally belongs to me. I should like also to thank Professor Suzanne Wemple for putting me in touch with Professor Riché. And at all times, I acknowledge a special debt of gratitude to Edmund Clingan, whose cheerful support and assistance have for many years enabled me to get through life without disaster.

Jo Ann McNamara

The risk of writing a history of daily life in the early Middle Ages must be carefully calculated. How can the ordinary life, in its habitual and humble aspects, be evoked from so scanty and disparate a collection of sources?* Although certain goods from Merovingian graves survive and are available to the historian, that cannot be said for the Carolingian period. At the same time, metal and ceramic objects, remnants of past lives which have resisted the ravages of time, are as yet poorly inventoried because archeologists have directed their most strenuous efforts to preceding periods. The frescoes and mosaics which decorated walls have almost entirely disappeared. Those which have survived provide only conventional religious scenes. Carolingian manuscripts are rich in miniatures, but they are not very useful for our study. Occasionally we can see in one a throne, in another the costumes of lay people, the fleeting image of a peasant or an artisan, but they leave us unsatisfied. Even the famous psalter of Utrecht, masterpiece of the school of Reims, which does present living scenes, sketches of town walls, palaces, animals, is of little assistance. Art historians have proven that the painter faithfully reproduced a manuscript of the late Empire without seeking, except in a few instances, inspiration from the realities of his own time.[1]

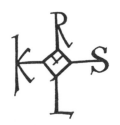

Written sources remain; happily they are not lacking. But here again we are dependent on the habits of educated men who leaned heavily on the books they used themselves. Carolingian writers, shut up in their work rooms, rarely looked out the window at the life around them. That reality, which was to them the shadow and symbol of another world, interested them little. Only the redactors of annals noted—alas, how dryly!—the events of their own times.

Despite the difficulties of the enterprise, the attempt to study the Carolingian world in terms other than wars, partitions, political and religious institutions is attractive.[2] All that, no doubt, was part of everyday life, but a re-reading of the texts gives them new clarity. Thus we have tried to outline the physical and human framework within which

* The translator's notes appear at the bottom of the pages to which they refer. The author's notes, citing sources used, appear at the end of the book, beginning on p. 293.

Carolingian man, from prince to slave, could live, to study the activities of the great and the humble, to perceive their material civilization, comprehend the Carolingian mentality and surprise the educated at their work. We shall also remind ourselves of the hardships of life and examine the manner in which Carolingians tried to cope with them. Some will think that we have devoted the better part to the aristocrats so that the commoners remain, as always, the silent majority. But our texts were written by educated men who were less careful to observe the people than to preach to them on the means to salvation. The *coloni* whose names are recorded in polyptichs, along with the dues they owed their masters, will always remain strangers to us. But perhaps we can lessen the gap with a new interrogation of the sources. New studies on alimentation, nutritional deficiencies, nausography—the study of sicknesses—may establish anthroponymic information and may also assist in clarifying inquiries on popular mentality, emotional patterns, the conception of time, dreams, etc. We are only at the edge of these new frontiers of historical research, and they are still badly charted.

Some readers will also think that our chronological limits are unsatisfactory. In truth, Carolingian civilization survived to the end of the Empire, continuing into the tenth century. The nations born of the partitions of those times felt themselves to be welded by the same destiny. In limiting the study to the period between the middle of the eighth to the end of the ninth century, we have followed standard practice, conformed to the guidelines for the series of which this book is a part, and, we must admit, taken advantage of the fact that the documentation for this epoch is richer than for the following period.

This work has been facilitated by monographs undertaken under my direction by students at the Universities of Rennes and Paris. I wish particularly to thank N. Baron, M.-F. Banchereau, G. Bansillon, J.-C. Berger, A.-M. Bolotte, B. Dusausoy, J.-L. Gacon, J. Guigue, S. Haquet, C. Labbé, Ph. Le Maître, J. Laurand, A. Pabou, G. Robert, C. Thiellet, J. Trevedy.

Pierre Riché

I

*The
Physical
and
Human
Setting*

The Carolingian Empire

Rerik
Hamburg
Verden
Osnabrück
Utrecht
Münster
Magdeburg
Gandersheim
Corvey
Dorestad
Essen
Erfurt
WENDS
Cologne
Hersfeld
Aix-la-Chapelle
St-Bertin
Nivelles
Liège
Fulda
Hallstatt
Quentovic
Arras
St-Amand
Stavelot
St-Riquier
Lobbes
Prüm
Mainz
Wurzburg
St-Wandrille
Amiens
Echternach
Corbie
Jumièges
Laon
St-Maximin
Trier
Worms
Rouen
Reims
Lorsch
St-Denis
Hautvilliers
Mettlach
Regensburg
MORAVIA
Paris
Metz
Meaux
Verdun
Strasbourg
Freising
Ferrières
Troyes
Augsburg
Le Mans
Sens
Langres
Mondsee
Redon
Rennes
Orléans
Murbach
Salzburg
St-Calais
Germigny-des-Prés
Auxerre
Luxeuil
Constance
Reichenau
Angers
Tours
St-Benoît
Flavigny
Nantes
Marmoutier
-sur-Loire
Besançon
St-Gall
St-Philibert
Noirmoutier
St-Martin
Dijon
Chur
de Grand-Lieu
Poitiers
Bourges
Nevers
Autun
St-Hilaire
St-Maixent
Lyon
St-Maurice
Müstair
Cividale
Limoges
Solignac
St-Yrieix
Aosta
Monza
Milan
AVARS
Bordeaux
Périgueux
Vienne
Pavia
Piacenza
Venice
Bobbio
Bologna
Ravenna
Lucca
Florence
Auch
Toulouse
Arles
Avignon
Gellon
Aniane
Narbonne
Spoleto
EMIRATE
Farfa
OF CORDOVA
Barcelona
Rome
Monte Cassino
ASTURIAS
Bari

The Carolingian Empire of the West
■ Archbishoprics
● Bishoprics
▲ Abbeys
···· Roads

0   100   200   300   400
kilometers

The Carolingian world can be envisaged readily enough by the twentieth century historian: a vast empire covering nearly nine million square kilometers, stretching over fifteen hundred kilometers north to south, from Hamburg to Barcelona, and over twelve hundred kilometers east to west, from Osnabruck to Nantes. This empire was divided into great territorial units entrusted to kings, prefects, and marquises. Some of these principalities were further divided into roughly two hundred to two hundred and fifty counties. But all of this, which seems clear enough to us, was by no means so clear to the Carolingians. They were each confined to their own social units, each to his own *patria*. The peasant saw no further than the limits of the domain he cultivated. The monk generally knew nothing but his monastery and its annexes. The clerk passed his life in the entourage of the bishop who ran his own diocese. And so forth. Nevertheless the literate Carolingian, who strove to look beyond the boundaries of his own *canton* and who had the luck to travel through different regions of the West, might have achieved a broader vision of the space in which he lived.

Carolingian Geography

For their limited geographical knowledge, Carolingians were dependent on the legacy of late antiquity. A survey of the catalogues of monastic libraries chiefly yields the names of Roman geographers: Julius Honorius, Solinus, Pliny the Elder, Marcianus Capella, Orosius, Isidore of Seville, or perhaps the "Geographer of Ravenna." The authors of geographical treatises of the Carolingian period, such as Virgil of Salzburg (writing under the name of Aethicus Ister) or Dicuil, author of a book on "The Measurement of the Earth," depended on these classics. To be sure, these two writers, both natives of Ireland, attempted to surpass their predecessors in geographical inquiry. Virgil even devised a theory of the existence of the Antipodes which seems audacious, almost to the point of heresy. But neither the one nor the other was able to extend his knowledge very far.[1]

Some Carolingians were able to perceive the contours of the known world from maps (*mappae mundi*) based on traditional geographical premises. In the middle of the eighth

3

century, Pope Zacharius had an annotated wall map drawn up in the Lateran palace. There was a similar map in the scriptorium of Saint-Riquier, and Bishop Theodulf had one placed in the refectory of the episcopal palace of Orleans "to nourish the spirits of his table companions by enabling them to become familiar with the immense universe under a reduced form." If, as is likely, Theodulf's map has been conserved in a manuscript of Ripoll, we can see that it represented the ocean surrounding an earth divided into five zones: an impassable torrid zone flanked on each side by temperate and glacial zones.[2]

Other *mappae mundi* were drawn on parchment. Generally they depict the world as a flat disc divided into three continents: Asia, Africa, and Europe, separated by the great rivers Tanais and Nile as well as the Mediterranean. Countries and towns were sited in each section, with Jerusalem at the center of the world and the terrestrial paradise to the east. A map found in the manuscripts of Beatus de Liebana's *Commentary on the Apocalypse* (787) adds an unknown southern continent to the other three.[3]

Confining ourselves to Europe, we can sometimes find mention of the principal lands: *Alamnia, Dacia, Germania, Saxonia, Fresia* (Frisia), *Grecia, Gallia, Italia,* and even *Britania* and *Scotia.* But any attempt to clarify these definitions or to discover what "Gallia" meant to the Carolingians requires recourse to antique descriptions. Thus, when the Bishop of Meaux, Hildegarius, described Gaul in the *Life of Saint Faro,* he repeated that it was bounded by the Alps, the Ocean, the Pyrenees, and the Rhine; that it was divided into seventeen provinces of which Belgic Gaul and Lyonnaise Gaul "still speak Celtic and which today are called Burgundy."[4] The latter remark was his only attempt to up-date the descriptions of Orosius or Isidore.

The Carolingians did, however, need more precise documents for military expeditions, for voyages, and for territorial partitions. Thus they arranged basic lists of names in *Itineraria,* antique road maps, the most famous of which are the "Table of Peutinger" and the *Notitia Galliarum* given to Charlemagne by Pope Hadrian along with a few up-dated accounts. Thus, at the end of the ninth century, a Bavarian clerk redacted a *Description of the Cities and Regions Situated to the North of the Danube,* in which he enumerated the Slavic peoples as far as the Vistula. About the same time, the Anglo-Saxon King Alfred ordered a description of Nordic lands to be taken from travelers' tales.[5] Other documents of this type may well have existed, but, unhappily, they have not come down to us.

The Frontier Peoples

In the absence of geographical treatises, we must turn to the chronicles to see how the Carolingians imagined the western world and the diverse peoples whom they encountered there. They spoke with fear and mistrust of the men living beyond the confines of the Empire. The Slavs, whom they found beyond the Elbe, seemed to them worthy of no other condition than slavery. Indeed they derived the word slave directly from *slavus*. When friends asked a returning warrior what he thought of the land of the Wends, he answered: "What do those little frogs matter to me? I could carry seven, eight, or even nine of them about strung up on my lance muttering I don't know what! It is a shame that our lord king and we should weary ourselves against such worms."[6] The relationship which some writers found between the names *Wends* and *Vandals* is equally significant.

They confused the Avars, who had been settled in the Danube basin since the seventh century, with the Huns and the Scythians. Adalbert, who had followed Duke Gerold there, described the Avar empire to Notker of Saint-Gall as a succession of nine concentric circles of the distance from Constance to Zurich, the last of which enclosed the booty which Charlemagne had seized.[7] Missionaries dispatched to convert this "irrational and unlettered people"—in the words of a council—received detailed instructions from Paulinus of Aquilea and Arn of Salzburg.[8] The chronicler also took notice of the Hungarians whose invasion compromised the initial results of the conversion. They passed for cousins of the Huns and Avars.[9]

Passing to the western boundaries of the Empire, we find another people who were feared and mistrusted, the Bretons.

This perfidious and insolent nation has ever been rebellious and barren of decent sentiments. Traitors to the faith, they are no longer Christian save in name, for of works, worship, religion, there is no trace. They have regard neither for children nor widows nor for churches. Brothers and sisters share the same bed. Brother takes the wife of brother. All live in crime and incest. They inhabit the forest and make their beds in the thickets. They live by rapine, like wild beasts.[10]

Thus Count Lambert expressed himself through the pen of Ermold the Black. The facile etymology of the Carolingians naturally derived the name of Breton from the stem *brutti*.

Similarly, to them, all Scandinavians were "the men of the north" (*Normanni*), that same north which was the domain of darkness, hence of the Devil. Before the great wave of invasions, they were known to the Carolingians as merchants and pirates, the two being commonly linked. But they were also neighbors with whom they could communicate. The chronicler of the *Royal Annals* was familiar with the domestic difficulties of Denmark.[11] However, from the mid-ninth century on, clerks, the chief victims of the invasions, could hardly find enough epithets to denounce the new barbarians whom God had sent into the Empire "because of the sins of the people and the iniquities of pastors and great men."

Francia

Turning our attention to the interior of the Empire, can we discern a coherent whole, a single community to which each individual could feel himself joined? A reading of the witnesses of the epoch compels us to doubt it. The Empire was formed of four great ensembles, each with a distinct personality: Francia, Germany, Aquitaine, and Italy. Francia was the center of the Empire, containing the palace, royal fiscs, and the great abbeys. After much strife, the sons of Louis the Pious ended by dividing this historic territory. Charles obtained western Francia from north of the Loire to the Meuse and the Scheldt, with Frankish Burgundy tacked on. Lothair held middle Francia from the Meuse to the Rhine, the future Lotharingia. Louis, called "the German," ruled eastern Francia whose principal axis was the valley of the Main, which sometimes retained the ancient name of Aus-

The Physical and Human Setting

trasia.[12] The Franks who occupied these three territories felt that they shared the same destiny and the same proud history, proclaimed by the prologue of the Salic Law redacted in the eighth century:

> Illustrious race of the Franks, instituted by God himself, courageous in war, in peace constant . . . , of noble stature, brilliant whiteness of skin, exceptional beauty, daring, swift and hardy, converted to the Catholic faith free of all heresy. . . . Long live Christ, who loves the Franks. . . .

Yet they remained different from one another. Lupus of Ferrières felt himself a foreigner whenever he ventured beyond the Rhine to Fulda. The political ideas of the redactors of the *Annales of Saint-Bertin* and the *Annales of Fulda* differ noticeably. In the south of eastern Francia, Bavaria long retained her independence under national dukes who strove to sustain her identity vis-à-vis the Franks and the Italians: "The Welches (that is, the Romans) are sots; the Bavarians are sages," noted a late ninth-century clerk.[13]

Beyond the lower Rhine lay Germania, above all comprehending the lands of the Saxons. No prince before Charlemagne ever dared venture into those frightful lands. It took Charlemagne thirty-three years of warfare to subdue them by terror and begin their conversion to Christianity. Still the Saxons kept their own laws and social hierarchy. Though the nobility assimilated with the Franks quickly enough, the people revolted repeatedly, and in 842, Louis the German had to face the *Stellinga** movement.[14] During the second half of the century Duke Liudolf, founder of the Abbey of Gandersheim and ancestor of Henry the Fowler, was to all intents and purposes independent. For the Franks, as witnessed by the Synod of Tribur in 885, the Saxons remained foreigners (*alienigenae*).

Aquitaine, south of the Loire, was a world apart, never really subdued by the conquests of Pepin and Charlemagne. The Franks had nothing but suspicion for these "Romans." Many a disparaging allusion could be cited regarding the people of Aquitaine. Pepin II, grandson of Louis the

---

* The *Stellinga* were a League of Saxon peasants.

Pious, was said to lead a frivolous life "after the manner of the Aquitainians;" the clergy of Aquitaine "knew how to devote themselves to riding, warlike exercises, and javelin throwing better than they could to divine services." At the death of Louis the Pious, the Aquitainians, "famous for the volatility of their temperament, began fighting and drinking." Abbo of Saint-Germain-des-Prés contrasted the proud and hasty Franks to the wily Aquitainians.[15] Though we do not possess any testimony from Aquitaine, it is probable that the sentiments of the people living there were equally hostile. The revolts repeatedly mounted against Charles the Bald are witness enough.

Particularism was equally strong within Aquitaine. The future Catalonia, so long dominated by Goths, then Arabs, and finally reconquered by the Carolingians, was beginning to shape its own personality. Refugees from over the Pyrenees, the *Hispani*, installed themselves there with their own laws. Counts of Gothic origin rendered judgment according to "Visgothic" law. In the west, the Gascons were far from being assimilated—the Counts of Toulouse and Bordeaux were responsible for protecting Aquitaine from their incursions. Still pagan, the Gascons in the Pyrenees resisted and sometimes ambushed the Carolingian armies. The episode of Roncevaux was not unique. The Gascon dukes further to the north were apparently reconciled to the Carolingians, but they retained cultural differences, even to their costume. When the little King of Aquitaine presented himself at Paderborn in 787, he wore the short round cloak, bouffant sleeves, large pantaloons, and spurred boots of Gascony.[16]

The Franks were equally ill at ease when they crossed into Italy. Like the Aquitainians, the Italians were unfavorably represented. We may attach little weight to Notker of Saint-Gall's remark on the homosexuality of the Cisalpines.[17] Yet there are other texts to confirm the Frankish suspicion of the Transalpine peoples:

> You Italians are satisfied to fill your stomachs with wine and abundant dishes and your high houses with yellow, shining metal. Gauls are never distracted by such cares, for their only desire is to subdue neighboring nations and gather their spoils as trophies

under their low roofs.

On his own side, the Italian feared to see one of his princes dressed like the Frankish aristocrats:

> Let this land of Italy and its inhabitants and the rivers which carress its ancient walls be enough for you. Let not ferocious Gaul or cruel Germany gather you to themselves nor deprive yourself of rule over a soil worthy of you.[18]

Beyond the ancient Lombard kingdom to which we have just referred, Italy contained many diverse regions: Romagna, or the papal state, Apulia, the duchy of Benevento, not to speak of the Byzantine lands to the south. But to the Frank it always appeared as a land made foreign by language and mentality, reached only after difficult traveling and, as we shall see, with risk to his health.

Diversity of Tongues

A traveler crossing the Carolingian Empire would encounter a series of distinct civilizations and mentalities. He would be forcibly struck by the peculiarities of language. Even within the borders of a single realm like western Francia communication was difficult: Basques and Bretons retained their own languages; Aquitainians, with many other inhabitants of Francia, spoke the *lingua romana*, a "proto-Roman" whose pronunciation varied from one place to another. Germanic speech was used in the north, in the diocese of Therouanne, while within the Germanic linguistic domain, islands of the Roman tongue persisted. Thus "Roman" was still spoken in several *vici romanisci* in the Salzburg region of Bavaria. And at Friuli, in the Chur region of the western Tyrol, Rheto-Roman, also called "Ladin," has survived for centuries.

Differences of dialect could also be found in the Germanic tongue which the texts call *lingua theotisca*, from which we derive the word *deutsch*. We know, for example, that the Saxons were unable to understand the Bavarians. Some texts have preserved the written forms of several regional dialects of Francique, the language of the Carolingian court.[19] The government found functionaries indispensable who were bilingual or trilingual, as were the princes. Charlemagne demonstrated his concern for imposing a norm on the Germanic language by outlining a grammar which has since been lost.[20] Louis the Pious, who could speak "Roman", used Francique by choice. Louis the German addressed Charles the Bald's troops at Strasbourg in 842 in *romana lingua*, while Charles repeated the same discourse in Francique to Louis' men.[21] To make themselves understandable throughout the Empire, the king's officers had to learn both languages, as we know Chrodegang of Metz did. In 844, Lupus of Ferrières sent three young aristocrats, one of them his nephew, to Fulda to learn the Germanic language.[22] Glossaries, the ancestors of our dictionaries, were available—that of Reichenau for example. The glossary of Cassel included 180 words designating parts of the body, names of animals, household utensils, and even maladies.[23] Finally, there were interpreters at the disposal of all those who did not command the necessary foreign tongues.

Different peoples of the Empire could communicate only in Latin, the language of edicts and administrative documents. This Latin adopted by Germanic kings had evolved since the fifth century. Germanic words enriched the vocabulary of war and construction while the whole was gradually transformed thanks to the variety of tongues in ancient "Romania." Charlemagne did attempt to restore the purity of the original Latin tongue, which remained the language of the church and its liturgy. Scholars, as we shall see, strove to learn correct Latin in conformity with the rules of the grammarians. And even if the results varied with the cultural milieu, even if written Latin was still influenced by the spoken language—Alcuin, finely lettered as he was, could not escape that—the result of the reform was still positive. A learned language was created, with an established orthography, a morphology, and a stable syntax.[24] Accordingly, the divorce between the Latin language and the Romance languages was in some sort liberating, accentuated by the early ninth century to such a point that the literate had to recognize that people no longer understood Latin and that it was necessary "for bishops to translate their sermons into the *rustica romana lingua* or *theotisca* so that everyone might understand what they were saying."[25]

This passage, from the Council of Tours of 813, was an admission of defeat. The literate wrote and spoke a language reserved for a small number of initiates. In Germanic countries, where no Roman substratum existed, clerks had long been accustomed to explain the rudiments of the Christian religion in Germanic languages. Soon it became difficult even in the monasteries to impose the Latin language on scholars who spoke a national tongue among themselves. Alcuin recognized that, to be understood by everyone, the Benedictine Rule which was read to the chapters would have to be explained in the vulgar tongue. An interlinear translation of the *Regula* was redacted at Saint-Gall. A bilingual edition of twenty-seven hymns from the Breviary, the Gospels, and the Treatises of Isidore was compiled at Reichenau.[26] At last, even religious texts were simply translated into Germanic without the inclusion of the original Latin. Bilingualism was of short duration.

Diversity of Laws

In addition to variations in culture and language, there was a diversity of law. The Carolingians respected the principle of personality of law which had pertained since the barbarians installed themselves in the West: to each people, its own law. Charlemagne "caused the laws transmitted until then by oral tradition to be recorded and consigned to writing for all the peoples placed under his dominion."[27] Other texts confirm this statement from Einhard. Charles had the Salic, Alamannian, and Bavarian Laws revised and the laws of the Saxons and Frisians redacted. By 802, he had commissioners at work completing the laws. The king reminded his judges that at each trial they should inquire as to which national law was going to be applied. The order implies that the judges were knowledgeable in all the different laws and in possession of their texts. The library of Duke Ewrard of Friuli included a corpus containing the laws of the Franks, Ripuarians, Lombards, Alamans, and Bavarians, with the "Breviary of Alaric," a compilation of the Theodosian Code always applied in southern France. For his part, Eccard,

Count of Mâcon, possessed the Gombetta Law applied in Burgundian lands, the Salic Law, and two examples of the *pacto romano*—that is, the above-named breviary.[28]

This diversity of legislation inherited from the past seemed to some clerks to be anachronistic. In his treatise *Against the Law Gombetta*, Agobard, Bishop of Lyon, wrote to Louis the Pious:

> I ask you, is it not in opposition to the divine work of unity that this incredible diversity of laws reigns, not only in each region and in each city, but in the same household and even at the same table? It would be pleasing to God Almighty that, under a single pious king, all men should be governed by a single law: that would be greatly to the profit of concord within the City of God and justice among the nations. There are no Barbarians and Scythians, Aquitainians, Lombards, Burgundians, Alamans, slaves and free men: Christ is all and is in all.[29]

This ideal of a united Empire, sharing the same faith, submitting to the same Christian law, was articulated often by the clergy. And the religious policies of the kings, the conversion of pagan peoples, moved also in this direction. Louis organized a mission of evangelization to Scandinavian lands and confided it to the monk Ansgar, who was named Bishop of Hamburg for that purpose. Salzburg became a center for missions sent into Moravian and Avar lands. A beginning was made on the evangelization of the Basques. The Benedictine Rule penetrated into Brittany, even to Landevenec, and supplanted Celtic usages.[30]

Hopes were raised during the first years of the reign of Louis the Pious that this goal of religious and political unity would be achieved. The monastic reformer Benedict of Aniane, the King's cousin Wala, and Bishop Agobard of Lyon labored for that end. But the fact of the different principalities (*regna*) which composed the Empire was against them. Was a proclamation of unity sufficient to efface these regional diversities and confound so many different peoples in a single state? When, under pressure from the aristocracy, Louis determined to divide his Empire among his sons, he was reverting to Germanic tradition. Without saying so, he was recognizing that the unified Empire was a theoretical construct. The clerics did not accept this decision but, grouped around the Emperor's eldest son, Lothair, heir to the imperial title, struggled long in vain. Successive partitions, particularly the partition of Verdun in 843, marked their defeat. Thus Agobard's disciple, Florus of Lyon, complained:

> Mountains and hills, rivers and forests, springs and rocky escarpments, and you, deep valleys, mourn the race of the Franks. . . . For so it has befallen them that all these peoples of the Danube, the Rhine, the Rhone, the Loire, the Po, all these peoples who once were united in the bonds of concord, must now, after the rupture of their alliance, suffer the consequences of this fatal divorce. . . . For a king, a kinglet; for a kingdom, the debris of a realm![31]

The drama of the Carolingian Empire is expressed there: on the one hand, the nostalgic dreams of the clerks; on the other, the constraining reality of diversity.

Carolingians
Abroad

2

Much traveling was needed if the Carolingians were to unite the diverse parts of their immense Empire, penetrating and dominating so many various regions. It is a commonplace that the Carolingian kings never stayed long in one place, going, like their Merovingian predecessors, from palace to palace to secure their food supply. To be sure, one biography of Louis the Pious informs us that the king had "decided to pass his winters, year by year, in four different domiciles. . . . Thus each of his domains, at the coming of its own year, had a sufficiency for the royal charges. . . ."[1] But this economic motive by itself is inadequate to explain the kings' movements. In addition to military campaigns, princes were constantly in motion to ensure the execution of their orders, to renew their subjects' oaths, and to make pilgrimages to leading sanctuaries.[2] Like Pepin, his father, Charlemagne traveled widely, but most commonly he was in Francia and Germania.[3] His sojourns in Aquitaine, Bavaria, and Italy were only episodes. And at the end of his reign he preferred to remain in his palace at Aix. His son, Louis, was a more sedentary emperor who confined his movements to the regions of Francia: Thionville, Ingelheim, Frankfurt. But Charles the Bald, who was obliged to force his realm into submission and then to defend it against the Normans, was continually in motion. For example, let us look at two years of the reign. In 865, he spent Christmas at Quierzy, moving to Ver in February and then on to Douzy. During Lent, he was at Attigny, at Ver, and again at Attigny. Then he had to go to Pitres on the lower Seine because of war with the Normans. Returning to Cologne, he proceeded soon after to Quierzy and Compiègne. In 867, he wintered at Compiègne and found himself on the Loire in spring. After Easter at Saint-Denis, he moved on to Metz. On May 19 he was at Samousey, moving to Attigny for hunting in the Ardennes. The army was convoked in August at Chartres; in September, after receiving a Breton prince at Compiègne, he passed to Saint-Vaast and to Orville. He was at Troyes on October 25, from which he went to Reims, returned to Troyes, and celebrated Christmas at Auxerre.

The king could not travel impetuously. If he meant to occupy one of his palaces, the *mansionarii* had to be ordered to prepare the necessary furnishings.* If he wanted to take advantage of his right to hospitality from bishops, abbots, and vassals, he had to announce his arrival some time in advance.[4] Notker of Saint-Gall describes the fever of a bishop who flew "like a swallow" to clean and decorate his church and even the streets after notification of the emperor's arrival. Leidrad of Lyon, who had transformed his episcopal palace, wrote to Charles that he had foreseen that he would visit him when he should come to Lyons.[5] No one received the emperor and his suite with unadulterated feelings, for the prince was usually accompanied by several hundred people. When Charles the Bald arrived at Auxerre, in 861, he occupied all the lodgings in the city. Lupus of Ferrières had to ask hospitality from the monks of Saint-Germain. The king's sojourns in episcopal houses created many abuses. In 845, the bishops meeting at Meaux requested the king's men to respect the episcopal residences, particularly by refraining from bringing women there. Hincmar asked the king to limit the requisitions of the *milites* in the sovereign's company. These were justified complaints, but they were in vain.[6] It was more practical and economical for the king to stay with the grandees. Though it can be shown that Charles the Bald delivered most of his charters during his sojourns in the great abbeys—Saint-Denis, Saint-Martin of Tours, Saint-Sernin of Toulouse—the moral and political advantages the abbots received from their royal host rarely compensated them for the heavy expenses they had to bear.

The Travels of the Great

Royal agents, from simple couriers (*scararii*) on constant call to the king's own representatives (*missi dominici*), were incessantly in motion. Charlemagne, in his general charges to the *missi*, assigned a very precise region of inquiry to

* Although the word *mansionarii* has other meanings, it here refers to that household servant who, according to Hincmar of Reims (*De Ord. Pal.*, 23), had the responsibility of preparing the king's residences for his sojourns.

each. In 798, Theodulf of Orleans and Leidrad of Lyon visited Vienne, Valence, Orange, Avignon, Nîmes, Maguelonne, Béziers, Narbonne, Carcassonne, Arles, Marseille, Aix, and Cavaillon.[7] Nor did lay aristocrats and even ecclesiastics hesitate to take to the roads to meet the king with the army or at his palace or simply to visit friends. Since these trips were very expensive, they sought the privilege of the *tractoriae*, a Roman institution still in use until about 865. *Missi* and royal vassals had this right to requisition lodging and provisions for their men and mounts.[8] A bishop could exact forty loaves of bread, three hogsheads of drink, one pig, three chickens, fifteen eggs, and fifteen hogsheads of forage per diem. Vassals, whose appetites must have been smaller, got seventeen loaves of bread, one hogshead of drink, and two of forage.[9] At the stages, the official traveler found fresh horses, *paravareda*, from which we get the word palfrey. Forage was of the utmost importance. When Lupus of Ferrières was dispatched on a mission, he requested the *tractoriae* from the king, expressing particular anxiety about forage. He further warned one of his friends to wait until summer because of the scarcity of forage. On that account, Lupus, who traveled much, was always anxious, whether it was a question of leaving for Germany, Italy, or some other royal residence.[10] When they could not move personally, aristocrats were always sending couriers with letters. Some idea of the organization of the courier system can be gained from a reconstruction of the epistolary dossiers of Boniface, Alcuin, Lupus, Hincmar, and many others. If haste was needed, the letter might be confided to a traveler or pilgrim. But generally it was preferable to trust to a known courier who could be recommended to the correspondent, wait for a response, and then return. There were complaints of letters lost or stolen, and some preferred to confide the message orally. As Einhard said, "A faithful man is surer than a letter, for all the world knows that a letter which escapes its carrier will divulge its contents, while a faithful man will resist torture rather than betray what has been entrusted to him."[11]

A designated courier had to be trustworthy and provided with a good escort. Nithard, in 841, was astonished to hear of the arrival of messengers from Aquitaine at Troyes carrying the crown and royal ornaments: "Who would not be amazed to learn that a fistful of men, almost without intelligence, had succeeded in carrying so great a quantity of gold and such an infinity of precious stones across such distances everywhere infested with brigands?"[12] In a letter to his brother, who was bringing him some manuscripts, Lupus recommended caution:

> We advise you to use the most vigilant precaution in choosing a road for, in the wake of the troubles which have erupted, brigandage is committed in the realm of our King Charles with impunity and there is nothing surer or more constant than violence and rapine. Therefore, seek out traveling companions whose numbers and courage will enable you to avoid groups of bandits or, if need be, to repulse them.[13]

Though traveling was expensive and dangerous, travelers were not discouraged. In addition to princes, aristocrats, and their agents, were there common men and women on the roads? Did they have occasion to move about? Despite our meager documentation on this point, we may answer in the affirmative. Free men, in answer to military convocations, were obliged to uproot themselves and go far from their homelands. The army which moved into Spain in 778 included not only Aquitainians and Lombards but also Burgundians, Bavarians, and Austrasians. In 793, Charles dispatched Aquitainians into southern Italy. In 806, the Saxons were required to send one warrior out of every six for the campaign against the Avars and Saracens. And, outside these obligatory travels—not to mention the massive deportations of Saxons to the interior of the Empire—we can occasionally perceive groups of peasants looking for better lands and kinder masters, slaves in flight, clerks who had broken their vows, "wandering" bishops, refugees from invasions, and so forth. We should also mention pilgrims who did not hesitate to travel thousands of kilometers through the Empire or outside of it to do penance or venerate a relic. On their journeys, these men and women were sure of finding hospitality as evening fell or at the end of a stage in a monastery or some simple *cella*. The reception of travelers, *peregrini, fratres supervenientes*, was the duty of monks and clergy. As we shall see, an entire network of hostelries facilitating the movements of both rich and poor had been constituted within the Empire.[14]

Land Routes

Kings, aristocrats, bishops, abbots, and commoners trod the roads of the Empire, following, in their turn, ways charted by the Romans and barbarians before them. Despite decay, the Roman network was still in place. Kings commanded counts and great proprietors to maintain these *viae publicae, viae regiae,* and *calciatae* (causeways). They reminded them that the money from taxes on merchandise—and these were numerous and diverse—were intended for this maintenance.[15] And where the ancient network was lacking, as in Germany, the Carolingians succeeded in creating coach roads over which armies and merchants could pass.

Let us suppose that a traveler wished to go to Spain from Magdeburg. It would take him some time to cross Germany to the Rhine, from which he could take the road from Cologne to Senlis, passing Paris, Orleans, Tours, Saintes, Bordeaux and, crossing the Pyrenees at Roncevaux, arrive at Pamplona. If he feared the Basques, he might instead take the Quentovic-Chalon transverse route, leaving Reims to descend the right bank of the river, the Rhodanian channel, to Nîmes, Uzès, and Narbonne. Gaining the pass of La Perche, he could follow the newly created *strata francisca* to reach Gerona and Barcelona. This was the route followed by Usuard, a monk of Saint Germain des Près, when he went looking for relics in Spain.[16] That way, also, passed the slave merchants who brought their human flocks from Slavic lands through Mainz and Verdun to the court of the Emir of Cordova. Pilgrims for Rome left the *transversale* at Langres and, passing through Besançon and Orbe, descended Lake Geneva, called the Lake of Saint Maurice, stopping in Le Valais and Saint-Maurice to prepare for the crossing of the Alps by Mont Joux, that is, the Great Saint Bernard. There they found a monastic hostelry. They could start off again toward Aosta on the Via Flaminia, then called the *via francigena,* through Aosta, Ivrea, Vercelli, and Pavia. Coming to Piacenza, they would cross the Po, head-ing for Bologna. Then, crossing the Apennines, they arrived in Tuscany where they might meet other travelers who had crossed the Alps at Mont Cenis because they had come from Vienne, resting in the monastery of Novalaise near Susa before taking the route to Turin and Pavia. Together, they could rejoice in having overcome the dangers of the Alps.

The Alpine Passes

The Alps had an altogether redoubtable reputation. Walafrid Strabo heaped praise upon a servant of Louis the Pious for daring to search for the Empress Judith in Italy. Sedulius of Liège pictured Bishop Hartgar crossing "the snowy fields and glacial roads" with a devoted escort. It was counted as a miracle that those who carried the relics of Saint Helena had little difficulty in crossing the pass at Mont Joux.[17] To be sure, these writers were indulging a taste for picturesque description, but literary convention mirrored reality. The first obstacles were the mountain climate and the sheer height. Only one who was hard-pressed indeed would cross the Alps in winter. To be sure, Pope Stephen II, the first Pope to go to Gaul, left Pavia in November, arrived at the monastery of Saint-Maurice during December, and arrived at the palace in Ponthion on January 6, 754.[18] But such a feat was rarely emulated.

When the Arab ambassadors arrived at Ivrea in October, 801, with the elephant Abul Abaz as a gift for Charlemagne, they thought it prudent to wait until spring at Vercelli before crossing the Alps.[19] Travelers needed the help of porters recruited from the local population. In describing the trip of Gerald of Aurillac across the Alps, Odo of Cluny spoke of the Marruci, who lived in the mountains and made their living by carrying baggage and the count's tents across the pass of Mont Joux.[20] But brigands lived there also and made the mountains frightful even in summer. The Alps were a fine field of action for outlaws. In 866, Abbot Hubert of Saint-Maurice, himself more a brigand than an abbot, took his men into the heights between the Jura and the Great Saint Bernard and forbade access to the armies of Lothair.[21] Finally, the passes opening the road to Italy were patrolled by princes, not only for strategic reasons but because they drew a fine profit from customs duties.[22] The traveler could take the sea route when climatic conditions or danger of attack forbade the crossing of the Alps. Pope John VIII went by sea from Rome to Arles, then by the road to Troyes.[23] But that voyage was much longer and more onerous.

The River Passages

Even outside the mountainous regions, Carolingian roads were beset with inconveniences. In winter, horses with simple wicker fittings rather than iron horseshoes slipped on the ice. After a rainy period, mud swamped the roads. The paths across the forests were poorly marked, and one might lose them as did the servants of Einhard between Seligenstadt and Aix.[24] The passage of the rivers was a major obstacle. On the great rivers, ferry service was assured as at Piacenza for the Po.[25] The Rhine could be crossed by a wooden bridge at Mainz. Burned in 813, it was reconstructed of stone, at least in its lower parts.[26] Charles the Bald ordered the maintenance of wooden bridges across the Seine at Charenton, Paris, and Pitres; across the Marne at Tribaldou near Meaux; and across the Oise at Auvers. The work was arduous, and he had to promise those who worked on the bridges at Charenton and Auvers that they would not be called up again.[27] Damaged bridges could be provisionally replaced by boats tied together, as was the case in 792 on the Danube or on the Seine in the spring of 841:

> On this date, according to Nithard, the river had overflowed. The fords had become nearly impassable, and the river guards had broken and scuttled all the boats. Moreover, Count Gerard (of Paris) had destroyed all the bridges which he had encountered. The excessive difficulty of passage wildly disturbed those who proposed to cross. . . . They said the current had carried merchant ships from the mouth of the Seine as far as Rouen. Charles made haste to Rouen, requisitioned twenty-eight ships and crossed the river with his army below the town.[28]

It was easiest to find a usable ford, but one had to know where they were, for more than one person drowned attempting to cross a river. Walafrid Strabo died falling into a water hole in the Loire.[29] Fords were supervised to ensure that travelers would not venture them in case of a flash flood. Kings took care that military convoys were provided with amphibious carts:

> Let our wagons, called *bastarnes,* which are intended for the army be well built [Charles recommended in the capitulary *De villis.*] Let the openings be securely covered with leather, so well sewn that, if they must cross water, the wagons can carry their provisions across the river without leaking.

We can observe this procedure during the Spanish campaign of Louis of Aquitaine. Carts divided into four compartments, joints sealed with wax, pitch, and tow, were drawn by two horses or two mules across the Ebro.[30] But the construction and maintenance of a bridge required at least a minimum of political organization. In the course of the ninth century such construction work became impossible. It became necessary to be content with fording rivers. Some clerks bringing relics of Saint Liborius from Le Mans to Saxony sought out a bridge so as to avoid wetting their feet and endangering their precious burden. Hardly had they stepped on the bridge they found when the planks broke and they had to seek out a usable ford.[31]

Waterways

In the absence of coach roads, more and more travelers used the waterways. Merchants carried grain, salt, iron, and barrels of wine by water on the Seine, the Loire, the Meuse, the Rhine, and the Danube. Abbots built their own fleets and looked for land holdings on the banks of rivers and lakes. The Abbey of Prüm, in 864, obtained an estate at Metz "on the Moselle in the place called port." Saint-Germain of Auxerre had four ships on the Loire.[32] Lupus of Ferrières asked the Abbot of Corbie for twenty trees and the loan of some skilled carpenters to aid his monks in building a better boat than they could buy. In four months the boat was completed and ready to take cargo up to Creil by way of the Seine and the Oise.[33] In Germany, ships regularly plied the rivers. Bavarians came down the Danube from Passau to Central Europe. Merchants of Mainz brought wheat in by water, along the Main. It was by ship that Boniface went on his final journey, and by ship Ansgar returned to Denmark in 826.[34] For military reasons, Charlemagne conceived the grandiose project of a canal joining the Rhine and the Danube from the Regnitz, a tributary of the Main, to the Altmühl, a tributary of the Danube. The work began in the fall of 793 but "because of the incessant rain, the land, which was marshy and naturally gorged with water, could not be stabilized for the building of a canal. No matter how much dirt the diggers removed during the day, during the night mudslides brought it all back." Archeologists have discovered the remains of this *fossa carolina* near the village of Graben: 1400 meters had been hollowed out.[35]

Most travelers used a combination of land and water routes. One of Einhard's trips may serve as an example. Going from the court of Aix to his Abbey of Saint Bavo in Ghent, he followed the old Roman road between the Meuse and Sambre from Maestricht. Arriving at Valenciennes, he took a boat on the Scheld, passing Tournai, and arrived at Ghent, where there was an important *portus* used by Frisian merchants. If he wanted to go from there to his Abbey of Seligenstadt, he would descend the Scheldt to its debouchment on the Rhine at Tile or Dorestad, and from there, on another boat, he could follow the course of the Rhine to Mainz. Then, via the Main, he would arrive at his destination fifteen days after his departure from Ghent.[36]

Voyages by boat were slower than by road. Thanks to the chroniclers, we can make some fairly precise calculations. In 875, Charles the Bald left Langres on the first of September and arrived at Pavia on the twenty-ninth of the same month. The following year, he left Rome on the fifth of January and arrived at Pavia three weeks later, reaching Saint-Denis by Easter. Einhard's notary took six days to cross the Alps from Pavia by Saint-Maurice to Valais. When necessary, however, travelers could go faster. In one night, Charles the Bald covered the thirty leagues between Saint Cloud and Lâon (120 km). Travelers generally covered 30

The Physical and Human Setting

to 40 kilometers a day. Clergy going from Le Mans to Paderborn left on May 1 and arrived on May 28, averaging 25 kilometers a day. Of course, when relics were being translated, there were numerous stops, and the journey moved at the speed of a procession.[37]

Speed depended on harnessing. The famous chariot (*carpentum*) of the Merovingian kings moved at the speed of the cattle pulling it. By preference draft horses were harnessed to those carts called *plaustra, carruca,* or *benna.*[38] Traction had already been increased by replacing the neck harness with the shoulder harness and a stiff brace (*armature*), which was padded to avoid hurting the animal and attached to the shafts of the vehicle. Miniatures from ninth-century manuscripts allow us to suppose that this invention was beginning to be employed. Permitting the replacement of frontal harnessing with harnessing in file, it would augment both traction and speed.[39]

If we were to join in the long meanderings of Carolingian travelers, we would be surprised at the wild monotony of the landscape through which they moved. Outside of a few cultivated clearings, a few slopes planted with vines, the forest dominated the vegetable kingdom, its boundaries giving way to heaths, swamps, and bogs. This landscape had barely changed since the days when the Romans had first conquered and then lost the west. The texts still talked about *silvae, minutae silvae* (coppices and brush), *mariscum, pastura, inculta, deserta*. And so it would remain, unchanged until the great land-clearances of the later Middle Ages. Occupied clearings were linked by roads. The population was clustered in towns and around abbeys and palaces. To go from one place to another required days and nights spent in traversing these apparently deserted and dangerously wild stretches.[1]

The Forest

To be sure, the forest landscape changed in response to climatic differences from the Mediterranean region to central Europe. Except for the dense regions of the Alps and the Pyrenees, the Mediterranean forest had been extensively thinned, even reduced to deserted second growth. Lombard kings had even found it necessary to protect trees in lands given over to pasture or where they were too eagerly sought for fuel and construction purposes. In Aquitaine, the forest cloak still spread over the lands of the Garonne, the Saintonge, and the Angoumois as well as the Massif Centrale. And beyond the threshold of Aquitaine, in the lands of the Loire, the forest held its own, giving way in part to the wastes and heaths of Maine and Armorica, "wooded haunts of savage beasts and swampy wastes" to repeat the expression of Ermold the Black. From the heights of le Perche to the lower Seine, the entire Neustrian countryside was filled with oaks, beeches, maples, birches, and other species of tree. Although historians debate whether the Beauce consisted of a forest riddled with clearings or a steppe, they agree that Brie was covered with trees. Its great forests had attracted the Merovingian kings to Paris, which had lost nothing of this ornament. Of the 4000 hectares of land which pertained to Saint-Germain-des-Prés, almost half was forested or otherwise uncultivated. To the east and north of the Seine, in Burgundy and Austrasia, the forest steadily deepened. These were the true frontiers, the oft-mentioned *Sylva Carbonaria**, the charcoal forest, and the Ardennes.

Let us then plunge into that immense domain of the ancient Hyrcanian forest, stretching from the Rhineland crags to Bohemia. The disciples of Saint Boniface, seeking a suitable site for their monastery, moved painfully through a beech forest at the borders of Hesse and Thuringia. For days on end, Sturm and his two companions forged ahead, sleeping in huts of branches behind thorny hedges which protected them from the wild beasts. They met no one but a few Slavs bathing naked near Fulda, who chased them away. The monks took no hurt beyond a bad odor. Finally, at the foot of the Rauschenberg, they found a favorable site for their monastery.[2]

How vividly this passage from the *Vita Sturmi* depicts the two faces of the Carolingian forest, its terror and its attraction!

Chief among the terrors of the forest were the wild animals who ruled there: stags and boars as well as bears, bison, buffalo (*bubalus*), aurochs (*urus*), and, above all, wolves. Texts are filled with references to the ravages of these beasts. In 846, a hungry wolf even got into a church in the Senonais during Sunday Mass.[3] No means could be neglected to frustrate these audacious animals: dogs were trained, traps were baited. In the month of May, by order of Charlemagne, wolf cubs were to be tracked down and either destroyed with poisoned powders or lured into concealed pits. The pelts of the slaughtered beasts were to be presented to him. In 813, wolf hunters were dispatched into every part of the country.[4] But in spite of all these measures, the wolf remained, until modern times, the scourge of the western countryside.

Princes and aristocrats hunted wild animals both for sport and to provide themselves with meat and furs. Kings

* *Sylva Carbonaria* was the Belgian forest, south of modern Brussels, which formed a natural boundary between the Scheldt river and the Ardennes (the site of the "Battle of the Bulge" in World War II).

jealously guarded their own hunting grounds, the *brolium* or, from the seventh century on, *foresta*—from which our modern word stems. In 800, when Charlemagne granted hunting rights to the monks of Saint-Bertin, he excepted "the forests set aside for our own use."[5] To secure these rights, the king charged his foresters with a survey of the reserves, particularly in the Vosges, the Ardennes, the forested Massif of the Oise and the Aisne. Hunters (*venatores*) were employed to maintain packs of hunting dogs, especially greyhounds (*veltres*), whose reputation reached even to Baghdad. Domain intendants were made responsible for fostering young dogs, while falconers (*falconarii*) furnished tame falcons. Hincmar mentioned the separate offices of hunters (*bersarii*), greyhound trainers (*veltrarii*), and beaver hunters (*beverarii*).[6]

Both lay and ecclesiastical aristocrats shared a passion for the chase. As soon as he began to emerge from childhood, a young man was trained to mount his horse, handle bow and boarspear, run the dogs, and cast the falcons. Bishops, abbots, and even simple clerks maintained sizable packs, in defiance of conciliar condemnation. Jonas, bishop of Orleans, was scandalized by this "dementia" which caused men to leave Sunday Mass for the chase and "to find the hymns of angels less pleasing than the baying of dogs."[7]

Nor did the forest interest only the great folk. The Carolingian peasant could not have survived without it, for there he found the wherewithal to nourish and warm himself.

The forest was not so unpopulated as one might have believed at first glance. It was the refuge of ascetic men and women who wished to flee the world. In the forest, they found the "desert" where they could pursue their vocations. In the middle of the eighth century, more than four hundred monastic establishments had been planted in the forest. This movement continued into the ninth century. In 817, the monastery of Benedict of Aniane was built "not far from Aix, where live the horned stags, buffalo, bears, and wild goats." In 800, Conques was founded, deep in the Rouergue forest. A road had to be cut into the rock to provide access.[8]

But in the end, the installation of monks signaled the

beginning of forest clearing and the transformation of the countryside. Already their presence alone offered reassurance in a hostile world. There were no better weapons than their prayers against the maleficent forces of paganism— woodland sprites, trolls and *Waldleuten*, sacred groves, enchanted springs and all the "forest murmurs" which, throughout the Middle Ages, incessantly bewildered the straying traveler.* And last but not least, the abbey or even the simple hermit's cell, promised safe harbor to all who went in fear of brigands, the cold, and the dark. There they could pass some hours of rest before taking the road again.

Man and Nature

The hostility of nature surely affected the Carolingian mind. Ninth-century men may have been more hardened to cold, heat, and humidity than we, but they were no less sensitive to climatic caprices. In a Germanic poem on Genesis, Adam, cast out of Paradise, complained of his sufferings from wind, rain, hail, and sun. Surely the Carolingians were the children of Adam. The redactors of the Carolingian *Annales* loved to connect natural catastrophes with political events. But occasionally they demonstrated a far from negligible store of meteorological knowledge. They noted a "soft winter" in 844, but "a very hard winter" in 845 brought famine to western France. In 846, the north wind blew until the month of May, endangering the harvest and encouraging the descent of wolves. At the end of May the Auxerrois was ravaged by floods. In 850 there were floods in winter and torrid heat in summer. In 858, the Meuse overflowed and washed away stone houses and walls. In 860, people suffered from snow and frost from November to April. The winter of 861 was very long, but it was rainy and mild in 863.[9]

That winter was a terrible season was never disputed. Every activity was suspended. A winter military expedition, with troops passing over a frozen river, was noted as an exceptional feat. Enemies occasionally did take advantage. For example, the Normans attacked Paris in the winter of 861.[10] But traveling was rare during the bad season. Here

* *Waldleuten* were "forest folk," cobolds, or German pixies.

is what Sedulius Scotus saw, with some lyricism, on his arrival in France in 848:

> The strident breath of white-faced Borea struck us with sudden blasts. . . . Aquilon* pitilessly ravaged the fields of the air, filling it with horrible cries and howls. . . . The languishing earth hid beneath a robe of white; the wooded mountain lost its hair, and, like the reed, the oak was forced to bend. . . . Lamentable spectacle! Borea in fury threw himself against us, learned grammarians and pious ecclesiastics that we are, while for his part, Aquilon spared no famous persons but tore into us with his cruel talons.

For all the polish of his classical readings, the poet still vividly transmits to us his terror in the face of hostile nature.[11] We can therefore imagine the joy that greeted the return of spring. A whole range of literary clichés, "the debate between winter and spring," the praise of the swallow and of the cuckoo, express this delight in renascent life.[12] Contemplating his little weed-choked garden at Reichenau, Walafrid Strabo was encouraged by the first warmth to take up his hoe.[13] Though the religious year began on December 25, for many folk spring was the real beginning of the new year.

Everything that has been said about the opposition of winter and spring, holds equally true for the duality of night and day. With the fall of night, everyone burrowed in. People who either had no lights or hesitated to use them for fear of fire, must, waking or sleeping, wait in darkness for the first light of dawn to be announced by the cock. Night is a time consecrated to sleep, said Hrabanus Maurus, but a time also which favors the exploits of thieves and bandits.[14] At night maleficent forces were set free and the spirits of the dead might come to disturb the living. Lupus of Ferrières recommended a new courier to his correspondents as "entirely suited to his state by his way of life except that he cannot sleep alone yet, I believe because of his nocturnal terrors."[15]

* Borea and Aquilon are poetic names for the north wind.

The Physical and Human Setting

Although the Carolingian west was predominantly rural in nature, the town continued to play a significant role in this society. The towns founded by the Romans did not disappear. Indeed, they grew so much that we might speak of an urban renaissance in the eighth and ninth centuries.[1] The emperors certainly loved to sojourn in their great rural domains, but many of them habitually spent weeks at a time at their courts in such great towns as Frankfurt, Worms, Regensburg, Pavia, and Verona.[2]

Northern Italy

As in the past, Italy, particularly the north, still presented the image of a very lively urban civilization. Pavia, the capital of the Kingdom of Italy, the *urbs regia*, was a busy marketplace as well as an administrative center. The Abbots of Nonentola and Brescia and the Bishop of Piacenza maintained warehouses there. Merchants came from Venice and from southern Italy. Aristocrats went there to purchase their silk clothing. Milan, the perpetual rival of Pavia, maintained an important market near Saint-Ambrose and the "five roads." As the will of Ansperto di Bassano testifies, businessmen and bankers made fortunes there. The walls, towers, the nine gates, the baths, the paved streets, and churches of the city were celebrated in an alphabetic poem of the mid-eighth century.[3] The monastery of Saint-Ambrose, founded in 789, was enlarged in the ninth century. The abbots and the bishops of Milan enriched the abbatial church, particularly adding the famous golden altar which we can still admire today. The Carolingian princes who ruled Italy chose Saint-Ambrose for their burial place.

Rome

To Italy and to the entire West, Rome remained the supreme city. Despite the destruction caused by war and the depradations of those who wished to put the stone to other uses, Rome retained her antique glamour. Walls, gates, triumphal arches, and baths abounded. The imposing mass of the Colosseum still dominated the quarter of the Forum, and, as a proverb of the day pronounced: "So long as the

Colosseum stands, Rome will stand; when the Colosseum falls, Rome will fall and, with her, the world." Transformed into houses or churches, many antique monuments were conserved by continuing habitation. The popes had frequently undertaken to restore aqueducts and church buildings. Between the reigns of Hadrian I (d. 795) and Leo IV (d. 852), nearly twenty churches had been reconstructed or restored, covered with mosaics and frescoes.[4]

The population of Rome had tended, since the seventh century, to desert the hills and to install themselves in the Campus Martius and along the Tiber, despite constant risk of inundation, leaving the hills to Latin and Greek monasteries. Only two of the hills, the Caelian and the Vatican, were still heavily used. The Caelian, where the Pope resided, was the center of religious and administrative life. The Lateran palace had been enlarged, as were the Cathedral of the Holy Saviour and the Baptistry of Saint John. Leo III had built state rooms featuring a mosaic decoration representing Saint Peter flanked by the Pope and by Charlemagne. All the boiling, intriguing world of administrative personnel directed by the *primicerius*, notaries, accountants, the paymaster general, masters of ceremonies, great dignitaries, vidames, archdeacons, *vestarius*, the librarian, the young cantors of the *Schola Cantorum*, ensconced itself as best it could in the inadequate and uncomfortable apartments.

The kings who came to Rome could no longer be housed in the Palatine palace, long since become uninhabitable. Therefore they lodged in the annexes of the Basilica of Saint Peter on the other hill, outside the walls of the Vatican. The Romans long remembered Charlemagne's visit of April 2, 774. Kissing each step of the great staircase which rose to the atrium of the Basilica, Charles presented himself before Pope Hadrian. They clasped hands and went inside to the *Confessio* where the remains of Saint Peter reposed. Near the same place, December 25, 800, the same prince received the imperial crown from the hands of Leo III.

The Vatican Basilica had several functions. There the suburbicarian bishops of Ostia, Albano, and Porto annointed the popes. When the crowning was over, the Pope, the Roman clergy, with representatives of the aristocracy and the dignitaries of the town, marched in procession to the

Lateran, following a well-defined itinerary: by the Campus Martius, the imperial forums always dominated by Trajan's column, the Forum, the Colosseum to San Clemente, decorated with new frescoes around 845. A dead Pope was escorted by a similar cortège to the pontifical necropolis at Saint Peter's. There he would be laid near the tomb of the first Bishop of Rome, a tomb which, over the centuries, attracted thousands of pilgrims from all over the West. All around the Vatican there were hotels, hospices, oratories to lodge these pilgrims. Anglo-Saxons, Frisians, Franks, and Lombards knew that they could find food and shelter in their national *scholae*. Built as it had been, outside the walls, the Vatican was vulnerable to riots and invasions. After the Arab raid of 846, Pope Leo IV built a great wall pinned on the mausoleum of Hadrian—the Castel San Angelo—which surrounded the basilica and the neighboring buildings, monasteries, and chapels, to rejoin the Tiber at the height presently crowned by the Hospital of the Holy Spirit. On June 27, 852, the Pope consecrated the walls, as he might a basilica, pronouncing appropriate prayers at each of its gates. Thus the Leonine City came to constitute a small town alongside the *Urbs*.

Outside the Aurelian walls, the great basilicas of Saint Paul-beyond-the-Walls, Saint Lawrence, and Saint Sebastian remained exposed to attack and could only depend on the help of the inhabitants grouped around them.* They were fortified at the end of the ninth century but, to preserve their relics, Pope Pascal I determined, on July 20, 817, to transfer the bodies of 2700 saints from the church cemeteries to a place within the walls. The abandoned tombs were never, however, entirely emptied and continued to draw pilgrims and relic collectors from all over the West seeking the precious remains of the saints. As we shall see, certain Romans drew substantial profits from the relic trade.

Can we estimate the population of Rome in the ninth century? During the late Roman Empire, the city contained about 250,000 people. According to some historians, it had

* Ca. 274 the Emperor Aurelian began the repair and enlargement of the city walls of Rome, a task completed by his successor Probus.

dwindled by Charlemagne's time to no more than 20,000. But the figure is still very large despite the spectacular drop. Rome remained the most populous town in the West. Immensely prestigious still, it was the ideal of all Carolingian towns.

The Towns of Francia

From the seventh century on, the old towns of the northern Empire, Neustria and Austrasia, overflowed their walls, and those walls were often allowed to fall into ruins. New settlements were born around funerary basilicas, abbeys, and simple chapels: Saint-Vaast, 300 meters from the city of Arras; Saint-Remi, 400 meters from the gates of Reims; Saint-Martin, 5 or 6 hectares around Tours; Saint-Médard and Saint-Crépin at Soissons. Some 15 chapels were built outside the walls of Metz and 8 within the walls. Paris followed a similar development. On the left bank, between the roads to Orleans and Melun, stood Saint-Séverin, Saint-Benoit, and Saint-Etienne-des-Grès. Saint-Geneviève on the hilltop, Saint-Médard, and Saint-Marcel were centers of population. On the right bank, Saint-Gervais and Saint-Paul on the road to Meaux, Saint-Merry, Saint-Martin, Saint-Georges, and Saint-Laurent farther on the road to Senlis, and Saint-Germain l'Auxerrois to the west of the Grand Pont were not isolated sanctuaries but invariably maintained monks, clerics, and other folk. We know that the right bank grew steadily through the Carolingian era, initiating an evolution which would mark the development of medieval Paris.[5]

Bishops and Towns

As Rome was saved by the residence of the Pope, so did other Carolingian towns owe much to their bishops. Even where a count or his adjutant had established headquarters, the bishop tended to become in fact the master of the town. Sometimes he had rights of possession over portions of the urban space. Bishops of the second half of the ninth century had minting rights and diplomas which gave them the power to raise taxes on merchandise. At Reims and Langres they were given the walls and gates of the city so as to obtain building supplies.

The Physical and Human Setting

Carolingian bishops were great builders. They enlarged cathedrals and laid out cloisters for the canons modelled after the one built by Chrodegang of Metz. In that town, the "bishop's house" comprehended both his own habitation and three churches. Around the cloister, there were a refectory, a dormitory, a kitchen, and rooms destined for the sick or for canons who had permission to sleep separately, two to a chamber. Aldric of Le Mans, a native of Metz, had a similar establishment in his town.[6] Moreover, he had an aqueduct built to spare the townspeople the trouble of bringing water directly from the Sarthe, a thing "which was never done before his time."

In a report to Charlemagne, Leidrad, Bishop of Lyon, noted works he had undertaken and completed: the restoration of the roof of Saint John's Cathedral and its neighboring church, Saint-Etienne; the reconstruction of the canons' cloister; the enlargement of the episcopal palace; and the restoration of a series of churches including Saint-Nizier, Sainte-Marie, and the monasteries of Saint-Martin d'Ainay, and Saint-Pierre.[7] Ebbo and then Hincmar transformed the center of the city of Reims. Gerfrid did the same for Lâon.[8] In the eight hectares of the city of Paris, the comital and episcopal palaces, the canons' quarters, the cathedral, the monasteries of Saint-Eloi and Saint-Bartholomew, the churches of Saint-Michel, Saint-Martial, Saint-Germain, Sainte-Geneviève, and Saint-Pierre, and the hospice of Saint-Christophe had accumulated. The revenues were divided, not without conflict, between the bishop and the chapter.

Like any good aristocrats, the bishops loved their comfort and furnished their palaces accordingly. At Auxerre, there was one dining room for the winter and one for summer, where the fresh air could be enjoyed. At Liège, if we are to believe the poet Sedulius, Bishop Hartgar constructed a vast room with gaily painted walls of gold, green, red, and blue which opened to the out-of-doors by means of windows made all of glass.[9]

The urban population lived by the bishop and for the bishop. The episcopal *familia* was composed of servants, notaries, young lectors and cantors of the school, canons and hospice keepers. All of these gravitated around this pastor whose authority was the more respected because of the support of royal power. Artisans, goldsmiths, occasional coiners, and masons when a job was on hand, also depended on the bishop. Merchants were regularly drawn to the towns and began to occupy their own quarters at Verdun, Regensburg, Worms, and Tournai. In some towns, like Nantes, Lyon, Vienne, and Arles, Jews were also becoming numerous.[10] Tavern keepers set up shop near the fair grounds and places of pilgrimage. Sometimes, too, prostitutes sought clients there. When Condeloc the Breton went to sell his wax in the market at Tours, a woman approached him and sought to bring him home with her, using the classic approach of claiming to recognize him as a childhood friend. It required the intervention of the monks of Saint-Martin to deliver him from "this snare of the devil."[11]

On religious feast days, the urban population gathered in cathedrals which were very often too small to hold them. Can we establish the population of the cities? As for Rome, we can make an attempt but without very precise results. Some 6000 people have been estimated for Metz, 5000 for Arras, 4000 for Paris. A chronicler spoke of "the crowded city," but this tells us very little, especially since it is the testimony of a person who had just come from a monastery or from the country.

The Portus

The scene presented above may be supplemented with urban agglomerations still in the process of formation. The *portus* was appearing along the great rivers: the Rhine, the Meuse, the Scheldt. There were ports where merchandise was unloaded, where boatmen stopped. There they found taverns where business could be done. Dinant, Namur, Huy, and Maestricht were no more than boat stops in the process of becoming little towns. At Dinant, the Abbot of Stavelot was beginning a rough process of distributing "allotments." Valenciennes was the center of a royal domain which was evidently growing in the ninth century. Ghent, at the foot of the Abbey of Saint-Bavo, was a fishing village whose importance was growing thanks to merchants carrying English wool, cloth, and lead. On the coast, the *vicus* of La Canche, Quentovic, possessed a mint and a customs house. The *portus* fostered the economic activity of the "Nordic Mediterranean." In the end, it would even succeed in rising above the Scandinavian invasions.[12]

Other centers of population, almost small towns themselves, contributed to the origins of medieval towns. Chief among these were monastic communities.

The Plan of Saint-Gall

In 820, Abbot Gozbert requested the delineation of the plan of Saint-Gall with a view toward the reconstruction of the monastery.[1] This plan presents a group of dwellings covering over 3½ hectares. If we were to stand facing the western entrance, we would have a building on our left which was probably intended for the Emperor and his suite. On the right we could see the sheepfolds and the shepherds' quarters; stables for goats, cows, and bulls; with houses for goatherds, cowherds and drovers, farm hands, and servants. To the right of the church, 40 meters further along, were a kitchen, cellar, bakery, and brewery for travelers and poor people. To the left, a kitchen, cellar, bakery, and brewery for important visitors. Still farther back were the hostelry and the extern school for young folk not intended for the monastic life. To the northeast there was a quarter for the infirmary: a hall where bleedings and purgations were undertaken, a kitchen and baths, and a medicinal garden with eight beds of plants whose names were listed. Adjoining this group, to the east, were the novice quarters with kitchens, baths, chapel, and infirmary. A house for visiting monks was projected for the same area. Not far away, the cemetery could be found, planted with fruit trees, followed by the monks' gardens with their eighteen beds of vegetables, the gardeners' house, and the close reserved for geese and poultry. Returning to the south of the cloister, we might see the quarters of the domestics and artisans: turners, coopers, brewers; the kilns for drying fruits and grain; the mill, the granaries, and the threshing floor.

The church, the cloister, and the abbot's house formed a central ensemble. East of the cloister, the monks' cellar on the ground floor was topped on the first floor by stores of provisions for the winter and the kitchen, joined

The Plan of the Abbey of Saint-Gall,
established for the Exposition of
Aix-la-Chapelle in 1965, B. N. Estampes

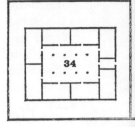

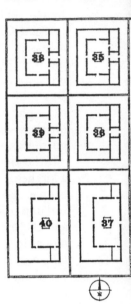

1. The church
   a) Ground-floor scriptorium with library above
   b) Ground-floor sacristie with wardrobe above
   c) Lodging for visiting monks
   d) Lodging for master of extern school
   e) Porter's lodge
   f) Vestibule for entrance to the hostelry for important visitors and to the extern school
   g) Vestibule for entrance to the monastery for all visitors
   h) Vestibule for entrance to the hospice for the poor and to the commons
   i) Lodging for the master of the hospice for the poor
   j) Monks' parlor
   k) Saint Michael's tower
   l) Saint Gabriel's tower
2. Annex for preparing sacred bread and oil
3. Monks' dorter with warming room below
4. Monks' latrine
5. Monks' bath and laundry
6. Ground-floor monks' refectory with clothing stores above
7. Monks' cellar with food stores above
8. Monks' kitchen
9. Monks' bakery and brewery
10. Kitchen, cellar, bakery, and brewery for important visitors
11. Hostelry for important visitors
12. Extern school
13. Abbot's house
14. Abbot's kitchen, cellar, and bath
15. Location for bleeding and purgation
16. Doctors' house
17. Novices' convent and infirmary
18. Infirmary kitchen and bath
19. Novices' kitchen and bath
20. Gardener's house
21. Poultry yard
22. House for keepers of chickens and geese
23. Goose yard
24. Granary
25. Workshops and artisans lodgings
26. Annex for artisans' lodgings
27. Mill
28. Mortars

The Physical and Human Setting

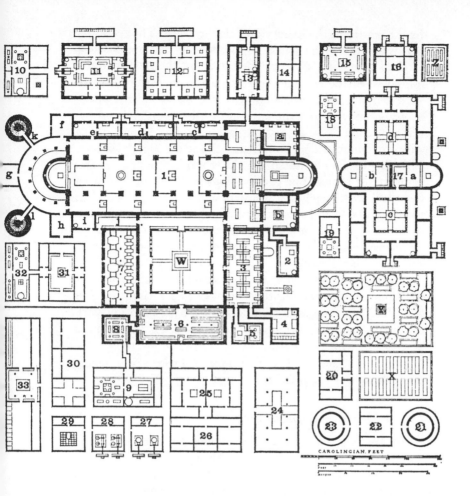

29. Court for drying fruit and grain
30. House for turners and coopers with threshing stage for grain for the brewery
31. Hospice for pilgrims and the poor
32. Kitchen, bakery, and brewery for pilgrims and the poor
33. Cow stalls and stable with lodging for cowmen and stable boys
34. House for the emperor's suite (identification uncertain)
35. Sheepfold and shepherd's lodging

36. Goat stalls and lodging for goatherds
37. Stable for dairy cows and lodging for dairymen
38. House for farm workers and servants attached to the emperor's suite (uncertain, cf. no. 34).
39. Pigsty and lodging for swineherds
40. Stable for mares and colts and lodging for stable boys
X. Monks' garden
Y. Cemetery and orchard
Z. Medicinal garden

Monastic Communities 37

by a corridor to the bakery and the brewery. The refectory was situated to the south, opposite the church, to keep kitchen odors at a distance. Below it lay the monks' wardrobe. East of the cloister there was a warming room, heated with a hypocaust, associated with the baths and the washhouse on one side and the latrines on the other.* Above the warming room, a dormitory was laid out for sixty-nine monks with a corridor leading to the church for the nightly offices. The abbot's house, north of the church, boasted several comfortable rooms. The ground floor included a front room furnished with benches, a fountain and a hearth, a bedroom with eight beds, and a corridor leading to the latrines. There were two other chambers above these. On either side of these apartments, porticos opened on the baths, the kitchen, and the cellar. Finally, the sides of the church gave access to a variety of vestibules, the porter's lodge, and those of the schoolmaster and visiting monks. The scriptorium, to the left of the apse, was divided in two by a partition with the library above. The monks' parlor was on the right as well as a hall for the poor.

Thus Saint-Gall constituted a little town where everything was provided for.

Other Monastic Communities

This plan was not a theoretical model for an ideal monastery. Recent excavations have confirmed that it did serve as guide for the reconstruction of part of the monastery. Moreover, a comparison between this plan and other familiar Carolingian monasteries demonstrates the presence of the same elements and the same desire for a comfortable establishment. When Ansegisus reconstructed Saint-Wandrille, he planned for a dormitory 60 meters long and 8 meters wide surrounding a cloister. The reception room below was to be paved, decorated with paintings, and closed in with glassed bays. The cellar and refectory would be on the east side, the major-domo's lodge on the north (encom-

* "Hypocaust" is the name for the open space below a floor through which hot air and steam could be driven to heat the room above.

passing the abbey's offices and the warming room). A portico joining these three buildings would surround the cloister, giving access to the archives on one side and the library on the other.[2] Also at Corbie, we can find the same arrangement around the cloister; refectory, dormitory, cellar, kitchen, warming room, infirmary, and abbatial house.[3] At Gellone, a more modest monastery, a novitiate, and guest house were added to the refectory, dorter, and infirmary.[4]

Around this core of buildings, a monastic town extended, composed of chapels and houses. At Saint-Riquier, in 831, 2500 houses were grouped into specialized quarters (*vici*): storerooms and accommodations for fullers, smiths, corders, tanners, cobblers, and men of all work (*servientes per omnia*). There was also a *vicus* for the *milites*, men hired for the defense of the monastery.[5] At Corbie, carpenters, masons, goldsmiths, fullers, and others are mentioned. The monastic *bourgs* of Saint-Denis, Saint-Martin of Tours, Saint-Germain-des-Prés, and Bobbio were imposing agglomerations. The taverns among the houses appear to have been a good source of revenue for the monks. They can be seen at Saint-Vaast, Saint-Philibert of Granlieu, Saint-Riquier (*vicus cauponum*), Compiègne, and indeed wherever pilgrims and merchants habitually passed through.[6] Like other towns, the abbeys held yearly markets, or at least simple weekly markets, and the taxes raised on these *telonei* were sources of great profit.

Thus monks, servants, artisans, and merchants formed a community comparable with that which we saw in the towns. There the abbot was chief and protector.

To defend the monastic town when it was threatened, walls were built which reinforced the urban quality of these monastic towns.[7] In some cases, two neighboring abbeys with a *portus* joined to form an important agglomeration. For example, the town of Ghent was born of the combination of Saint-Pierre of Mont-Blandin, between the Lys and the Scheldt, Saint-Bavo, on the right bank of the Scheldt, and the boatmen's quarter. The same phenomenon can be seen on the Aa: on one side, Sitiu, better known as Saint-Bertin; on the other, on the heights, Saint-Omer, with a merchant quarter between the two. The whole was enclosed with a wall about 879. The town of Saint-Omer was already taking shape.

The Monastic Population

Can we end this brief glimpse at the monastic communities with an estimate of the number of their inhabitants? Chroniclers who wished to praise some particular monastery tended to puff up the numbers with references to hundreds of monks. Thus Jumièges was said to hold 900 monks, although a list from the year 826 contains only 114 names. As we have seen, the dormitory of Saint-Gall made provision for 70 monks. Some 72 monks can be counted for Ferrières; 70 at Saint-Wandrille, and 84 at Charroux. Adalhard of Corbie claimed 300 monks for his monastery with 150 auxilliaries. At Saint-Bertin there were 60 religious and 112 servants. In 832, under Hilduin, there were 150 monks at Saint-Denis. Some 120 religious are known to have been at Saint-Germain-des-Prés in 820. Therefore, except for Corbie and Saint-Riquier, where the number of monks reached 300, the numbers for the great monasteries range between 70 and 150, which is modest enough. To this number we must add servants, temporary domestic personnel, the poor, and the foreigners who resided briefly in the hostelry. Thus the population of a monastery was very unstable, but it rarely surpassed a thousand persons.

Like the monastic communities, royal residences sheltered more or less numerous populations of peasants, artisans, clerks, and functionaries within their walls. We know of more than two hundred and fifty such residences within the Empire. Some, like the palaces of Pavia and Regensburg, once the homes of the Lombard and Bavarian princes respectively, were tucked into towns. But the great majority of these residences were established on the grounds of rural plantations, recalling the great *villae* of late Roman and Merovingian times. Not all of these residences were palaces in the juridical sense of the term. Some simply housed a royal representative who supervised the peasants and artisans and directed the exploitation of the land. A palace, or *sedes regia*, was designed to receive the king and his suite for weeks or months at a time. The palace was intended to serve for religious ceremonies, to house the hunt, to shelter general assemblies or the preparation of a military expedition.[1]

The Carolingian Palace

6

In the reign of Pepin, the palaces of the Oise and the Aisne—Quierzy, Verberie, and Compiègne—were the most frequented, along with those more to the east, Attigny, Ponthion, and Samoussy. Charlemagne preferred the Meuse palaces of Herstal, Duren, and Aix and, above all, the Rhenish palaces of Frankfurt and Worms. After the burning of the latter in 793, he had Ingelheim built, about 9 kilometers from Mainz. In addition, he had a more distant palace built at Nijmegen on the Waal and one at Paderborn in Saxony. In Aquitaine, Louis occupied four palaces in rotation: Angeac, Ebreuil, Doué-la-Fontaine, and Chasseneuil.[2]

These palaces have all disappeared and are now little more to us than names in acts or chronicles. But following the old descriptions, archeologists have begun to assist our view of these residences by opening up excavations at Quierzy, Doué-la-Fontaine, Annapes, and Paderborn.[3] Sometimes, too, the texts help us. The inventory of the fisc of Annapes is quite precise. The royal apartments (*sala regalis*) were built of stone: three rooms, surmounted by ten small rooms on another floor, with a cellar below. There were two wooden porches. In the court stood seventeen wooden houses, including two granaries, a bakery, a stable, and three granges. The villa of Triel, as described in a letter, included a "well-constructed house with a chimney, an upper room (solarium), a porch, a cellar, a cupboard, three wooden rooms and three of mud, a grange, and eleven stables. The court was enclosed with a stone portal."[4]

The discomfort of these rural residences could hardly have satisfied the kings and their suites. If we are to believe the text of a manuscript from Laôn, a palace worthy of the name should include reception rooms, dining rooms for both summer and winter, baths, "a gymnasium equipped for the practice of various crafts," and so forth.[5] Moreover, there must be a chapel and lodgings for clerks, guest apartments, rooms devoted to administration, a royal treasury (for the safekeeping of valuable objects, cloth, and books), and quarters for soldiers. Desirous of rivaling the emperors of the East, Charlemagne determined to enlarge his modest residence at Aix into a palace worthy of an imperial residence. This was accomplished between 794 and 870.[6]

The Palace at Aix

Four groups of buildings were constructed in a great square of 20 hectares, recalling the Roman camp with *decumanus* and *cardo**. At the northeast, the reception room (*aula regis*), 47 by 20 meters, occupied the place of the present city hall of Aachen, flanked by a tower housing the archives and the treasury. Patterned after the *aula palatina* at Trier, this room may have been decorated with paintings representing modern and ancient heroes, as was the great hall at Ingelheim.[7] Assemblies of the great gathered there, and foreign ambassadors were received. It was entered by a portico, divided by an *absidiola*, and two symmetrical staircases, like the entrance still to be seen in the ninth-century Asturian palace of Naranco. To the east rose the battlements of the residence of the king and his family, with the king's own chamber on the first floor. To the southeast there was

---

* In a Roman camp, the *decumanus* was the main east-west street and the *cardus* ran north-south.

a bathing area comprised of several pools fed by a spring called Quininus, which provided 55-degree water. In the reign of Pepin the Short, the old Roman baths had been restored and the old pagan idols removed from their places. The great pool could accommodate a hundred bathers. A gallery ran between the *aula palatina* and the religious buildings to the south, and in the center of this gallery rose a house with a monumental porch, the official entrance to the palace, seat of the tribunal and the garrison.

In the south we find the buildings devoted to worship arranged in the form of a Latin cross. At the point of intersection, 30 meters high, the famous octagon chapel still stands, the masterpiece of its architect, Eudes of Metz. The octagon was girdled by an ambulatory whose sixteen tiers of groined arches were surmounted by a gallery. Following the practice of the Byzantine emperors, the king and his household assisted at the offices from the height of this gallery. But in contrast, Charles, "wishing to give to God what was God's," had his own royal chair in the west, not on the altar as had the *Basileus*. From there, he could see the altar of the Savior facing him with that of the Virgin, around which his servitors were grouped, just to one side. He could admire the marble colonnades from Rome and Ravenna, topped by their Corinthian capitals, the massive bronze balustrades, and the mosaics of the cupola representing Christ in majesty praised by the twenty-four old men of the Apocalypse. In the west, the octagon was lengthened by an annex of three stories, ancestor of the great *Westbau* and a vast atrium of exedras like that at Saint Peter's in Rome. There were two small basilicas north and south of the octagon, one called "the Lateran," where the councils of 817 and 836 were held. The other seems to correspond with the Byzantine *metatorium*. Theoretically, these two basilicas were reserved for the clerks of the chapel. They could be reached through a portico from the *Curia*, a small building constructed east of the rotunda.

This vast palace ensemble was surrounded by a four-gated wall. Merchants had established their houses beyond, with a market; the establishments of the bishop and abbot and those of vassals and great dignitaries like Angilbert and Einhard were also in this area. The latter even commanded

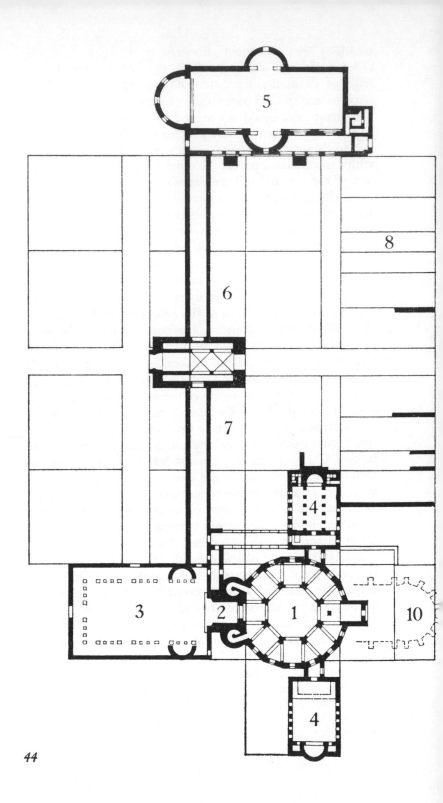

44

The Palace of Charlemagne at Aix-la-Chapelle
(after L. Hugot)

1. Palace chapel
2. Porch flanked with two turrets
3. Atrium
4. Small lateral basilicas
5. Aula palatina
6. Porch above the judgment hall
7. Barracks of the milites: royal corridor above
8. Probable location of palace
9. Baths
10. 14th century Gothic choir

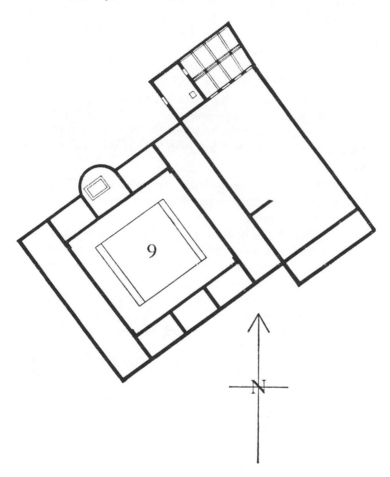

his own chapel where he kept relics sent from Rome. There was also a cemetery with its own chapel, a hunting park surrounded by a wall, and a menagerie. The whole palace was under the surveillance of a *mansuarius* who kept order in the town, not always an easy task.[8]

Other Palaces

Charlemagne passed the last years of his life at Aix. He died there and was buried in the chapel, perhaps in the antique sarcophagus decorated by a depiction of the rape of Proserpina. Though crowned at Aix in his father's lifetime, his son Louis preferred to summer at Ingelheim, Thionville, or Compiègne. Though Lothair I and Lothair II continued to live at Aix after the partition of Verdun, Louis the German passed the winter at Regensburg and the summer at Frankfurt. There, in 852, he built a chapel attended by a dozen clerks. As for Charles the Bald, at the end of his life he chose the palace at Compiègne as his principal residence. His chapel there, served by a hundred clerks, was a copy of the chapel at Aix as testified by John Scotus who left us a detailed description.

> Charles wondrously built a splendid temple
> —A temple constructed with great variety on columns
> of marble—
> Where a life of high magnificence occupied the talents of a hundred clerks, day in and day out.
> Look at the curves of the polygon and the deployment of the arches,
> The regular conjunction of the sides, the capitals and the bases,
> The turrets, parapets and paneling, the maze of rooftops,
> The oblique windows where pools of light filter through the glass,
> The paintings of the interior, the pavements and the varieties of stone;
> All around the porches, sacristies, pastophories,
> People going up and down all around the altars;
> The charged luster of the lamps and the high crowns,
> Gems aglitter on all things and the gold gleaming red,
> The draperies and tapestries surrounding the temple on every side. . . .[9]

The Physical and Human Setting

If we are to understand the condition of life in the Carolingian epoch, we must attempt to estimate the size of the population. To be sure, we have no statistics at our disposal, and the estimates of contemporaries are useless. For example, at the siege of Paris during the Norman invasion of 885, 40,000 assailants were said to be opposed by only 200 defenders. In any case, numbers had only symbolic value for clerks: a small group of people becomes a multitude; a town is always "populous."[1] Our only statistical information is furnished by the polyptichs which enumerated the inhabitants—men, women, and children—occupying the lands of an abbey. Fifty years ago, F. Lot estimated from such a source that the domain of Saint-Germain could boast a density of 34 to 39 inhabitants per square kilometer. He believed that if these proportions were extended to the whole of the territory corresponding with present-day France, one could claim 18 to 20 million inhabitants.[2] In fact, however, it is most imprudent to extrapolate on the basis of such fragmentary pieces of evidence. Recent studies suggest that, though the European population expanded slightly from the seventh to the ninth centuries, density was very unequal from one region to another: 34 inhabitants per square kilometer between the Yser and the hills of the Boulonnais; 20 inhabitants in the northern regions; 9 to 12 in the environs of Lille; 4 in the Moselle Valley.[3] Certainly, the Carolingian Empire was generally underpopulated, and certain areas were nearly barren of inhabitants.

From such a base, is it possible to determine what demographers call "population dynamics"—that is, rates of mortality, births, and marriages?

Mortality

Carolingians normally died at what we would today consider an early age. Charles the Bald died at 54, Louis the Pious at 62. Einhard was thought to have attained an advanced age when he died at 65. A lifespan of 70 years was exceptional. Thus we can understand why Charlemagne, who was never sick and who died at 72, made such an impression on his contemporaries.[4] One needed a strong constitution to survive the first years of life. Even in princely

47

families, infant mortality made heavy ravages. In 875, Richilda, the wife of Charles the Bald, was brought to bed of a stillborn child. Again pregnant in February 876, she bore a child who lived only six months.[5] Pastors were disturbed by the many infants who died before they could be baptized. A three-year penance was imposed on priests who "by their negligence excluded the new-born from the kingdom of God."[6]

Famine regularly struck the population, causing the deaths of adults and children alike. Shortages could be caused by floods which delayed the sowing, winters which lasted too long, late frosts which destroyed the first crops, torrid summers which dried up the vegetation, and even an invasion of grasshoppers in 873. Carolingian annals often describe the catastrophic effects of the greater famines. In 793, the hunger was so terrible in Burgundy and Francia that "many died." In 868, the dead in Burgundy were counted in the thousands: there were not enough men left to bury them all. In the county of Sens, 56 persons died in one day. In 874, "a third of the human race died in Gaul and Germania." In the effort to feed themselves, people were forced to eat earth mixed with a little flour and fashioned in the shape of bread. In Saxony, the hunger was so pressing that they ate their horses. There were even outbreaks of cannibalism: "Some welcomed the hungry into their houses, killed them, and put the bodies into the salt tub . . . . " "Men ate men; brothers ate brothers, and mothers their children." The hungry were tormented by hallucinations: "In this same year (793) one could see in various places that spring, false wheat in the fields or covering forests and swamps in enormous quantity. It could be seen and touched but not eaten."[7] The king was forced to take steps against hoarders, fixing a maximum price for wheat. Penitentials modified the penalties for theft rising out of necessity, citing the Book of Proverbs: "Men do not despise a thief, if he steals to satisfy his stomach when he is hungry" (VI. 30).

Malnutrition caused yet further deaths when followed by an epidemic. The plague which ravaged the west in the middle of the eighth century was a choking disease. But, so far as we know, chroniclers rarely described the

The Physical and Human Setting

nature of the pestilences they reported. In 836, the flower of both the ecclesiastic and lay aristocracy died in Italy.[8] Against such a scourge men could do nothing. As we shall see, hygiene and medicine were powerless to allay illness. One could do naught but multiply one's prayers and await the end.

Birth Control

Once a crisis passed, the demographic curve generally exhibited at least a temporary correction. But even when people married very early, births barely compensated for the declines. Though it is impossible to estimate the rate of fecundity, the idea of what we call birth control is evidenced in capitularies, conciliar canons, and penitentials. So effectively could men and women "fool nature" to avoid the advent of a child that large families were rare. Still, conforming to long-established tradition, the church allowed sexual relations only for the purpose of procreation and forbade all types of contraception. Church authorities prohibited all sexual behavior which they believed to be nonprocreative, including *coitus interruptus* and the *retro* position in which the man lies beneath the woman.[9] Theodulf wrote, in his chapter "On Fornication against Reason":

> They call it pollution, or the abominable sin—the deed of lying with a woman in an abnormal fashion. That is why we read that Onan, son of Judah, was struck down by God for spilling his seed on the ground after he had penetrated his wife.[10]

Penitentials then in use put forbidden relations between married people on the same plane as the taking of abortive potions by women:

> The mother who kills her child, whom she is carrying in her womb, before the fortieth day after conception will fast for a year, and for three years if it is after the fortieth day.[11]

Herbal potions, well known since antiquity, might be contraceptive or abortifacient. Roman and Byzantine doctors whose writings were known to the literate provided a wide variety of recipes on this subject. They recommended fern roots, willow leaves, epimede, rue, mixtures of aloes, gillyflower seeds, ginger, pepper and saffron, spermicidal unguents, and pessaries of different sorts. Although they classed them as *maleficia*—that is, products of magic—Carolingians made use of all these potions. Confessors were instructed to ask penitents: "Have you drunk any *maleficium*, that is, any herb or other product to avoid having children, or have you given such a drink to another?" In pastoral rounds, bishops were to look out for women who performed abortions or "sorceresses" who furnished potions for that purpose:

> If anyone, to satisfy their own desires, or through hatred, did something to a man or to a woman which would impede their having children, or gave them any drink so that they could not, he engender or she conceive, this must be held to be homicide.[12]

This text would be repeated for centuries in the canon law. Nevertheless, church legislators showed their awareness that misery might be the cause of a mother's refusal to bear a child:

> A woman who kills her child by magical practice, by drink or any art, will do seven years penance. If she did it from poverty, the penance will be reduced to three years.[13]

If, in spite of these precautions, a child came into the world, some people did not hesitate to kill it. Infanticide, even if committed involuntarily, was often denounced and punished. Some women, fearing to reveal the child of adultery, drowned it at birth. In 780, a village girl of Bischofsheim found the body of a newborn child in a pool of water. Soon the peasants accused a nun from the monastery of having caused her child to disappear. It required the intervention of Saint Leoba to unmask the guilty party—a poor woman whom the nuns had taken in.[14] Parents smothered children under the weight of blankets or by placing them between the mother and father in bed.

It was considered a lesser evil to abandon a child, usually at the door of a church. Priests even publicly encouraged adulterous women to abandon their children rather than commit murder.[15] Many such children were received into monasteries. In 787, a priest of Milan founded the first orphanage known to us. Wishing to stop parents from killing children whose birth they wished to conceal, and thereby exposing themselves to eternal damnation, Datheus established a hospice where the children of adultery were entrusted to nurses, baptized, and instructed until they reached the age of seven.[16]

The only acceptable way to limit births was periodic or total continence, for, it was often recalled, marriage was instituted not for men "to satisfy lust" but to assure the continuation of the species. In his treatise, "On the Education of Laypeople," written at the request of an aristocrat, Jonas, Bishop of Orleans, devoted an entire section to the question of marriage, so that his readers "could learn to conduct their conjugal life honestly."[17] Jonas reported the reflections of certain laymen:

> Our wives are bound to us legally; if we wish to use them at any time for our own good pleasure, it is no sin. . . . God created the genital organs so that married persons can have relations between them. How can it be wrong that these relations are motivated by pleasure?

To such men and to others, who more scrupulously inquired of the priest when they could "meet" their wives, Jonas replied that the church forbade relations between spouses during certain periods: forty days before Christmas, forty days before and eight days after Easter and eight days after Pentecost; the eve of great feasts, Sundays, Wednesdays, and Fridays; during the wife's pregnancy and until thirty days after she has given birth if it was a boy and forty days if it was a girl; during the menstrual period; five days before taking communion. One can see, with a little calculation, that there were not too many days left.

Everything touching sexuality was considered impure. Church tradition, with a new interest in the Old Testament, particularly Leviticus, only served to reinforce this clerical position. However, some account was taken of extenuating circumstances in determining the sanctions against transgressors. Thus, a man who "met" his wife during Lent would be required to do a year's penance, but, if he was drunk, the penalty was reduced to forty days.[18] Preachers and hagiographers supplied examples of lay persons who had followed the duty of continence even to excess, such as the father of Gerard of Aurillac, to whom an angel issued a reminder that he ought to "know" his wife so that a child could be born to them.[19]

Sexual License

These extreme cases were, it is true, quite rare. More commonly, laymen were not very scrupulous in observing the prescriptions of the church, or else they tended to seek compensations outside of marriage. Many aristocrats had concubines, either slave or free. Jonas deplored this: a husband should not be allowed to do what is forbidden to the wife; if a servant becomes pregnant, she holds her mistress in contempt.[20] But the contrary example was set by persons of the highest rank. Did not Charlemagne have numerous concubines until he had reached an advanced age? Had not Charles the Bald enjoyed intimacy with Richilda before he married her?[21] Moreover, Germanic custom recognized *Friedelehe* (from *fridila*—well-loved), a union of limited duration, concluded without transfer of tutelage or dower, simply marked with the morning gift (*morgengabe*) which every man was expected to make to one who had shared his bed. Great proprietors could, without much constraint, satisfy their caprices with slave girls or free women living on their domains. To exemplify the virtue of Gerald of Aurillac (d. 909), his biographer related that, seduced by the charm of one of his peasants, the young man made a rendezvous with her one evening. Thanks to God, however, she then appeared so ugly to him that he let her go. Moreover, fearing a return of temptation, he arranged her marriage, freed her, and gave her a plot of land.[22]

The story, here so edifying, generally ended otherwise. Many did not content themselves with the love of servant girls but frequented prostitutes who kept houses near the great pilgrimage centers—Saint-Martin of Tours, for example—or even in villages and the royal palace itself. When Louis the Pious installed himself at Aix, he was obliged to chase out the evil-living men and women who cluttered the courtyard.[23] A capitulary in the year 820 forbade them lodging in the palace or the houses nearby:

> Any man in whose house prostitutes have been found must carry them out on his shoulders to the market place where they will be whipped; if he refuses, he will be whipped with them.[24]

If we accept the evidence of Germanic law codes and penitentials then in use, sexual license spread through all the ranks of Carolingian society. The Germans were very careful of the honor of their wives, and any attempt to shame them was harshly punished. In the law of the Alamanni, it cost a man six sous if he pulled off the headdress of a young girl out walking. If he raised her dress so as to uncover her knees, six sous. If he turned it up all the way, twelve sous. If he took it off, forty sous. The penalties were doubled if married women were molested. Lombard law applied the death penalty to a man who took the dress of a woman who was bathing and forced her to go home naked.[25] In the penitentials, illegitimate unions of young people, adulteries among married folk, rapes, guilty relations between laymen and nuns, monks and lay women, monks and nuns, were all foreseen and penalized. Sexual deviations made up an even longer catalogue: the brother who deflowered his sister, the son who had guilty relations with his mother, sodomites, lesbians, men guilty of bestiality—all parade before us like a pre-Dantesque inferno.[26] One can only hope that the occasions upon which a confessor had to deal with these diverse aberrations were rare. In that tone, Theodulf, Bishop of Orleans, warned them:

> Many crimes are enumerated in the penitentials, crimes which it is not proper to make known to men. Therefore, the priest should not interrogate them about all of them, for fear that the penitent will fall yet further, on the instigation of the devil, into vices of whose existence he had formerly been ignorant.[27]

The Christianization of Marriage

Carolingian bishops and canonists sought to remedy sexual

licence by placing a higher value on marriage through Christianization. According to the earlier Germano-Roman traditions, marriage had generally consisted of two civil formalities: betrothal and nuptials. Betrothal was defined as a promise constituting a legal bond, a contract of transfer between the fiancé and the clan or guardian of the young girl. The fiancé publicly engaged himself to provide a dower. The guardian gave over to him the symbols of his authority. If the engagement were not respected, the fiancé would draw the vengeance of the family upon himself. For example, a certain Stephen promised to marry the daughter of a Count Regimund in the presence of her relatives and friends. He changed his mind, however, and delayed the delivery of the dower. Accordingly, the fiancée's clan pursued him. Usually, the dower consisted of moveable and immoveable goods, recorded in a written document, the *libellum dotis*, samples of which have been preserved in formularies: "It pleases me to give you, before the wedding day, something of my goods, to denote certain lands in certain places . . . to do with as you will. . . ." The second step was the marriage itself, consisting of the execution of the contract, the remission of the fiancée on the occasion of a banquet and various festivities. Then, on the day after the nuptials, the husband would bestow the morning gift on his wife.[28]

Normally, Christians also liked to have the benediction of a priest. But that act, which was imposed in the East from the fourth century on, was in no way obligatory in the West. Nevertheless, the church, as the guardian of the sanctity of marriage, attempted to intervene as the guarantor of its stability. In the first place, the clergy denounced the rape of maidens and provided for the annullment of marriages to which the wife had not given her consent. Moreover, they ruled that girls who had passed fifteen or sixteen years of age could not be married without their consent. Secondly, they commanded that marriages be performed with a certain publicity. The council of Ver, in 755, commanded "that all lay folk, whether noble or not, should celebrate their nuptials publicly."[29] This emphasis on publicity can partially be explained by the need to avoid such marriages between relatives as were classed as "incest." Indeed, marriage was prohibited to persons to the seventh degree of kinship. As in most tribal societies, exogamy was the rule, and both civil and religious law underwrote this principle. Thus Charlemagne's capitulary of 803 condemned laymen "who soil themselves with incestuous nuptials, contracting such marriages before the bishops and priests have, with the elders of the people, diligently researched the consanguinity of the future wedded pair."[30] Blood ties were often invoked by persons wanting to divorce, but the bishops sought to avoid frequent dissolutions of unions. They understood that, in a society founded on kinship and lineage, descent from a common ancestor united everyone. This necessitated many inquiries in rural communities where marriages were commonly made between neighbors. But they also understood the difficulties which might arise from this procedure. In practice, they were obliged to bend the rules and accept marriages between relatives to the fourth degree. Nevertheless, spiritual relatives were added to the natural relatives under the prohibition as a *diriment impediment*: a godfather could not marry his goddaughter, nor a godmother her godson.*

To ensure the stability of marriage, the church also spelled out some conditions under which divorce would be authorized: the bad conduct of a wife or the impotence of a husband. But inquiries were necessary in these cases also. The famous politico-religious affair of the divorce of the Emperor Lothair II provides an example of the first instance.[31] Wishing to give one of his concubines the title of wife and queen, the Emperor accused his legitimate wife, Theutberga, of having had incestuous relations with her brother, Abbot Hugh of Saint Maurice-en-Valais, a person, we are told, of evil repute. Once the Queen's champion had victoriously sustained the ordeal of boiling water—one of the classic "judgments of God"—the divorce could not be accomplished.[32] Pope Nicholas I, sustained by Hincmar, Archbishop of Reims, used the occasion to clarify church doctrine regarding divorce. An impotent husband was to establish the proof and cause of his condition, for impotence was often believed to be the result of sorcery. He could

* *Diriment impediment:* those impediments which render a marriage null and void, generally consisting of some personal incapacity, a defect of consent or consanguinity.

then be treated by exorcism. Many wives came to Hincmar striving to prove, with written memoirs where possible,
that their husbands were incapable of conjugal relations
with them. The husbands retorted that the wives lied.[33]

Sterility, or any other malady in a wife, could not be a
cause of divorce. To be sure, in answer to an inquiry by
Boniface, Pope Gregory II answered that a man who could
not have relations with his wife could remarry if he found
it impossible to practice continence.[34] But that was an exceptional case. Even in Germanic lands it was generally
expected that the man who engaged himself in marriage
must cleave to his wife "even though she were sterile,
deformed, old, dirty, drunken, a frequenter of bad company, lascivious, vain, greedy, unfaithful, quarrelsome, abusive . . . , for when that man was free, he freely engaged
himself."[35]

II

The
Powerful
and the
People

The "powerful" who dominated Carolingian society were called by many names: *optimates, primores, magnati, sublimes, illustres, majores, potentes*. This small group constituted the aristocracy who had succeeded in the course of the eighth century in imposing themselves through force and diplomacy on the people. During the Carolingian centuries, they controlled the sources of wealth and occupied the principal religious and civil posts.

The Aristocratic Family

How could a Carolingian aristocrat be recognized? To begin with, by his family. He was "of noble blood," "the issue of an illustrious lineage," of good stock—that is, a gentleman. Through his ancestors he sprang from the Merovingian aristocracy who had been allied to the Austrasian family of the Pepinids. The all-powerful mayors of the palace: Pepin II of Herstal, followed by his son, Charles Martel, had successfully overcome internal and external threats with the help of their Austrasian and Neustrian companions. In return, they endowed them with lands and dignities—comital, episcopal, and abbatial; they gave their daughters, sisters, or at least nieces to them in marriage. To be sure, Charles' son, Pepin, called the Short, depended primarily on the support of the church and the papacy to make him powerful enough to supplant the Merovingian family. But he would not have dispensed with the faithful followers who had linked their fortunes with those of the Carolingians. With the support of this handful of nobles, the Frankish kings governed their realm and finally their Empire. It has been estimated that the members of about twenty-seven families, most of whom came out of Austrasia, monopolized the highest posts. Among them we might note the Etichonids of Alsace, the Rorgonids who were solidly entrenched in Le Maine, the Widonids who held counties and duchies in Brittany and Italy, the Girarids, the Unrochids.[1] Once they had grasped the royal crown, the Carolingians felt themselves to be tightly bound to these families. To be sure, their coronation was a source of extraordinary power. The consecrating bishop had bestowed the crown, sceptre, and other insignia of their rank upon them. But when the ceremony had ended, they resumed their ordinary garments and their habitual way of life.

Descendants who took pride in their illustrious ancestors maintained the same names from generation to generation. Martel's grandson bore the name of Charles, then it passed to the grandson of Charlemagne, and so forth. Similarly, the name of Guillaume, founder of Saint-Guilhem-du-Désert, conqueror of the Muslims at Orbieu, was passed to his grandson, issue of the marriage of Bernard of Septimania with Dhuoda. These ancestors of this famous family were praised by Dhuoda in the *Manual* she composed for young Guillaume when, at the age of sixteen, he was preparing to become a vassal of Charles the Bald. She instructed her son to pray for all who, on both the paternal and maternal sides, had contributed to the fortune of the family. After listing these ancestors, the mother wrote: "When a member of the stock (*stirps*) dies, you must have his name added to the list of the deceased for whom we must pray."[2] Similar lists (*libri memoriales*) were kept in abbeys founded by aristocrats in order to preserve the memory of their benefactors.[3]

The Carolingian family still retained much of the character of a Germanic clan. The father, or in his absence the maternal uncle, was all-powerful. Nothing could disparage his authority. Dhuoda even suggests that the respect due a father should be the model for the fidelity due a king. Young Guillaume owed his opportunity for political prestige and material wealth to his father, Bernard. It would be an unpardonable crime to rebel against a father. Though she did not name him, Dhuoda was making allusion to the son of Louis the Pious who was in revolt against his father, the Emperor. Some priests, like Hrabanus Maurus and Hincmar, devoted treatises to the respect owed by sons to fathers.[4] Still the young were tempted to take the places of aging men. Bavarian law stipulated that a chief's sons should not seek to replace their father so long as he retained his potency, his ability to help the king, lead an army, mount a horse and carry his arms, so long as he was neither blind nor deaf.[5] In describing the life of Charlemagne's family, Einhard described him as a model Germanic father. The Emperor venerated his mother Bertha and loved his sister

Gisela. He did not want to be separated from his sons and daughters: "He never dined without them or travelled without them." His love for his daughters was such "that he did not wish to give them in marriage to anyone, neither to one of his own nor to a stranger. He kept them all near him in his house until his death, saying that he could not relinquish their society. But, happy in some respects, he had to suffer the evil results of this conduct." The last phrase alludes discreetly to the liaisons of Bertha and Rotruda with some of the court nobles.[6]

In the royal family, bastards were cherished as well as legitimate children. Charlemagne, who had many concubines and many bastards from them, assured them all brilliant futures. And he was deeply affected when one of them, Pepin the Hunch-backed, rebelled. Louis III was so pained by the death of his bastard Hugues, in 880, that he renounced his pursuit of the Normans. Charles the Fat attempted to transmit his crown to his bastard Bernard. In 888, Arnulf, bastard of Carloman, did become King of Germany.[7]

Aristocratic Marriage

Although women held an inferior position in Frankish society, the noble woman played an important role in the bosom of her family. From her youth the noble woman was the object of rivalry since aristocratic lineages were so often united by political marriages. From the beginning of their history, Carolingian princes set the example: the fortune of the Pepinid ancestors stemmed from the marriage of Begga, Pepin the Elder's daughter, and Anchesigel, son of Arnulf of Metz. The mayors of the palace and their royal descendants made marital policy the chief means of reinforcing their clientele. Thus most of the great families of the Empire enjoyed blood ties with the Carolingian family. The Girards and the Guillaumes descended from Charles Martel; Pepin the Short's sister married Odilo of Bavaria; Bertha negotiated a marriage between her son, Charles, and the daughter of the King of the Lombards; the same Charles, by marrying Fastrada, reconciled himself with the Alamannian princes. Nithard says explicitly that the young Charles the

Bald married Irmentrude, niece of the powerful Alard, "to draw the greater part of her people to himself."[8] And if a family hesitated to make a particular alliance, the deed could be accomplished by the act of abduction, an old Germanic custom which had not yet died out. A vassal of Charles the Bald ravished one of Lothair's daughters in 846. One of Charles the Fat's councillors snatched the rich heiresses of Alamania and Italy to give them in marriage to his friends.[9]

Could such a marriage, undertaken as an association of interests, come to include conjugal love? That is a difficult question to answer. Certainly some couples were happy, but the chroniclers, who were chiefly interested in sorrow, did not record their names. Charlemagne sincerely mourned the death of Hildegard who gave him eight children during twelve years of marriage. The widower Einhard found it hard to console himself for the loss of a wife who had helped him in the administration of the household.[10]

The importance of women depended entirely on this double role of mother and helper. Men venerated the women who presented them with heirs. According to Regino of Prüm this was the great merit of Louis the German's wife, Emma.[11] And if a wife was sterile, a man like Lothair II might try to repudiate her for the sake of the concubine who had borne him children. Charles the Fat attempted to obtain a divorce on the grounds that his wife, Richarde, was barren.[12]

Whether or not her own desires were satisfied, a wife was expected to be an active collaborator in her husband's enterprises. Dhuoda, an abandoned wife, never had a reproachful word for her husband Bernard. On the contrary, she venerated "her lord and master" and reminded her son how useful she had been in his enterprises, though they were no more than "borrowing silver from Christians and Jews."[13] Bertha, the wife of Girard of Vienne, and Ingelberga, the wife of Louis II, accompanied their husbands on their warlike expeditions. Likewise, Carolingian queens did more than play an important role in the organization of the palace. Crowned like their husbands, they became their associates on the throne, *consortes regni*. To take only two examples, Louis' wife, Judith, and Richilda, wife of Charles the Bald, actively pursued their husbands' policies. At the end of the ninth century in southern France, a diploma attributed the title of Countess to the widow of the Count of Toulouse, Raimond. A similar title was held by the widow of the Count of Catalonia, Sunifred. Thus, after the example of their queens, the wives of the high aristocracy began to acquire political functions equal to those of men.[14]

In the *Manual* addressed to her son Guillaume, Dhuoda repeatedly insisted on the young man's right to a place with his lord Charles. In a single sentence, she summed up the essentials of the art of aristocratic living:

> If you would be a useful servitor with your companions-in-arms at the royal and imperial court, you must fear, love, venerate, and cherish the illustrious ancestors and relatives of the King, your lord, whether they derive their high nobility from their ancestors or have acquired their offices thanks to marriage. In every action, seek their advantage and execute their orders faithfully, with your spirit as well as your body.[15]

In effect the aristocracy fulfilled the double role of councillor and faithful follower.

The Duty of Counsel

Allusions to the council and to councillors are easy to find in the writings of the period. From king to simple seigneur, no lords ruled alone. They had to surround themselves with their leading men and school themselves to heed their advice. Charlemagne himself, as we shall see, never acted without taking counsel. His successors, endowed with less grand personalities, were often influenced by members of their entourage. Louis the Pious' cousin, Wala, sought to direct his affairs at the beginning of the reign. Count Adalbert enjoyed such authority with Lothair that "no one dared to deviate in the slightest from his advice."[16] The very young Charles the Bald declared that he could do nothing without the support of his grandees. In 843, the king invited the members of the Council of Coulaines to guide him with their advice and to defend him against "the enticements which might overcome him because of his youth and inexperience of power." While we do not go so far as to say with Fustel de Coulanges that "Charles the Bald was the leader of followers whose followers made the law," we can assert that the engagements made at Coulaines influenced Charles' policies very heavily, at least at the beginning of the reign.[17]

Among the great, the ecclesiastical aristocracy was not last to offer counsel. From the reign of Louis on, the episcopate was "in the limelight."[18] In his *De institutione regia*, Jonas of Orleans (d. 842) formulated the policy of the bishops, and his line was followed by the reforming councils of 829. The bishop, who crowned the king, must render account to God for the conduct of the prince. Princes should conform to the words of the prophet Haggai (II.12) and "interrogate the priests on the law." If a king exceeded his power and became a "tyrant," bishops could inflict penance on him. This happened to Louis the Pious at Attigny in 822 and, above all, at Soissons in 833. Having recognized his faults before the bishops who favored Lothair, Louis was condemned to perpetual penance. In fact, he was restored to his dignities within a year, thanks to his other two sons and their adherents. But the precedent was not forgotten. After Louis died in 840, and again after the partition of Verdun, the bishops, disquieted by the dislocation of the Empire, proposed a "program of concord" between the brothers and revived their periodic meetings. At Yutz, in 844, the bishops under the presidency of Drogo of Metz, one of Charlemagne's bastards, exhorted the kings, proposed reforms to them, and demanded that they do penance for their past errors. They renewed these paternal counsels at the Assembly of Meerssen in 847 and again in the same palace four years later. One of the most active among the ecclesiastical councillors was the Bishop of Reims, Hincmar. He reminded King Louis in a letter that bishops must keep watch over kings and direct them toward their salvation. He referred to the book of Kings, recalling that Samuel the priest had crowned Saul but had then chosen David to replace him because of his infidelities.[19] Therefore bishops had the power to correct and even to replace kings. "Bishops, by virtue of their ministry and the sacred authority vested in them, ought to unite for the direction and correction of kings so that the mighty ones of different realms and the people confided to them might receive the support of their counsels." This declaration, signed by forty-five bishops at Savonnières near Toul in 859, testifies to the high ambition of the ecclesiastical aristocracy.[20] But such declarations of principle had little effect. Despite their temporal power and their moral authority, bishops did not control kings, and the great folk considered little beyond their own immediate interests.

. . . and of Fidelity

The success of the episcopal program of government depended on the magnates' observation of one of the chief duties of the aristocracy: to keep faith with their lords. The aristocratic quality *par excellence* was respect for the given word. A chieftain had his duties to his faithful followers, and a faithful follower who denied his lord was behaving like a slave, to use Nithard's expression.[21] In fact, the whole history of the ninth-century aristocracy is a tale of fidelities given and withdrawn according to circumstances and changing interests. The famous episode of the "field of lies" comes readily to mind. In 833, Lothair was so successful in corrupting his father's sworn followers that during a single night all of Louis' men transferred their tents to Lothair's camp. Or we may remember Charles the Bald, rudely abandoned by the Gauzbertids in 858.[22] Representatives of the greatest families did not hesitate to change sides. In 838, Gerard, Count of Paris, pledged his faith to Charles. He moved to Lothair's party two years later. Bernard of Septimania awaited the issue of the battle of Fontenoy so that he could do homage to the winner—whom he later betrayed. Guenelon, Bishop of Sens, who had crowned him king, went from Charles' camp to Louis', and his name became eponymous for "traitor*." "The common good" did not move the aristocratic conscience. They dreamed of nothing beyond the interests of their families, the growth of their power, and the increase of their goods. "Each followed the

---

* Later his name appeared as "Ganelon," the traitor in *The Song of Roland*.

path which pleased him, striking out amidst dissensions and quarrels," wrote Nithard in the conclusion of his book.[23] The clans stood in opposition to the court and to one another within the realm: the clan of Wala, and then of Adalard, against the clan of Welf, the clan of Robert the Strong, the clan of Boso, and so forth. Above all, the princely families plotted amongst themselves. Rebel heads fell and new treasons were provoked by the executions as families sought to avenge their dead. One of the chief resorts of the politics of the time was the old Germanic *faida*, which we call vendetta.

Landed Property

The aristocracy disposed of immense wealth in land acquired by conquest, gifts, or purchases. The Carolingian family itself was in the lead with properties extending from the valley of the Oise to the Rhineland. W. Metz has been able to isolate more than a thousand names representing everything from palaces to simple rural households. Grouped together into "fiscs," these domains were not of equal extent. The fisc of Annapes and its attendant villae* covered 2850 hectares, while that of Snellegem surpassed 7000 hectares.[1]

Other aristocrats, whether or not they were related to the Carolingian family, were equally well endowed. The testament of Fulrad, Abbot of Saint-Denis, indicated that his family had ten estates in Alsace, eight in Lorraine and six in the Saar basin. The Welfs were masters of immense domains north of Lake Constance; the Etichonids were proprietors of a large part of Alsace; the Unrochids, who were related to the latter, had groups of estates in Alamania, Friuli, the Toulousain, Flanders, and elsewhere. Gerald of Aurillac possessed lands in the Auvergne, in the southeast, in Poitou, and in Spain. He could, according to his biographer, go from Puy-Griou to Sarlat sleeping only in his own castles.

Thanks to the surviving documents, the landed wealth of abbeys can be more precisely evaluated. Saint-Germain-des-Prés possessed more than 30,000 hectares; Saint-Bertin more than 10,000 hectares; Fulda tallied more than 15,000 hectares. The Council of Aix of 816 indicated that the great establishments controlled from 3000 to 8000 manses—a manse† had an average extent of 12 hectares—and this figure might well be doubled. A church of secondary importance might hold from 1000 to 2000 manses, while a modest establishment commanded 300 or 400. In the *Notitia de servicio monasteriorum* of 819, Louis the Pious listed the monasteries of the Empire with military and fiscal responsibilities proportionate to the wealth of each.[2]

---

* *Villae* were large farms comprising fields and villages.
† A manse was a single-family farm, see p. 102 below.

Domain Administration

All the great proprietors took an active interest in the good administration of their estates, for they drew their power from that source. They consulted theoretical treatises like those of Palladius or Columella who recorded Roman methods of exploiting land to the best advantage. They maintained archives of their property deeds and charters of donations, supplemented by the occasional fabrication of a forgery. Up-to-date inventories (*descriptiones*) were maintained, and minute accounts of rentals were established.[3] For these tasks they employed personnel whom they hoped were qualified.

They were following the highest example. Carolingian kings expected the *judex* who directed each fisc to furnish regular accounts of the state of the *villae*. Around 811, Charlemagne ordered the *missi* to collate "a descriptive inventory of the fiscs, so that we may know what rights we possess in making our demands of each one."[4] We still have five of these inventories (*brevium exempla*) for royal fiscs in the north of France: Annapes, Vitry-en-Artois, Cysoing, Somain, and Triel. The investigators had surveyed the condition of the work buildings, furniture, utensils, annual harvest expectations, number of animals, and so on.[5] Charlemagne or Louis of Aquitaine, anxious to ensure a good yield, promulgated a capitulary of sixty-nine articles (the famous *De villis*) to recall the principles of sound exploitation and correct the abuses of the intendants.

Encouraged by the king, great ecclesiastical proprietors also attempted to assemble precise records in order to estimate the revenues of their vast holdings. About 813, an important document was redacted on order of the Abbot of Saint-Germain-des-Prés and became known as the "Polyptich of Irminon." Villa by villa, the number of tenants were listed with their holdings, the names of the peasants and their children, and the rents they owed in service and in kind. The abbots of Saint-Pierre of Ghent, Saint-Armand, Saint-Bertin, and Saint-Remi of Reims redacted *brevationes* of the same type.[6] If an unfortunate series of events caused the depopulation of the domains, they would lose all their economic value. In such a case, the proprietor would undertake a new survey of the revenues, as was done at Prüm after the Norman invasion of around 892.[7] Thanks to Adalhard, Abbot of Corbie, we can even delineate administrative details. In his *Statuta*, redacted about 822, he followed the increasingly standardized procedure of distinguishing the revenues reserved to the abbot and his house (*mense abbatiale*) and those destined for the monks (*mense conventuelle*). The latter were subdivided by office: the cellarer had charge of the material sustenance of the monks, the refectory, mills, breweries, bakeries; the chamberlain (*camerarius*) saw to the clothing of the monks, the maintenance of the church and sacristy; the monk in charge of giving welcome to pilgrims and the poor had to supervise their lodging. When travelers became too numerous, he had also to seek means of providing for them beyond the allowance for daily distribution.[8] In short, everything appeared to be foreseen. We can see yet another example of good management in the Constitution of the Abbot of Saint-Wandrille, Ansegisus. He had an extensive list of supplies owed by each group of villae to the abbey. For example, the domains of the Boulonnais and Ternois annually owed sixty monastic habits, twenty pieces of white linen for shirts, enough leather for five pairs of sandals, twenty hogsheads of beans, twenty-one cheeses weighing seventy-five pounds each, a thousand eggs, two hundred pounds of wax for the church and two hundred pounds of tallow for lighting.[9] The examples could be endlessly multiplied.

We have seen that the great folk traveled much. Proprietors provided for the storage of the harvests in granaries to ensure their ability to feed themselves and their large entourage on the road. They made provision for firewood and wine for the court. Thanks to a *corvée* for transport, the Abbot of Saint-Bertin could have his wine delivered from the Rhineland every year.* Einhard, a lay abbot, announced his intention to go to Aix by asking his overseer to put the house in order, laying in cereal, grain for beer, wine, cheese, and so on.[10] Inventories, statutes, and administrative correspondence all bear witness to the Carolingian striving for order and organization.

Fear of Shortages

The texts are full of testimony to the daily difficulties of administration behind which lurked a nagging fear of a

---

* *Corvée* refers to labor dues regularly exacted from a peasant as part of the price of his tenure.

failure of supplies. The letters of Lupus of Ferrières are very significant in this respect. He complains of a lack of grain, wine, and salt. He did not have enough money to buy clothes. In order to make a trip, he had to borrow money from an aristocrat. It is true that his monastery was not among the most heavily endowed. It is also true that he was trying to regain the profitable *cella* of Saint-Josse, near Montreuil-sur-Mer, which the king had given to one of his lay followers.* Still, "I have only enough grain for two more months, the sick complain, and the guests are without assistance. I shall have to sell the altar vases," he wrote to his correspondents in high places.[11]

We know that these abbots had to be tirelessly on guard against the usurpations of neighboring monasteries. They entered into law suits over disputed lands, and blows were sometimes exchanged. Even the richest landlords were sometimes overcome with the same cares. Their constant fear of shortages is astonishing. The revenues drawn from these abbeys should have been quite sufficient for the maintenance of the monks, their *familia*, and those whom they assisted. We are obliged, therefore, to imagine constant waste or embezzlement as well as inability on the part of the master to make himself obeyed.

Such conditions explain, though they may not justify, the cupidity and even avarice of the aristocrats, an avarice continually denounced by moralists. The Emperor himself condemned those who forced the poor to sell their land or who promised to secure exemptions from military service in exchange for a gift of land. Conciliar canons fruitlessly deplore the fact that rich laymen sought every opportunity for impingement on the goods of the church. Charles Martel set the example, and his successors, hoping to secure the fidelity of the magnates, emulated his policy at the risk of drawing celestial anger down on their own heads.[12] Thus the wife of one of Charles the Bald's followers was upset by Saint Remi in a dream after the king had given her husband land belonging to the church of Reims. A king might use lands taken from a church or an abbey to recompense his vassals or to indemnify a bishop deprived

---

* Lupus, like some other ninth-century and tenth-century writers, uses the word *cella* to refer to a small oratory with a small land grant attached for the support of the occupant.

The Powerful and the People

of his seat.[13] For clerks, too, displayed mighty appetites, though in principle they should have set an example of disinterestedness.

> Can he be said to have quit the world who never ceases to increase his property by any possible means . . . , who, pushed by cupidity, recoils neither from perjury nor the bribery of false witnesses, who seeks out cruel and greedy lawyers and, when he has acquired the property, cares less how he got it than how much he kept?[14]

Ecclesiastical Treasures

Clerks and monks were not forbidden to acquire wealth intended to fatten the capital of their church, embellish the liturgy, or help the disinherited. Outside of their landed property, churches disposed of moveable goods which constituted their "treasure," produced by the *cens*, the *decima*,* fines and offerings of the faithful (*oblationes, donaria, munera, elemosynae*) in the form of coins of precious metal, jewels, silks, and so forth.[15] This treasure was confided to a guardian who had to foil the plots of thieves, who might even pierce the walls, and pilgrims who might take advantage of crowded days to seize some precious object. Like the *descriptiones* ordered by landlords for their domains, inventories were redacted by bishops or abbots giving, often with much precision, descriptions of each object—its shape, weight, value, and the name of the donor, if he were a prince. Here is a short extract from the inventory ordered by the king for the Abbey of Saint-Riquier in 831: the church possessed four gold chalices, two great and thirteen small silver ones; two gold patens, four large and thirteen small silver ones and one of gilded bronze; forty brown chasubles, five of black silk, three of Persian silk, one of silver; six tapestries, three curtains, four silk cushions and a linen table cloth embroidered with silk.[16] One might say that the treasure served as a bank account. Lupus of Ferrières sold part of the treasure of his church to buy grain. The monks of Saint-Denis raised 688 gold livres and 3250

---

* The *cens* is a rent and the *decima* a tithe.

silver livres to purchase the liberty of their abbot who had been taken prisoner by the Normans.[17] These treasures drew the covetous attention of the magnates as well as the pirates, and the princes were in the lead. In 841, Lothair invaded le Maine and forced the clergy to hand over the treasures from all of the churches. In 877, Charles the Bald raised the tribute destined for the Normans by drawing from church treasures "as much as fortune had bestowed upon them."[18] The proprietors themselves were tempted to turn the reserves to their own uses and, as Charlemagne complained, "to sell the sacred vessels to the Jews."[19] Rothade of Soissons pawned a gold chalice decorated with pearls to a tavern keeper and a crown of gold to the Jews.[20] Hincmar of Laon was accused of having despoiled his church treasure to provide his followers with bucklers and spurs of precious metal.[21]

The Treasures of the Laity

In the absence of exact documentation, we are less well instructed on the moveable wealth of the lay aristocracy. It was certainly substantial. The laity sought to imitate princes, showing their power by flaunting the luxury of their trappings and arms, their imposing trains, or the wealth of their art collections. That model of the pious layman, Count Gerald of Aurillac, astounded his contemporaries by the modesty of his clothing and the simplicity of his life-style.[22] A literate layman—and we believe that there were learned laymen—might exercise his patronage by commissioning luxurious copies of manuscripts. They had psalters and bibles and even, occasionally, a library.[23]

The testaments of two of these lay aristocrats, Ewrard of Friuli and Eccard of Mâcon, furnish us with some idea of their wealth. The first sprang from the Unrochid family, engendered by Louis the Pious. He determined in 865 to divide his moveable goods among his four sons and three daughters. He designated in detail what each would receive from the treasure of his private chapel, his private collections, and his library.[24] If we leave consideration of the books until later, we can see that Ewrard possessed nine swords with gold-ornamented guards and points, six baldrics of gold, precious stones, or raised ivory, three *broignes*, a

The Powerful and the People

helmet with hauberk, greaves, gauntlets, spurs of gold and precious stones, four richly decorated curved poignards (*facila*).* He had silk and gold civil and liturgical vestments (dalmatics, chasubles). Vases of different shape were cut from marble or horn or covered in gold and silver. Among other items, Ewrard also left ivory and crystal reliquaries, small portable altars, censers, handbells, ceremonial coronets, and ivory tablets.

Eccard of Mâcon, of the Nibelung family, first married Richilda, the widow of Count Boso, and then married Albegunde. He had no children with these two wives, and, accordingly, around 880 he distributed his wealth and his books among his wife, nephews, certain lay aristocrats, bishops and abbesses, about twenty people in all. Supplementary descriptions enable us to reconstruct some of the luxury objects: a sword from the Orient, cloths of various colors, signet rings (made of antique intaglio), "Saracen" tablets, etc. He had everything that the generosity of princes and the stocks of merchants from the East could provide.

The aristocracy did not accumulate these luxurious objects in their treasuries for aesthetic pleasure alone. They were acquired ultimately to enable noblemen to make gifts. Generosity was deemed to be a quality of nobility as, inversely, avarice was, along with cowardice, considered to be an aristocrat's most grievous fault. To celebrate births, marriages, and political alliances, a man would open his treasury, confident of the reciprocal generosity of his counterpart. This practice of exchanging gifts, the potlatch so much studied by ethnologists, was one of the most characteristic features of Carolingian social life. When Pope Stephen came to Reims in 816, he distributed presents of gold and vestments to the Emperor, the Empress, and the royal children as well as to the courtiers. In exchange, the Emperor gave him two cups, horses harnessed in gold, a silver vessel, and a coat of purple and white linen. As Ermold remarked: "The prelate gained four times the value of the gifts he brought from Rome."[25]

* A *baldric* is a strap worn over the shoulder from which a sword can be hung. *Broignes* are leather jerkins reinforced with metal rings and studs. *Greaves* are pieces of armor extending from ankle to knee. A *dalmatic* is an open-sided outer garment worn under the chasuble when celebrating a pontifical high mass.

The
Lay
Aristocracy:
A Life
of Sport
and War

10

All free men of the Carolingian Empire owed military service—the service of the host—but, in fact, since the middle of the eighth century, the heavy cavalry had become the "queen of battles." The landed caste, who controlled the wealth, thus constituted the principal element in the army.[1] Arms and equipment cost dear. By about 800, a horse was worth forty sous, the price of eighteen to twenty cows. A man might sell a farm and a slave to cover the cost of a horse and sword. A cone-shaped helmet of boiled leather (*galea*) cost six sous; a brogne (*lorica* in classical Latin or *brunia* in the vulgar tongue, a leather tunic covered with iron plates) twelve sous; a buckler (*scutum* or *ecu*) made of leather-covered wood or wicker, in a round form or triangular shape designed to cover both head and body of the horseman, cost at least two sous. A two-meter lance, oak with a sharpened edge, two sous. A double-edged sword, 0.90 to one meter long, designed for both cutting and thrusting (*spata*), was seven sous. Finally, the knights' armaments were completed with a shorter sword (*semi-spata*) carried on a belt. In addition a knight had to provide mounts and arms for his squire, provisions for three months of campaigning, and so forth. Given these conditions, it is easy to see that it required endowments of important estates to assure the recruitment of the heavy cavalry.

Athletic Training

The young aristocrat was destined from infancy to go to war. Commenting on Vegetius' *On the Military Art*, Hrabanus Maurus wrote:

> Today we see that in the houses of the great, children and adolescents are raised to support hardship and adversity, hunger, cold, and the heat of the sun. They are familiar with the popular proverb that "He who cannot achieve knighthood at puberty will never do it, or only with great difficulty, at a more advanced age."[2]

As soon as a boy reached puberty and was capable of managing arms, about fourteen or fifteen years old or earlier, his father presented a sword to him. Thus he entered

74

into the society of adults. This sword, whose handle and sheath were often richly decorated, became his companion. He gave it a name and kept it even to the grave.[3] In a fresco from San Benedetto de Males, an aristocrat holds his sword like a cross between his hands.[4] His other companion was his horse, which he would not abandon at any price: "Kill my mother, I don't care!" cried an Aquitainian aristocrat to a Saracen. "Never will I give up to you the horse you demand. He was never made for the reins of a wretch like you!"[5]

The first lesson in a young man's training for war was to learn to mount his horse. Gerald of Aurillac "became so agile that he could leap onto the back of his horse with an easy bound."[6] He devoted himself to violent exercise: archery, the quintain, simulated combat.* Nithard relates how Louis and Charles organized military games at Worms in 842:

> Everyone participating in a particular spectacle assembled in one place with the rest of the crowd ranged on each side. Soon, Saxons, Gascons, Austrasians, and Bretons in equal numbers flung themselves into a swift gallop, one against the other as though straining to come to grips. Then one group made an about-face and, protected by their bucklers, feigned a desire to fly from their pursuing comrades. Next, reversing their roles, they, in turn, took up the pursuit of those from whom they had fled before. Finally, the two kings, with all the youth on horseback, threw themselves into the midst of the clamor and, brandishing their lances, charged among the fugitives, striking first one and then another.[7]

The hunt was another form of combat training. Charlemagne wanted his sons to learn to mount their horses, handle arms, and hunt according to the Frankish custom. Ermold advised the young Pepin to "enjoy the pleasures of the forest, use dog or falcon to pursue the game animals where

* A quintain was a mannequin mounted on a swivel "holding" a shield and a sack of flour. When a jouster hit the shield improperly, the quintain would turn, delivering a blow on the back with the flour.

they live." The same Ermold depicts a hunting party near Ingelheim in 826. The Empress Judith, who accompanied her husband, could hardly keep the young Charles, then aged three, out of the action:

> When Charles saw the animal, he howled to join in the pursuit as was his father's custom. He begged for a horse; he loudly demanded arms, a quiver full of swift arrows. . . . Had not his mother and his tutor restrained him, he would, with the obstinacy of all children, have started out on foot. . . . But the others in the party who were chasing the young animal caught it and brought it alive to the young prince. Then he seized weapons of his own size and struck the trembling beast. . . .[8]

The mother's fears were not frivolous. Hunting was a dangerous sport: long since grown up, this same Charles in 864, his nephew King Carloman in 884, and countless others died in the course of hunting parties. But then the risk made the game more thrilling. Until their dying days, nobles remained attached to the chase and left the care of their dogs and falcons to their heirs. Before surrendering, the defenders of the tower at the siege of Paris in 885 put their falcons to flight rather than deliver them to the enemy.[9]

The Warrior Life

The greatest hunt is the hunting of men, warfare. Every year in the month of May when fodder was ready to be cut for the horses, the king made rendezvous with his magnates. The month of May is thus designated in Wandalbert's calendar: "By ancient law, the chosen recruits should be put to the test of camp and battle in May; then they should attack the proud enemy with knights and footmen." In fact, the convocation of the host took place between May and June. Charles wrote to his vassals:

> Know you that we have convoked the general pleas this year in eastern Saxony, on the river Bode, in the place called Stassfurt. We enjoin upon you to come

The Powerful and the People

there on the fifteenth calends of July (17 June), with all your men, well armed and equipped with arms and baggage and all the furnishings of war, with sufficient dress and provisions. Each knight is to have a buckler, lance, longsword and short sword, a bow and quiver full of arrows. Each should have in his carts utensils of all kinds and provisions for three months to take from this meeting place. . . .[10]

All the military formations grouped at such convocations: counts with their men, vassals with their subordinates, the heavy cavalry, the light cavalry, and the foot. They were not to be late. "Any man called to the army who does not arrive on time at the designated place will be deprived of meat and wine for as many days as he has delayed."[11] Every free man of the Empire was bound to this host service. Those who refused were struck with the heavy fine of sixty sous—the price of twenty mares or thirty cows—payable immediately, unless they had sworn before witnesses that they were invalids.

If the aristocrats were impatient to go into combat, we may be sure that the bulk of the army, who formed the infantry, regretted leaving their families and the pursuit of their agricultural activities. Those men were in haste to return home to bring in the harvest and the vintage. A multitude of deserters in the course of a military campaign (*herisliz*) suffered the death penalty. Charlemagne was aware of the difficulty of imposing military service on everyone. In 807, he restricted the call to the host to the proprietors of three manses (an average of 40 hectares) or more. In 808, he agreed to call only those who possessed four manses. The rest would group together to send one man at the common cost for each four manses.

It is difficult to estimate the size of the Carolingian army: suggestions have ranged from thirty thousand to a hundred thousand—a very large margin of error! The most conservative list only three thousand cavalry and six to ten thousand foot, by which they explain the sluggishness of Charlemagne's conquests. Low numbers would account for the fact that it took thirty years to subdue Saxony. But we must recognize that Charlemagne did succeed there where Rome had failed.[12]

The king and his staff made careful preparations for all his campaigns. They never engaged themselves until they had studied the reports of spies from enemy country and the best maps at their disposal and until they had accumulated all the equipment necessary for a lengthy campaign. Thus, when he decided to free the west from the Avar peril which had threatened them since the seventh century, Charles directed the army to proceed in two bodies on either side of the Danube, while a flotilla sailed down the river bringing provisions and standing ready to rescue men in trouble. Nithard, who followed the expeditions of Charles the Bald, noted the care with which the king and his councillors prepared a campaign before they began it. These kings took account of the military talents of the men at the head of their armies. They placed most of their confidence in the elite troops, the *scarae*, small units of heavy cavalry led by the king's sons, the young paladins, who could mount a rapid offensive wherever danger was most pressing.[13]

Once assembled, the army began to march toward the theatre of operations. They were obliged to march slowly so as not to be separated from the carts, *basternae*, carrying their provisions. Covered with leather to facilitate river crossings, these contained flour, wine, salt pork, hams, and tools (axes, adzes, drills, hatchets, picks, shovels, and catapults). To draw such heavy carts (a cart of wine weighed nearly half a ton), the horses must have been furnished with shoulder harnesses. Pillage was forbidden until the lands of the enemy were reached. Each soldier was held responsible even for breaches committed by horses in the fields. If they needed grain, they were to ask the peasants for it under the right of *fodrum*. If it were stolen, although the peasant was unable to go to law personally, he could act through the intermediacy of his count or parish priest. But how could soldiers be prevented from looting? Carolingian soldiers do not give the impression of being well disciplined. They sold their arms to merchants following the army and got drunk on the money. Those who were caught under the influence were made to admit the fault and henceforth condemned to drink water.[14]

As soon as they were in enemy territory, soldiers and officers alike could unreservedly give themselves up to the

The Powerful and the People

joys of looting. Listen to Ermold the Black describe the Breton expedition:

> Like the serried ranks of thrushes and other birds who fly over the autumn vineyards pecking at the grapes . . . did the Franks . . . flood over the province despoiling it of its treasures. They ferreted out everyone alive hiding in the woods and marshes or concealed in ditches. Men, sheep, and cattle were led away. The Frank carried his ravages everywhere. The churches, as the Emperor had commanded, were respected. But everything else was put to the torch.[15]

The hardships of the march, where forests, bogs, and mountains favored enemy resistance, encouraged the high command to practice a scorched earth policy and to massacre all who fell into their hands. In this manner, Aquitaine, Brittany, Saxony, Septimania, and many other regions were ruined for decades.

Ideally, if they had their choice, aristocrats preferred other forms of combat. They had been prepared since infancy for more decisive engagements. But their training had deceived them: great battles, featuring massive charges, are rarely found in the annals of the age. The most famous remained the battle of Fontenoy-en-Pusaye (June 25, 841) which one witness called a mighty contest. "Never had anyone seen such massacre among the Frankish people," said one chronicler.[16]

> Neither dew nor showers nor rain ever fell again on that field where the most battle-hardened warriors had perished, mourned by their mothers, their sisters, their brothers, and their friends. On Charles' side and Louis' too, the fields were as white with the linen garments of the dead as they might have been with birds in the autumn.[17]

Thus, in Latin verse, did another witness add his pathetic lamentations. It was rare that the total submission of an enemy could be won in a summer's campaign. It was sometimes necessary to trick the men into staying through the winter. It was often necessary to besiege towns or strongholds for a long time. The siege of Barcelona lasted seven months, that of Pavia nine months. War machines, rams, catapults, stone-throwers, rolling towers, trebuchets (a new weapon employed at the siege of Angers in 873), had to be disposed around the fortifications.[18] Meanwhile the adversaries, following immemorial custom, hurled insults at one another.[19] "Machines multiplied their heavy blows, the walls were battered on every side, the battle raged more violently than ever. . . ."[20] Finally the moment came when, weakened with famine, the besieged surrendered. The outcome of a military campaign was rarely negative. To be sure, many of the shining elite of the Carolingian aristocracy fell in battle. The catastrophes of Suntelgebirge in 782, of Roncevaux in 778, remained in all men's minds. But for every such disaster, Charlemagne completed many a successful conquest. The Franks could live on the booty they took from the enemy. The prince and his grandees would divide the spoils. Consider the cries of joy which greeted the news of the capture of the Avar treasure: "No war in the memory of man ever reported such booty, such a weight of riches."[21] Fifteen carts, drawn by four bulls each, were filled with gold, silver, and clothing. When the spoils taken from the Saracens, arms and clothing, were divided among the captains, one received a silken habit and another a "sword of Indian origin." The collections of the great aristocrats were largely amassed from these prizes of war.[22]

Poets celebrated the wealth gained, the victories achieved. "Poor and rich, powerful laymen and clerks in orders, all cheered, whatever their age, rank, or sex."[23] But not every battle was deemed worthy of praise; above all, those which opposed Franks to Franks were deplored. "This battle is not worthy of celebration, it was not one to be put to music," said the poet of Fontenoy.[24] But battles against pagans were sung according to the Germanic custom, in Latin or in the vulgar tongue. The victory of Pepin over the Avars, of Louis the Stammerer over the Normans—the *Ludwigslied*—and even the disaster of Roncevaux, were rapidly transformed into legends.[25]

Without a doubt, war was a game to the aristocracy. "There the Franks played," wrote the poet of the *Ludwigslied*. But it was also a holy work when directed against pagans and enemies of the church. Kings were accompanied

The Powerful and the People

by military almoners: "Every bishop chanted three masses and three psalms: one for the king, one for the Frankish army, and a third for the present situation." Before leaving to fight the Avars, Charles ordered his army to fast and pray for three days in barefoot procession.[26] The Carolingian army sought to resemble the armies of the Old Testament, and the warriors emulated the Maccabees.[27] In the *Ludwigslied*, Louis III prefigures the Christian knight, the vassal of God. It was God who called Louis and asked his help for his people, oppressed by the men of the north. Louis accepted, took leave of God, raised his gonfanon against the Normans, and spoke to his *leudes:* "God has sent me here and given me my orders. . . ." Singing a holy canticle he led his men into the combat, and all joined together in singing the *Kyrie Eleison.*[28]

The Lay "Order"

Defining the just and holy war, clerks linked the aristocracy with ecclesiastics and monks. A link was necessary for, very often, in this clerk-dominated society, laymen suffered from what we would call an inferiority complex. Clerks always considered the lay condition as a concession to human weakness. Those who lacked the moral fibre to live in celibacy and poverty had to take wives and look after their goods. They constituted the carnal category as against the spiritual. "Great distress is born in the hearts of laymen," wrote Paulinus of Aquilea. "They say: what good is it to me to learn to read Scripture or frequent priests or attend the churches of the saints? If I were a clerk, I should then do what clerks do."[29] Laymen asked themselves if they could be sure of eternal salvation and felt the need of a rule of life which could bring them, like the clerks, to Paradise.

To answer this need, clerks composed "mirrors," treatises of edification, which were to serve the laity as "rules" served monks and canons. In his *Book of Vices and Virtues*, Alcuin addressed himself to Count Guy, assuring him that a lay habit and worldly activities would not close the gates of Heaven to him if he practiced the Christian virtues.[30] Paulinus of Aquilea sent a "book of exhortation" to Eric, Marquis of Friuli, through which he might "as a layman" train himself for the "work of God." Around 828, Jonas of Orleans wrote a little book for Count Matfrid—a book whose title, *Institutio Laicalis*, reflects its intentions. As a parallel, he addressed his *Liber de institutione regia* to Pepin, King of Aquitaine, recalling the duties of a Christian prince. This treatise can be counted with all the other "mirrors of princes" written by Alcuin, Sedulius Scotus, Smaragdus of Saint-Mihiel, Hrabanus Maurus, and Hincmar. Finally, the laymen themselves tried to send their children into public life with counsels of good conduct. Between 841 and 843, Dhuoda, wife of Bernard of Septimania, wrote a manual for her son Guillaume who was entering Charles' service at the age of sixteen, which he "should read and re-read and consider as a mirror in which he could find reflected in all security the salvation of his soul in the midst of the multiple occupations of the age." She asked Guillaume to read the manual in turn to his younger brother Bernard when he should have reached an age to understand it.[31]

All these "mirrors" proposed, each in its own way, a similar program of education, to fit princes for the governance of the realm and to give all laymen the means of governing themselves.[32] Aristocrats were to take up arms against vices, which were listed with descriptions of their ravages. They were to practice the virtues conforming to their rank: justice toward subordinates, generosity toward the church and the poor, protection of the poor, and good counsel to princes. They were to respect the sanctity of marriage and regulate their conjugal life according to the rules defined by the church. Finally they were to consecrate the strength of their arms to the service of right and faith. Then they could be sure of their salvation. As Paulinus of Aquilea reminded them, Christ shed his blood, not for priests alone, but for the whole human race, for all those who served him with all their might.

Laymen, then, had a well-defined function in Christian society. They formed an "order" beside clerks and monks. The word begins to appear in different texts of this period.[33] Thus the resurgence of the old Indo-European concept of a tripartite division began to insinuate itself into the literary reflections of a Christian society seeking its own equilibrium. With the orders of monks devoted to prayer and consecrated to pastoral work, the order of the laity was not insignificant. We could almost call this a "promotion of the laity," at least of the aristocratic laity, those who called themselves the *bellatores*, the *milites*, the *militia saecularis* who were thus distinguished from the herd, the mass of men who worked and of whom no one spoke.

Bishops and Abbots

All aristocrats cherished the dream of snaring a bishopric or abbacy for their children, not only for the material advantages pertaining to these offices but also for the high consideration accorded ecclesiastics in a sacrally oriented society. Since Clovis' time, Frankish kings had the right to appoint their bishops. They were not slow to exercise this *concesso regalis* to secure faithful councillors—or at least so they hoped. According to Lupus of Ferrières, "The king drew on the clerks of his palace as had been the custom of his ancestors."[1] As soon as a bishopric was vacated, the great folk rushed to besiege the king or the queen on behalf of relatives and friends. Notker of Saint-Gall has given us some excellent examples drawn from life. When Charlemagne determined to bestow a bishopric on a man of humble rank, he had to resist the pressure of his entire entourage:

> The officials of the palace, always ready to spy on the unfortunate and report the trespasses of others, impatient of every restraint and envious of one another, busied themselves among the Emperor's familiars in hopes of influencing his choice for the bishopric. . . . Queen Hildegarde dispatched the leading people of the land to him and finally went herself to solicit the place for her own clerk. . . .

On another occasion, a rich and noble clerk received a bishopric from the king:

> Mad with joy, he assembled a crowd of public officials in his house, made an ostentatious display for the people of the diocese who had hastened to congratulate him, and prepared a splendid banquet for all. Stuffed with food, gorged with wine, and engulfed in drunkenness, he failed to appear at the nightly offices. . . .

The chronicler adds that the Emperor revoked his decision and gave the bishopric to a more worthy clerk.[2]

Charlemagne surrounded himself with remarkable clerks who labored at reforming the kingdom's religious life. He knew how to choose well-trained men who were both pious and adept at carrying out his policies. They were entrusted with diplomatic missions, appointed as *missi*, and entered among his vassals. The episcopal office he bestowed upon them was classed as an *honor* as was the office of count. If they were charged with infidelity, they could be deprived of it. However, though Charles was able to keep his bishops in hand, the results for his successors were less felicitous. A bishop of aristocratic birth, like the great laymen, had his own clientele. He was eager to secure good places for his relatives and friends, to provide them with jobs and wealth. He had a tendency to confound the wealth of the bishopric with his own personal fortune. He sought to transmit his office to a brother or cousin in the absence of a son. Through the course of the ninth century, the bishops progressively emancipated themselves from royal tutelage. After the example of their fellow aristocrats, they became temporal lords in their own right.

High-born abbots and abbesses mirrored the experiences of the bishops. To begin with, the kings confided the monasteries to men and women who were related to them by blood or linked by the bonds of fidelity. The great monasteries of northern and eastern France such as Saint-Denis, Corbie, Saint-Riquier, Fulda, or Saint-Gall were reserved for friends of the prince.[3] Some of these people could accumulate several abbeys. Alcuin was abbot of Ferrières, Saint-Loup, Sens, Saint-Josse, Flavigny, Cormery, and Saint-Martin of Tours. Einhard was lay abbot of Seligenstadt, Saint-John the Baptist of Pavia, Saint-Wandrille, Saint-Servais of Maestricht, Saint-Pierre, and Saint-Bavo of Ghent. Aelisacher directed the abbeys of Saint-Riquier, Saint-Aubin of Angers, and Saint-Maximin of Trier. Charlemagne's sisters and daughters also received abbeys, and, after him, many a Carolingian princess was dowered in this manner. In the ninth century, the great folk competed eagerly to gain these sources of income or to keep them in their families.

Worldly Life

Carolingian bishops and abbots, whether employed by king or count, lived in a style which was almost indistinguishable from that of lay aristocrats. Though prohibited by

canon law from shedding blood, it often happened that they
found themselves, out of duty or choice, participating in
warlike expeditions. As we saw above, the prince expected
them to furnish contingents of soldiers when the host was
convoked. But some among them, like Odo, Abbot of
Corbie, did not hesitate to join in the fighting themselves.
Lupus of Ferrières wrote to him: "I am often most anxious
about you, recalling your habit of heedlessly throwing
yourself, all unarmed, into the thick of battle whenever your
youthful energy is overcome with the greedy desire to
conquer."[4] For his own part, Lupus did not love war and
answered the royal convocation only against his inclinations: "I, as you know, have never learned how to strike an
enemy or to avoid his blows. Nor do I know how to execute
all the other obligations of military service on foot or horseback. Our king does not have need of warriors alone."[5] He
preferred his manuscripts and his studies to warfare. The
same lamentations flowed from the pen of Claudius, Bishop
of Turin:

> In winter, I do not get a single moment of leisure to
> devote myself to my favorite studies, for I am always
> en route to the palace. Then in spring, with my
> parchments under my arm, I go down to the coast to
> fight the sons of Hagar and the Moors. By day, I put
> my sword to work, and by night I employ my books
> and my pen. Thus do I seek fulfillment of my
> dreams.[6]

Arn, Bishop of Salzburg, complained to Alcuin that
the need to carry out his temporal charges prevented him
from the proper performance of his pastoral duties. Alcuin
himself deplored that "men who ought to be free to serve
God must travel so far," but he answered with a string of
scriptural citations stressing the duty of obedience to secular power.[7] In vain did Aldric of Le Mans ask the king that
he might abandon his offices and devote himself entirely to
the service of his clergy and people. In 829, the bishops
gathered in council to demand greater liberty to fulfill their
duties toward God.[8] Numerous examples illustrate the crisis
of conscience which afflicted the Carolingian clergy. But
at the same time we must recognize that many were se-

duced by the charms of the active life and its attendant advantages.

How many, in effect, enjoyed a life of luxury on the model of the great lay nobility! In their comfortable palaces, they supported squires and flunkeys, kept sparrow hawks and falcons. They gave sumptuous receptions and upheld the reputations of their tables. Sedulius has given us a lasting memento of one feast given by the Bishop of Liège:

> The noble brothers who were assembled there relished their vacation from pious work. Thou, illustrious Bacchus, brought us new pleasure. In joyous cups, you bring the kiss of peace and capitivate the wise. . . . Let each one down two pints! Let each drinker recite a verse in iambic, and then let everyone take up the sixth voice in chorus.[9]

When Notker of Saint-Gall described a prelate, sitting on soft down cushions, dressed in the most precious silks, calling in the most accomplished singers provided with all sorts of instrumentalists, he was not simply giving way to his own taste for picturesque anecdote.[10] Jonas of Orleans also described his colleagues, "who demand diverse dishes capriciously, lavishing praise on the cooks who prepare the most delicate dishes, and who, with their bellies swollen with good cheer, faces flushed with the finest wines, open their mouths, not to praise God, but to bellow great howls of laughter."[11]

For his part, Alcuin complained about the presence of actors and citharists at the feasts held by bishops and abbots and advised them to give precedence to the writings of the Church Fathers over Germanic poems.[12] Many abbots and even more abbesses pursued the worldly and luxurious life of great aristocrats. The fact is certified by the repeated attempts of capitularies and conciliar canons to restore order. One cleric is accused of having a special chamber for his servants; another would rather play than pray, and another wrote amorous poetry, *Winiloedes*.[13] One was buying silken clothes while another kept his door open to men and women alike. One used the pretext of a pilgrimage to Tours or Rome to leave his monastery and debauch himself while yet another plotted to overthrow abbot or abbess. The very structure of the Carolingian monastery, its personnel recruited from the aristocracy, young nobles more or less forced into a vocation, and ruled by lay abbots and abbesses nominated as we have seen, made the enforcement of a regular way of life almost impossible.[14]

Reforming Efforts

Still, in closing, we must take notice of the efforts of Charlemagne and his successors to take cognizance of these abuses and suppress them. Charles ordered his *missi* to remind the ecclesiastics among them that they must not forget that they had "quit the world." "And there must be more ways in which those who have quit the world can be distinguished than that they do not carry arms and are not publicly married."[15] Kings and bishops gathered in council to reiterate that monastic claustration was intended to be absolute and that monks and nuns should, above all things, tend to the service of God.

Raised there until he went out to found a monastery on his own lands, Benedict of Aniane knew the court well. He attempted to impose the rule of Saint Benedict on all the abbeys.[16] Thanks to the help of Louis of Aquitaine and his bishops, he succeeded in reforming Saint-Martin of Ainay at Lyon, Micy near Orleans, Cormery, Saint-Savin on Gartempe, Gellone (Saint-Guilhem of the Desert, near Aniane), La Grasse, Psalmodi. When Louis became Emperor, he installed Benedict at Inden (presently Cornelimunster, 6 kilometers from Aix-la-Chapelle), which became the model abbey for the Empire where many came to receive their training. "Louis put Benedict at the head of all the monks of the Empire so that he might reform Francia by his salutary example just as he had instructed Aquitaine and Gothia in the rule of salvation."[17] Thus, Ardo, Benedict's biographer, believed that an attempt at monastic centralization was intended which did not exactly conform to the Benedictine tradition. What is more, in 817, the abbots and monks gathered at Aix approved an 83-chapter capitulary codifying the usages and customs of the monasteries in accordance with the Benedictine rule.

Inspectors, supervised by Benedict, were charged with the enforcement of the capitulary. We know that they encountered resistance. Moreover, Benedict of Aniane's death in 821 and the political difficulties of Louis the Pious favored abbots and abbesses who, doubtless, considered these reforms, imposed upon them from above, to be excessive and did not wish to abandon their accustomed ways. In the latter half of the ninth century, the Benedictine rule as reworked by Benedict of Aniane was hardly applied anywhere. When Gerald, a lay aristocrat of Aquitaine, wanted to establish a monastery at Aurillac in 890, he could find few monks worthy of the name. He sent some young nobles to Vabres in Rouergue, where the rule was in force, for instruction. But as soon as these aristocrats returned home, their lack of discipline began to cause gossip.[18] A survey of monastic conditions was undertaken for the Synod of Trosly in 905. The bishops there deplored the fact that lay abbots had installed themselves in monasteries with their wives, children, hunting dogs, grooms, and men of war, squandering the monastic revenues.[19]

The only way to reconstitute monastic life was to separate it radically from the world. In 863, Girard of Vienne founded a monastery on his own lands and determined to submit the foundation to the Pope's authority with the abbot being elected by the monks. Guillaume the Pious, Count of Mâcon, followed this example in 910 when he installed monks on his lands at Cluny. This time, however, the abbey was not submitted to the Pope but to the apostles Peter and Paul, which released it effectively from the control of any power, whether lay or ecclesiastical. We know what success awaited Cluny and its importance in the monastic reform movement of the tenth century. By then, the hour of the royal and aristocratic monasteries had, for the time being, passed away.[20]

The court might be defined as the geometrical space in which lay and ecclesiastical aristocrats gather around their princes seeking gifts, favors, and places. We have already described the framework of the court, the palace in which the king and his entourage lived for months at a time, guided by the exigencies of the moment to a choice of summer and winter residences suitable for hunting, ceremonial feasts, or general assemblies. Now we can attempt to recapture certain aspects of life at court as evoked by writers living near the king.[1]

Life at Court

12

Court Service

Before the king arrived with his household, certain domestic personnel, clerks, vassals, and *mansionarii* had already prepared the palace and laid in sufficient reserves to entertain the king and his suite. The two most important court dignitaries, the senescal (*senescalus*, or senior valet) who was the "supervisor of the royal table" and the butler (*buticularius*), then took charge of the palace economy. The constable (count of the stable) and his adjutants, the marshals (*mariscalci*), supervised the provisioning of the stables.[2] The king's first concern was the installation of his "treasure" in his private apartments, a responsibility entrusted to the chamberlain (*camerarius*), who was consequently one of the most powerful dignitaries at court. Everything needed for ordinary or extraordinary expenditures was stored in the "chamber": booty won in battle, tribute from "protected" peoples, ambassadorial gifts, church donations, and the "eulogies" of the great folk; in addition, there was money derived from direct imposts and the more fruitful indirect revenues (from the *telonei*, the passes where tolls were collected), fines from the *bannum*, and annual gifts from abbeys.* Ingots of precious metals were also deposited there before being issued to the heads of the mints to strike silver coinage. The "chamber" was a veritable warehouse filled with coffers of jewels, gold, crowns, silken stuffs, and luxury goods brought to the palace by accredited merchants,

* "Eulogies" are greetings, expressed by gifts; the *bannum* is the law court.

and even priceless illuminated manuscripts commissioned by the king from scribes and painters. Charlemagne's testament, recorded by Einhard, gives us some idea of the importance of his "camera."[3] This treasure was still what it had been under the Merovingians, the *instrumentum regni*, the source of rewards through which the king sought to secure the loyalty of the aristocracy. It is not, therefore, hard to see why the *camerarius*, or chamberlain, was considered the second man in the Empire in the time of Louis the Pious.

Not far from the chapel in another part of the palace, the king installed his office—if we can use so pretentious a word. The demands of imperial administration required the speedy installation of another treasure, the archives, in which copies of correspondence were saved with the reports of the *missi* and royal diplomas.[4] These archives were the source for Bishop Ansegisus' compilation of the capitularies in 827.

Since the reign of Pepin, clerks had become familiar with Latin, the administrative language, and were trained to follow formularies in drawing up acts under the direction of the chancellor (*cancellarius*). Notaries were expert in the writing of *tironiennes*, medieval stenography, while scribes were trained in cursive or the new minuscule hand.[5] Theodulf sketched the silhouette of the little notary, Erchambald, "girdled with the tablets hanging at his sides, re-reading in a chant, the letters which had been dictated to him."[6] In addition, the king used private notaries for help in preparing his discourses, questions to ask the *missi*, articles to be negotiated with bishops, abbots, and counts during the general assemblies. Charlemagne aimed at the restoration of the administrative rescript to the place it had held in the late Roman Empire, and still held in Byzantium. We believe that was the chief goal of his intellectual policies. But such efforts ran against the grain of the barbarian tradition where pride of place was given to oral communication and foundered in the incapacity of his lay functionaries to learn to read and write. Nevertheless, in reorganizing his palace offices, the Emperor created a precedent which the French monarchy would not forget.

There were close links between the chancellery and

the chapel, since the same clerks worked in both offices. But the clerks of the chapel performed essential services of their own to the court. They guarded the relics which accompanied the king, such as the famous cape of Saint Martin—which gave its name to the royal oratory (*capella*)—and maintained religious services for the king and his household. Charles attended chapel every morning and evening, even returning at night to hear the offices. He sang along with the clerks in an undertone and, if we are to believe Notker of Saint-Gall, personally indicated the moment for singing psalms and responses to individual clerks.[7] He desired his chapel to be a model for all churches, insisting on the rigorous use of Roman chant which Pepin and Charles wished to spread to the whole Empire. The king even introduced the innovation of adding the *Filioque* to the chanting of the Credo, which did not entirely please Pope Leo III.* The chapel became even more central to the palace under Louis, called "the Pious." "The army of palatine clergy," to use an expression of the king, grew great and often pursued its own policies. One of the leaders of the imperialist party was Hilduin, Abbot of Saint-Denis and arch-chaplain in 822. In his shadow the young Hincmar was formed. This arch-chaplain even gave himself the title "Archbishop of the Sacred Palace." This enviable place was occupied in turn by Fulrad, Abbot of Saint-Denis, Angilram, Bishop of Metz, and Hildebald, Bishop of Cologne. The arch-chaplain was the Emperor's principal councillor in religious matters, assisted in the appointment of bishops and abbots, and participated in the preparation of the assemblies which debated liturgical and theological questions.

The King and His Magnates

The arch-chaplain's role of councillor was shared by the

* *Filioque*, meaning "and the Son," is a phrase describing the procession of the third person of the Trinity equally from the first two persons. The phrase, a specific denial of the Arian heresy, was first added to the Creed after the conversion of the Visigoths in Spain and spread to Frankland in the eighth century despite papal disapproval. Although never used in the Byzantine church, it was added to the Creed officially approved by Rome in the eleventh century.

other lay and ecclesiastical dignitaries of the palace. No king worked alone. Rulers knew how to follow the advice of serious persons and to entrust them with diplomatic and military missions. The seneschal Egihhard was among those who died at Roncevaux; the seneschal Audulf was dispatched to Brittany in 786; the butler Eborhard was charged with the mission to Bavaria in 781; and the chamberlain Adalgisus went to Saxony in 782. Jeremy, who was chancellor in 813, accompanied Jonas of Orleans to Rome in 825; Louis the Pious sent his chancellor, Aelisachar, on missions to Armorica and Spain. A notary or an usher might also be taken into the king's confidence.[8] He could also seek counsel from those who had been convoked for general assemblies (*conventus generalis, placitum generale*): counts, abbots, bishops, and other vassals. Charlemagne's assemblies coincided with the gathering of the troops in May or June. Later they were dissociated and held at another date. Sometimes, if the circumstances warranted, he might even call a second assembly.

> All the great ones came together in assembly, the most considerable clerks and laymen, to deliberate and make decisions, the least considerable to give adherence, sometimes after deliberation but always by their own intelligent decision, not under force or through blindness.

Thus Hincmar explained the "ideal" assembly to the young prince Carloman in 880.[9] It was not conceived as a popular assembly even though several hundred persons might be encamped in the palace for days or even weeks. The king might organize the *conventus* into two sections, one lay and one ecclesiastical, and then collate the results of their deliberations. These would then guide the king in the redaction of a series of articles (*capitula*) which would constitute the capitularies to be approved by the assembled participants. There is no doubt that in the course of the initial deliberations he took the advice of his customary councillors and friends who had come for that purpose.

Attendance at the general assembly was obligatory: the members were convoked by letter, and it was dangerous to ignore the orders of the king. No more could one quit the court without the prince's permission. Some people complained of this. Lupus of Ferrières remarked to one of his correspondents that he had been at court for four months without having left the king for a single day. Frothair of Toul was at court more often than in his bishopric. The aging Alcuin invoked his failing health to excuse his absence. Likewise, Einhard cancelled his journey to Compiègne in 830 under pretext of ailing kidneys and spleen complicated by violent enteritis.[10] Some have, in fact, interpreted this as a "diplomatic malady" which enabled Einhard to avoid taking sides between Louis the Pious and his son Lothair.

Even in ordinary times, when no assembly was in session, the court buzzed like a noisy hive from morning to night. Ushers had to restrain the petitioners besieging the royal apartments. The clerks were always seeking a bishopric or an abbey. As Lupus of Ferrières wrote to a friend: "Rumors run among us that palace clerks proudly express their ambition to obtain monasteries to which no responsibility is attached, for the sake of satisfying their own duplicity by oppressing the servants of God." He himself was not disinterested:

> Last year, thanks to the efforts of my friends, I was presented to the Emperor and received with much kindness by him and the Queen. And now—that is, the 10th of the kalends of October, first indiction— I am on my way back to the palace. The Queen, who has great influence, has summoned me, and many people think that they will soon confer some dignity upon me.[11]

As yet unbeneficed vassals, those who were not *casati*, awaited the good will of the king*. According to Einhard, he had to begin receiving the petitioners introduced by the count of the palace before he was barely awake.[12]

Foreign travelers were welcomed and held in high regard, which, according to the king's biographer, "constituted a heavy charge not only on the palace but on the whole realm." Among these foreigners, we must not overlook the ambassadors and their suites who had, since Pepin's

* See p. 267 below.

reign, appeared regularly at court. Embassies came from the Emperor in Byzantium and the Caliph of Baghdad, from the Arab emirs of Spain, the Anglo-Saxon kings, from Saxon, Scandinavian, and Bulgar chieftains. The gifts they brought fattened the king's treasure, the aristocracy formed alliances with men from far away, and Carolingian culture was enriched by new influences. Charlemagne took advantage of the presence of clerks from the East to have Greek hymns translated into Latin and to have an organ constructed after the model of the instrument brought in the Byzantines' baggage.[13]

Diversions

Life at court, though it may have appeared rather rude to travelers from Baghdad or Byzantium, was not lacking in diversions for body and soul alike. Sport occupied a central position in the schedule. Charlemagne was an excellent swimmer and brought all his palatines with him into the pool at Aix:

> Whenever there was bathing, the society was numerous; aside from his sons, he bade his magnates, his friends, and sometimes even his crowd of bodyguards to share his frolics. It sometimes happened that he had as many as a hundred or more people in the water with him.[14]

Hunting in the forests of the Vosges, the Ardennes, or Franconia occupied a great part of the autumn and winter. To honor the ambassadors from Baghdad, Charles organized a hunt for the auroch, a wild ox which terrified the Asiatics. When the Danish Prince Harald came to Ingelheim, Louis the Pious took him to a hunt on an island in the Rhine:

> Then the wood echoed throughout with the baying of dogs. Here the shouts of men resounded, and there sounded the accent of the horns. The beasts were found and fled across the brakes. . . . Ardent Caesar himself killed a crowd of beasts, striking them with his own hand; the agile Lothair, in the flower of

his youth, finished several bears with his own hand. . . .[15]

Reserves of savage beasts and even menageries were maintained in the palace environs. Ermold described an area enclosed in solid walls near the palace of Aix. It was populated with various species of birds as well as savage beasts. The king, with a small company, went there to hunt deer, bucks or hinds. Even in winter, he chased birds there with his falcon. Doubtless, it was there in that closed park that Charlemagne installed the lion and the bear sent to him by the princes of Africa along with the famous elephant, Abul Abaz, sent by the Caliph of Baghdad in 802. He was kept alive until 810, and his bones were conserved at Lippenham until the eighteenth century.[16]

Meals occupied a great part of the day for men fatigued by their physical exertions. Charlemagne was a great eater and often mentioned the inconvenience of the fasts imposed by the church. He loved the roasted meat which his huntsmen thrust on a spit, and he would not obey the advice of doctors who recommended that he eat boiled meat.[17] In general, Carolingians ate a lot, indeed, too much, according to moralists. Milo of Saint-Amand, in a poem dedicated to sobriety, humorously described the palace kitchens: "these kitchens, smoking day and night, and the cooks all sooty and blackened by the smoke."[18] Though often the subject of raillery, the head cook was a great personage. Clerks who knew their Old Testament reminded their readers that it was Nebuchadrezzar's chef who besieged and pillaged Jerusalem. The chief of the cup bearers had a still heavier responsibility, for meals were liberally washed down. Though Charlemagne had a personal horror of drunkenness, he could hardly thwart the ingrained habits of the Franks: "Goblets of pure thick wine passed from hand to hand." Many sought the privilege of drinking from the king's own cup.[19]

Carolingian kings knew very well how to treat their guests. The luxury of their table and the generous provisioning of banquets played an important part in the politics of prestige. The biographer of Charles' bastard, Hugues of Rouen, evoked the feasts at court and the pleasure which they gave.[20] To entertain the convivial guests and, perhaps, to discourage too much relaxation, musicians played profane as well as sacred music on their lyres and zithers. They accompanied mimes who made the company laugh at their sallies.[21]

Poets leaped at the opportunity these banquets provided for descriptions in the antique mode. Such a gathering of the prince and his familiars lent itself readily to a profile. Such descriptions are not lacking in Theodulf. Charlemagne, fatigued, seating himself at table, his sons removing his mantle and sword while his daughters offered him flowers and fruit. Thyrsis (Megenfred), the great chamberlain, stood at the king's side; the arch-chaplain, Hildebald, "his spirit fulfilled, his visage serene, his heart pious," came to bless the king's food and drink. Flaccus (Alcuin) was there: Flaccus, the glory of our poets, explaining the sacred dogmas of Scripture and making game of the difficulties of verse. Only Homer (Angilbert) was missing. Lentulus brought apples in a basket while the little Nardulus (Einhard) ran here and there like an ant. Menalcus (Andulf) arrived, surrounded by bakers and cooks carefully bearing the elements of the feast on platters which would be presented before the royal seat. Eppinus (Eberhard) came, charged with precious flagons of wine. Finally Alcuin blessed the table, and each fell to the feast. When it was over, Theodulf, surnamed Pindar, recited his verses which charmed all the world except for Wigbod who, a little drunk, shook his great head. The king called him, his knees wobbled and gave way under the prominent mass of his belly: "The gait of Vulcan and the voice of Jupiter."[22]

As we can see, Theodulf gave the king's familiars names drawn from classical antiquity. Other writers drew surnames from the books of the Old Testament: Charlemagne was David, Hildebald of Cologne, Aaron; Fredegisus, Nathanael; Einhard, Beseleel. In Louis the Pious' time, Lothair was called Joshua; Louis the German, Jonathan; and, obviously, Charles, the youngest, Benjamin.

The Women of the Court

All the aristocrats who stayed at the courts of Charlemagne and his successors remembered their happy times with marked nostalgia. These princes knew how to make an art of living which was not understood at any other barbarian court. They were sensible of the charms of the princesses, the wives and daughters of Charlemagne and the consorts of Louis the Pious. Carolingian poets sang the praises of women. Thus Sedulius, the Irishman, lauded the beauty of the Empress Ermengard, wife of Lothair I:

> Her voice is pure as gold and clear as the note of zither. Her skin is as roses mixed in snow. Her blond hair circles her head like a chrysolith. Her eyes are lively, her white neck like milk, lilies, ivory. Her graceful hands are like the snow.[23]

But Alcuin warned one of his disciples to be on guard against the "crowned doves who fly about the chambers of the palace."[24] It was sound advice when we remember that Charles' daughters willingly allowed themselves to be courted by the magnates, that Bertha was seduced by Angilbert and Rotruda by Count Rorigon, and that the aging king himself installed his concubines at the court. When he came to the throne, Louis the Pious had to send his sisters into monasteries and chase away the prostitutes installed at Aix.[25]

The habits of the new king were more austere, but he was not insensible to women. He could not support himself in continence after being widowed from Ermengard in 818. The most beautiful of the aristocratic girls were presented to him, and he chose the Bavarian Judith, of the Welf family. Was this Judith Louis' evil genius; did she bewitch the king while she betrayed him with Bernard the chamberlain and other men? Such rumors circulated among the supporters of Lothair, Louis' eldest son and the sworn enemy of the queen, his stepmother: "The young men laughed, and the old men suffered to see the paternal couch soiled, the palace dishonored, the name of the Franks smirched, the lady of the palace delivered up to puerile games in the very presence of men in sacerdotal orders," wrote Agobard.[26] "Calumnies of the imperialist party!" answered Judith's defenders. But the partisans of Lothair, headed by Wala, Abbot of Corbie, would not accept Judith's young son, the future Charles the Bald, as a claimant to part of the Empire. Therefore, they let loose a violent campaign of defamation.

The Caste-Consciousness of the Aristocracy

The aristocracy held a privileged position in the realm. It depended on their intimacy with the king as well as on their own wealth. Aristocrats were jealous of their place and made other social classes feel the differences which separated them. Already they were moved by the spirit of a caste. At one point, theologians, drawing upon certain of Saint Augustine's theses in a discussion of predestination, were apparently inclined to believe that "social predestination" also existed.[27] It was not through merit that one was born noble, free, or slave, and therefore no one should seek to change his condition. Further differences existed in the bosom of the aristocracy itself. The great, who stemmed from the royal family or issued from illustrious ancestors, mistrusted the petty nobility. At the end of the ninth century, Charles the Simple was accused of being too friendly with Haganon, "who was born of obscure parents." The great nobles warned him that they would desert his council if he retained his favorite. The fact is, Haganon was a petty noble.[28] Until the eleventh century, kings were obliged to govern with the help only of the greatest and most famous aristocrats.

If the high aristocracy had so little consideration for the *hobereaux,* we can imagine how deeply they mistrusted the people.* They looked askance at the clerks of low extraction whom Charlemagne tended to keep in his entourage. Ebbo, Louis the Pious' foster brother, was the son of a freed slave†. Through the Emperor's favor he became Archbishop of Reims, but he was not allowed to forget his servile origins: "The Emperor gave you liberty, not nobility," his enemies reminded him, ". . . for that would not be possible."[29] Speaking of the Bishop of Constance, Abbot Waldo of Reichenau wrote: "I can never recognize a superior of inferior birth to my own while I still have three fingers on my right hand." The opinion of the inferior classes simply did not count. To those who would invoke the adage, *Vox populi, vox dei,* Alcuin retorted that the people should be

---

* *Hobereaux:* petty gentry or squireens.

† A foster brother was the wet nurse's son, customarily raised with a noble as a servant-companion.

directed, not followed.[30] The fact that a man of the people might have become a priest did not entitle him to more consideration. A proprietor in need of a chaplain sought out the bishop and told him, "I have a clerk here who was one of my slaves, and I have freed him. I want you to ordain him as a priest in my service." An ordinary clerk was, in fact, the servant of a noble. He might serve at table, prepare wine, lead the dogs to the hunt, and hold the ladies' horses. If he had learning, his patron used him as a secretary or steward. If he performed his functions badly, he could be beaten like any domestic servant.[31] Priesthood did not lead to social promotion in the Carolingian epoch.

Occasionally, a few clerks in the name of Christianity reminded the nobles that, great and small, all men were born of the same father. Thus spoke Theodulf of Orleans of the people:

> Their sweat and their toil made you rich. The rich get their riches because of the poor. But nature submits you to the same laws. In birth and in death you are alike. The same holy water blesses you; you are annointed with the same oils; the flesh and blood of the lamb nourishes you all together.[32]

Speaking of the humble flock, Jonas wrote:

> The weakness of their bodies, the deformities of their appearance, the dirt of their clothes, and the inferiority of their resources ought not to prevent us from recognizing in them men, absolutely twin to ourselves.

These are commonplaces drawn from the teachings of the Church Fathers, but they served as reminders to those orders which are found in all epochs when the pride and exploitation of the great oppress the weak. In their capitularies and in their councils, the princes and the bishops repeated tirelessly to the powerful that they must not forget the duties they owed to the people.

In contrast to the handful of powerful folk who governed, made war, and prayed stood the vast majority who worked modestly and in poverty. Despite our paucity of sources, we shall try to discover this "silent majority": essentially rural people living in villages on lay and ecclesiastical domains. Then, too, there were townspeople, artisans and merchants, mostly Christian or what passed for Christian with a sprinkling of Jews who, as we shall see, played an active role in the economy (for which they received royal protection).

Carolingian jurists divided the people into two groups: free and non-free. The first were under oath to the king; they owed him military service and participated in judicial assemblies. Personally or as part of a family unit, they were responsible for their own acts. They could travel freely throughout the Empire and marry where they pleased. The others, the non-free, had no rights. They were under the coercive power of their masters and enjoyed no judicial guarantees against unlimited punishment. Their marriages could be dissolved, and they or their children could be sold. In all things, their master acted for them. Contrary to what has often been claimed, slavery had not yet disappeared from the West. Quite the opposite: the wars of conquest had given it new stimulus. Gangs of slaves were not infrequently encountered on the roads, en route to be sold within the Empire or abroad. Yet another servile group worked on rural domains or as artisans in the towns. These were slaves by birth, whose parents were slaves or who issued from a marriage between a free man and a slave woman. In addition, someone might be condemned to slavery for debt or as a punishment.[1]

However, this judicial distinction does not really describe the social facts of differing conditions of life. Some free men were far more miserable than some slaves. Some former slaves, who had been freed from servitude, continued to live as they had before emancipation. These were men of an intermediate status to whom modern historians apply such terms as "semi-free." To understand the lives of these people, we must seek to construct their social and economic framework, beginning with a study of the rural folk who constituted four-fifths of the population.

Carolingian People

13

The Rustics

Rustics experienced an extreme diversity of conditions from small proprietors through tenants to day laborers. The image of the *colonus,* installed with a tenure on a great domain and bound to certain dues and labor services, is far too simple for our purposes. Historians attempting to trace a profile of the Carolingian peasant have depended primarily on sources drawn from the classic lay and ecclesiastical domains north of the Loire. Accordingly, they have tended to overlook the fact that a middle class of free, land-owning peasants lived in western and southern France, Italy, and Germany.[2]

Small Proprietors

We have many acts relating to the sale, purchase, or donation of small properties, or allods, to use the Germanic word. They reveal the peasant and his family, installed on their land, their "manse." This word, derived from *mansio,* house, appears in the seventh century, designating a piece of land sufficient for the support of a family. It is echoed in the Provençal *mas.* It corresponds to the Germanic *hube* and the Anglo-Saxon *hide,* which Bede defined as *portio unius familiae.* Later, the word is used for the unit upon which dues and charges were based, a median of about 12 to 16 hectares.[3] The possessor of a manse could dispose freely of the fruits of his labor and transmit his land to his children. The owner of at least four manses had to answer the convocation of the host while the less fortunate pooled their resources to send a man to the army. The lands of these free peasants were often threatened by the powerful, who employed many pressures and pretexts to satisfy their unending greed. The small proprietor could never afford to relax his vigilance if he hoped to keep his lands. Thus a Neustrian peasant gave some of his cultivated land, fields, and pasture to Saint-Germain-des-Prés. His four children continued to work this paternal land as *coloni,* while retaining an allod of four *bonniers.*[4] Sometimes a peasant who wanted to augment his holding might address a "prayer" (*precaria*) to the abbot to remit land to him which he could cultivate for his lifetime (from which we derive the expression "precarious title.") At his death, he was to remit all his goods to the monastery. In fact, through the abbot's negligence, his children might succeed in keeping the lands together. The Council of Tours, in 813, expressed concern over the abuses risked by this practice of parceling out ecclesiastical property.

Free men might acquire full ownership of land taken from the wastes. In 799, in Germany, a man named Liudger bought a parcel of woods and meadow. After bringing it under the plow, he exchanged that *hoba* against another waste without renouncing his rights over the land he had already cultivated.[5] In 845, a household obtained a field from the Abbot of Saint-Julien of Brioude. They farmed it and, after five years, divided it into two parts: one to be returned to the abbot and the other to remain in the farmers' hands. The agreement was duly registered in a charter recording the terms of the division.[6] In the Narbonnaise, Gothic peasants received land reconquered from the Muslims which, under the *aprisio* system, they could cultivate with the assurance that it was hereditary.* More than once, Carolingian princes had to defend these *aprisionaries* from the jealousy of the great proprietors and the malevolence of Frankish counts. In his *preceptum pro Hispani*, 844, Charles the Bald reiterated that these peasants could sell, exchange, and bequeath these goods as they wished.[7]

Tenants and Hired Hands

If the *pagenses* were unable to support their families from their own lands, they could take up other properties as tenants.† For example, the *libellari* of northern Italy were peasants who had concluded a rent contract, or *libellum*, with a great proprietor. According to the antique system, the lease was issued for 99 years or for two or three generations (emphytheotic leases)**. Thus, in the year 862, lands of a domain of Bobbio were cultivated by 47 free peasants, assisted by agricultural workers, who retained their revenues

---

* *Apprisio* is land appropriated from wasteland.
† Pagenses are peasants.
** In Greek, emphytheotic means implanting, here referring to the colonists.

except for certain quantities of wheat, wine, and sheep remitted annually to the landlord. Similar rents can be found at Montierender and at Prüm. In wine-producing regions, the vine grower kept half the vintage for himself.[8]

Peasants with their own lands to work could still, at certain times of the year, engage themselves to more powerful land owners as hired hands. At Corbie, the monastery gardeners appealed to the peasants for help in exchange for meals and transportation home at the end of the work. Similarly, on the lands of Prüm, certain peasants called *prebendarii* were asked to perform several labors in return for their subsistence or prebend.[9] Such an arrangement was of mutual advantage: the proprietor got the necessary supplementary labor, and the poor peasants could be sure of eating their fill for several days and earning a little money.

It is very clear that there were great inequities among the free peasants. Some rich peasants owned four or more manses and a team of draft animals. They could clear a profit in years of scarcity by selling wheat and wine at higher prices. But, on the other side, the poor who could not pay their debts pawned their harvests before they were reaped. These men were forced to become *coloni* on the great domains.

Tenants of the Domains

We know these *coloni* well, thanks to polyptichs which have been preserved. They lived on land not directly cultivated by the master (*mansus indominicatus*, or reserve), disposing of tenures of varying sizes with a house, stables, granges, kitchen garden, vineyard, farmland or pasture. In addition, the tenant could turn his pigs into the reserve forests for acorns and gather his firewood there. He could pasture his beasts on the meadows or fallow lands. The lands he worked rarely formed a single parcel but lay dispersed over different areas of the domain, obliging him to adjust his seasonal movements in at least minimal agreement with his neighbors. The holdings of the tenants were not all of the same extent. One peasant might cultivate ten times as much as another. Through purchase, exchange, or independent clearance, one peasant might augment his holdings so as to live easily on dozens of hectares while his neighbor had to be content with a little patch of land. A manse originally intended to support a single family might end by having two or three families installed on it while not far away other manses lay empty. The domain proprietor was not always to blame for such a situation. One abbot offered to install tenants crowded on a few manses on the waste lands. They refused because they lacked the necessary animals or equipment. Or, as often happened, they preferred to remain within their familiar horizons, however difficult.[10] The general picture of the manse system from domain to domain and even on the same domain was thus irregular.[11] Beside the lands reserved for the peasants, other lands might be given to new occupants by the owner or even to slaves.

Most often, the slaves (*mancipia*) worked on the master's reserve. They were lodged in the buildings of the villa and tended the cattle, cultivated the kitchen gardens and orchards, manufactured agricultural implements, and spun and wove textiles. They married one another and saved up a small nest egg in hopes of obtaining their freedom sooner or later. The masters of the domains often noted that this servile work was poorly performed. Perhaps they blamed the precarious conditions of a slave's life, for they gradually developed the custom of installing them on their own tenures. These "settled" slaves lived much as the free tenants did, and when such a slave was freed by his master, he rarely left the domain. Because of reverence for the patron saint of the church or more or less fearful deference toward his former master, he agreed to take up a tenure on the domain and be mixed among the other tenants in the future. Thus a social category of rural serfs was slowly created, the "men" of one lord or another, who owed him rents and labor services.[12]

Rents and Services
Every tenant was obliged to pay rents in silver or in kind and to perform certain services on the lord's reserve or face the loss of his land. Every year the peasants sent certain pieces of silver, poultry, or small animals to the court. They had to deliver certain manufactured articles: stakes, tools, boards, or pieces of cloth. Annually, a tenant worked a piece of land assigned to him on the reserve arable. The

vilicus or *mayor* in charge of domain exploitation allotted each tenant a parcel, called *ansange* in the north, which he was required to farm from the ploughing to the storage of the harvest. In addition, the tenants had to help the laborers on the heaviest days: hay making, harvest, and vintage. Finally, the tenant might have haulage duties, transporting tuns of wine, firewood, wagon loads of grain and hay from the villa to the abbey or the market.[13]

These were the general prestations due from the peasants. However, we must not forget that these exactions varied enormously within the domain from one holding to another. The peasants on a *mansus ingenuilis* had fewer obligations than those who had the misfortune to hold a servile manse, though they might not be slaves themselves.* Moreover the rules varied even among the holders of the free manses. For example, the inventory of Staffelsee, the domain of the Bishop of Augsburg in Bavaria, lists the following requirements for twenty-three *manses ingenuiles*. In one year five of them delivered two cows plus animal transport when required; six had to supply fourteen hogsheads of grain, four suckling pigs, a piece of linen from the workshop, two chickens, ten eggs, one setier (approximately eight pints) of linseed oil, a setier of lentils—in addition to five weeks of work, three days of ploughing, cutting, bringing in one cartload of hay from the lord's field, and messenger service. Six others owed two days of sowing and harvesting, in addition to mowing three cartloads, hauling wine, spreading manure on the lord's fields, and delivering ten carts of wood.[14]

In the same way, prestations differed from one domain to another. In some cases the peasants worked very little: at Arnheim they did two weeks in May and two in the fall; at Saint-Pierre-de-Gand, nothing. On the other hand, at Boussignies, they had to report twice a week with their yokes. In general, when the dues in kind were light, the labor services were heavy. Thus, at Nouailly-en-Berry, the tenants redeemed themselves from payment of three deniers and continuous transport service to the army by

* *Ingenuilis* means free: obligations of land parcels were stratified by custom, regardless of the tenant's social status.

The Powerful and the People

delivery of nine chickens, thirty eggs, loads of faggots and lathes, and two sheep. But they still had to plough eight rods of land in fall and twenty-six in spring, help bring in the harvest, repair the fences, and deliver two carts of wood and one of provisions to Angers and Paris.[15]

We could give many more examples. The texts mirror the lords' preoccupation with the need to ensure a labor supply. But from the peasants' point of view, it is clear that they were rarely worked to death. Rather, they enjoyed long periods of time to cultivate their own lands, and, beyond what was entered in the registers, they disposed of sufficient revenues. Moreover, we know that in good seasons, they sold the surplus of their harvest and frequented rural markets near their villages and even sold their wine and wheat over considerable distances.

The Village

Let us now turn our attention to the village, *vicus*, where the free men lived and the hamlets where the houses of tenants clustered. A peasant's house, *casa* as opposed to the *domus*, was built of those materials which came readily to hand. In southern France and in Mediterranean lands generally, houses were built of stone (*casa petrinea*), usually a single storey built over a cellar.[16] Elsewhere, and much more commonly, wood (*materia*) and clay were used. It has been noted that the Germanic word *wand* (wall) comes from *wanden* (plaster) while the words for stone wall (*mauer*) and tiles (*zeigel*) come from the Latin, *murus* and *tegula*. Bavarian law provides fines for each element of a house which was burned: twelve sous for the column supporting the roof, six sous for other interior posts (*winchilsul*), three sous for corner supports and interior and exterior beams sustaining the walls.[17]

These wooden houses were easily dismantled. From parts of houses excavated in Germanic villages like Gladbach and Warendorf, we can see that the posts made up a frame within which the walls were formed by woven wooden lathes daubed with mud. The roof, which was probably thatched, was reinforced by wooden posts acting as external buttresses. The house generally formed a single room divided into compartments.[18] Such houses were built in rectangles of various sizes: from twenty meters long at Warendorf to three or four meters at Gladbach. Compartmental divisions enabled the peasant to dispose of two or three rooms for his family and his animals. These chambers opened into a central room where the family ate and, perhaps, slept. A place was reserved at the center of the rural house for the hearth with an opening in the roof to allow the smoke to escape.

In some cases, a more efficient organization was provided by the building of annexes. Texts mention steam rooms, rooms kept particularly warm (*pislum*), rooms which could be locked with a key, (*screona*, from which we derive the old French *escrègne*, a chest with a lock).[19] A palisade or hedgerow protected the whole against prowlers and particularly against beasts.

Within, the house was furnished with a bed laid out on the beaten earth floor, where the householder slept with the smallest children (who were thus in danger of smothering), a few benches, and the furniture necessary for meals. Everyone rose at daybreak. The father and older sons worked in their own fields or those of the lord. The wife and daughters baked bread, fed the poultry, tended the sheep, wove pieces of cloth, gathered wood, and occasionally helped with the haymaking. They never tilled the soil. Gerald of Aurillac questioned a woman he encountered working a field. She explained that the season of sowing had come upon them while her husband was sick and she was alone. Gerald gave her money to engage a day laborer, explaining that "women should not do the work of men, for God has a horror of what is against nature."[20]

The exigencies of agricultural work and the communal spirit of Carolingian people made periodic reorganization possible. The peasants agreed jointly on the dates for ploughing or sowing, the placement of moveable fences to protect the crops, the release of cattle onto the communal pasture, and the mating of mares and stallions. The free men among them regulated the inevitable conflicts arising among neighbors by participation in the judicial assemblies presided over by the count or his delegates. They also gathered to give their oaths to royal representatives. All too briefly, scattered texts sometimes allow us a glimpse of these

rural communities in action, jealous in defense of their accumulated rights. No stranger, arriving in the village, could
settle there unless he was welcomed by all. A single refusal
would force him to clear out after three notices. But if he
were admitted, he then shared rights over the pastures,
waters, and communal roads.[21]

The Rural Priest

In principle, peasants were obligated to attend Mass every
Sunday as ordered by king and bishops. Even cowherds and
swineherds were supposed to be freed from their work to
join with Christian people.[22] Great efforts had been made to
multiply rural churches and supply a priest for every two
or three villages and hamlets. Domain proprietors had
chapels built among the buildings on the reserve for slaves
and tenants.[23] Nearly all of these churches have by now
disappeared, but they once acted as community centers for
peasant groups.[24] After Mass, contracts were concluded
orally or even in writing. If the priest was trained to draw
up an act, he would be asked to serve as notary. In the
atrium leading to the church and sometimes even in the
church itself, women and men danced, and not all their
songs were hymns. The curate himself was invited to join
in these profane celebrations. Usually a man of modest back-
ground, the priest was glad to share the pleasures of the
peasants. They invited him to the tavern and to wedding
suppers and, if his voice was good, he might even lead the
singing.[25] They excused his weaknesses and made the wife
who kept his hearth welcome among them. In a synodal
statute Theodulf cautioned rural priests:

> Do not go drinking and eating in the tavern. Do not
> sport with women. No, rather accept the invitation
> of the father of a family to dine pleasantly with his
> wife and children. For this charity and the carnal
> nourishment he offers you, you may give him the
> spiritual food of your discourse.[26]

Relations between pastor and flock were more difficult when the priest attempted to collect the *decima,* a tithe
of one-tenth of their personal revenues ordered by the Carolingian princes. Naturally enough, the contributors were in

no hurry to bring the priest what they owed. In some regions, priests had to issue lists of recalcitrants and forbid
them entry into church. Refusals were punished with a fine,
and further delay would result in the laggard's goods being
placed under seal. A final refusal would bring him before
the count's court.[27] In addition to the *decima*, a priest might
have a manse of twelve *bonniers* (about 15 hectares) with
four slaves to cultivate it. This at least was the standard at which they aimed.[28] In fact, many rural pastors were
poorer than their flock. The proceeds of the *decima*, meant
to fill their storerooms, which were often located within
the church building itself, were often confiscated by great
proprietors, ecclesiastical as well as laymen. Then the priest
must seek another source of livelihood and might become a
usurer or pawnbroker. Councils might deplore this state of
affairs, but, it would seem, the same bishops did little to relieve the condition of the rural priest.

Peasant Resistance

The peasant's acceptance of the charges which weighed
upon him was not always docile. Despite the poverty of
our documentation on this point, we can catch glimpses of
protests, occasionally discern the resistance of peasants. Conflicts often erupted between the proprietors of forests and
their peasants over rights to pasture or wood cutting. A
royal arbiter was needed at Saint-Gall to restore the peace.
After long discussions on both sides, "it was decided that,
according to ancestral custom, everything from this spot to
that pond . . . will be common to all, to cut wood, feed
pigs, and pasture sheep. . . ."[29]
    Moreover, peasants often refused to perform due ser-
vices on the pretext that they had fallen into desuetude.
Then the written acts which had originally consigned them
had to be rooted out.[30] After the Norman invasions, the peasants protested the effort of one proprietor to augment the
cens.[31] In 864, Charles the Bald complained that tenants on
royal and ecclesiastical domans had refused to undertake
new cartage services for marling*: "And, for the service of

* Marling is fertilizing with soil composed of clay &
carbonate of lime.

the hand, they do not want to thresh in the grange, although they do not deny that they owe the service of the arm."[32] In this same Edict of Pitres, Charles denounced persons who had sold their manses to neighbors or to the parish priest, keeping only their houses, so that they could refuse the services due on the tenure they occupied.

Some peasants even sought to leave the domain. A Breton lord demanded that the Abbot of Saint-Sauveur-de-Redon repatriate a group of peasants who had deserted his lands.[33] The biographer of Gerald of Aurillac recounted:

> One day, Gerald met some of his *coloni* on the road who were leaving their homes to depart for another province. After he had recognized them and asked where they were going, they told him that they were leaving his lands because, although he personally had done them nothing but good, they had been mistreated there. The soldiers with Gerald advised him to punish them and make them return to the lands they had deserted. But he did not wish to do that. He let them go where they would and even gave them liberty to travel.[34]

Capitularies and chronicles all mention slaves who escaped from their masters' authority. If they were caught, they could be birched or imprisoned.

But can we speak, as have some historians, of peasant revolts in the Carolingian period? Certainly, some capitularies occasionally mention *conjurationes* and even *conjurationes servorum*.[35] In fact, however, these movements appear primarily to have been manifestations of self-defense against bandits or invaders. In 884, Carloman commanded villagers not to band together against depredation but to confide their cause to the curate or the count's subordinates.[36] In 859, the *vulgus* of the lands between the Seine and the Loire formed a *conjuratio*, but that experience led the people to disaster. In Frisia, on the other hand, the peasants refused to submit to the exactions of the Norman chiefs on the grounds that they had already paid Louis. They armed themselves and succeeded in thrashing the Normans.[37] But this success was all too rare. In 882, an army of peasants occupied the monastery of Prüm, which had been abandoned by the monks. But the Normans quickly exterminated these unarmed people who were ignorant of all military tactics.[38] And the public powers, mistrusting these outbreaks of spontaneous resistance, forbade the peasants to carry arms. "If a serf is found wielding a lance, let it be broken over his back."[39]

The Merchants

Although the commercial classes of the Roman and Merovingian periods had vanished, there were still some merchants who were called *negociatores* or *mercatores* in the texts. What should we understand by these names? In general they describe the peddler frequenting local or regional markets as well as the international trader. Contrary to long-established belief, the Carolingian economy was not self-sufficient. Exchange existed on every level.[40]

Local and Regional Markets

Local markets, usually held every eight days on Friday or Saturday in towns or larger villages, drew anyone with a surplus of agricultural produce to sell or a need for manufactured goods not available in the town shops. While Pepin was still mayor of the palace in 744, he ordered the bishops to establish market places, *legitima fora*, where they did not exist already, and place them under the control of the public power. These markets had become so numerous a century later that Charles the Bald had to order his counts to make lists noting which of them had been established by his predecessors and which of them were being conducted irregularly.[41] The king was anxious to police the markets, not only to provide security but to protect the sales taxes which fed his treasury. Only reluctantly did rulers consent to allow certain abbeys or bishoprics to open their own markets during the middle of the ninth century.

The volume of transactions at these markets was not very large. Local potters, smiths, and weavers sold their products in exchange for agricultural produce such as chickens or eggs. The medium of exchange was the *denier*, a piece of silver from which is derived the French word for commodity (*denrée*). In addition, there were peddlers who regularly went from one market to another, like the *pauperculus* who led his salt-laden ass between Orleans and Paris.[42]

More important markets lasted for several days around an annual feast day. One of the most ancient of these fairs was that of Saint-Denis around the ninth of October. In addition, there were fairs at Pavia, at Chappes near Bar-sur-Aube (which once drew the Norman pirates), at Saint-Maixent (founded in 848 by Pepin), and at Cormery on January 24.[43] Business was done in a field in the monastic enclosure (*bourg*). To protect their tranquility, the monks marked boundaries beyond which the men and women attending the fair were not to trespass. This point was marked by a cross at Saint-Philibert of Granlieu.[44] When they had completed their transactions, peasants from far away would generally pause to venerate the patron saint whose feast it was. The day often ended in a tavern where they might drink too much. One drunken peasant from Stavelot lost the two cows he had bought at the fair.[45]

Some of the merchants who frequented these fairs could be called professionals. For themselves, or on commission from particular aristocrats, abbots, or princes, they would transport provisions or equipment from one end of the Empire to another by cart or by boat. They can be seen in northern Italy and in the Austrasian towns, at Bonn, at Mainz, Verdun, in the ports of Dorestad and Quentovic, as well as Rouen where an important flotilla lay. They worked in partnership with Frisian merchants or even with Arabs from Spain. Their principal commodities were wheat, wine, salt, and iron. Always on the watch for abundant harvests, these merchants bought wheat for re-sale at a good price in times of dearth. One of these important grain markets was Mainz where Franconian wheat came by the Main and could be transported by water on to Frisia. In Ermold's dramatization, the Vosges said to the Rhine: "O Rhine, if you did not exist, my granaries would be intact, full of the grain produced in our fertile country which you carry off to sell overseas while our own unhappy peasants suffer, alas! from hunger." Then the Vosges complained of the Alsatian wine which left her slopes to be sold abroad.[46] Great proprietors who could not consume the yield of the vintage on the spot confided it to merchants who sold the wine directly to regions where vines grew less readily or passed it through the fairs of Saint-Denis. Saxons and Frisians regularly appeared there to provision themselves.[47] The salt necessary for the preservation of meat and fish was transported from the Atlantic (Batz, Guerande, Bourneuf) or the Mediterranean salt marshes (the Sigean pool). Every year the sources changed. In 817, the Bishop of Sens complained of the high price of salt because heavy rain had obstructed its collection. These hazards did not affect the extraction of mineral salt at Reichenthal in the Bavarian Alps, Styria, Wich in Lotharingia, and Halle in Saxony. Salt-makers' boats descended the Danube to Mautern from which they could extend their voyage as far as Moravia.[48] Other minerals, particularly lead and iron, were also transported and sold and sometimes even smuggled for use as weapons. Charlemagne had to forbid commerce in arms more than once. The capitulary of Thionville, in 805, listed the markets affected by the prohibition: Bardovic and Scheessel in Saxon lands, Magdeburg and Erfurt, and, farther south, Hallstadt on the Main, Forsheim, Fremberg, and finally Regensburg. "No one is to carry either arms or armor there to be sold. If any are found with such things, all their goods will be confiscated. . . ."[49]

Professional Merchants
There were some merchants who looked beyond the frontiers of the Empire. There were others under the direct supervision of the crown, which protected them and monopolized their enterprises. The *preceptum negotiatorum* of 828, which might be called a charter in favor of merchants, demonstrates the royal interest in merchant privileges.[50] There the Emperor informed the bishops, abbots, dukes, counts, gastalds, vicounts, centeniers, *missi*, and other officials of France, Burgundy, Septimania, Italy, Tuscany, Rhaetia, Bavaria, and the Slavic fringe that he had conceded certain privileges to those merchants who arrived every May to provision the imperial "chamber," that is, to furnish the Emperor and his entourage with the rare and precious objects which were stored in the royal treasury. Such merchants were to be exempted from military service; their

teams and boats were not to be requisitioned; and they were to be free of diverse taxes, particularly internal *telonei*. These *telonei*, an inheritance from the late Roman Empire, were levied on most commercial operations and transport. Royal agents levied the *rouage* (*rotaticum*) on wheeled vehicles, the *portage* (*portaticum*) on back packing, the *saumaticum* on beasts of burden, and the *barganaticum* on barges. *Pontage* (*pontaticum*) had to be paid for crossing a bridge and *éclusage* (*exclusaticum*) for passing through a sluice.[51] But the palace merchants were free of all these duties. They had to pay only the 10 percent on the ports of Quentovic and Dorestad and the dues at the mountain passes. Great aristocrats also had their favored merchants whom they sought to provide with similar immunities. Alcuin recommended his *negotiator* to the Bishop of Coire so that he could transport goods to sell in Italy without obstruction. The Bishop of Passau had his *negotiatores sancti*, and the great abbots of Saint-Denis, Flavigny, Saint-Germain of Auxerre, and Jumiège all had their designated merchants whose activities were protected.[52]

Northern Merchants and Mediterranean Merchants

Professional merchants seeking to extend their fields of action beyond the frontiers of the Empire made free contact with the great centers of international commerce in the north, the Mediterranean, and the Orient. In the ninth century, the Baltic was the center of an important trade network controlled by Frisians and Scandinavians. Ships loaded with beaver and marten furs left the ports of Hedeby, Birka, or Reric and debarked at Hamburg, Bardovik on the Elba, Bremen on the Weser, or Dorestad on the Rhine. Frisians ascended the Rhine, establishing depots at Cologne, Strasbourg, Worms, and Mainz, where they used the pilings of the wooden bridge to dock their boats. Bishop Ansgar took ship at Cologne to begin his evangelic mission in Denmark and followed the trade route to Birka in Sweden on the Baltic coast.[53]

Scandinavian incursions disrupted these exchanges but did not end them. The Normans were merchants as well as pirates. At the height of these invasions in 873, the King of Denmark asked Louis the German to protect the merchants coming and going on the shores of the Baltic. Before the silting of its channel, Bruges, whose name probably derives from the Norwegian *brugge* or port, was indebted to the presence of northern merchants for its original development.[54]

At Birka, the great emporium of the north, merchants could buy products from Asia which came across the Russian plain. However, they were linked more directly to the Orient by the Mediterranean routes. Despite the opinions of Pirenne, Mediterranean commerce was never broken by the Arab invasions. Jews, particularly the Radanites (those who knew the routes or Rah Dan), who are mentioned by the Master of the Post Ibn Khordabeh, sought eunuchs, woven cloth, bearskins, marten fur, and swords in the Frankish realm to sell in Egypt. They carried musk, aloes wood, camphor, and cinnamon from the Orient to Constantinople and then on to the West.[55] Several chroniclers evoke these Jews, installed at court or in an episcopal household. Isaac the Jew was Haroun-al-Raschid's ambassador at Aix, and even more memorable was the Jew who sold a rat embalmed with diverse aromatics to a bishop for an enormous sum by pretending that it was an extraordinary animal imported from Judea.[56]

Jews were not the only ones interested in Oriental commerce. Venice, theoretically a Byzantine possession in northern Italy but practically independent, sent her own merchant vessels to seek out silks and spices. The wealthy family of Partecipazio who ruled the town from 811 to 870 got part of their fortune from commercial ventures overseas. In his will, Doge Gustiniano Partecipazio (829) said that he had invested 1200 livres in maritime activities. In 840, Lothair I concluded a treaty with the Venetians to import Oriental products into the Kingdom of Italy at Comacchio and Pavia. Trade flowed incessantly between the Po Valley and Venice. In 860, one chronicler noted that, the sea being frozen, merchants had to abandon their ships and send their goods to Venice by cart.[57] The great center for redistribution of Oriental products was at Pavia. Gerald of Aurillac stopped there on his return from a pilgrimage to Rome, and, hearing of the presence of a rich aristocrat, Venetian merchants came to offer clothes and perfumes to his men. Gerald learned that the mantle of precious silk which he had bought in Rome was cheaper there than at Constantinople. Seized with scruples, he had the difference relayed to the Roman merchant.[58]

From Italy, goods passed on to Gaul. Theodulf noted that silks of many colors, incense from Saba, ivory from the Indies, balm from Syria, and leather from Cordova could be had in the market at Arles.[59] Spain likewise received these precious goods from the Mediterranean or the African routes.

The Slave Trade

The slave trade was the most important element in the Oriental commerce. From the eighth to the ninth centuries, the slave trade did not abate. To the contrary, the penetration of the Carolingian armies into Slavic lands had opened up a new supply.[60] Both Jews and Christians went out to buy slaves in Bohemia or the land of the Wends and transported them across the Empire through Raffelstatten, Regensburg, Mainz, and Verdun to the Mediterranean ports. Abbot Stürm of Fulda encountered such a slave gang on its way from Thuringia to Mainz. About 870, the monks of Sithiu (Saint-Bertin) enroute to Rome passed a caravan of merchants from Verdun conducting slaves to Spain. Slaves were sent also to Marseilles, Venice, Aquilea, and Rome. Around 750, Venetians bought slaves at Rome and sold them to the Muslims. In 870, the monk Bernard noted six ships at Tarento filled with nine thousand slaves destined for Egypt and Africa.[61] There was the greatest demand in the Emirate of Cordova, particularly after Al Hakam I (822) decided to fill his militia, his administration, and his harem with five thousand slaves.

The Carolingian kings could not remain insensible of this traffic, and they did try to control it. Pepin forbade the sale of both Christian and pagan slaves. In 779 and 781, Charlemagne tried to regulate such sales. They were to be concluded in the presence of a count or a bishop and were prohibited beyond the frontiers. Louis the Pious made the same recommendations when he extended his patronage to Abraham, a Jew of Saragossa. In 845, the bishops who met at Meaux expressed anew their dissatisfaction with Jewish and Christian sales of slaves. They expressed a desire that

Christians should redeem them, so they could be baptized rather than sent to augment the rank of the infidels, "the Empire's most ferocious enemies."[62] Bishop Agobard of Lyon was scandalized when he learned that the Emperor had forbidden the slaves of Jews to be baptized without their masters' permission. He announced himself ready to give twenty or thirty sous, the price of a slave, to save the souls of these unfortunate persons. He further accused the Jews of Lyon of stealing children in infancy to be castrated and sold to Spain. The charge may not have been groundless. At least one merchant of Verdun is known to have transformed slaves into eunuchs before conducting them to Spain.[63]

Commercial Conditions: Prices

On the level of the regional market or on a grander scale, commerce was subject to the normal laws of exchange and regulated by established prices and measures. Even in those cases where barter was used locally, it depended on comparative evaluation. Thus a piece of land was described as being "worth 6 deniers, or the price of 6 deniers in food, clothes, wax, or beasts."[64] A seller at Pamplona informed a buyer in 835: "I have received from you in payment one cow, a woolen mantle, and twelve cheeses, the equivalent of 4 sous and 1 trien (a third of a sou)." This is a continuation of the *adaeratio* system of antiquity.

We can therefore, make some evaluation of the prices of a variety of goods.[65] In 794, cereal prices were:

oats: 1 denier the hogshead
barley and spelt [a kind of wheat]: 3 deniers
rye: 4 deniers
sifted flour: 6 deniers

These prices were imposed by the king. Real prices, in fact, depended on the harvest. At Prüm in 900, rye was worth 2 deniers a hogshead, whereas at Sens in 868 it was 7½ sous, or 90 deniers.

Again in 794, at two pounds to a loaf, 1 denier would buy:

23 loaves of oats, or
20 loaves of barley, or
15 loaves of rye, or
12 loaves of wheat

Animal prices:

> 1 ram: 4 to 12 deniers
> 1 sheep: 12 to 15 deniers
> 1 cow: 14 deniers
> 1 ox: 24 to 108 deniers
> 1 bull: 72 deniers
> 1 horse: 240 to 360 deniers

The price of a horse here is dramatically higher than the rest, but we do not know what sort of a horse was in question. Draft horses were certainly cheaper than war horses. A farm dog was worth 12 deniers.

Clothing prices:

> 1 piece of linen: 4 deniers
> 1 piece of serge: 12 deniers
> 1 sheepskin cloak: 12 deniers
> 1 sable roque: 120 deniers
> 1 short mantle: 120 deniers (price fixed in 808)
> 1 double mantle: 140 deniers
> 1 marten or otter cloak: 360 deniers
> 1 monk's cowl: 60 deniers

Arms prices:

> 1 sword: 60 deniers; with scabbard, 84 deniers
> 1 helmet, 72 deniers
> 1 cuirass: 144 deniers
> 1 lance and 1 buckler: 14 deniers

Slave prices:

> 1 male slave (in Italy in 725): 144 deniers
> (in 807): 170 deniers
> (at Lyon at the same time): 240 to 360 deniers

These indicators, drawn as they are from a variety of sources over a very broad span of time and space, can provide no more than a very approximate scale of values. Moreover, scholars who have interested themselves in the question of Carolingian prices have discerned an uneven but definite rise in prices through the period. That is why Carolingian kings periodically intervened in the control of commercial enterprises to fix a ceiling on prices.

They also commanded that transactions take place in the daytime before witnesses. The only exception were sales of food and forage, which could be made at night to a hurried traveler. Anyone who bought a horse, an ox, or any other beast of burden was to be given the identity of the seller and his place of origin.[66] In addition, efforts were made to define dishonest profit in terms of the specific transaction:

> Anyone motivated by cupidity to acquire grain or wine which he does not need at the time of the harvest or the vintage—for example, the purchase of a hogshead for 2 deniers which will be held back until it can be resold for 6 deniers—must be accused of seeking what we would call dishonest gain. On the other hand, if they made the purchase out of necessity—to keep it for their own use or to distribute it to others—we would call that an act of business (*negotium*).[67]

Thus Charlemagne condemned hoarding and speculative maneuvers effected in periods of dearth. At the same time he defined the just price which must be freely applied. Thus, sales made at a price lower than the real value in Italy because the necessity of the moment had put the sellers under pressure would be invalidated after an investigation by the *existimatores*. In 850, and again in 865, Louis II reiterated the same guidelines for the "just price." The bishops at the Council of Paris in 829 denounced both lay and ecclesiastical aristocrats who imposed a lower price at the harvest or vintage than that which peasants could have realized at a later time. Thus, contrary to what we have often supposed, it was not believed that commerce in itself was bad. There was no social stigma placed on the merchant who enriched himself honestly. But he must respect certain moral principles. When the soldiers of Louis III, the Young, sacked the town of Verdun in 879, it was because the merchants had refused to sell them provisions at the just price.[68]

The "just price," which was also called the "market price," depended on normal supply and demand, but it was difficult to enforce in periods of shortage. That was why Charlemagne, who may have been familiar with the legislation of the late Roman Empire, intervened to fix maximum prices. After the famine of 793 had pushed prices up, Charles declared at the Council of Frankfurt that:

> no man, lay or ecclesiastical, shall ever, in time of plenty or dearth, sell grain more dearly than the pub-

licly defined price of a hogshead: a hogshead of oats to be 1 denier; a hogshead of barley, 2 deniers; a hogshead of rye, 3 deniers; a hogshead of wheat, 4 deniers. If he wishes to sell it in loaves, 12 wheat loaves of 2 pounds each should be 1 denier; 15 of rye in the same weight, 1 denier; 20 barley loaves and 24 of oats for the same sum.

The king himself set the example, prescribing that the grain furnished by his own fiscs was to be sold at a lower price: 2 hogsheads of oats for 1 denier; 1 of barley for 1 denier; 1 of rye, 2 deniers; and 1 of wheat, 3 deniers.[69] In 805, he again fixed food prices and prohibited the sale of grain outside the Empire. In 806, he overhauled the price scales, and there we can note a rise: 2 deniers for a hogshead of oats; 3 for spelt mixtures (*spelta disparata*), 4 for rye; and 6 for a hogshead of sifted wheat.[70] Finally, the Emperor determined: "The same hogshead must be applied to all, so that everyone uses equal measures and equal hogsheads."

Measures

That last remark brings the difficulties of Carolingian standardization into focus. If the spirit of the law were to be obeyed, weights and measures would need to be equal, and this was not the case.[71] The Carolingian world had inherited the Roman system of measures, but these were not used consistently. Length could be measured either by the Roman foot (0.296 meters) or the foot of Drusus which was a little longer (0.333 meters). The league was used for long distances, and according to various authors it ranged from 2.5 km to 4 km. Other Carolingians might measure in miles: 1.5 km to 1.8 km for the Roman mile and half that for the German mile.[72] Surfaces might be measured in square acres, 120 feet divided into 12 rods (*pertica*), or in *ansanges*—about 40 rods to the Bavarians—*mappas* (which were larger), or *jugera*. The seventh century introduced the *bunuarium*, a fundamental agrarian measure favored by the Franks in the ninth century—except in Lotharingia and Brittany—covering about 10 acres (*arpents*).

Capacity was most commonly measured in hogsheads, *modius*, whose contents varied from 20 to 70 litres depending on time and place. The hogshead was divided into three tercels (*terciolus*), or into sixteenths, setiers (*sextarius*). The setier held two *hemina* or four quarts. Moreover, specific products required special measures: the *corbus* or *corbeille* (12 hogsheads) for spelt, the *staupus* for mustard, the *situle* (8 setiers) for liquids. Finally, the *carrada* was used to measure not only hay and wood but honey and beer. Weights were defined either by the Roman pound of 327.45 grams or the Carolingian pound, 445 to 491 grams. An ounce was a twelfth of a pound.

Carolingian kings tried to impose some order on this great diversity. Pepin desired stable measures, like stable prices. In the "General Admonition" of 789, Charles wrote:

"equal and exact measures should be employed by all so that, in cities as in monasteries and villas, just and equal amounts will be bought and sold." To give more force to this aspiration, he added a citation from the Book of Proverbs (20:10): "My soul detests two sorts of weights and two sorts of measures." In the capitulary *De villis*, he instructed his intendants to use "hogsheads, setiers, situles of 8 setiers, and a corbus, equal to those which we have in the palace."[73]

We know that the palace would fix new standards of measurement since, in 794, reference was made to "the public hogshead, newly established." Charles also fixed a new weight for the pound.[74] But it is hard to know if these attempts to standardize weights and measures had any effect. The bonniers formerly in use had disappeared by the tenth century. The successors of Charlemagne consistently commanded standard measures, but only within their own states. In 854 Charles the Bald commanded the counts to survey diligently their weights and measures, but, in these areas as in others, he could not make them obey.[75] The most common condition was the regionalization, even the localization, of measures.

Money

By the time the Carolingians came to power, gold money had disappeared. The sou (*solidus*), bequeathed them by the Roman Empire, survived for a while in the barbarian kingdoms in the form of the *triens* (a third of a sou). It continued to be current in Byzantium (nomisma) but no longer circulated beyond Italy. It was replaced with silver *scettas*, struck in England and Frisia or, after 660–670, by a small piece of silver, about twenty millimeters in diameter, which took the old Roman name, denier. What is more, the power to mint money had been lost to the crown and was controlled by the private mints of abbeys, cities, and individuals.[76]

Pepin, who understood that revenue, as well as power, could be derived from the striking of coins, imposed coinage in his own name from 755 on and undertook the regulation of its fabrication.[77] Charlemagne continued Pepin's efforts, dividing the livre into twenty sous and the sou into twelve deniers. He had silver deniers struck in his name. He imposed the denier on Italy, where gold money was still struck (capitulary of Mantua, 781). In 794, he announced the creation of a new denier: "As touching the denier, let it be known that we have decided that these new deniers will have currency in every place, every city and in all markets, and will be accepted by everyone, for they carry our name and will be pure silver of good weight."[78] We know these weights from the coinage which we have found. They were 25 percent heavier than the earlier deniers (1.60 grams as opposed to 1.27).

For centuries, this standard determined the monetary system of the west. The sou became fictitious money, for accounting purposes only. The only coinage actually minted was the denier and, more rarely, its subdivision, the obole or half-denier. The system was also adopted by King Offa of Mercia, and it was so successful that England remained faithful to the duodecimal and vigesimal system (1 shilling equals 12 pence) until 1970.

This replacement of light deniers by heavy deniers, which may have been caused by a drop in silver prices, required a new definition of the weight of the pound, raising it by about 25 percent over the Roman pound. This standard was not very well received. Princes had to be on the watch constantly for counterfeiters, and those who passed counterfeit money.[79] Charlemagne threatened recalcitrants with a 15 sou fine if they were free men and a beating if they were slaves. Counts and bishops were warned that they faced the loss of their offices if they did not apply the reform. The weight was slightly augmented again when Louis the Pious issued his own *novi denarii* around 819:

About the money which was the subject of an admonition about three years ago, when we fixed a
date after which a single coinage would be used and
all others would cease to have currency, we now
decree . . . that we agree to a delay, until Saint Martin's day, for the execution of our order . . . so that,
on that day, this coinage alone will have currency in
our realm.[80]

In 864, Charles the Bald issued a similar command, declaring:

that no one, moved by hope of gain or avarice, will
take our decision lightly; by 1 July everyone is to
have changed their silver into the new money, and
from that date, only the new deniers will be
accepted.[81]

He added that he would take measures against anyone striking deniers in any but the licensed mints.

In effect, the success of the monetary policy depended on the king's high-handedness with the coiners.
Twenty mints can be counted before 794 and thirty by the
end of the eighth century. In 805 and again in 808, Charles
reiterated his right to restrict the mint to his own palace, but
he did not enforce it.[82] Charles the Bald listed ten mints in
his realm: Quentovic, Rouen, Reims, Chalon, Sens, Paris,
Orleans, Melle, Narbonne, and the Palace. But after the
reign of Louis the Pious, bishops and abbots were conceded
minting rights: Corvey in 833; Hamburg in 834, and Prüm
in 861. As the years went by, individual mints multiplied,
and by the end of the century counts, too, had succeeded in
usurping the right of coinage.

Now let us try to penetrate into such a workshop.[83]
There ingots were cut into as many pounds as were wanted.
They were hammered down until they had been reduced
to the thickness of a franc and then cut into little squares
of the proper weight and finally rounded with further hammer blows. The matrices (dies) were fashioned by engravers
who used puncheons to imprint the royal monogram, the
effigy of the Emperor, or the name of the minter on either
side. Thus a die found at Melle, now in the Niort museum,
bore the legend *Carlus rex Fr*. The reverse of one of Louis
the Pious' deniers bore the imprint of two hammers and two

dies circled with the word *Metallum* (Melle), the location of the mint.

Then the coin could be struck: a blank was placed between two dies and printed with a single blow of the hammer. The minters were specialized workers whose different operations were strictly supervised. The Edict of Pitres witnesses:

> On the first of July, counts will receive five pounds of silver at Senlis which will be provided from the royal reserve for the striking of the new money. Each of them will arrive accompanied by witnesses, his viscount, and the moneyer responsible for the striking. The silver is to be weighed in their presence and its purity proven. The weight of the silver is to be restored in minted deniers six months later at Senlis. These deniers are to be weighed on the same scale in the presence of the same witnesses.[84]

Since the monetary patterns bore the royal monogram on one side and the names of different places on the other, numismatists have wondered whether the royal mints were not itinerant. Recent researchers have come to the conclusion that coins were struck in several shops in the environs of the established mint. These were, according to J. Lafaurie, "mills" operating to order where technicians with sufficient competence to guarantee uniform fabrication were concentrated by royal command. These workshops provided a living for their directors, who collected a tax on each striking.

Once it was struck, the coinage was put into circulation. Studying 114 treasure hoards buried between 752 and 888, numismatists have hypothesized that monetary circulation was generally regional. Thus 57 workshops were represented in the treasure found at Glisy-lès-Amiens: 113 pieces were struck at Quentovic, one of the most active workshops in Gaul, with 14 from Amiens, 39 from Reims, 35 from Rouen, 31 from Saint-Denis, 27 from Saint-Quentin, 21 from Paris, 18 from Laon, and 14 from Soissons. Pieces from the workshops of Chartres, Orleans, Auxerre, Maestricht, Huy, Namur, Dinan, or Mouson are rarer. None came from eastern France.[85] The monies struck by the king of western Francia were equal in weight to those struck by the king of eastern Francia or the Emperor, but they bore different legends and seem to have had an entirely different pattern of circulation. When Lupus of Ferrières went to Rome in 849, he tried to provide himself with Italian silver money which was alone acceptable on the other side of the mountains. There we have one of our oldest examples of international exchange.[86]

Except for Scandinavian regions, Carolingian money did not circulate beyond the imperial frontiers, for it could find no takers. The entrenched currencies were the Muslim dinar and the Byzantine nomisma, both struck in gold. Historians have wondered why the Carolingians adopted monometallism in silver and only very rarely made coins in gold (the medallion coin of Uzès and some pieces from Dorestad and Aix). The flight of gold to eastern lands has been mentioned, but this is contradicted by the existence of the Carolingian treasures.[87] Gold had not disappeared, but it had been converted into ingots or ornaments. Gold was sold at a value tied by agreement to silver: "In our realm, a pure gold pound is not to be sold for more than twelve pounds of silver," declared Charles the Bald in 864.[88] The Carolingians held to silver money because they held reserves from their mines in the Harz, Bohemia, Melle, and Poitou. And they wished to encourage regional exchanges by providing stable money of good alloy adopted to the new commercial situation. Indeed, the creation of the silver denier signaled the revival of commerce within the Empire.

Another index of the importance of money is the existence of interest taking and usury. Many contracts and letters show us the borrowers and lenders, who often come out of the abbeys.[89] Some people put their lands in gage to secure a loan (mort-gage) or even pledged themselves, becoming slaves if they failed to meet their payments on time. This commerce in money disquieted the public powers. In 806, Charlemagne defined usury: "It is usury when anyone is repaid more than he gave out—for example if he gave out ten sous and reclaimed more. . . . A loan is just only when the repayment equals what was furnished."[90] In another capitulary, he punished usury with a fine of 60 sous. Counts were ordered to apprehend usurers and bring them before the bishop's tribunal. For usury was forbidden in Deuteronomy: "You will not exact interest from your brother, not for silver nor for goods nor shall anything be lent at interest." Priests who practiced usury, even under an assumed name, were to be punished. All these interdictions on usury were collected by Regino of Prüm in his *De synodalibus causis*.[91]

The Jews

Importance of the Jews

What was forbidden to Christians might be permitted to Jews. Jews had been living in the West since the end of the ancient world, and in the eighth and ninth centuries they could be found in the areas where they had earlier taken up residence: the Italian towns like Rome, Ravenna, Pavia, and Lucca and such Gallic towns as Lyon, Vienne, Arles, Chalon, Mâcon, Uzès, Narbonne as well as Soissons, Nantes, and farther north in Aix and Frankfurt.[92] In these towns they entered a variety of trades: merchants, goldsmiths, doctors, and even tax collectors. In addition they might possess rural properties of vineyards or fields. Indeed, Pope Stephen III complained in a letter to the Archbishop of Narbonne that Jews who owned land were employing Christians as agricultural laborers. The acts preserved in local cartularies give witness to many Jewish owners of vineyards at Vienne and Mâcon. For example, a Jew named Justus gave a field and a vineyard to the Chapter of Mâcon in exchange for a small farm and vineyard in a different location.[93]

Jews could be found in the entourages of aristocrats and princes. They were charged with embassies to the East, returning with cloth, perfume, and spices. Louis the Pious particularly protected them, taking them under his *mainbour* and conceding exemption from the *telonei* to them as merchants of the palace. A *Magister Judaeorum* was given charge of protecting them. For that purpose, Evrard was sent with the imperial *missi* to Lyon to regulate conflicts between Christians and Jews. He ruled in favor of the latter, as we are informed by Agobard, one of the few bishops hostile to the Jews. In a letter to the Emperor Louis, Agobard complained of the "insolence of the Jews" and the protection they found in the palace. On their side, the Jews took pride in displaying the rich cloaks the court ladies presented to their wives. They obtained the Emperor's permission to change the market day from Saturday, which was their Sabbath. They were also permitted to build new synagogues and to prohibit the baptism of their slaves. In 841, Agobard's successor Amolon took up his predecessors' battle against the Jews and demanded a revival and enforcement of the measures taken by Roman emperors and Barbarian princes against them.[94]

Tolerance toward the Jews

In fact, there was no persecution of the Jews in the Carolingian period. The attitude of the author of the *Annales of Saint-Bertin* who blamed the Jews for the death of Charles the Bald and the Norman conquests of Bordeaux in 848 and Barcelona in 852, was exceptional.[95] Jews continued to live undisturbed in the midst of Christians. They wore no particular costume and spoke the same language as everyone else. They regularly celebrated religious offices in the synagogue. Even their given names bear witness to their integration into Carolingian society. Certainly there were many Davids, Abrahams, Eleazars, Isaacs, Josephs, Nathans, Samuels, and Sedechias, but for every Nathan there was a Donatus, one Isaac called himself Gaudiocus, and so forth. This practice of latinizing Hebrew names continued well into the tenth century.[96] Moreover—and this was what disturbed the Bishops of Lyon—the Jews had attracted some Christians to themselves. Christians in their service, both slave and free, were in danger of being proselytized. In towns, it was not uncommon to find Christians who had "Judaized." Sometimes they had begun by dining with Jews and beginning to learn their doctrines. As Agobard wrote:

> While we, with all the humanity and goodness which we use toward them, have not succeeded in gaining a single one to our spiritual beliefs, many of our folk, sharing the carnal food of the Jews, let themselves be seduced also by their spiritual food.

Christians in Gaul and Italy needed reminding that it was a sin not to respect the sabbath. What is more, some of them went instead to the synagogue, saying that they preferred the sermons of the rabbis to those of their own curates. There they learned that Jesus had been a young Jew, a teacher, who was hung as a magician and buried in a cabbage patch. Meanwhile their wives learned that the Jews, descendants of the patriarchs and prophets, were God's own people practicing the only true religion.[97]

The Jews and Christendom

To the great scandal of their bishops, some Christians did not hesitate to convert to Judaism. The most famous case was that of the Deacon Bodo, of the Alamanic people, who had been raised in the palace from his youth. In 838, he received the Emperor's permission to go on pilgrimage to Rome and used the occasion to sell all his companions except his nephew into slavery. He then had himself circumcised, let his hair and beard grow, took the name Eleazar, and married a young Jewess. Being unable to return to the Empire, he took refuge at Saragossa.[98] Bodo-Eleazar exchanged several letters with a Cordovan layman, Paul Alvare, originally a Jew himself, who accused the neophyte of converting other Christians. From this epistolary dossier of 840–841, we can glimpse the arguments used by Jews and Christians to sustain their respective beliefs. Bodo said that he himself had quitted "that reprobate and abject faith, lying and accursed, detestable, abominable and vile," to turn from idolatry to the worship of the only God because he had been scandalized by the immorality of the Catholic clergy and the contradictions of Christian beliefs. When he was in the palace, he had known fourteen Christians who professed opinions which diverged from their faith. Alvare responded that he knew seventy-two varieties of heresy but tried to refute Bodo's arguments by commentaries on passages from the Old and New Testaments.[99]

The clerks of the Empire did not remain inactive but sought to respond in kind to the Jewish arguments. Agobard urged the clergy to go to the synagogues to preach and informed the Emperor of the conversion of several young Jews. He even admitted that some Jewish parents had fled with their children to Arles to protect them from the intemperate zeal of the Lyonnaise clergy. Alerted by the Jews, the Emperor did intervene to prevent an attempt at more or less forcible baptism. Amolon, in his much-copied *Book against the Jews*, presented a small dossier of scriptural arguments which preachers could use.[100] However, he was obliged to recognize the failures of the "Christian mission." The bishops at the Council of Meaux, led by Florus and Amolon, vainly urged Charles the Bald to pass anti-Jewish legislation which would prohibit mixed marriages and the construction of new synagogues and limit the paternal rights of Jews.[101] Charles the Bald refused. Even discrimination in the law courts between Christians and Jews was becoming attenuated. Under Charlemagne, a Jewish complainant had to furnish as many as nine witnesses, but his successors were less exigent. A capitulary falsely attributed to Charlemagne, which doubtless dates from the ninth century, puts Jews provided "particularly painful ordeals for Jews," but it does not appear to have been enforced. On the whole, Jews were treated about the same as other subjects. In their own interests, princes welcomed them with a tolerant spirit. The Jews were rich, and their wealth profited the Empire. Charles the Bald's tax of 877 imposed on merchants specified that Jews would pay 10 percent of the value of their merchandise and Christians 11 percent.[102]

The conversion of the Jews could not really be expected until the end of time: "Though the Synagogue is not yet joined to Christ, it will be when the nations have reached their fulfillment." This was the feeling of Amalarius, who passed as a friend to the Jews and was even accused of inviting them to liturgical ceremonies.[103] Like many other literate Christians he took advantage of the religious knowledge of Jewish rabbis. Through his veiled allusions we can glimpse the existence of Talmudic schools in Italy and the Rhineland where learned Jews could refute the doctrinal affirmations of the Christians.[104] Alcuin had attended a religious discussion in Pavia between the Jew Lullus and Peter of Pisa. The text of this controversy had been transcribed. It was also mentioned by Claudius of Turin, who advised readers who questioned his account of Biblical times to consult the texts retained by the Jews. Nourished on the Old Testament, Carolingian culture felt very close to the Jewish tradition. Frankish liturgy, morality, religious laws, and even the politico-religious system resembled Jewish custom so closely that some historians have conceived of an "occult influence of Judaism on the Christian conscience."[105]

III

*Technology
and
Domestic
Occupations*

Carolingian society was comprised of three groups: those who fought, those who prayed, and those who labored. The latter group was held in small esteem by the Carolingian aristocracy. Theodulf was right to remind the powerful that they were too inclined to despise the working world while their own wealth was founded on the sweat and labor of the poor. The magnates were not "idlers" in the antique sense of the word, but they did believe that only the professions of battle and prayer (the *opus Dei*) were worthy of them. They abandoned the physical work of supplying food, clothes, lodging, and other consumer products to others. Even the original effort of monasticism to dignify manual labor was rarely echoed in the religious literature of the period. Monasteries disposed of a sufficient number of laborers to undertake very specialized activities. Even the rural priest was expected to have some servants to relieve him of the necessity for manual labor. Individual bishops and abbots who did work with their hands, were exceptionally motivated to mortify their pride or to undertake a penance which would remind them that work is a curse which the sin of Adam imposes on all.

Carolingians and the Working World

Nevertheless, manual laborers and their tasks were mentioned so frequently in the texts that we might almost suggest a "Carolingian labor renaissance."[1] Charlemagne had a horror of laziness and idling. He commanded that alms be refused to able-bodied beggars who did not work. He desired all his subjects to give thanks for all their benefits once a week and issued very precise regulations regarding the Sabbath rest for that purpose. In the general *Admonitio* of 789, he devoted a chapter to the world of labor:

> Let no servile work be done on Sunday and no one be required to work in the fields on that day: none should cultivate the vine nor plough the fields, nor harvest, nor make hay, nor prune the hedges, nor clear forests, nor cut trees, nor dress stones, nor build houses, nor work in their gardens, nor attend law courts, nor hunt. Only three sorts of cartage will be authorized on Sunday: deliveries to the army,

deliveries of provisions, and, if the need should arise, the burial of the lord. Women should not work at cloth: none should cut out clothing, nor do needle work, nor card wool, nor pound flax, nor wash clothes in public. For all must be obligated to rest on the Lord's Day. Everyone, in all places, should congregate to celebrate Mass in church and thank God for all the good things that he has given us on this day.[2]

The cycle of rural labor was celebrated by poets and painters. In contrast to the representations of the months in antique and Byzantine manuscripts, the painter of a Salzburg manuscript around 820 abandoned the use of allegorical figures in favor of a realistic depiction of people at work.[3] When the Emperor wished to give new names to certain months of the year, he used characteristic agricultural activities. June was the "month of fallow," July the "hay month," August the "wheat blade month," September the "forest month," October the "vintage month."[4]

The Agrarian Calendar

To Carolingians, agriculture was the very essence of labor. The very word meaning to work, *laborare*, passes into modern French as *labourer*, to work the land. Theodulf, commissioning a painting of The Earth for his episcopal palace, envisaged a beautiful, strong woman suckling a child. Among her attributes were baskets of fruits, cymbals, chickens at her feet, and cows. He explained that the cymbals represented the noise of rural implements, the chickens indicate the seed which the Earth takes into her bosom only to return it in abundance. The submissiveness of the oxen testified to their understanding that they owed her their fodder and would have nothing without her.[5]

Regional differences make it difficult for us to reconstruct the Carolingian agrarian calendar. However, we can determine the cycle for the northern regions of Europe by collating the Salzburg miniatures with contemporary poetry. In January, man is numbed by the cold and the fields contract; but by February spring is in the air. In March the vines are pruned, and in April animals are put out to pasture and the soil prepared. In May forage is collected for the cavalry and the vines tied to props. June is the month for ploughing, in contrast to antiquity when ploughing was done in October or November. July is the time for hay-making and August for hay harvest. In September and October, peasants collected and pressed the grapes and sowed grain. In November wine was put into barrels and grain threshed; the pigs were brought in from the pasture to be slaughtered in December.

Tillage, Sowing, and Harvesting

Agricultural techniques had changed little since the end of antiquity. The coming of the Germans was not followed by an agrarian revolution. Peasants still used very rudimentary equipment, generally being content with wooden tools. The inventory of Annapes mentions only a few instruments of iron: two scythes, two sickles, and two spades were available for the whole of this great domain. Generally the peasant had a reasonably efficient plow to till the earth, a traditional instrument which we can see in all the manuscripts of the period.[6] The tool was guided with one hand and a goad brandished in the other to make the two oxen move. The ploughshare, sometimes reinforced with a metal cap, could turn over the earth superficially. In some texts we find mention of the *aratrum* and the *carruca*. These may be references to the mould-boarded plow apparently known already to the peasants of Central Europe. Such a plow had great advantages in that it permitted deep ploughing of the heavy soil of the great northwestern plains. However, great quantities of iron, a rare and expensive metal, were needed in its manufacture. Ermold the Black once longed to employ Danish idols for the purpose: "The iron of which your gods are made would be a boon to the cultivation of the fields. Why don't you make a plow? A wheeled plow to turn the earth would benefit you far more than that God."[7]

Having only a simple plow, peasants had to spade up their fields periodically to restore their fertile elements. Manure would have helped them avoid that labor, but progress in the use of fertilizers was practically nonexistent. Generally, they were content to burn the stubble. A single innovation was the introduction of marling, mentioned in an incidental remark in a capitulary of 864. But the peasants resisted it because they would have to haul the marl. As Charles the Bald wrote, "Peasants refuse to haul marl and do other things which they do not like, perhaps because they did not transport marl in the past. But in many places marl was transported in the time of our grandfather (Charlemagne) and our father (Louis)."[8] Some texts mention manuring the reserve as a labor service, but this precious fertilizer was primarily used for the kitchen gardens.

Under such conditions, the soil was exhausted quickly and could not be used in successive years. A field had to be abandoned to fallow for two or three years before it could be used again. We do not know whether the traditional biennial rotation—fallow one year, cultivated the next—had become standard or if rotation had become triennial. Historians debate this heatedly. Indeed a few texts mention winter wheat and spring wheat, with one field sown with maslin (a mix of wheat and rye), rye, or barley in the autumn and the other sown with oats in the spring. The third field would be left fallow. But even if this novel technique was beginning to be employed in northern France, it had not spread very far. As G. Duby wrote:

> We must suppose the use of a wide range of systems, from strict triennial rotation to an erratic slash-and-burn: tillage practiced here and there for several years in a row after burning the brush at the forest edges until the soil was completely exhausted.[9]

Carolingian agriculture required great spaces because of its itinerant nature. June, or "fallow month" to use Charlemagne's name, was the time of tillage for the great majority of peasants, at least in northern lands. After an initial ploughing, the fields were harrowed before the autumn sowing. According to a text from Redon: "The good farmer first prepares the land, cutting trees, burning trunks, and then finishes by drawing his *aratrum* over the land, tracing the furrows. If he has contoured the land carefully, he may return home knowing that all will be well."[10] Once the fields were ready, the sower, with his sack full of seeds, walked over the area, throwing them broadcast. Generally the seeds were rather lightly sown and at best could be expected to yield about two bushels of grain to the hectare. Harrowing helped hide the seeds, but the birds got their share. Once the grain began to ripen, peasants used mobile barriers to protect their fields from large and small animals as well as men. Charlemagne's revision of the Salic Law punished those who broke the posts supporting a trellis or drew harrow or plough across a field where the grain had sprouted.[11]

Harvest time varied by region. In Charlemagne's calendar, August was "wheat-blade month." The harvester seized a fistful of blades and cut them with a sickle. Women tied the sheaves, gathered and piled them up to wait for the carts which carried them to the barn, sometimes covered and sometimes not. The designer of the plan of Saint-Gall designated a place where "the harvest will be threshed," a floor (*aera*) where the grain could be separated from the chaff with a flail or be trampled by beasts. Adalhard desired that wheat should be delivered to Corbie in sheaves so that he could use the straw. But many peasants limited themselves to sending only the grain which they owed.

The Mill

Corn chandlers received the grain for grinding. At this point, the problem of watermill installations must be considered. It has been believed that proprietors were obliged to replace muscle power with hydraulic power because of a scarcity of slaves.[12] However, we have seen that slaves were still numerous. Moreover, free tenants were expectd to grind and sift barley and grain, regularly reducing it to flour. Nevertheless, in the sixth century water mills began to appear in some places, and their use spread. Barbarian laws mention proprietors who built milldams on rivers for the establishment of a mill. By the ninth century, most of the great domains owned water mills. Fifty-nine were cited in the Polyptich of Irminon for the Paris region, of which eight were of recent construction. The royal inspector at Annapes noted five mills. Adalhard devoted a chapter to the mills of Corbie, some equipped with three to six wheels. Millers were directed to keep them in good repair, clearing the sluices and providing millstones. For this work, they were allotted full tenures and discharged from all other duties.[13] Some villages were named for their mills: Mulhaus in Franconia, Mulinheim (modern Seligenstadt) where Einhard's intendant sent the grain from his domain. This suggests that the water mill was considered to be a rare and costly installation.

Yields

Cereal cultivation demanded a series of painful tasks for a rather modest return. Historians seeking to calculate harvest yields have produced lists of very slender figures. The year that the royal inspectors came to Annapes, 64 percent of the spelt reaped the year before had been sown, 40 percent of the wheat, 38 percent of the barley, and 100 percent of the rye. This represents yields of 1.8, 1.7, 1.6, and one for one. This is astonishing compared to a median yield of 8 for 1 in the late Roman Empire. Perhaps that had been a particularly bad year with the crop damaged by a late frost or heavy rainfalls. Certainly, other texts for the end of the ninth century give higher ratios (one mentions 3 and 4 for 1). However, the debate must remain open and inconclusive until we have more numerous and precise numerical indicators for various areas in the Empire.[14]

Clearing

Peasants might attempt to increase the arable area by attacking the forest or bringing heaths and marshes under cultivation. But what they won on one side was lost on the other. For the forest was a source of inestimable wealth for Carolingians and all medieval men. There they found nourishment from small game, wild fruits, cranberries, mountain ash berries, apples, pears, prunella, chestnuts, mushrooms, and honey from wild swarms. The forest furnished them with litter for the stable, forage for beasts, beechnuts and acorns for pigs. From the forest they drew wood, not only for heating but for construction: beams, shingles and lathing; sabots, tools, and tableware were made of wood; charcoal was necessary for working forges; resinous torches provided light; oak bark was used for tanning and pitch for caulking.[15]

Still, the forests extended so widely that large clearings could be undertaken without risk. Wishing to safeguard his forests, Charlemagne instructed his intendants: "If spaces must be cleared, let them be cleared, but the fields must not be permitted to increase at the expense of the wood. Where there should be wood, do not allow too much to be cut and damaged." However, in 813, the king ordered the intendants of the fisc to put their men to work on forest clearing.[16] From the seventh and eighth centuries, abbeys unhesitatingly pursued the effort of clearance. Polyptichs and charters often mention "assarted" lands. The Abbot of Fulda bought lands collectively cleared by some peasants. "Guests" were installed in the fields to bring them under cultivation. Entire domains were created from recent clearings. During the Carolingian period, the Bishops of Salzburg and Passau began the clearing of portions of Bavaria beyond the Enns.[17]

In the southern part of the Empire, land reconquered from the Moslems was put into cultivation by the monks of Roussillon and the Aude valley and by the *Hispani*, Gothic refugees who were accorded important privileges by the Carolingian kings (for example, the right of *aprisio**). Thickets, brambles, stubble, vegetation tangled with undergrowth which could not easily be destroyed, gave way to land prepared for tillage (*ruptura*). Water channels were laid out and pastures planned. Charles the Bald encouraged this expansion of cultivation in his capitulary *Pro Hispanis* and promised that all the cleared land would be freely owned by the newcomers:

> It is our further desire to reward those who have rescued the desert lands from aridity and delivered them to cultivation, in whatever country they may be, by granting them all that they have cleared within their "aprisions," that they may keep it and possess it freely on condition that they always perform the royal services due in the county of their residence.
>
> They are perfectly free to sell their aprisions, to exchange them, give them away, or leave them to

* See p. 103.

their descendants; if they have no sons or nephews, their other relatives will succeed as heirs according to their own law. . . .

They are authorized to conserve and possess these goods in peace, tranquilly, according to ancient custom, to pasture animals upon them, cut the wood, bring in the water necessary as the need arises, according to ancient custom and without anyone's opposition.[18]

Refined Cultivation: Vines, Vegetables, Orchards

As new monasteries were created, they continually spread viniculture in the West. Abbots and princes were very careful to possess vines and to honor their guests with samplings of the year's wine. From olden times, the vineyards of Italy were famous. A growing reputation was enjoyed by the wines of the Paris region and the Loire. Alcuin called Theodulf "the father of the vines." Rhine wine was sufficiently important for Louis the German to specify his ownership of the vineyards in the Treaty of Verdun, 843.[19] Even in lands like southern Brittany where the climate was unpropitious, abbots planted small vineyards near the abbatial buildings.

At all times, viniculture is an enterprise for the wealthy. It requires much hand work and very attentive care. Moreover, a vineyard must be leased on a long-term basis since it takes five years for a new vine to produce a full yield. Proprietors often entrusted the cultivation of the vineyards to tenant farmers who paid rent in kind (*métayers*). These peasant *vinitores* had to plant and fence the vines, train them on their props, and collect the vintage. October was the "vintage month" (*windumenmonath*). Grapes were cut and carried to the press where they were generally pressed by foot. Charlemagne attempted to forbid that practice: "The pressings from our *villae* are to be in good condition. Let our intendants ensure that our vintage should not be stamped by foot but that all should be done with propriety and decorum." The juice was poured into barrels which had been prepared in advance. Carpenters had built hogsheads (*pontae*) coated with pitch and banded with iron hoops. The plan of Saint-Gall depicts large and small barrels ranged in the cellars. Once the vintage was finished, proprietors planned its sale. Convoys of boats or carts were organized. Studies of the Polyptich of Irminon, for example, have shown that the Abbots of Saint-Germain des Prés sold most of their harvest. The most productive domains for wine were located near rivers where it was easy to move the barrels to the boats headed for Saint-Denis where a wine fair was held in October, or to Rouen and Quentovic from which they could be sent to England.[20]

The Carolingian diet depended on an abundance of vegetables. Every individual from simple peasants to abbots and bishops kept a garden near their houses.[21] The plan of Saint-Gall designated the rows for vegetables (*olera*), listing the different types to be planted there: onions, leeks, garlic, shallots, celery, persil, coriander, chervil, anet, lettuce poppy, sariette, coleseed, parsnips, carrots, cabbage, beets, and lamb's lettuce. Some of the same vegetables are also mentioned in the capitulary *De villis* and in Walafrid Strabo's poem "On the Cultivation of Gardens." There the monk of Reichenau pictured himself hard at work as winter ended. He pulled up the nettles, destroyed the mole hills, prepared the soil, and traced the vegetable furrows with planks of wood, crushing the clods with a forked hoe and spreading fertilizer over all. Spring rains and moonlight did the rest. Gardening demands daily attention, for weeds push up vigorously and caterpillars and insects threaten to destroy everything. One morning a gardener monk of Redon saw his whole plantation ravaged by caterpillars.[22] At Corbie the *hortulani* monks contracted for specially trained laborers to care for their four gardens outside the cloister. They were instructed to till the soil, sow, weed, thin, hoe, and repair the fences. We also have a list of their tools: pickaxes (*fossorii*), spades, hatchets, sickles (*falcilia*), and so forth.[23] Good seeds were always being sought by these gardeners. When the monks of Reichenau could not find leek seeds in Francia, they requested some from a distant abbey.[24]

The orchard, too, was near the house, combined with the garden or next to it. The designer of the plan of Saint-Gall had the original notion of planting the orchard in the monastic cemetery. It included apple, pear, plum, medlar, laurel, chestnut, fig, quince, peach, hazelnut, almond, mulberry, and walnut trees. In addition to these, the capitulary *De villis* mentions cherry and rowan trees [akin to mountain ash] and specifies several varieties of apple both sweet and sour, under their Germanic names: Gozmaringa, Crevedella, Sperauca, Geroldinga.[25] Fruit trees were protected by law: 3 sous fine for cutting down a tree outside the close, 15 if it were in the close. Abbots confided their care to specialists. At Corbie, two servants were assigned to the care of the newly planted orchard. At Bobbio, the harvest was supervised by the "guardian of the fruit."[26] These fruits were exported over great distances. Lupus wrote pleasantly to Abbot Odo of Corbie:

> By a messenger whom you know well, I am sending you the peaches I promised. If, as I fear, he should devour them or if he complains that they were stolen, compel him by your prayers to deliver the pits at least (if he hasn't gulped them down as well) so that at last you may have your little share of the most succulent of peaches.[27]

Stock Breeding

Stock raising was always of the utmost importance in Germanic civilization. We need only read the laws redacted in the seventh and eighth centuries to be convinced of it. Severe penalties were imposed for the theft or mutilation of cattle. Moreover, the size of herds, the different species of cattle, and the responsibilities of herders and their dogs were described in some detail.[28] Like their ancestors, Carolingians were more interested in cattle raising than in agriculture. The instructions relative to livestock are numerous and precise in the capitulary *De villis:*

> Let them have a care to the stud horses—that is, the *waraniones*—guarding against leaving them in the same pasture too long, lest their health deteriorate. If any individual is more apt or more experienced at this work, let him offer us his advice at a convenient time before the season for joining the stallions and the mares begins.

And let all the mares be watched with care and separated from the foals at the proper time. And when the fillies have multiplied, let them also be separated out to form a new herd.

And let care be taken that our foals be brought to our palace by Saint Martin's day in winter (11 November). . . .

Let each intendant discover how many foals should be put in the same stable and how many studmasters ought to be put there to care for them.[29]

When we remember how important his cavalry was to him, we can readily understand why Charles wanted to improve the yield of his herds. Nor did he neglect the meat-producing cattle and sheep. Each villa was instructed to maintain cow byres and sheepfolds, stables for nanny and billy goats. Oxen and ewes were to be specially fattened.[30] Nor can we say that the great ecclesiastical proprietors were less careful of stock breeding because they needed less meat. Like laymen, abbots and bishops needed horses for riding and traction and other beasts for carrying their baggage. Their meat fed the monastic *familia*, their guests, and the infirm. Gravy flavored their vegetable dishes, and fat was used for lights. Bishops and abbots were as careful as laymen of their stock. Aldric, Bishop of Le Mans, was proud to leave a greatly augmented herd for his successor: eighty flocks of mares with their stallions, two hundred flocks of cows, ewes, goats, or pigs distributed among the different villae belonging to the church of Le Mans. When the Abbot of Fulda received land in Frisia, its extent was measured by the number of beasts it could support: sixteen ewes, fifteen cows, twelve oxen, and forty sheep.[31]

In summer the animals were put out to pasture on the fallow lands reserved for this purpose (*pascus*). One or more herders with sheep dogs (*canes pastorales*) guarded against thieves by day and against beasts by night. Pigs were raised in the open air, kept in nearly a wild state in the forest where they fed on acorns, beechnuts, chestnuts, and berries. The size of a wood might be measured by its pigs. In the Paris region, a hundred pigs were generally equated with 153 hectares. The fall of acorns in autumn enabled them to put on weight for the winter, while some pigs were raised in proximity to the mill to be specially fattened. Each domain included stables and barns (the plan of Saint-Gall indicates about 1500 square meters for these). There the buildings for sheep, goats, pigs, comprise a vestibule giving on to an internal court where the stables were. Cattle and horses were housed in larger buildings. Neatherds and stablemen lived in a house contiguous to them which held additional stables and a storehouse for hay on the second floor.[32]

The hay which would be needed for winter feeding was gathered from the humid fields in July. It was forbidden to send animals out before the haymaking. We can evoke the work of the mowers from texts and illustrations.[33] Men, furnished with a great two-handed scythe and a grindstone at their waists, cut the grass. Women tied it in sheaves and loaded the carts. The work had to be done quickly. In fact, it could not have required too much of the peasants' time, for the field was always smaller than the arable land. Despite the abbey's name, the reserve of Saint-Germain-des-Prés, comprised no more than 91 hectares of grassland to 4630 hectares of cultivated soil. In other abbeys, it was stated that the fields were to comprise the lesser part of the domain. The proportion varied. It might be as high as 20 percent as in Coyecques in Artois, a dependent villa of Saint-Bertin, or only 1.5 percent as at the villa of Lobbes at Leernes in Brabant.

Great proprietors and simple peasants alike encouraged the preservation and efficient use of their herds. Intendants were given careful advice in letters. Einhard once complained that the pigs which were sent to him were too small and gave instructions on the slaughtering of oxen. A bishop in Swabia wrote:

> Let the sheep be given daily the dues of twelve tenants in salt and a good mix of food so that they will be ready on my arrival. Take the pigs owed by the serfs and see that they are well nourished with flour. Take the geese and stuff them.[34]

Annalists note epidemics of animal diseases as catastrophes on a par with human epidemics.[35] Monks copied tracts on the veterinary arts, and the people recited magical formulae to save sick or lame beasts.

Let every intendant ensure that he has good workers in his district: workers in iron, gold, and silver; shoemakers, turners, carpenters, shieldmakers, fishermen, birdcatchers, soap makers, . . . workers who know how to make nets for the hunt and for fishing and for catching birds, and other workers who are too numerous to list.[1]

These orders of Charlemagne, in the capitulary *De villis*, demonstrate the sovereign's seemingly innovative desire for specialized labor. Without going so far as the German historian Dopsch, who speaks of an "industrial revolution," we should notice that the activities of artisans attracted the interest of educated Carolingians.[2] Technical treatises were recopied in the *scriptoria*, and the pen of John Scotus Erigena ranked the *artes mechanicae* with the *artes liberales*.[3] His disciple Manno defined the *mechanica ars* for a friend in Laon. Other learned men did not think themselves too good to write a verse explaining how to make a vase.[4] Moved by a love of creativity, Carolingian aristocrats surrounded themselves with workmen who were artists in their trades.

The Corps of Artisans

Like the royal villas, all the great monasteries had their corps of artisans. At Saint-Riquier, they were settled in agglomerations (*vici*) which were the forerunners of the specialized quarters of the medieval towns. There were blacksmiths to furnish the monastery's ironwork (*ferramenta*). Fullers and pelterers worked with felt (*filtra*) and skins. Shoemakers and saddlers plied their craft.[5] At Corbie, there were six smiths, a fuller, two goldsmiths, a parchment maker, and four carpenters. At Bobbio, Wala made provision for a chamberlain to direct the work of the saddler, parchment maker, and turner, when he planned to adopt the usages of Corbie. The plan of Saint-Gall provided for workshops and artisans' houses in one quarter of the monastery. Turners, harnessmakers, saddlers, shoemakers, and polishers and furbishers of swords (*emundatores*) were settled around the house and "*officina*" of the chamberlain. Down a further row worked smiths (*fabri ferramentorum*), goldsmiths, and fullers.[6]

Certain artisans were given land in return for giving the lord a percentage of the work they produced. For example, at Boissy-en-Drouais (Eure-et-Loir) the *colonus* Antoine was to furnish six javelins, the *colonus* Ermenulf (a smith) six lances, etc. We know that smiths were settled on the lands of the Bishop of Salzburg, shoemakers as well as glassmakers "housed" on the domain of Fulda. At Aurillac, a young man was set to learn the trade under a smith of the domain.[7] Though the specialized quarters devoted to particular trades had not yet appeared in the towns, the artisans already had their workshops there. Texts mention goldsmiths at Lucca, Pisa, Monza, Pavia; blacksmiths at Monza—one of whom is called "magister"; and a tinsmith at Lucca. Besides goldsmiths, we can see furriers and iron workers and tailors in ninth-century Milan.[8] Artisans and merchants are mentioned as part of the population of Worms.[9]

Many artisans were in the service of aristocrats to furnish them with the luxury products they loved. Magnates actively sought out sculptors, goldsmiths, painters, enamelers of free or servile condition. When Angilbert built Saint-Riquier and Gerald built Aurillac, they imported specialized workers.[10] Ebbo of Reims recruited artificers for his town and gave them lodging. His friend, Louis the Pious, offered him a slave who was a goldsmith.[11] Royal goldsmiths were famous. Lupus of Ferrières dispatched one of his servitors to Saint-Denis to perfect his art because "the news had gone abroad that the Abbot Louis employed very skillful goldsmiths."[12] Thanks to inscriptions we have the names of some "masters" who directed teams of workers: "magister" Ursus, sculptor of Ferentillo, and "magister" Wolvinus, the goldsmith to whom we owe the famous altar of Milan.[13] As in earlier periods, the blacksmith and the goldsmith were the most valuable artisans of the Carolingian age. Both were protected by wergelds greatly surpassing those for other subjects (40 sous according to Alamanic law).[14]

Blacksmiths

The smith, fusing his metal in a shower of sparks to produce elaborate weapons, was depicted as a sorcerer. A figure to be admired and feared, he retained this reputation into modern times. A chronicler describing a comet which crossed the sky in 808 found it natural to compare it with a mass of melted iron throwing off sparks.[15]

These artisans were as scarce as they were celebrated. In all the lands of Montierender and Prüm and the domains of Annapes, there were neither forges nor smiths. Carolingian civilization was based on wood. As we have seen, agricultural implements were rarely made of metal. Iron was rare, and its production was reserved to certain privileged domains. The king, for example, possessed forges for which he expected an annual accounting from his intendants. He also possessed iron and lead mines.[16] Minerals to feed the forges were extracted from established lodes in the Vorarlberg, Rhaetia, and the Lahngau.[17] In addition some smaller mines existed. It is likely, for example, that from his domain at Ferrières Lupus extracted a small quantity of minerals for export.[18] The desire to keep arms in use is a more plausible explanation for the absence of metal objects in Carolingian tombs than any religious consideration.

The "striking force" of the Carolingians depended on the blacksmith. In a much-quoted passage, Notker of Saint-Gall described the reaction of Didier, King of the Lombards, to the iron-armed soldiers of Charlemagne: "The iron, alas! the iron shakes the strength of our walls and the courage of the young; iron destroys the experience of the old. . . ." Louis the German astonished the Norse ambassadors by preferring iron weapons to their gold.[19] Other people did well to envy Carolingian weaponry which issued from the smithies with such solidity and bite. Archeological finds have enabled us to study the technique of manufacturing the longsword. For the heart of the sword, the smith soldered and hammered strips of soft iron and vaporized iron into a squared bar. Then in the front of the charcoal-fueled forge, he soldered the different elements to ensure the strength of the core. The edges were formed separately from a bar of homogeneous metal and joined by welding. The whole was then shaped with a whetstone or file. Apparently freeing himself for once from his antique models, the painter of the Utrecht psalter sketched the polishing and grinding of a longsword.[20]

Here we cannot fail to summon up the celebrated figure of Germanic folklore, Wieland, as described in the Scandinavian saga:

> The King said, "The sword is good," and he wanted it for himself. Wieland answered, "It is not especially good; it must be made better; I shall not stop till then." The King went away in good humor. Wieland returned to his forge, took up a file, and cut the sword into little pieces which he mixed with flour. Then he released some birds who had been hungry for three days and gave them the mixture to eat. Placing their excrement in the front of the forge, he smelted them and cleansed the iron of all the dross it still contained, and then he forged the sword anew. This sword was smaller than the first one . . . , but it fit the hand as well. The first sword Wieland had fashioned had been greater than was customary. Again the King sought out Wieland, examined the sword, and affirmed that it was sharper and better than any he had ever seen. They went down to the river; Wieland took up a tuft of wool three feet long and of the same width and threw it into the river; he held the sword lightly in the water and the tuft was carried against the edge and the sword cut the tuft of wool as smoothly as the current of the water itself. . . .[21]

Frankish swords had a great reputation in the East as well as the West. Radanite* Jews came to buy them; the Muslims who captured the Archbishop of Arles in 869 demanded 150 mantles and 150 swords as ransom.[22] We have already remarked Charlemagne's fear of contraband arms sales on the eastern frontiers of the Empire. Norsemen were so keen to buy or steal swords that Charles the Bald threatened with death those "traitors to the fatherland and to Christianity" who gave arms to the enemy. But despite the law, Carolingian swords appeared in the north, for Scandinavian archeologists have found them.[23] Some of them even bore the name of the smith, Ulfert, framed with

* See p. 115.

two crosses.[24]

Besides the blacksmiths, foundry workers fashioned bells to be hung in church steeples. Notker of Saint-Gall speaks of a monk who was specially trained in bronze work and who received a quantity of silver to make a bell whose tone would be purer than any yet produced. But he dishonestly kept the silver for himself and was satisfied to use the traditional alloy of copper and tin.[25] Once a bell was founded, the names of the abbot or bishop who had commissioned it and of the artisan were inscribed on it. Founders were also commissioned to make the doors and balustrades which decorated churches. Einhard praised the beauty of "the balustrades and massive bronze doors" which Charlemagne, reverting to antique tradition, installed in the chapel at Aix and which are still visible. The remains of a foundry discovered near the palace suggest that the work was done on the premises.[26]

Goldsmiths

Wieland, we are told, had as much skill in working with jewels, gold, and silver as he had in forging swords. Alamanic law placed the same wergeld of 40 sous on both smiths and goldsmiths. For if iron was rare in the Carolingian Empire, the inventories of church treasures suggest that gold was not. Gold coinage was abandoned more for economic reasons than for lack of the yellow metal.[27] Gold was provided by antique treasures and booty taken from enemies. In 898, King Arnulf authorized the gold-washers of Passau to harvest gold from running waters. Around 862, the poet Otfrid of Wissem who wished to praise the Franks wrote: "Brass and copper and even, marvel of marvels, crystal, are drawn from the land of the Franks. You can judge yourselves of the quantity of gold and silver which they collect on the shores."[28] Ermold already speaks of the Rhinegold which is not just a pretty legend. Silver came from the mines of the Harz, Bohemia, and the lode at Melle, rich in argentiferous lead. Some new mines were opened. Louis the Pious gave the Abbey of Montierender a domain from his fisc from which they could extract lead.[29]

When aristocrats wanted some precious object made,

they gave ingots and slabs of gold from the store in their chamber to the goldsmith. We can study the tools of the artisan—one might even say the artist—from barbarian tombs: a graphite receptacle (for melting the metal), pincers, chisels, files, hammers, small anvils, and scales. Thin leaves, reduced to a width of several tenths of a millimeter, were used for precious metal work. In her manual, Dhuoda incidentally pictured the skill of the *fabricatores metallorum* awaiting the right moment and the perfect temperature for the fashioning of gold plaques.[30]

A wooden core was used in the making of a reliquary statue. The golden statue Salamon of Brittany sent to Hadrian II has been lost, but the methods of the goldsmiths can be studied from the reliquary of Sainte-Foy-de-Conques, partly fashioned at the end of the ninth century. All the goldsmith techniques which are called "barbaric" were perfected by these artists, who made fibulas, belt buckles, sword guards, chalices and patens, votive crowns, book bindings, altar pieces which can still be admired in the museums of the world, settings of gems, sapphires, emeralds, jasper, topazes, carbuncles of colored glass, and channels for the enamel in cloisonné.[31]

An artist had also to know how to re-set antique and oriental jewels newly admitted into the collections of the nobles. The ewer Charlemagne gave to Saint-Maurice of Agaune, where it can still be seen, was decorated with enamelling which may have come by way of the Avars from the Byzantine Empire. Augustus' cameo, mounted on Lothar's cross, was kept at Aix-la-Chapelle, and that of Judith crowned the reliquary called "Charlemagne's jewel box" which Charles the Bald gave to Saint-Denis.

The Carolingian goldsmith was not limited to techniques transmitted from master to pupil. He also had treatises from antique or Byzantine texts copied in the abbeys, an aspect of the technological revival of Carolingian times which cannot be neglected. The catalogue of the Reichenau library, established in 822, listed a *Mappae clavicula de efficiendi auro*. Treatises on "the working of gold and silver" and on "the founding of metals and wax" are listed for Corbie, Laon, and Saint-Quentin. A manuscript from Lucca, written at the end of the eighth century, gives us a notion of the contents of these technical books. From them, the working of gold leaf, silver, and tin could be studied. ("Take a long thin leaf of good quality. When it is beaten thin, fold it in two and beat it. . . .") They describe methods to transform leaves into gold thread; gild iron; give copper a gold color; cast lead or glass; fashion a gold collar; weld metals of silver, copper, tin; mold bronze; write in gold on parchment, glass, or marble.[32]

Though nothing, or nearly nothing, remains to us of Carolingian edifices, we do know something of the many projects that were undertaken in this period. During the reign of Charlemagne we can count 232 monasteries, 7 cathedrals, and 65 palaces which were constructed or reconstructed.[1] We have already seen works in progress at Lyons, Le Mans, Reims, Auxerre, and Rome. Indeed, some bishops and abbots were so seized by a passion for building that they became a cause for anxiety. Thus, in 812, the monks of Fulda complained that they were becoming exhausted by the labor which Abbot Ratger demanded for the construction of sumptuous and superfluous buildings.[2] New liturgical developments, the translation of relics, and the creation of new chapters of canons were all occasions for the undertaking of grand projects.

Wood and Stone Construction

Most Carolingian monuments have disappeared because they were built of wood. "From my forests, palaces and churches are built; it is I who provide the choicest beams," says the Vosges to the Rhine in Ermold's poem. Many texts make reference to these wooden (*ecclesia lignea*) or frame churches (*ecclesia ligneis tabulis fabricata*).[3] Occasionally a lucky archeologist can still discover the traces of a church and the foundations of cabins in a peat bog. Town houses as well as peasant houses were built of wood. Sedulius emphatically described the discomfort of such a dwelling in which he was lodged at Liège:

> Our quarters are sunk in perpetual night. No rays of enchanting light shine into the interior. No robe of color ever drapes these walls. Neither key nor lock keeps anyone from entering. No bursts of paint make the vault shimmer. It is drowned in a dense shadow. But, if you made the sad rain fall, O Neptune! it would pierce our roof with glacial dew. When savage Eurus* howls, the old house trembles and quakes. . . . Believe me, such a house is not for sages who love a dazzling burst of light; it is fit only for owls or a pack of blind moles.[4]

* Southeast wind.

Was the royal palace also wooden? In part, at least, it was, for chroniclers noted some of the accidents which befell princes: the cave-in of a portico or the collapse of a beam.[5] However, kings did seek to build their own residences and chapels more solidly. The royal residence at Annapes, "very soundly built with three rooms," facing seventeen wooden houses in the interior of the court, has disappeared. But we may still admire monuments built "in the Roman fashion" at Aix, Germigny, and Steinbach, or even the little rural houses of the Grisons.

When they could, builders replaced wood with stone. Thus Einhard had a basilica built at Seligenstadt to replace a little wooden church (*lignea modica contructa*). Louis the Pious had the cloister walls of Charroux rebuilt in stone. Benedict, who had first had to content himself with wooden structures at Aniane, replaced them with a great church with marble porticos and columns in 772.[6]

Planning

Architects prefaced the beginning of a construction job with studies and blueprints, as in all times, based on the architectural treatises of late antiquity. There were many copies of Vitruvius' manuscripts in monasteries, and Einhard recommended that author to one of his pupils. The abridgement of Vitruvius by Faventinus was also read. Formulas were in use for the construction of walls and bridges.[7] In planning the reconstruction of his monastery, the Abbot of Saint-Gall had a model set up. It was not a purely schematic design but exactly built to a forty-foot base scale. The contemporary plan of the palace of Aix-la-Chapelle, which has been reconstructed, was modeled on the grill pattern of ancient towns. A central square of 360 feet divided into 16 smaller squares, flanked by an isoceles triangle on the east.[8] It was also possible to execute a wax model, as at Saint-Germain-d'Auxerre, for a study of the elevation.[9]

The architect had several formulas to choose from. The classic basilica plan of the apse can be seen at Steinbach and Saint-Pantaleon in Cologne. A plan based on the Latin cross, with a transept between apse and nave, could be imitated from Saint Peter's in Rome. Architects added a second apse at the end of the nave in the great abbeys of Agaune, Fulda, and Saint-Gall. Another solution was a tripartite edifice with a forenave, which archeologists call the western projection (*Westbau*), rising to two stories (a vestibule and a higher church with galleries) as we can still see at Corvey. To the east beyond the nave, another sanctuary rose above the crypts guarding the relics of the saints. Nor was the central plan neglected; it was adopted for the church of Germigny-des-Près constructed by Theodulf. Finally, the architect of Aix combined the Latin cross plan with the central plan, inserting the famous octagon into the intersection.[10]

Once begun, the works were supervised by a lay or ecclesiastical master of the works who recruited workers on the spot or ordered transport to move them from job to job.[11] The hagiographer of Saint Maur depicts the construction of Glanfeuil, noting the assemblage of *artifices et operarii*, carpenters and masons under the direction of "a clerk knowledgeable in the art of construction."[12] Chroniclers also note the difficulties of the workers' lives. Sometimes exploited by the master of the works, they were abandoned as soon as they could be spared or fell victim to industrial accidents.[13] In Italy, the laws of the last Lombard kings gave detailed regulations for the work of masons and established a "salary scale" in money and supplies.[14]

Building Techniques

We know little about building techniques. Certainly, if a wooden structure was planned, material must first have been sought in neighboring forests. *The Life of Saint Pardoux* helps us to see this part of the work. The master of the works for the church of Saint-Aubin at Guéret dispatched his carpenters to the forest. They cut the wood (in Latin, *materia*, from which derives the French word *mérain*), which was loaded on carts and returned to the works. But when they measured the beam, they found that it was a foot and a half short of the intended length. The superintendent ordered that the carpenters be whipped. However, Saint

Pardoux intervened with a miracle which provided the measure and even surpassed it. The excess was cut off and hung in the church as an object of veneration.[15]

If a stone building was intended, material might be sought in quarries, but, more often, it came from the ruins of Roman monuments. Thus Ebbo of Reims was authorized to use stones from a wall at Reims to build the church of Notre Dame. Einhard used sandstone from a Roman *castrum* for his church of Seligenstadt. The monks of Saint-Wandrille searched for stones from Lillebone, and those of Lehon in Brittany took them from the ancient town of Corseul.[16]

Once the stones had been brought to the works, masons (*maciones, cemetarii*) cut and assembled them. Lime kilns, mentioned in texts, have been retrieved by archeologists. Ansegisus of Fontenelle rebuilt the dormitory of Fontenelle "in fine worked stone joined by a mortar of lime and sand."[17] The finest display was reserved for the bases of walls, pillars, and arches. Many walls were constructed in a decorative manner set off by brick chains in the antique fashion. Einhard ordered one of his intendants to have a specialist make 60 bricks 2 feet long and 4 fingers thick, followed by another lot of 250 of the same shape but smaller—half a foot and 4 fingers by 3 fingers.[18] In the great edifices only the lower floors and crypts were vaulted. The framework thrown over the nave was covered with tiles supplied by the tenants. Where lead was available, *tabulae* of that metal were laid on the roof. Writing to an abbot, Einhard expressed the anxiety he suffered over the roofing of the church of Saint-Marcellin. He estimated the cost at thirty livres. Lupus asked an Anglo-Saxon king to forward some lead to him at Etaples to finish his church at Ferrières.[19] The roofs of buildings in progress were covered with shingles (*sandulae*) fixed on lathes (*axiles*). Every year the tenants of Saint-Germain-des-Prés had to contribute 40,000 shingles and 20,000 lathes to the monastery. Princes and bishops issued reminders that the roofs of rural churches must be regularly renewed.[20] The carpenters and roofers were directed by a *magister carpentarius*. A sketch of these specialized workers can be found in a manuscript from Reims.[21]

Decoration

While the building was being raised, other artisans were preparing the decoration. Glaziers set pieces of painted glass in lead moulds (*vitrearii* or *vitri factores*). Stained glass windows commanded admiration at Fontenelle, Beauvais, Reims, Auxerre, Liège, and Rome. The monks of Reichenau appealed to one master glazier to come and teach his art to their young monks.[22] One part of a manuscript of Lucca, which we have already cited, was consecrated to the technique of glass painting.

Bronze workers cast the balustrades and doors Mosaic artists laid out the pavements or the cupolas. Sculptors dressed stone or marble in the chancels, ambulatories, and ciboria. In a bas-relief in Ferentillo, we can still see the image of "Magister Ursus," cane in hand, directing his sculptors.[23] Though the quarries at Saint-Béat closed at the beginning of the eighth century, marble could still be recovered from ancient monuments. Thus when Count Conrad and his wife Aélis decided on the reconstruction of the Abbey of Auxerre, the monks collected marble from Arles and Marseilles and had it sent by water. For his own part, Charlemagne had several kinds of marble shipped from Ravenna and Rome, not only for Aix but for Saint-Riquier as well.[24]

All the walls of the palace and churches were covered with frescoes recalled to us by witnesses at Malles, Reichenau, Trier, Auxerre, and Rome. The first storey of the porch of Lorsch was painted with a trompe-l'oeil decoration in the antique fashion: a low wall painted in a checkered pattern supported columns crowned by an architrave.[25] Poets described the frescoes that decorated refectories and state rooms. At Ingelheim, scenes from antiquity and Frankish history could be viewed. One text describes paintings of armed men, agricultural workers reaping or gathering grapes, fishermen standing in their barques, and hunters setting their traps or chasing does and harts.[26] Painters also depicted mythological scenes: the sun and the moon with radiating hair; winds, months, or seasons displayed either nude or clothed.[27] Alas, it has all disappeared. Still, despite their distrust of the cult of painted images in church which we shall consider further on, we can see that Carolingians fully appreciated the beauties of artistic forms.

The experienced painter had to know how to prepare the ground on which he was to place his colors. At Auxerre a thick coat of sand mixed with lime and ferruginous clay was covered with a thin layer of lime on which four colors were painted. Yellow ochre, red ochre, white, and green were preserved on this sample. The painter had to compose harmonious forms and fill in their outlines artistically. He must know the rules of colors and proportions fixed by the ancients, particularly Vitruvius.[28] A pictorial code directed him to paint in a prescribed manner: a lord would be shown carrying his arms; the apostles would be shown with their attributes (Matthew has a beard, Peter is bald, James and Zebedee are young).[29] When John the Deacon described his portraits of Gregory the Great's parents in Rome, he indicated that he had no intention of realistic representation but meant to paint figures according to the conventional canons of physical beauty.[30] Bishops and abbots were responsible for choosing painters and supervising their execution of the work. The Abbot of Saint-Wandrille had a painter travel to Cambrai to ornament the refectory. The Bishop of Toul, Frothair, asked a friend to send him all the orpiment (yellow arsenic), indigo, minium (red lead), lazur, prasin, and mercury he could spare for the paintings to decorate his new church.[31]

Time of Construction

The construction of buildings required much money and many men. It was understood that such a work would go on for a long time. The foundations of the Cathedral of Cologne, one of the great Carolingian edifices, were first laid about 800—91 meters long and 20 meters wide. The church was consecrated in 870.[32] The Cathedral of Reims, undertaken by Ebbo about 816, was consecrated in 862 under his successor, Hincmar. Sometimes, to encourage or frighten the workers, monks might announce that the patron saint had appeared to them in a dream to complain of the slowness of the work.[33]

Construction continued in the second half of the ninth century, but, before new edifices could be raised, it was necessary to surround villas, abbeys, and palaces with walls and to establish fortified points of resistance. The chronicler of the miracles of Saint-Bertin helps us to see the construction of the *castrum* of Saint-Omer. Once the site was measured, the forest between Saint-Omer and Saint-Bertin was cleared, providing construction material while obliterating an area in which an enemy could take cover. Ditches were dug around the abbey and ramparts of earth raised, surmounted by palisades of wood.[34] In more exposed areas, *castra* were raised as well, wooden towers resting on a stone substructure.

Furnishings

The furnishings of Carolingian dwellings, whether rural cottage or palace, did not differ much from those of later times. People used wooden benches with cloth upholstering (*bancales*), chairs with backs (covered with cushions), and sometimes armchairs. Leafing through illuminated Carolingian manuscripts, particularly Gospels, we get some idea of the variety of these wooden seats, decorated with marquetry.[1] Some of them were collapsible, in which case they were made of metal, like the *sella plicatilis* (folding chair) at Pavia, whose iron mountings are decorated with gold overlays or inlaid enamel work.[2] Thrones were symbols of temporal or spiritual power reserved for great personages.[3] Archeologists have been able to compare the throne painted in the psalter of Charles the Bald with the throne given by the Emperor to Pope John VIII which is still preserved at Saint Peter's in Rome.[4]

Furniture and Clothing

17

Rooms and Dormitories

Despite the claims of Ermold the Black, who fed too well on antique memories, Carolingians used chairs at the table rather than couches.[5] In the refectory of Saint-Gall, the planner showed tables and benches. Before the abbot's table, in the form of a **U**, the guests' table was laid. When the Bishop of Augsburg visited Saint-Gall in 908, he covered the monks' seats with down cushions, surrounded the reader's lectern with painted images, and covered the tables with cloths of vivid colors.[6] The beds in the dormitory of the same monastery were arranged in staggered rows.

Charlemagne directed that each of his villas should have a complete store of bedding: covers, eiderdowns, and sheets.[7] The inventories of Triel and Annapes list mattresses, feather pillows, sheets, bolsters, covers, and counterpanes.[8] The latter item (*lectaria*) could also be used to guard against the cold when one got out of bed. When they chanted vigils in winter, the monks of Aniane carried them with them.[9] Animal skins were also used as covers. Wooden chests (*scrinia*) served for the storage of clothes and precious objects, jewels and papers. Families, both spouses and children, slept together in a bed under which they placed a little bottle of holy water to ward off the attacks of the devil. A cradle (*berciolus*) was placed nearby in such a way that it could be rocked from the bed.[10] When great folk traveled, their portable beds and tents were part of the baggage.[11] They also brought drapes (*cortinae*) and tapestries (*tapetia*) which ordinarily hung on the walls and beams of their chambers.

Kitchen and Tableware

Moving to the kitchen, we find andirons, chains, and pot-hooks (*cramaillas*) around the hearth (*fornax*). There were also iron and leather cauldrons, salt basins, bread bins, and many wooden utensils.[12] A buffet (*toregma*) held lead plates and pots of tin, lead, iron, and wood.

The texts make no mention of pottery tableware, but archeologists have brought pottery remains to light and have begun to date and classify various types.[13] As a result, we know of Badorf pottery (near Cologne) which was made between 720 and 860, characterized by simple designs of little squares and triangles imprinted with a fine paste and the aid of a roller. Pitchers with handles, narrow-necked bottles, pot-bellied amphorae with a pair of handles, have been reconstructed. In the middle of the ninth century, a new type appeared, decorated in a red color, called Pingsdorf pottery. At Zelzate, at the mouth of the Scheldt, money was kept in a kind of flat gourd with two handles made in the domestic workshop. At the same period, local workshops were producing pots with a hand-shaped spherical bulge which, according some archeologists, were intended for use over peat fires. The discovery of shards glazed with lead at Doué-la-Fontaine (Maine-et-Loire) and painted ceramic at Beauvais adds to our knowledge of Carolingian pottery in France.[14]

Glass vases are rarely found. Their production re-quired highly sought-after artists. An Anglo-Saxon abbot wrote to his compatriot, Lull of Mainz, asking him to send workers to make some *vitrea vasa* (glass vases).[15] In northern Gaul, glass workers (*vitrearii*) were settled on holdings near Douai and in the Aisne. Glass kilns are mentioned in texts, and the techniques of manufacture had not changed since Merovingian times.[16] Eccard's will mentioned an ampula (that is, a small glass vase) and a chalice of blue-tinted glass. His contemporary, Ewrard, also mentioned glass chalices in his testament.

Both of these texts also mention various kinds of vases made of marble, gold, silver, horn, swamp wood, or maple wood decorated with silver or gold. With the traditional *phiali, calices,* and *scyphi,* we find *hanaps* (tankards), a word of German origin, and, above all, silver *garali* from which the word "grail" is derived. The Reichenau glossary distinguished the *poculum,* a drinking vessel, from the *craterus,* reserved for wine, which other texts call *copa.* The *botilia,* bottle, is also mentioned. Aristocrats also had ewers of silver with basins for washing hands, used for secular and liturgical purposes, spoons and knives.[17]

Clothing

Clothing of Commoners and Monks

Each social group had a distinct costume. This custom, which would last for centuries in the West, was already prevalent in Carolingian times.[18] A prelate who wished to disguise himself as a peasant, according to Theodulf, dressed in a hooded headdress, a shirt of rude linen, and a loose garment. He wrapped his legs in narrow strips of cloth (*bandelettes*) and shod himself with heavy shoes. To complete the disguise, he fastened a knife at his belt.[19] A monk's habit was not unlike that of a peasant, but it had more pieces. A rule in the year 817 provided that a monk should receive two shirts (*camisia*) annually, two cloaks (*cuculla*), and a *capa* (a vestment to which a hood was often attached). In addition, he had four pairs of stockings (*pedules*), two pairs of drawers (*femoralia*), a belt (*roccum*), two cloaks falling to the heel, wooden shoes and sheepskin mittens for winter.[20] Annually at Corbie each monk received three tunics (two white and one colored), two pairs of boots, three pairs of pants, two pairs of stockings, gloves, two mantles. Every three years, furs, capes and head coverings were replaced. Cast-off garments were distributed to the poor in the hostelry.[21] The monks of Monte Cassino had three tunics (two thick ones for winter and a light one for summer). They had three mantles as well—but no cowled ones because Abbot Theodomar considered that they cost too much in Italy.[22] Clerks on the other hand, were not supposed to wear cowls except for protection against the cold. Neither were they supposed to have a layman's mantle (*mantellum* or *cotta* without a hood); rather, they should dress in a very simple costume.[23] Gerald of Aurillac, who lived like a clerk, achieved a "proper compromise between vain pomp and gross rusticity." He dressed in woolen or linen clothes and wore a headdress which his biographer curiously styled a *tiara*.[24]

Aristocratic Clothing

Lay aristocrats wore clothing fashionable in their own countries. The people of Aquitaine wore a tunic, bouffant pantaloons, and boots.[25] Italians favored ample vestments, whereas the Franks loved tightly cut costumes. Einhard tells us that Charlemagne was faithful to his Frankish costume:

> Occasionally, on feast days, the Emperor consented to don a garment interwoven with gold, jewel-decorated shoes, a golden fibula to fasten his garment, a golden crown, and jewels. But on other days, his dress differed little from those of the common people. Near his body he wore a shirt and linen drawers; over them, went an embroidered silk tunic and trousers. He had leggings around legs and feet, while a vest of otter or rat skin protected his shoulders and chest in winter. Finally he donned a great blue mantle.[26]

His successors and other princes who lived in the Frankish fashion wore the same costume. When Harold the Dane came to Ingelheim in 826, Louis the Pious gave him a costume which Ermold the Black described in detail: a tunic decorated with jewels, cinched by a belt, with tight sleeves; a slit mantle held by a pin; white gloves; a baldric falling over the hip holding the sheath of the sword. . . .[27] This description corresponds to the manuscript portraits of Lothar and Charles the Bald and the fresco of San Benedetto of Malles.[28]

The aristocratic feminine costume is known to us from manuscripts and the descriptions of court poets.[29] The women threw a great mantle over a large-sleeved tunic.

They achieved a tighter fit with a jeweled belt, sometimes weighing as much as three pounds.[30] A gold bandeau and a jeweled headdress held their veils. The jewels especially attracted the attention of the poets: collars and pendants falling to the belt can be seen in certain manuscripts. When Hathumod's biographer described the youth of the future Abbess of Gandersheim, he said that she disdained all the objects which the fortune and rank of her relatives could procure for her: beautiful coiffures, ribbons, hairpins, gold buckles, broaches, necklaces, bracelets, rings, girdles, boxes of perfume, and so on.[31] Carolingian women could spend many minutes at their toilettes. Though we have no Tertullian to denounce the luxury of these women, here and there we can learn from the revelations of moralizing clerical critics of coquettish abbesses.

Clothing Manufacture

Carolingian men and women got their new clothes from the same workshops. Women worked linen and wool individually or in teams. They sheared the sheep, washed the fleece, carded the wool with thistles, combed it, spun and wove it.[32] Flax was harvested everywhere and delivered regularly. It was then steeped, washed, beaten, and woven into linen.[33] Women subsequently dyed the bolts of cloth with woad, madder, or vermillion.[34] They next delivered up the lengths of linen (*camsiles, panni, drappi*) or made them up into shirts, drawers, or girdles. Some domains specialized in the fabrication of textiles. Ansegisus of Saint-Wandrille once calculated that a certain *pagus* would furnish 60 pieces of clothing and 20 *drappi* for the making of shirts; another would give two *drappi* for shirts. Eight domains of Saint-Germain-des-Près were regularly expected to provide clothing.[35]

Aristocratic women occupied their leisure by weaving and spinning. Charlemagne expressed his wish that his daughters not become idle sluggards. He had them taught to work wool, handle the distaff and spindle, and "made them learn all things which pertain to honest women." He often praised the skill of certain princesses or abbesses in making woven veils, brocades, or gold-embroidered stuffs for princes or bishops. Judith wove a *peplum* for her royal husband. Irmentrude, according to Sedulius, was a perfect expert in Pallas' art.[36]

Some artisans specialized in the working of hides, and to them were provided the skins of cattle, deer, sheep, or wolves. Each monastery provided itself with boots, shoes, "galoshes" with wooden soles, from its own workshops. Fur vests were made from sheepskin, marten, mole, otter, and beaver fur. Some of these came from great distances, like the beaver skins from the Black Sea which Louis the Pious gave to the Abbot of Fontenelle.[37]

Clothing Exports

Some clothing was made for commercial purposes. We cannot fail to mention the famous "Frisian" mantles which historians have discoursed on so long.[38] In 796, Charlemagne complained that King Offa of Mercia sent him cloths of different lengths.[39] According to Notker of Saint-Gall, Charlemagne resented that the short mantles were as costly as long ones: "In bed, I cannot cover myself with them; on horse, they do not protect me from rain or wind, and when I satisfy the needs of nature, my legs freeze."[40] Were they from Frisia or already of Flemish or English origin? Or even of Syrian provenance? We could debate the origins of *panni frisonici* at great length. Nor have recent discoveries of archeologists at Birka and in Holland yet succeeded in clarifying the question. Frisians were intermediaries rather than manufacturers. They also imported shirts, called, *berniscrist*, from across the channel.[41]

Carolingian aristocrats were even more interested in bolts of silk (*pallia*) which came directly from the East or through the Italian distributors in Pavia and Venice.[42] When he was in northern Italy, Charlemagne mocked his courtiers returning from Pavia in rich silken habits. He led them such a race over the hunting fields that rain, thorns, and rents soon ruined the luxurious stuff.[43] Those magnificent garments princes received as gifts from Byzantium or Baghdad were passed on to their followers or added to the treasuries of great ecclesiastics and laymen to be worn on feast days. Aristocratic wills and the inventories of church treasuries enable us to imagine the wealth and variety of these *pallia transmarina.*[44] When they were exhumed, the remains of Bernard of Italy, buried at Saint-Ambrose in Milan in 818, were wrapped in a mantle of white silk damask more than fifteen meters long. The list of Angilbert's acquisitions for Saint-Riquier mentions garments for both secular and ecclesiastical usage: 78 luxurious draperies included 24 silk dalmatics, "Roman" albs, and brocade *amices*; 5 stoles and 10 brocade oraires; 5 silk cushions; 5 silk mantles, 10 of purple, 6 of *storax* (silk cloth decorated with crosses); a peach-colored chasuble; 15 brocade chasubles and 6 of sendal (light silk). Some of these *pallia* were decorated with the figures of exotic animals. Paul I sent Pepin a mantle decorated with peacocks. Gregory IV had vestments ornamented with lions in the midst of trees and griffons. At Arles, Theodulf was offered *pallia* of different colors with a cow following a bull and a calf, a design that the poet thought to be of Arab origin.[45] These cloths can still be admired in the treasuries and museums of Europe and particularly in the fabric museum of Lyon.

Lighting and Heating

Lights

Manmade light was costly and inefficient for the scribe who wished to continue copying after sundown, the lord who sat late at table, and the monk preparing for nocturnal offices. Some abbeys charged particular tenants, called *luminarii* and *cerarii*, with the provision of fat and wax for that purpose. Coastal monasteries took advantage of fish and whale oil, and some domains specialized in the furnishing of lighting products. One villa of Saint-Wandrille had to supply 200 pounds of wax, 180 of oil, and 8 hogsheads of fat. The *coloni* of Bitry owed the Abbot of Saint-Germain-des-Prés only 22 pounds of wax or 8 setiers of oil.[1] Torches and candles were numbered among the customary dues of tenants. Olive oil in the Midi and walnut or poppy oil in the north was used to fill lamps which differed little from antique lamps, though they appear to have been considered luxury lighting. Wax appears to have been principally reserved for lighting the sanctuary. Gerald of Aurillac reserved the candles remitted to him for the altar and chapel reliquaries while instructing his servitors to make the customary torches of resinous birch bark.[2] Torches and candles were fixed on metal cressets and candelabra. In church, as we can see in manuscript paintings, lamps were attached to a ring which could be raised and lowered by cable. The church of Aniane was lit by seven gold candelabra, seven silver lamps on a ring, and seven lamps before the altar, "so well that it seemed to be broad daylight," noted one monk. The bishops of Auxerre could dispose of several silver rings and chandeliers in their churches. Angilbert gave Saint-Riquier thirteen silver rings with lamps, two gold rings, six silver lamps and twelve of tin. The inventory of Saint-Trond, of 870, numbers seven chandeliers, five silver lamps and seven tin ones.[3] Many lamps burned night and day before the reliquaries. We can well understand the emotion and wonder of the faithful, accustomed as they were to poor torchlight or even just the light of their own fire, when they penetrated into the bright sanctuary.

Heating

"This year winter was so hard that we could not get wood for heating, and nearly a third of the people died."[4] Leaving the chronicler sole responsibility for his statistics, we are content to note that the heating problem recurred annually for Carolingian man. While the poor were glad to find wood and turf which gave more smoke than heat, architects of palaces and abbeys planned chimneys in some of the principal rooms. The plan of Saint-Gall indicated a central or lateral hearth (*caminata pyrale*) in each dwelling room with smoke escaping through a hole in the roof. The abbot's house, the guest apartments, and the infirmary were also heated. A room called the warming room (*calefactoria domus*), furnished with hearth and chimney (*evaporatio fumi*), communicated directly with the basilica.[5]

Such rooms can be reconstructed for Saint-Denis and Saint-Wandrille. At Corbie monks would warm themselves and dry their habits before and after the offices. They chattered or became drowsy while reading "because of the sweetness of the heat."[6] Apparently, no heat was provided for the scriptorium, and more than one scribe complained of fingers numbed by a cold. A refusal to warm oneself was proof of asceticism. Saint Pardoux, a monk of Guéret, rejected heat from any source but the sun's rays. Only as he grew old did he occasionally submit to the use of "hot stones," the ancestors of our grandparents' "bricks."[7] This custom, which was apparently not very widespread, was revived later in Ottonian palaces. Great quantities of wood were required from the peasants to feed the fires in palaces and abbeys. Charles the Fat authorized the monks of Saint-Germain of Auxerre to remove two cartloads of wood daily from the forests of the fisc.[8]

Hygiene and Body Care

Baths, Bleedings, and the Use of Simples

The planner of Saint-Gall reserved space for a bath room next to the warming room. Two other baths were to be placed near the infirmary and the noviciate. Contrary to what has been said so often, medieval men were not neglectful of body care. Any palace worthy of the name enjoyed both cold and hot baths. To prove that Gottschalk, a prisoner at Hautvilliers, was truly undeserving of his interest, Hincmar of Reims noted that the monk refused to warm himself or to wash himself.[9] Every Saturday Carolingian princes would change their clothes and bathe. This was, no doubt, dictated by Germanic custom, for in Scandinavia today Saturday is still called "bath day."[10]

The baths were near the cloister at Saint-Denis and Corbie. The monastic rule of 817 decreed that their use was to be supervised by the abbot. The "statutes" of Murbach suggested abbatial supervision as the common baths were being replaced by individual tanks. The sick were allowed regular baths except during Lent, the rest of the monks at Christmas and Easter.[11] In effect, not to bathe was an ascetic exercise. Among the punishments inflicted on public penitents was a prohibition on bathing.[12]

Carolingians used simple and traditional methods to guard the body from the illnesses that menaced it. We can get an idea of what they were by a glance at the infirmary depicted in the plan of Saint-Gall. In the principal building there was a warming room (*pisalis*), a dormitory, a refectory, a room for the seriously ill, and lodging for the staff of the infirmary. There were three other structures in the complex: the kitchen and bath room, a chamber for bleeding and prescription of potions (furnished with a chimney and benches), and finally the physician's house with a room for the dangerously ill, where the pharmaceutical chest was kept. A medicinal garden was laid out near this house. Thus, bathing, bleeding, and the use of simples were connected in the prevention of sickness.

Bleeding (*flebotomia*) was practiced regularly. Monastic rules insisted that its use be moderated and that eating and drinking be restrained on the occasion.[13] Anxiety that the pallor of the religious was caused by bleeding too frequently was expressed by a capitulary of 789.[14] Physicians were advised to consult a book attributed to the Venerable Bede to determine the most favorable day. Their clumsiness was criticized: "Who dares to undertake a bleeding should see to it that his hand does not tremble," one reads in a manuscript from Laon.[15]

The use of medicinal herbs, simples, had not changed from ancient usages. Lay estates and abbeys included beds for medicinal herbs in their gardens. Such a *herbularius* planted near the infirmary at Saint-Gall boasted sixteen species of plants. In a poem, Walafrid Strabo outlined the uses of various simples: aurone healed gout; fennel was recommended against constipation, coughs, and eye maladies; chervil arrested hemorrhages; absinthe reduced fevers; pennyroyal helped cure sunburn; parsley was a diuretic.[16] Simples were not to be taken indiscriminately but restricted to the proper time in the year. A Laon manuscript recommended August for sage seasoned with pepper, September for betony and pepper, October for savin and salts, November and December for savory for the stomach, and so forth.[17]

The virtue of local plants was reinforced by pepper and other spices from far away, like cinnamon. The Echternach manuscript cited below prescribed several medications based on spices. Herbs, cinnamon, and 56 grains of pepper should be used to cure insomnia; studs of cloves, myrrh, aloes, and incense for headaches; herbs and 24 grains of pepper cut into wine (spiced wine or *pigmentum*) for kidney ailments; ammoniac salt, different types of pepper, oregano, hyssop, and ginger for eye trouble. Similar recipes were provided in other texts. A spoonful of honey, vinegar, mustard, and 10 grains of pepper daily would solace the liver. Stomach flatulence could be diminished with the juice of boiled apples, honey, and 20 grains of pepper. This type of medical advice abounds everywhere, even in Latin and German bilingual manuscripts.[18]

Nutrition

Carolingians, with their close communion with nature, were great partisans of dietetics. They preserved the lessons of Roman and Merovingian treatises. Multiple copies were made of the physician Anthymius' book, *De observatione ciborum,* written for King Thierry.* A certain Grimaud, preceptor and count of the palace, addressed a *dieta ciborum* to the king.[19] When he learned that Bishop Hincmar was a convalescent, Pardulf, his colleague at Laon, gave him dietary advice: avoid excessive fasting, recently caught fish, and freshly killed poultry. Beans cooked in grease had purgative virtues.[20] Medical calendars summarized considerations appropriate to each season and month. To avoid colds in winter, one should eat hot food, exercise, avoid

---

* King Thierry, son of Clovis, was king of Austrasia, 511–534.

frequent hair-washing, and purge continually. In March, baths should be taken but bleeding avoided. In April, one should be bled and eat fresh meat but avoid "roots." In May, one must avoid beer and never drink water on an empty stomach. In June, sage was not to be eaten, but a full glass of water on rising and boiled milk should be taken. In July, humors of the brain should be averted by abstaining from sexual relations, and so forth.[21]

Medicine

When overwhelmed by a serious illness, one should seek a physician. Princes maintained physicians in their homes: laymen, clerks, or Jews. Thanks to their own learning, some abbots and bishops, like Pardulf of Laon, could doctor themselves. Medicine was included in the training programs of clerks despite canonical prohibitions against bloodletting which closed the exercise of that art to clerks.[22] For some learned men, medicine was the eighth "liberal art." Monastic libraries possessed medical manuscripts copied from ancient treatises. At Echternach, for example, scribes made collections borrowed from the aphorisms of Hippocrates, Galen, Soranus, Heliodorus, and Justus. Laon was an active center of medical study where they used Marcellus Empiricus and Oribasus.[23] More than thirty Carolingian medical manuscripts are catalogued in the Bibliothèque Nationale, and a study of them yields a good idea of the medical knowledge of the period.[24] It was poor enough, compared to the Byzantines and the Arabs. Scientific descriptions of illnesses, veterinary treatments, pharmaceutical recipes, and magical formulae for healing are all mixed in together. Somewhat surprisingly, there are also gynecological treatises, though monks had little consideration for the female sex. Some works on surgery mention the names of instruments and give instructions for operations.[25] Those who were caring for soldiers wounded in battle were advised to utilize such works. According to Abbo, the iron hand replacing the right hand which Count Eudes, hero of the siege of Paris, lost in battle was hardly less strong and vigorous than the original.[26]

Carolingian men and women were haunted by the fear of hunger.[1] Aristocrat and peasant alike, all dreaded the months of shortage before the harvest and sought to store up reserves. But they did not have equal opportunities.

To Each His Menu

The peasant picked vegetables from the patches near his house—peas, vetches, and beans. In addition, he combed the underbrush, marsh, and river for supplements to his diet.

Monks, in obedience to the Benedictine rule, got one meal in winter and two in summer: a *collatio* at noon and *cena* in the evening. The monastic rule prescribed a daily pound of bread, a hemin of wine (between a quarter and half a liter), or double that amount of beer. It forbade the monks to eat fruit or lettuce between meals. Each meal included three dishes (*pulmentaria*) of dairy products and vegetables.[2] At Reichenau, sick monks could request *warmosium*, a dish apparently made of cream and leeks.[3] Feasts, held in the great monasteries on holy days or royal anniversaries, consisted of a special meal called the *refectio*. Poultry, such as stuffed chickens and geese, and cakes were distributed.[4] This scandalized the Breton ascetics, who ate only barley bread—and that mixed with ashes, bowls of gruel, and vegetables, denying themselves even fish and shellfish.[5] On Saturday and Sunday, they accepted a little cheese thinned with water. At Guéret, Saint Pardoux refused all poultry, preferring to eat the mushrooms the peasants brought him.[6] Walafrid Strabo recommended a more moderate frugality: "some salt, bread, leeks, fish, and wine; that is our menu. I would not spare even a glance for the splendid tables of kings."

Princes and aristocrats could not forego meat, particularly roasted meat. Charlemagne took an aversion to his doctors because they advised him to give up his accustomed roast meat in favor of boiled meat. Spicy dishes were particularly appreciated at the tables of the great: "This table covered with pimentoed meat is a far cry from the insipidity of boiled food and softly pressed curds of milk," wrote Theodulf in a description of a meal at Aix-la-Chapelle.[7]

Main Ingredients

Though Carolingian menus have not survived, we can study the principal ingredients of the diet of the time.

Bread, particularly white bread, was the dietary base of the most privileged classes as well as monks and canons. At Corbie, 450 loaves were baked every day, and the oven at Saint-Gall was reputed to have a capacity of nearly 1000 loaves. While white bread was kept at Saint-Denis for monks and guests; the servants had to be content with rye bread. In the same monastery, some flour was kept back to make what the text calls *pulempta*, or polenta (porridge). Finally a gruel made of barley or oats was used by many peasants as a substitute for bread.[8]

Meat was brought in from the hunt. When Gerald of Aurillac's cook lamented that he had no meat, a deer happily came to fall at his feet. That enabled him to prepare "a delicate repast, worthy of his lord." In addition, the flesh of cattle, sheep, and even goats was consumed.[9] Pork occupied a special position of its own. At Corbie, an entire chapter of Adalhard's *Institutiones* was devoted to pork. He figured that 600 pigs a year would be consumed in the refectory, with 50 reserved to the abbot.[10] Monastic cellarers and royal intendants had pork smoked or salted to ensure provisions of meat through the winter. While such parts as tripe had to be consumed swiftly, salted pork (*baccones*) hung in the *lardarium* of Corbie waiting for several months to be eaten.

When they wanted to be sparing, Carolingians ate fish. Charlemagne advised his intendants that "when the fish in our ponds are sold, new fish should be put in their place, so that there may always be fish." In the palace, fish dishes were prepared for service with condiments. It was considered good manners to eat them without turning them over.[11] The cellarer at Reichenau supplied the fishermen with nets, indicating which fish were in season in the Rhine, and paid them with a cup of wine for their catch.[12] Though many texts mention fish and fisheries, few are informative about the varieties of fish. The Abbot of Saint-Denis was supplied with fat fish in Cotentin and flat fish in Ponthieu; conger eels were caught in the Rance; 200 eels, a much sought-after food, had to be delivered to the Abbot of Saint-Germain-des-Prés each year.[13]

When there was a feast, eggs, geese, moorhens, and chickens flowed into the kitchens of the great lay and ecclesiastical aristocrats. Charlemagne protected himself against a possible shortage of fowl by ordering that his great estates should maintain a stock of at least 100 hens and 30 geese, while the smaller farms should have 50 hens and 12 geese. It has been estimated that in the year 893 the Abbey of Prüm controlled 2000 farms with a production of roughly 20,000 eggs a year.[14]

Dairy products were more difficult to procure unless they were preserved in the form of butter and cheese. A bishop who was entertaining Charlemagne substituted cheese for the fish which he lacked. He was astounded when the Emperor removed the crust, which the clergyman considered the best part, before eating it. While thanking his host, Charles asked him to send two carts of the cheese to Aix each year. Monks consumed large quantities of cheese. The tenants of Saint-Germain-des-Prés furnished them with 160 *pensae* of cheese. If, as we suppose, a *pensa* was roughly 75 pounds, that would represent 12,000 pounds. The estates of Boulogne and Therouanne sent 21 *pensae* to Saint-Wandrille. Ten sheepfolds were designated to produce cheese at Corbie. When entertained by the Bishop of Utrecht, Alcuin said he had been given an excellent meal of honey, gruel, and butter, for, he said, the Frisians have neither oil nor wine. Fat and lard were generally replaced by butter during days of abstinence and Lent.[15]

Turning to a discussion of vegetables, we find two categories. The term legumes (*legumina*) referred to the vegetables which grew in the fields: beans, lentils, peas, green beans, chick peas, and other types of edible herbs. Roots (*olera*) grew in the kitchen gardens: leeks, garlic, onions, carrots, etc. The capitulary *De villis* and the plan of Saint-Gall include exhaustive lists of the garden stocks. The bishop's gardens provided vegetables for the canons' table, the most common being beans and leeks. The tenants of Saint-Denis had to supply the abbey daily with "crushed herbs for the preparation of legumes."[16]

Everyone appreciated fruits. Complaints were common against the schoolboys who devastated the orchards. The redactor of the capitulary *De villis* lingered over the names of certain types of apples: sweet apples and sour apples; apples for immediate eating and those for keeping. Intendants planned for the provision of fruj ʒ over as long a period as possible. At Bobbio, there was a *custos pomorum* in charge of fruit storage. Charlemagne advised the possessors of vineyards to hang grapes from hoops in order to preserve them.[17]

Let us end this glance at Carolingian alimentation with a reminder of the importance of honey and spices. Not only was honey used to sweeten food, but it was the base for many drinks: hydromel (mead), honeyed wine, and mixtures of honey and beer. On the royal domains, there was a special supervisor for the honey harvest. Certain estates specialized in its production. Saint-Wandrille designated 8 estates for regular deliveries of honey. Einhard wrote his intendant to complain that the honey harvest had fallen below the yield he had expected.[18]

Carolingian cuisine depended heavily on spices and condiments. Pepper, cummin, cloves, and cinnamon were purchased from merchants in touch with the Orient. A text of uncertain date mentions the monks of Corbie going to buy 100 kilos of spices in the shops of Cambrai. Cinnamon, galanga, cloves, mastic, and pepper reached the market at Mainz.[19] A ninth-century manuscript from Echternach provides a recipe for *garum*, a fish-based condiment which had been well known in antiquity. It begins:

> Mix fish, salt, and anise; stir daily, mixing in some herbs—mint, Greek fennel, laurel, sage, etc. Take the whole from the fire when half-cooked, strain, and preserve in well-sealed vases.[20]

Drink

> "Hey, boy! rinse my glass, pour the wine, get out the best! In the name of Almighty Christ, toast me with a cup of what they bring you, friend!"

This poetic fragment from a ninth-century manuscript is no simple echo of the Bacchic poems of antiquity but mirrors the daily reality of wine. Every class of society drank heavily, even to excess.[21] Abbots and bishops set the example: "At Angers, they say, an abbot lives, and the first man's name he bears. They say he wished, all by himself, to equal all the Angevins in drink. Eia! Eia! Eia! Glory, eia, glory to Bacchus."

These verses by some *écolâtre* or schoolboy correspond to the observations of Theodulf of Orleans: "A bishop who keeps his gullet full of wine should not be permitted to forbid it to others. He ought not to preach sobriety who is drunk himself."* We know that, without going to such excess, Alcuin did not distrust beer and wine, for he tells us that he used them to clear his throat before teaching or singing. While staying in England, he sent several butts to his monks of Saint-Martin, praying one of his pupils to drink in the place of one who was living so sad a life, far from his habitual sources of merriment. One of them, nicknamed the "cuckoo," followed his advice only too well and earned the reproaches of Arn of Salzburg. Alcuin wrote to him: "Unhappy me, if Bacchus drowns my cuckoo in his flood!"[22] Taverns were intrinsic to rural and urban life. Even the curate was no stranger to the village tavern. They were found in market places, places of pilgrimage, on royal domains, episcopal and abbatial estates. Drinking contests were common: "Does drunken bravado encourage you to attempt to out-drink your friends? If so, thirty days fast," admonishes a penitential.[23] "I have lost all hope in life and my soul is sorely troubled, for I have no wine," wrote a scholar on his way to the market to exchange his grammar book for a couple of drinks. "But no one would buy it or even look at it."[24] Perhaps the poem was a joke, but it echoed a daily preoccupation. Similarly, a parody of the Salic Law in "popular" Latin levied fantastic fines on those who drank too much. Bilingual conversation manuals, whether Latin-Greek or Latin-Germanic, always began with "Give me a drink."[25]

Moralists warned against the maladies provoked by drunken excesses. Civil and religious law condemned the intoxication of priests, laymen, soldiers, and penalized those

* The director of a cathedral school bore the title *écolâtre*.

who participated in religious or secular associations devoted to drinking bouts (*potationes*). But people still drank, at every hour of the day, on every occasion, to celebrate the closing of a bargain or the feast of a saint.[26]

But what did they drink? Wine for a certainty. We have already seen the care lavished by bishops and abbots on their vintages and their anxiety to cart or ship in a supply if the harvest fell short. During the Norman invasions, fleeing monks often attempted to bring their casks but rarely succeeded in the effort. In 845, returning to their monastery, the monks of Saint-Germain gave thanks to God and their patron because the Normans had not touched their wine and the supply would last until the next harvest.[27] They needed wine for the Sacrifice of the Mass, but it was also served at the monks' and canons' meals, and better wine was kept in reserve for passing guests. The Council of Aix in 818 attempted to limit each canon to a fixed quantity of wine.[28]

Some considered it a penance to have to content themselves with beer if wine was lacking. Installed at Liège, Sedulius Scotus could never accustom himself to the regional beer and begged his bishop to send him some bottles of wine. He wrote in praise of a certain Robert, who had 1000 barrels of wine of the highest quality in his caves, and the abbot thanked him by sending him 300 bottles of Moselle.[29] In the northern and eastern regions of the Carolingian world, however, beer was a popular drink. It was made in part from cereals reduced to malt in the maltery (*malatura* or *camba*), boiled down, and mixed with hops by specialized craftsmen.[30] The regulations of the Abbeys of Saint-Denis, Saint-Trond, Corbie, and others gave instructions for the furnishing of breweries and the brewing of beer, which they called *cervisia*.* The guest house on the plan of Saint-Gall had its own brewery. Beer like wine could not be kept very long. The amount to be consumed had to be produced on order.

There are scattered references to other fermented drinks. Lupus of Ferrières recommended cider (*pomaticum*) to his correspondents, made either from wild apples or pears. Mulberry wine, hydromel, or some other beverage made partly from honey was also available.[31]

* *Cervisia* is a common type of beer for the period.

Many people simply drank water. Fearing a shortage of pears and an equally severe shortage of beer because of a bad grain harvest, Lupus of Ferrières wrote: "Consequently, let us make use of a healthy, natural drink which will sometimes be of benefit to both body and soul—if it is drawn not from a muddy cistern but from a clear well or the current of a transparent brook."[32]

Carolingian bishops and abbots display much concern for the provision of drinking water. Until Aldric built his aqueduct, water from the Sarthe was being sold at a penny a hogshead.[33] The Abbot of Saint-Denis was preoccupied with the constant care of the Crou River which passed through the monastery.[34] The best solution was to control the water from a spring and bring it to the cloister or kitchen fountains through conduits. But that was not always possible. The monks of Laon complained that they had nothing with which to quench their thirst but non-potable water: "Bacchus is not there to soothe throats dessicated by summer, and now we must fill our bellies with unhealthy water. . . ."[35]

Without a doubt, this was an age obsessed with wine.

IV

Cults
and
Cultures

In so vast and diverse a place as the Carolingian universe, we must use the word "beliefs" in the plural. Christianity was preached everywhere, but it had not yet eliminated the vital remnants of ancient faiths rooted in the Roman, Germanic, and Celtic past. The entire history of the Carolingian church, indeed of the medieval and even the modern church, is the history of a permanent and persevering combat with superstition. Animistic and magical practices had their adepts among the people and even among the clergy. How could it have been otherwise? Men and women surrounded by savage nature felt themselves to be dominated by unseen forces. Above all else, they strove to soothe their anxiety and ensure the safety of body and soul through rituals. Their daily life and daily work bound them to the soil. Their incantations aimed at rendering Mother Earth fecund and marking her mysterious cycles through the changing seasons.

Religious Beliefs and Attitudes

20

Paganism and Pagan Survivals

Paganism still had strong roots in those parts of Germany which had just been painfully won over to Christianity.[1] Sacred enclosures, groves, stones, and springs still had their cults despite the efforts of kings and missionaries to destroy them. Boniface felled the sacred oak of Geismar, as did Charlemagne the Saxons' Irminsul, the tree which was believed to uphold the vault of heaven. The sylvan cults of the *nimidas* were proscribed, and sacrifices in honor of the Germanic gods Odin and Donner were forbidden. The Saxon capitulary of 785 threatened Draconian measures against idolatrous practices:

> . . . Whoever delivers the bodies of the dead to the flames, following the pagan rite, and reduces the bones to cinders, will be condemned to death. . . .
> . . . Whoever invokes springs or trees or forests or makes offerings to them in the pagan manner, or hold feasts in honor of demons, will be fined 60 sous if noble, 30 for an *ingenu* (free man), and 15 for a *lite* (bondman). If they do not quit themselves faithfully immediately, they will be excluded from the services of the Church until the debt is fully paid. . . .

> . . . We ordain that the bodies of Christian
> Saxons are to be borne to our church's cemeteries and
> not to the tumuli of the pagans. . . .[2]

But aside from these extreme cases, a decadent
paganism survived everywhere, characterized by various
superstitions without reference to particular cults. As in
antiquity, men still celebrated the beginning of the year by
marking the calends of January. In 742, Boniface complained
to the Pope that he had learned that singers and dancers
dressed as beasts made their rounds day and night performing sacrilegious incantations even on the steps of Saint
Peter's Church in Rome.[3] The prosperity of the year was
thought to depend on organized festivities and exchanges of
gifts. The feasts called *Spurcales* in February, the celebration
of nature's renewal in spring, and observances of the summer
solstice in June all provided occasions to commune with
nature in drinking bouts and sexual irregularities. The re-
generation and renewal necessary for the re-commencement
of the rhythms of daily life were represented, as in many
"primitive" societies, by a feast or an orgy.[4] Other superstitions were part of the fabric of everyday life: the flight of
a rook, the appearance of a little mouse, or a sneeze commanded special attention. Favorable days must be chosen for
traveling and for spinning. Even without clearly remember-
ing the goddess, people waited for Venus' day, Friday, to
marry.

Pagan superstition was particularly attached to cults
of the dead. In the middle of the eighth century and at the
end of the ninth, texts show the funerary wake, *dadsisas*,
giving way to dancing, singing, and eating. In effect, the
dead had to be appeased so that they would not trouble the
living. In some places, a piece of money was put into the
mouth of the corpse, or even a host, in durable memory of
the old custom of an obol for Charon.[5]

Magic and Sorcery

These traditional folkloric superstitions are not very serious
in comparison to the magical practices of which sorcerers
and their disciples were guilty. Capitularies of the eighth

and ninth centuries denounce magicians, enchanters, diviners, dream interpreters, and fortune tellers without much distinction for their different functions.[6] Special mention was sometimes made of *tempestarii* who could call up storms. In his treatise "Against the Erroneous Opinions of the People Regarding Hail and Thunder," Agobard reported that when thunder was heard in his neighborhood, nobles and peasants, young and old, believed that men called *tempestarii* had used enchantments to unchain a magical wind. The harvest destroyed by such storms was said to be given by the *tempestarii* to men who came in flying vessels, the ancestors of flying saucers, from a land called Magonia. Agobard added:

> We have even seen several madmen who believe that such absurd things are real and display three men and a woman to the assembled crowd, saying that they fell from these vessels sailing on the clouds. For several days they kept them in irons and then brought them before me to have them stoned.[7]

Agobard, who did not believe in sorcerers, tried to convince such men of their errors. But belief in sorcery was too widespread. Intervention by the public powers was called for. The Council of Paris in 829 devoted an article to the subject:

> Certain very pernicious evils are assuredly remnants of paganism such as magic, judicial astrology, sorcery, *maleficia* (witchcraft), or poisoning, divination, charms and belief in the guidance of dreams. These evils should be very severely punished according to the Law of God. For there can be no doubt that people exist, and we know of several, who through prestidigitation and diabolic illusions so imbue human spirits with a taste for their philtres, flesh, and phylacteries that they are apparently rendered stupid and insensible to the evils brought upon them. It is also said that their *maleficia* can trouble the air, bring down showers of hail, predict things to come, steal the fruit and milk of some folk to bestow it on others, and do an infinity of such things. If any people of this sort, men or women, are discovered, they should be punished all the more

rigorously in that they have the malice and temerity not to flinch from the public service of the demon.[8]

In 873, Charles the Bald learned that sorceresses and sorcerers had caused the deaths of several persons and ordered his counts "to seek out those responsible for the crimes."

> If they are found guilty let them perish, man and woman, as law and justice require. But if they are only suspect . . . , subject them to the judgment of God. Let them be put to death, not only the guilty but the men or women who were their accomplices, so that even the memory of so great a crime will be made to disappear in our kingdom.[9]

Women were always thought to be particularly disposed toward sorcery. Regino of Prüm described the nocturnal ride of the sorceresses obedient to Diana and condemned those who believed in it. He spoke of women "who pretend that their charms and *maleficia* give them the power to change the dispositions of human beings from hate to love and vice versa or to take their goods away through ligatures."[10] Salic law fined anyone who called someone a *herbugium** or who accused someone of carrying a bronze cauldron to a sorcerers' gathering. There was a higher fine for accusing a free woman of being a witch (*stria*) and eating human flesh. There are similar penalties in Lombard law and the Saxon capitulary of 789.[11] Yet someone who wanted a woman dead might easily get his way by accusing her of witchcraft. That was the fate of Bernard of Septimania's sister, who was condemned by Lothair to be put into a cask and thrown into the Saône in 834, *more maleficorum*. In the same period, partisans of Lothair accused their enemy, the Empress Judith, of having ensnared her husband with artful charms and diabolical power.[12]

Maleficia appeared in many forms. It could impede the growth of another's grain by magic powders, as Agobard once reported, or incantations. It rendered a neighbor's cattle sterile or brought harm on others through making knots in a dead person's girdle.[13] Love potions to excite a husband's

* A *herbugium* is a witch's helper.

Cults and Cultures

passion or attract a lover were made from sperm, menstrual blood, and aphrodisiac plants. Denouncing a nun who had had recourse to a sorcerer, Hincmar copied the composition of some potions: bones of the dead, cinders and ashes, hair, pubic hair, different colored strings, various herbs, snails and snakes were used in *maleficia,* sterilizing potions, and abortifacients.[14]

By far the most popular magical practices were those designed to protect and cure. Prisoners seeking to be free of their bondage, or peasants who feared that their horses would injure themselves, all recited the formulae preserved in Germanic texts.[15] Sick children were carried to the peak of the roof while medicinal herbs were cooked to the recited incantations.[16] Amulets and phylacteries endowed with particular characteristics were sold to anyone who wanted their protection. At Rome in the middle of the eighth century women bound phylacteries with ribbons on their arms and with cords on their legs.[17] Models of human limbs were hung from trees or placed at the crossroads to procure the healing of an arm or leg.[18] Finally, magical divination was practiced continually by methods inherited from antiquity: paying heed to the direction of smoke, or examining the excrement or liver of animals, climbing to the rooftops, interpreting dreams or opening books at random.

Even priests had recourse to auguries and spell-casters or interpreted dreams.[19] Some of the manuscripts which the monks copied carry the magical squares which predicted the course of an illness by combining the letters of the victim's name and the number of the day on which he fell ill.[20]

It was impossible to root these magical practices out of the popular soul. The Church christianized them and attempted to restore to God what had pertained to the Devil. Just as they consecrated trees and fountains to the saints, they replaced pagan incantations with prayers for rain, the fertility of the fields, and the recovery of the sick. The Pater and the Credo could be recited while gathering simples. A swarm of bees could be called in the Lord's name and secured by three repetitions of the Pater. We still have some incantatory formulae used for healing various maladies such as hemorrhages, dropsy, and eye diseases. Here is a so-called *Adjuratio contra malas oculorum:*

✝ Alias ✝ nec lia ✝ nec gallina ✝
supra rypa maris sedebat macula ✝
✝ famuli tui illius sive alba, christus ✝
✝ spergat; sive rubra, Christus deleat ✝
✝ sive nigra, Christus deficiat ✝ Ayos ✝ Ayos
✝ Ayos ✝ sancta crux ✝ Amen ✝[21]

Astrology

No survey of Carolingian beliefs would be complete without notice of the importance men attached to the stars and the meaning of their revolutions, despite denunciations of popular astrology as superstition. Many thought that the moon influenced the course of illness: an illness begun in the new moon would last a long time, but sickness would end quickly if begun in the second quarter. An illness in the fourth quarter indicated that death was near.[22] One evening Hrabanus Maurus was at home preparing a sermon. Hearing a great clamor, he asked what it meant and was told that the people were helping the moon which was in eclipse:

> Horns were blaring as if calling for war, and pigs were grunting. People were throwing arrows and missiles at the moon while others were hurling fire from all direction at the sky. . . . They claimed that the moon was being threatened by I don't know what sorts of monsters and would be devoured if they did not help. In pursuit of the same end, other people began to break the pots they had brought with them.[23]

Here we have a description of that *Vince Luna,* "Victory to thee, O Moon," which church councils denounced regularly but apparently in vain. Nor would people begin the activities of the day without considering the pattern of the constellations. There were days on which it was bad to work and others on which it was bad to be bled or bad to plant vines. The literate understood the calendar of what were called "Egyptian days" and could explain it to the illiterate.[24]

Learned men, too, were attentive to maps of the heavens which they depicted on parchment or on silver tablets. Charlemagne had a tablet in his palace representing the earth, the planets, and the stars. In 810 he commissioned several manuscripts reproducing the various constellations, and these have been preserved to our own day. The works of Aratos, translated into Latin, were found in several libraries.[25] This interest did not spring from simple scientific curiosity. Before he undertook any expedition, the Emperor questioned the heavens. He asked Alcuin and Dungal the Irishman to explicate the moving stars, the position of Mars, and eclipses of the sun.[26] Heavenly motions always presaged important events. Einhard wrote that there were "frequent eclipses of sun and moon" during the three years before the death of Charlemagne. "For seven days in a row, a black spot could be seen on the sun." In 837 a comet appeared under the sign of the Virgin and in twenty days traversed the signs of Leo, Cancer, and Gemini. Louis asked Einhard and other learned men to explain it. The biographer of Louis who is known to us only as "The Astronomer" says:

> Since the Emperor Louis, who was very attentive to such phenomena, first spotted it, he could not rest until he could consult with a certain sage and with me, who pass for having some learning in these matters. . . . "Go," he said to me, "to the palace terrace and then return quickly and tell me what you noticed, for there is a star I did not see last night. . . ."

Louis asked them whether this sign announced a change of reign or the death of a prince and praised God for the warnings supplied in this manner. A little further along, the biographer noted that a comet, appearing in the sign of Scorpio, announced the death of Pepin, while an Emperor's death was foretold by an eclipse of the sun. Nithard noted a comet which rose to the center of Pisces and disappeared between the constellations of the Lyre and the Drover at the very time when the Oath of Strasbourg was taken. The partition of the Empire in 843 was announced, according to Florus of Lyon, by a comet whose long, flamboyant mane filled the skies with fires of baleful splendor.[27] A cultivated man like Lupus of Ferrières did not hesitate to write to a monk:

> As to the comets which have been seen, there seems

to be more to fear about them than to discuss. Since Holy Scripture says nothing about them, we must think, even fear, what the experiences of the Gentiles taught them concerning the apparition of these heavenly bodies; and they report that comets foretell epidemics, famine, or war.[28]

Simple folk or clergy, Carolingians never ceased to scrutinize the heavens in search of presages. Year by year, chroniclers noted the meteorological events which, to them, were disquieting *prodigia*.

Carolingian Marvels

Illiterate or learned, Carolingians felt themselves to be in daily contact with the supernatural. God was constantly intervening in the affairs of the world which He created and which was, in any case, only a reflection of true reality. Prodigies are reported as though they were as natural as the succession of day and night. Man could not ignore their significance. The supernatural presented itself to all human senses: armies of fire and flame were seen in the heavens; beer transformed into wine could be tasted; perfumes spread mysteriously during a procession of relics, and diabolical spirits gave off a nauseating odor. . . .[29] Though it was forbidden to interpret dreams, visions were welcomed by the faithful as salutary warnings. Receipt of such visions was recorded by monks and clerks and given wide publicity. In 828, Einhard learned at the palace at Aix that the Archangel Gabriel had appeared to a blind man and ordered him to record a dozen articles in the form of a miscellany and to present the compilation to the Emperor. Louis the Pious was insufficiently attentive to the message. Consequently, in 874, his son Louis the German envisaged him plunged into infernal torment "because he did not follow the twelve articles" dictated by the angel. The tone of Gabriel's text is unknown to us, but it is likely that it contained moral counsels rather than political.[30] A poor woman of Laon was ravished by ecstasy and taken by a man dressed as a monk into a sinister place where she saw the Empress Ermengard imprisoned in water by three millstones, one on her head, one on her chest, and the third on her feet. She also saw Beggo, one of Charlemagne's relatives famous for his avarice, obliged to drink liquid gold while the demons mocked him: "All your life you have thirsted for gold and your thirst was never quenched. Now you will drink until you are satiated." In "The Vision of Wettin," Walafrid Strabo recounts a voyage to Hell (where he shows priests who abandon the treasures of the soul for sumptuous tables), to Purgatory (where Charlemagne expiated his impurity), and at last to Paradise (where dwelt the temperate and virginal).

Carolingians depicted the afterlife in a graphic manner. Charles the Fat had a vision of evil bishops burning in valleys of pitch, sulphur, lead, wax, and soot. Black demons tried to seize him with hooks of fire; fire-breathing dragons sought to engulf him. Escaping, he found himself on a mountain where all sorts of metals were melting together. Then he was in a valley where two springs flowed, one boiling and the other frigid. There Charles saw his father, Louis the German, condemned to be plunged into one or the other on alternate days. Reaching Paradise at last, the prince was dazzled by a great light surrounding the elect who were sitting on a topaz of extraordinary grandeur.[31]

In the Carolingian world, the forces of good and evil were in constant confrontation. The Devil was always seeking to extend his realm. Satan was, in the words of Paulinus of Aquilea, "a liar, inventor of sickness, creator of pride and all vices, counsellor of all turpitude."[32] He took advantage of human weakness to ravage the earth, destroy crops, decimate flocks with sickness. Thus it was, according to Einhard, that Satan's instrument spoke through the mouth of a "possessed" young girl. Though she was illiterate, she discoursed in Latin, criticizing society and morals.[33] The Devil could also be seductive, disguised in the form of an angel of light. Thus disguised, he visited Charles, son of Louis the German, and invited him to communion. With the bread, the Devil entered into the prince and made him mad until he was cured by the use of relics. When the Devil took possession of a house, the stones wept; houses were destroyed by fire, and hidden sins were revealed to priests who came to asperge haunted places with holy water.[34]

In this world, where Heaven mixed with Hell, where time and eternity were confounded, death was a fearful but familiar accident. Men and women accepted it with resignation but not without emotion. Carolingian poets composed "laments" (*planctus*), to deplore the loss of dear ones, particularly if they were warriors or princes. At the death of Charlemagne's beloved wife, Hildegard, "the brazen hearts of the warriors were wrung, and their tears ran down between buckler and sword." The Abbess Hathumoda was accompanied to the grave by her weeping nuns. In the face of death or other catastrophes, people expressed their feelings in sonorous moans and despairing gestures: "All the clergy were in tears, the monks wept, cries of sorrow filled the air. . . . Women tore their hair, struck their naked breasts with their fists, and tore their faces with their nails. . . ." Thus Abbo described the reaction of the Parisian population to the arrival of the Normans in 885.[35]

On the day of their anointment, Carolingian kings were entrusted with the mission of leading their people to salvation. They had to be given the means of knowing the Truth and renouncing pagan beliefs and superstitions. It was a great ambition. Artisans, merchants, and the rural masses were to be instructed in the Christian religion while pagan populations in newly conquered regions were to be evangelized. Charles sought to imitate Josiah who, "preaching, correcting, exhorting, struggled to bring the realm which God had entrusted to him to His true worship."[1] The king desired that the men and women of all his lands should be instructed in the Christian message. For that, he needed well-trained clerks.

Religious Training of the Clergy and Instruction of the People

21

Clerical Training

Charlemagne's Educational Policies

This is the context in which we must understand Charles' "educational policy," a policy his successors would follow until the end of the ninth century. In the absence of new testimony, it has long been debated whether Charles had decided to reorganize the schools before he met Alcuin at Parma in 781. The first text known to us is the order for the opening of schools in the *Admonitio generalis* of 789, twenty years after Charles' accession. Episcopal and monastic schools had been in existence since the sixth century, but they had succumbed to the blows of the eighth-century crisis and had not been restored.[2] The king ordained "that schools be established where children can learn to read; that psalms, notation [the stenography of the age], chant, computation, and grammar should be taught in every monastery and bishopric and that these institutions should obtain carefully copied Catholic books."[3] Such a program of studies resembled that taught in earlier times: reading, chant, calculation, and Latin. The innovation was the obligation to open schools in every monastery and bishopric. The Emperor followed it up with a recommendation that mature men should be given the responsibility of recopying psalters and missals. This introduces another aspect of the reform to which we shall later return.

The difficulties in enforcing the decision were attested by the numerous reports which followed. A *Letter on the Need To Cultivate Letters* required all bishops and abbots to choose men with the will and capacity to study and ask them to instruct their fellows. In 794, the Council of Frankfurt recommended that bishops undertake the instruction of their clergy. Though there is no further mention of schools after 800, *missi* and bishops were ordered to guide the instruction of clerks and supervise examinations, as we shall see. The great reforming councils of 813 again urged the training of the clergy, with a view to the further instruction of the people and the celebration of the liturgy. The Council of Chalon again outlined the familiar program of letters and Holy Scripture.[4]

Educational Policy after Charles

Restoration of the schools, linked to the instruction of the people, was one of the major cares of bishops and abbots under Louis the Pious. The Emperor and his advisors knew that the best way to mould the urban clergy was by constraining them to form around the bishop a community that would observe the rule of the canons. This rule, redacted by Chrodegang of Metz in the middle of the eighth century, obliged the clergy to perform the offices, devote time to Scriptural readings, and preach publicly. Chrodegang refused ordination to those who were incapable of such tasks.[5] Charlemagne aimed at regrouping the clerks of episcopal centers into chapters of canons, but he had met with lively resistance from clerks and priests who preferred to maintain their independence and refused so monastic a life style. Guided by Benedict of Aniane, Louis the Pious tried to revive the reform. Indeed, it had become more necessary than before because monasteries had been forbidden to receive secular pupils and were to reserve the monastic schools for novices. In each cathedral school, readers and chanters were made masters who must verify the progress of their clerks.[6] In 818, bishops were reminded that they ought to instruct clerks who did not live in the community. In 822, at Attigny, the same preoccupation appeared: "We ask that the schools, to which we have not been as attentive as we should have been, be restored." In 829, at Paris, the bishops requested schools "for the honor and utility of the Church" and to train "soldiers of the Church," that is, pastors. After the death of Louis the Pious, in 845, the bishops who met at Meaux reiterated that a master who could instruct the priests should be permanently appointed.[7] We can see that it was not easy to command respect for royal decisions.

The same educational policy was extended to Italy. In 824, Lothair complained that religious learning had disappeared everywhere because those to whom it had been entrusted were negligent and indifferent. He determined to regroup the schools into eight centers: Turin, Pavia, Cremona, Verona, Vicenza, Cividale, Florence, and Fermo.[8] We don't know why he was moved to attempt this first outline of an Italian educational map nor the extent of the application of these reforms. We do know, however, that a year later Pope Eugenius II decided to install masters who could teach letters and doctrine in all his bishoprics and parishes.[9] Thus Lothair's decisions were extended to the Papal States.

Finally, in 829, the bishops suggested to Louis the Pious that he establish "public schools" in at least three parts of the Empire. This singular expression is puzzling. Did they mean schools open to all, lay and clerical, where students might obtain a broader education than the episcopal schools proffered? It seems likely. In 859, the Council of Savonnières recommended that the "public school" be directed by the bishop and consecrated to "divine and humane sciences," which reflects the program generally followed elsewhere.[10]

Program for Clerical Instruction

It was, we must admit, a modest program. There was never any question of giving clerks the liberal arts education available in the great monastic schools. Bishops and princes aimed at training the clergy to take up and carry out their pastoral duties. A Carolingian priest should know Latin, the language of Scripture, and liturgy. He was not asked to spend long hours over Latin grammar but to be able to say Mass and recite prayers without committing such barbarisms as that of an eighth-century Bavarian clerk who baptized *in nomine patria et filia* ("in the name of the nation and of the daughter.")[11] He should memorize the Credo and the Pater, understand the prayers of the Mass, know how to modulate psalms according to the division of the verses, know how to read homilies and have some of them by heart.[12] In the absence of punctuation marks in manuscripts, all but the most cultivated had difficulty reading. Even the palace clergy did not always understand very well what they read.[13] Where manuscripts were lacking, as they often were, prayers and sermons had to be entrusted to memory. A priest should know how to chant without trying to gain a facile success in imitation of profane singers. Agobard denounced cantors who, thinking themselves at a theatrical performance, affected an exaggerated sweetness in their singing: "They say that music makes demons flee, but we should be aware that such songs welcome them into the heart." The favored chant was the Roman chant which, with some difficulty, had been introduced into the Frankish realm by Pepin and Charlemagne and which was gradually replacing the varied liturgies of the West. Roman clerks were brought to Rouen to train the clergy of the town when the reform was applied, and a similar reform was applied at Metz thanks to Chrodegang. From there, it spread to Lyon. Leidrad expressed his satisfaction in a report to Charlemagne:

> As soon as I took up the governance of the above-named church at your command, I employed all the power within my small means to procure clerks for its service, so that, by the grace of God, there are now a great many. That is why your piety made it a duty and a pleasure to grant my request for a clerk from the church of Metz. Thanks to him, with God's help and the support of your favor, the *ordo psallendi* has been restored in the church of Lyon so that as far as our strength allows we now perform all that the rule exacts for the perfect execution of divine offices according to the rite of the sacred palace. Thus I now have schools of cantors, and most of them are so well trained that they can in turn train others. . . .[14]

This concern for unification extended beyond the liturgy to the administration of the sacraments: baptism, penance, communion, and unction for the sick. The priest had to memorize the prayers of the Roman liturgy and needed to possess a few indispensable books. Thus Riculf, Bishop of Soissons, commanded his priests to own four samples of the baptismal ceremony, texts for the consecration of baptismal fonts and holy water, and the text for the rite of burial.[15] In planning his pastoral visits, Regino of Prüm proposed to ask each priest certain questions: "Had he at his disposition a copy of the Creed, and the Sunday orisons according to the tradition of the orthodox Fathers? Did he understand them thoroughly and could he instruct the people in them? Had he a martyrology so that he could announce the exact birth days of the saints to his people?* Had he the forty homilies of Gregory the Great? Had he read them studiously, and did he understand them? Had he the Roman penitential?"[16]

Examinations

To verify the knowledge of priests, bishops strengthened their "learning controls."[17] Before ordaining a priest, bishops would verify the moral and intellectual qualifications of the petitioner. A manuscript of Wissemburg gives us a typical questionnaire:

> Question: Why do you wish to be ordained a priest?
> Response: To announce the word of God, give baptism, and efface sins through penance.
> Q. Why do you sing the Mass?
> R. To commemorate the death of the Lord.
> Q. How do you sing the Mass?
> R. I offer the bread, which is the body of Christ. . . .

The clerk under interrogation should also comment on the Pater and Credo and know the different vices he was to combat.[18] On Holy Thursday, when priests went to the episcopal city for their Holy Oils, the archdeacon was to question them particularly about the rite of baptism. But, in 818, ecclesiastical authorities announced that the size of the dioceses and the multiplication of parishes had made it impossible for all priests to make the journey. In addition, some of them were sending delegates to procure the Sacred Chrism. On the other hand, priests were supposed to attend the diocesan synod once or twice a year. The bishop had

---

* Saints' feasts commemorate their heavenly birthdays, when they died on earth.

extracts from the Pastoral Rule of Gregory the Great read to them there, or a homily on the Gospel, and organized examinations for the clergy. Theodulf instructed priests to bring some clerks with them to the synod, bearing linens and sacred vessels to demonstrate how well they acquitted their ministry.[19] Bishops were supposed to move about their diocese, making pastoral visits and inspecting the work of the priests. The priests dreaded these visits, for they had to provide for the bishop and his suite. In 844, Charles the Bald intervened to protect the curates of the Septimanian parishes from episcopal exactions. The costs were to be divided among five parishes and the prestations precisely defined. Bishops must limit the number of servants and horses they brought with them. Some bishops had arrived with veritable herds of horses, which they nourished at the expense of the curates and sold in the course of their pastoral rounds.[20] Another reason for fear was the episcopal inspection and the examination which followed. Regino of Prüm, in a *Manual* written for the Bishop of Mainz, outlined questions to ask clerks and laymen with extracts of canonical citations relating to these questions. When the bishop was too occupied with his political or administrative cares to travel, he was replaced by archdeacons in their own archdiaconates. Gauthier of Orleans ordered them to examine the priests for their knowledge and their fashion of celebrating Mass and administering baptism.[21]

The bishop's responsibility for his diocese extended also to supervision of wandering clerks moving from one region to another. Each priest arriving from another diocese was supposed to present a letter of recommendation from his bishop. Kings mistrusted these men preaching from province to province. Their pleasure with success that outshone the local priests was balanced by fear that heresy was being propagated. They remembered the famous Adalbert and Clement the Irishman who had aroused the passions of the abused masses in the mid-eighth century. Adalbert, fortified with an angelic vision and a letter from Christ which had fallen from Heaven, went about building chapels and raising crosses in fields and near fountains. He distributed his own nails and hair as relics, claiming that the hierarchy and the sacraments were unnecessary. Clement had preached that Christ descended into Hell to liberate believers and unbelievers alike, even those who had worshipped God as idolaters. The Council of Soissons in 744 and the Roman synod of 745 condemned these adventurers and their disciples.[22] But new Adalberts and Clements were always to be feared. Popular heresies, like those described by Ratramnus of Corbie, were always reappearing here and there.[23] Thus for security it was necessary to supervise foreign clerks and make them submit to examination. A text dating from the reign of Louis the Pious gives us a glance:

> Where were you born? Where were you educated and tonsured? Did you travel from one parish to another, or were you educated in one parish? Who ordained you? Did you pay to be ordained? To what church were you appointed . . . ? When you baptize, do you know how to distinguish the use of the masculine and feminine, singular and plural? How do you confess the Trinity and the Unity of the divine persons? Was Christ consubstantial with the Father? Is he eternal like him . . . ?

These last two questions were certainly designed to seek out the tenets of Adoptionism, a heresy condemned in 794 which still had disciples in the ninth century. The questionnaire pursued the subject of baptism and the resurrection of the dead, and, each time, the proper response was included—as though they feared that the interrogator might not be sure of the answers.[24]

Popular Instruction

A solid religious education was both a weapon in the struggle against pagan survivals and a means of ensuring each of the faithful an opportunity for personal salvation. To that end, Charlemagne and his successors labored with zeal and perseverance. It would be tedious indeed to recapitulate all the articles in all the capitularies consecrated to popular religious training. From the mid-eighth to the ninth centuries, they are very numerous and full of repetitions. We need only note that the most frequent concern is for the two principal steps in the initiation of a Christian, baptism and preaching.[25]

Baptism and the Instruction of Children
A child was supposed to be baptized as soon as it was born.

Because of variations in rites from one region to another, Charles issued a questionnaire to all his metropolitan bishops about 811, inquiring into the manner of performing the sacrament and explaining it to the faithful. Some of the answers have been relayed to us.[26] From them, we can see that children were baptized immediately at birth only in cases of necessity. Parents were generally advised to wait until Easter eve or Pentecost. The priests used their Lenten sermons to remind parents and godparents of the essentials of Christian dogma. They were also asked to recite the Pater and the Credo. In lands not yet conquered by Christianity, neophyte adults had to be instructed before baptism. Paulinus of Aquilea had seen mass baptisms of unprepared persons in Saxony and spoke out against them: "Christ never said, 'Go, baptize all nations and then teach them my precepts,' but 'Go, teach and then baptize.'" Alcuin suggested that the Saxons denied their baptism because no care had been taken to root the faith firmly in their hearts. From a formulary in the Germanic tongue, we have the text of a priestly interrogation of a pagan neophyte:

Do you renounce the Devil?

I do renounce him.

Do you renounce the works and the will of the Devil?

I do renounce them.

Do you renounce the blood sacrifices, idols, and gods which pagans take for gods, idols, and sacrifices?

I do renounce them.

Do you believe in God, the Father Almighty?

I do believe.

Do you believe in Christ, the Son of God, the Savior?

I do believe.

Do you believe in the Holy Spirit?

I do believe.

Do you believe in God Almighty, in his Trinity and in his Unity?

I do believe.

Do you believe in the Holy Church of God?

I do believe.

Do you believe in the remission of sins by baptism?

I do believe.

Do you believe in life after death?

I do believe.[27]

Baptism was always performed by triple immersion in the baptismal font or the baptistry annexed to the episcopal church, sometimes reconstructed on a pagan model.[28] Only a bishop could administer confirmation. Rural children waited for the pastoral visit to be confirmed.

At the moment of baptism, the child received his Christian name. By onomastic inquiry, we can trace the changing fashions in names. In aristocratic families, a boy generally received his grandfather's name, but in other milieux children were often given some variation of their parents' names. Thus in Irminon's polyptich, the sons of Aldaldus were called Aldoardus and Aldoildis; the sons of Madalgaudus, Madalcarius, Madalgis, Madalberta, Madalgudis. Some parents whose own names were Germanic preferred more Christian names for their children: Clementia, Bona, Benedictus, Deodata, Natalis. Sometimes they borrowed names from the Old Testament: Abraham, Benjamin, David, Samuel, Joseph, etc. Someone should undertake a comprehensive study of the symbolic, indeed magical, significance of these names.[29]

Once baptized, children had to be instructed by their parents and godparents. They attended religious ceremonies with them and had the chance to profit from the preaching offered to everyone. Charlemagne would have liked children to learn reading and writing at the parish schools. The Council of Mainz of 813 recommended that parents send their sons to monastic or presbyterial schools to learn the Credo and the Pater so that they could teach them to others on their return home. If they could not learn them in Latin, then they should know them in their own tongues. Theodulf of Orleans expressed the wish that priests should hold schools in every farm and village, "*per villas et vicos.*" They were to turn away no children entrusted to them by the parents to learn letters but were to teach them, exacting no salary and limiting their gain to occasional small gratuities which the parents might offer. At the end of the ninth century, one of his successors, Gauthier, again directed each rural priest to open a school, "if at all possible." Some rural schools were actually opened at Reims and Soissons, where the priest was asked to segregate boys and girls—a feeble glimpse of the education of girls.[30]

Preaching

Where there was no school, education had to be gained by ritual and preaching. Capitularies and councils relentlessly reiterated that preaching is the principal care of bishops. "Clearly, the health of the people is founded primarily on teaching and preaching," Alcuin said. "Preach, preach, in season and out."[31]

Bishops were to preach in the cathedrals, and if they were prevented, they must provide a clerk as substitute. Whenever the question of clerical duties arose, the texts put preaching in first place. As we have seen, clerical training had been designed to that end. Occasionally, as Alcuin reminded Charlemagne, the *boni laici* could also preach. Sermons were to be preached in the vulgar tongue, so that everyone could understand them. They should be adapted to the particular audience, as Gregory the Great advised in the sixth century in his frequently cited *Liber pastoralis*.[32] Careful advice was given to preachers setting out among the pagans. In a celebrated letter, Daniel of Winchester explained how Boniface might convince the Germans to convert. Through discussions with the pagans, the preacher should bring them to speak of their own gods as never having existed. They should be shown that nearly the whole of humanity embraced Christ:

> If their gods are powerful, how can they explain the fact that Christians possess lands richer in grain and oil, the most fertile regions, leaving them only glacial countries? All this should be explained in sweet and moderate tones, without irritating and controversial passion.

Similarly, when Ebbo of Reims was sent out among the Danes, Louis the Pious recommended patience and moderation, supplying him with the general line of his preaching.[33]

For those already converted to the faith, the content

of sermons must differ. Theodulf of Orleans counseled his priests: "Those who know Scripture must preach Scripture. Those who do not can at least urge, 'Separate yourself from evil, do good, seek after peace.' " There we have the *schema* for two types of sermons. Preachers were assisted in explication of the Scriptures with homilies which digested and simplied them and with the sermons of the Church Fathers. Paul the Deacon and Alcuin composed such works. Fourteen homilies designed in the ninth century for recitation at great liturgical feasts have been preserved in Italian manuscripts. They were inspired by Augustine, Gregory the Great, Bede, and Caesarius of Arles. Priests were advised to procure and use homilies.[34]

Some of these homilies might be limited to consideration of certain truths of the faith:

> Let every bishop have homilies for the instruction of the people. They should reaffirm the fundamental articles of the Catholic faith, the eternal rewards of the good and eternal damnation of the evil, the future Resurrection and Last Judgment, stating what is needful to achieve salvation and what causes its loss.

Those who did not possess the necessary texts were to confine themselves to a simple re-statement of essential Catholic truths. The final chapter of the *Admonitio generalis* of 789 paraphrases the Credo: "Let priests preach honestly, without inventing or recounting to the people new things which may be uncanonical and according to their own taste rather than Holy Scriptures."[35] This is followed by definitions of God, the Trinity, the Incarnation, the Redemption, the Resurrection, and the Last Judgment with a list of vices and virtues appended. In other texts, like a letter of Hrabanus Maurus to Aistulf of Mainz, themes are given for sermons which are more moralistic than dogmatic. Christians are urged to forsake pride, vaingloriousness, lust, and avarice and embrace chastity, humility, modesty, and charity. Priests should remind them to pay the tithe, burn candles, take communion, confess themselves, attend Mass on feast days rather than working, not to chatter in church and to abstain from pagan superstition.[36]

These counsels were, perhaps, not urged in vain, but

they tended to fall on a distracted ear. To regain their auditors' attention, preachers illustrated the sermon with examples drawn from the lives of saints. Alcuin wrote two versions of his life of Saint Willibrod: one in verse for the educated and another in prose for monks to which he appended a homily which could be read to the people. At Saint-Riquier, there were two texts of the life of the founder of the abbey. One was written in good Latin; the other was longer, in a style and language more accessible to the people.[37] However, utilization of these hagiographic texts in popular preaching was relatively rare, reserved for feast days and pilgrimages. Bishops appear to have mistrusted this literature whose origins they could not control.

Even when delivered in a language which everyone understood, moralizing sermons risked the loss of the listener's attention. There are constant complaints of inattention and particularly of chattering in church. Priests then sought to assert themselves by threatening disobedient Christians with the Last Judgment and the torments of Hell: "Fear the tortures of Hell so that you may avoid them."[38]

The education of the people was all too often reduced to a moral negative. They were told what they should do, no doubt, but above all what they should not do. Respect for external prescriptions was reinforced by the legalism of the Old Testament. Infractions of the law were punished, the interests of social groups were preferred to individual spiritual progress. Priests and bishops eventually have the image of policemen enforcing laws rather than of spiritual guides leading each one along the road of faith. Laymen were reluctant to place too much reliance on a clergy which was frequently ignorant, worldly, or over-eager to collect tithes. Many preferred to place themselves in the care of monks. Already conflict between the two clergies over the pastoral domain can easily be predicted.

The Architects of the Revival

Carolingian educational policies had a well-defined and limited goal: to create a clergy capable of guiding the people. However, the ultimate results surpassed the initial aim to constitute what has been called the Carolingian Renaissance. Let us leave definitions of the term "Renaissance" to the debates of the erudite and be content to say that in the middle of the eighth to the end of the ninth century, literary production was greater than it had ever been before in the northern domains.[1]

Foreigners

This revival did not suddenly begin with the advent of Charlemagne. It was prepared and advanced by intellectual advances in Spain, the British Isles, and Italy. It was assisted by the arrival of foreigners in Francia. Spaniards, fleeing the Arab occupation, settled in Gaul with their manuscripts and their learning. Leidrad and Agobard in Lyon, Claudius at Turin, Benedict of Aniane at Aix, Theodulf at Orleans, and Prudentius at Troyes bore witness to the cultural traditions of the Visigoths. Charlemagne returned from Italy in the company of Transalpine scholars: besides the aged Peter, grammarian of Pisa, there were Paul the Deacon, monk of Monte Cassino and one-time teacher at the court of Pavia; Paulinus, grammarian become Bishop of Aquilea; and Fardulf, a poet who ended his career as Abbot of Saint-Denis. Nor did Anglo-Saxon culture lack representatives in the Frankish world. One of them, Alcuin, was a foremost architect of the Carolingian Renaissance. Master of the schools at York, he visited Italy when he was thirty-seven and met Peter of Pisa at Pavia. Thirteen years later, in 780, he met Charles on a new journey at Parma and passed several years with him before returning to England. In 793, he settled permanently in Francia, receiving several abbeys, including Saint-Martin of Tours, and died in 804 at the age of sixty-nine. His pupil Fredegisius succeeded him and later became chancellor to Louis the Pious. Anglo-Saxon Bishops of Sens and Bremen and the Abbot of Echternach joined their compatriots whom Boniface had settled in the abbeys of Germany. Finally, the literary revival was animated by a group of Irish (*Scoti*): Clement and Dungal at Charlemagne's court; Dicuil, who followed the lead of another Irishman, Virgil of Salzburg, in his interest in cosmography; Sedulius Scotus, who arrived in Liège about 884; and, above all, John Scotus Erigena whose very name proclaims his Irish birthplace. A protegé of Charles the Bald, John, with other Scots, revived the school of Laon, making it a center of Greek studies and philosophy. The Irish were astonishing, sometimes even scandalous, because of their free speech, worldly science, and intellectual audacity: "These were incomparably learned men. They cried out to a crowd of customers, "If anyone desires wisdom, let him come to us and receive it, for we are here to sell it." Or, as another chronicler tells us, "Defying the separating sea, nearly the whole of Hibernia has emigrated to our coasts in a hoard of philosophers."[2] Relations were sometimes strained between these different groups of foreigners and between them and the Franks. They were jealous of one another, digging at one another in epigrams and accusing one another of doctrinal deviations. Harmony did not always reign in the Carolingian Republic of Letters.

But thanks to the influence of these strangers the rather modest Renaissance of Charlemagne's day expanded under his successors, though it affected only a small elite in some monasteries and privileged bishoprics. The great centers of study were situated in the north and east of the Empire and in Italy. They owed their success to a well-stocked library, a particularly learned master, or the personal relationships they cultivated with other scholars or with the court. Under the abbacy of Hrabanus Maurus, pupil of Alcuin, the school of Fulda shone but declined after him. Lyon had the luck to receive the Spaniards and to command a scriptorium where hundreds of manuscripts were recopied.[3] At the end of the ninth century, the school of Laon lost its renown, but thanks to John Scotus' pupil, Heric, Irish learning soared anew at Saint-Germain of Auxerre. On-going centers like Saint-Gall, maintaining themselves continuously for decades, were rare indeed. Moreover, the cultural map of the Carolingian Empire had many blank spaces. Aquitaine did not participate in the movement at all except in that part of Septimania which was in contact with Catalonia. Provence had no center of study. On the other hand, paradoxically, Armorica was modestly enriched by the monasteries of Redon, Saint-Pol-de-Leon, and Landevenec before the Norman invasions erased it all.[4] Finally, we need hardly say that only those ecclesiastical and lay aristocrats who possessed both wealth and leisure were affected by the movement at all.

The Role of the Court

Princes, from the reign of Pepin on, encouraged the intellectual revival, urging the clergy to recover their taste for study to provide better religious instruction for the people. Under the influence of Italians, Anglo-Saxons, and Irish, they sought to make the court a cultural center comparable with the bygone Lombard court at Pavia.[5] Historians have talked of "the palace school" and even "the Palatine Academy." But what can we make of that? Did Notker of Saint-Gall invent from whole-cloth his famous picture of Charlemagne lecturing the lazy young aristocrats and commending the pupils of more modest estate?[6] Certainly there was a school at court for the training of future clerical workers and a choir-school for young clerks of the Chapel. Alcuin addressed a poem to Charles describing the cultural activities of the court:

> Sulpicius conducts his white flock of lectors, teaching them not to misplace their accents. Idithun trains the children in sacred chant, teaching them how music is shaped in a combination of feet, numbers, and measures. Then come the scribes and the doctors.

The poet spoke of the palace children (*pueri palatini*), particularly Charles' daughter Gisela: "who studies the stars in the stillness of the night. . . ."

All the young people who lived with princes had a chance to learn.[7] Charles himself set the example. As Einhard said:

> He cultivated the liberal arts passionately. Full of veneration for those who taught them, he heaped honors upon them. He followed the grammar lessons of the deacon Peter of Pisa, then in his old age. In other disciplines the master was Alcuin, called Albinus, himself a deacon, a Saxon of Britain by origin, the most learned man of the age. [Charles] devoted much time

and effort to learning rhetoric, dialectics, and above all astronomy from those about him. He learned to calculate and applied himself attentively and sagaciously to the study of the stars in their courses. He tried also to write and habitually kept tablets under the pillows of his bed with leaves of paper so as to use his leisure moments in practicing the tracing of letters; but he had begun too late, and the result was not very satisfactory. . . .[8]

In addition, his biographer noted that Charlemagne wished his children, both boys and girls, to be initiated into the liberal arts. Young aristocrats who were sent to the court also profited. All the princes who succeeded Charlemagne were literate, which caused Heric of Auxerre to say to Charles the Bald: "The palace deserves the name of school, for every day one spends as much time on scholarly exercises as on the military arts."[9]

As to the "Academy" which we owe to Alcuin's pen, it was limited to the small circle of scholars around the prince. These lovely souls read occasional poems and exercised themselves by solving puzzles and a type of riddle made fashionable by the Anglo-Saxons. Thus, Alcuin asked the young Pepin, "What is a year?" "A cart with four wheels." "What horses pull it?" "The sun and the moon." "How many palaces has it?" "Twelve." "Who are its guardians?" "The twelve signs of the Zodiac." Or, again: "I have seen a woman with an iron head, a wooden body, and a feathered tail carrying death." "The woman is a soldier's arrow." "Of what does man never tire?" "Profit."[10]

Besides these parlor games which seem a little too "cute" to us, scholars occupied themselves with serious problems. They discussed true wisdom, the significance of astral revolutions, and theological questions. Charles asked Fredegisius if ghosts or the unborn had any true existence, and the clerk responded with a treatise dedicated to him but destined for the entire court. Such discussions would be pursued at table and even in the bath.[11] Charles the Bald defended John Scotus against his detractors and took a personal interest in the Irishman's philosophical work. Nor was he disdainful of the court poets who addressed verses to him "in the form of designs" (*carmina figurata*), ancestors of our crossword puzzles. The famous "Eclogue on Calvitia [Baldness]" had

146 verses each beginning with the letter C. Whatever we may think of them, these displays of verbal virtuosity were very successful.[12]

The Tools of the Revival
Copyists' Workrooms

> Here should they sit who reproduce the oracles and sacred law, that they may be guarded from any frivolous word for fear that their hands and even they themselves may lose themselves among frivolities; they should strive to render the books which they execute correctly, that their pens may follow the right road.[13]

Alcuin had these verses inscribed on the door of the scriptorium of Saint-Martin of Tours. Every great monastery or episcopal household had such a scribal workshop. From one end of the Empire to the other, clerks and monks and even layfolk were employed in this labor. We must thank thousands of specialists for the thousands of manuscripts—nearly eight thousand have been preserved—written between the eighth and ninth centuries.[14]

Here, again, the impulse came from above. Charlemagne and his assistants issued precise directives for the recopying of badly written manuscripts and encouraged the adoption of that more readable and regular minuscule hand which has been dubbed "Carolingian." This new writing appeared in several workshops at about the same time, so that we cannot make an exact determination of its origins. Little by little, it replaced ancient scripts and naturally imposed itself upon the West. Across the centuries, it was recovered by the printers of the Renaissance to give us our present "lower case" typography.[15]

Let us imagine these scribes at work in their shops, surrounded by their materials: parchment leaves laid in chests, horns of ink, quills, erasing knives, etc. The parchment had previously been prepared by trimming the skin of a calf or sheep. Plunged into a bath of lime for several days, the skins were then stretched and scraped on both sides, cut, and finally tinted purple for luxury manuscripts.[16] Since parchment was very expensive, the scribes sometimes used leaves on which an incomplete manuscript had already been written or which had been carefully scraped. These palimpsests, more numerous in Germany and Italy than in western France, have enabled us to discern antique or pre-Carolingian texts under the Carolingian writing, old texts that would otherwise have been lost to us. Once prepared, the parchment was marked by pinpoints. In this manner four leaves could be ruled at once; when folded, these made the eight folios of a *quaternion*. Then the scribes got to work. Sitting on a bench with their feet on a stool, they placed the parchment on a writing desk or even on their knees. Sometimes they had the manuscript from which they were to copy on one side, but more often they wrote from the reader's dictation. Before beginning they tested their pens, tracing a few letters of the alphabet or the first verse of a psalm on the margin. Occasionally, being unable to exchange remarks among themselves, they wrote personal reflections in the margins of the text they were copying: "How hairy this parchment is!" "It is cold today." "This lamp gives poor light." "I don't feel well today." "It's time to start work." "It's dinner time." And so forth.[17] Scribal work was hard, particularly in winter, but how joyful they were when it was finished!

> Even as the sailor, fatigued with his labors, rejoices when he sights the familiar shore toward which he has so long aspired, so does the scribe exult who sees the long-desired end of the book which has so overcome him with weariness. The man who does not know how to write makes light of the scribe's pains, but those who have done it know how hard is this work.[18]

At the end, they recommended their souls to the readers who would come to know the manuscript.

Scribes rarely worked alone. In the great scriptoria, the copying of a single manuscript was distributed among a team under the direction of the head of the workshop. A copy of Titus Livius, executed at Tours, bore the names of eight copyists at the bottom of each book. Even when names are missing, it is easy enough to recognize changes of handwriting whether each scribe reproduced part of the model or they took turns at the task. Thus the work advanced rapidly. The length of execution of a manuscript varied with the facility of the copyists. One scribe boasted of having written the Salic Law in two days, and another claimed to have completed Augustine's commentary on the Epistles of John in seven days, an average of thirty pages a day. In general, it took two or three months to copy a manuscript of normal size.[19]

When the manuscript was finished, it had to be reread and corrected. Since the scribes might be beginners, or inexperienced, or even practically illiterate, errors abounded. Some scribes copied texts in mechanical fashion, entirely ignorant of the content. Florus of Lyon, who deplored the mistakes of copyists who, he suspected, slept at their writing, has left us an exemplary psalter. Some scribes describe their own incompetence and ask the reader to correct their mistakes or pray their master to undertake the work. In any case, the head of the shop reviewed the manuscript, corrected punctuation and spelling, underlining incomprehensible words in some places and giving the proper form in the margin, etc. Attentive study of these manuscripts thus allow us to reconstitute the arduous work of the scriptorium.[20]

If the completed manuscript was to be a luxury psalter, a gospel commissioned by a bishop or prince, or an antique literary or scientific work, the scribe was succeeded by the painter. He decorated the initials, lined up the pages, and, according to his own taste or the style of the school in which he was trained, painted leaves that had been kept in reserve.

By comparing the styles of the illuminators, we can establish the characteristics of the schools of Tours, Reims, Metz, and others. But the illustrations also demonstrate that painters, like other artisans, sometimes moved from shop to shop. Thus Lupus of Ferrières recommended a certain painter to one of his correspondents.[21] And although the techniques of illumination differed from those of the muralist, it is not unlikely that the painters constituted a coherent community distinct from that of the scribes.

Once the manuscript was copied and decorated, it was assembled. Leaves and quartos were arranged into a *codex* and, if the book were an expensive one, protected with a binding. This was a new technique which made great progress in the Carolingian period. Particularly rich bindings, for a special manuscript like a Bible or liturgical book, could be provided by goldsmiths or ivory workers. The binding boards of the sacramentary of Drogo of Metz or Charles the Bald's psalter were praiseworthy anonymous works.[22]

Libraries

What we have already said about the fabrication and ornamentation of manuscripts explains well enough why books were so carefully cared for and why they constituted so important an element in church treasuries. The library was specially located beside the scriptorium.[23] Here books were stored in chests or, less commonly, in armoires locked with a key which was confided to the *claviger librorum*. As with inventories of liturgical objects, book catalogues were compiled and updated periodically. The catalogue of Saint-Gall started with a list of 284 volumes, growing through several adjustments to 428.[24] The librarian divided the books into different groups: Bibles, liturgical works, the Fathers of the Church, canon law collections, grammars, poetry, history, Roman and Barbarian law codes, medicine, and so on. Sometimes he noted the state of the manuscript: "well written," "old," "impossible to read." Most especially, he kept "loan sheets" in the form of a gloss. As in all ages, books entrusted to a reader were in danger of disappearing. The monks of the community received regularly, and during Lent particularly, books for reading in the warming room or the schoolroom.[25] The reader was expected to take care of the book. Indeed, a work was often finished with a remonstrance by the scribe or donor: "This book was given to God and his Mother by Bishop Dido [of Laon]. Anyone who harms it will incur God's wrath and will offend his Mother." In spite of all the risks it entailed, some books were also loaned outside. Thus one scriptorium might appeal to another library, near or far, for a certain work which it lacked and hoped to copy. Lupus of Ferrières procured manuscripts he did not have from Prüm, Fulda, and Tours, engaging himself to return them as soon as they had been copied.[26] Many borrowers were not so scrupulous, however. Hrabanus Maurus complained that the scribes of Utrecht had not returned the copy of a commentary on Saint Matthew which he had lent them. Walafrid Strabo sent a copy of his cosmography to a friend with these words: "Read it, copy it, and return it."[27] Discussions about unreturned books were never lacking between the neighboring monasteries of Saint-Gall and Reichenau. Different methods were employed to avoid this forgetfulness. The book itself might carry a warning: "Dear reader, remember to return me to Saint-Nazaire [of Lorsch] for I cannot bear to belong to another master." Or, more stringently, a deposit could be exacted. No precaution, however, prevented books from disappearing either because they were kept by the borrower or stolen in the course of transference. Thus we have no way of knowing whether the 40 books which went out from the library of Cologne in the middle of the ninth century, of which we have a list, ever returned to their coffers. To replace lost books or obtain books they had never had, bishops and abbots were always on the hunt for manuscripts.[28] The librarian of Murbach inscribed in his catalogue all the books which he had found to add to the 335 his collection already possessed.[29] Appeals were so regularly made for the services of well-known scriptoria that certain abbeys like Tours, Saint-Denis and Saint-Gall were noted as regular "publishing houses." Monasteries also benefitted from the donations of certain aristocrats who possessed rich libraries. Thus many manuscripts, originally commissioned by laymen from different scriptoria, eventually made their way into ecclesiastical libraries.

The Life of the Schools

Educational Methods

At the "second week of his life," that is, in his seventh year, a child was ready to begin his education. That does not mean that children were not received into monasteries at even younger ages. Many parents offered their sons or daughters when they were barely weaned, although, theoretically, the child could confirm or deny his parents' decision on reaching the age of reason. But at the beginning of the eighth century, this liberal custom was abandoned. The parents' choice was held to bind the child all his life so that he could not take from God what had been given to him. The gift, of course, included not only the child but the lands which accompanied the oblate. Though many accepted the reception of children without vocations—a practice which was not without danger to monastic life—some violently contested it. The most famous example was Gottschalk, the son of a Saxon count, who had been offered to the Abbey of Fulda at an early age. Reaching adolescence, he asked to be restored to liberty. The abbot, Hrabanus Maurus, refused and sustained the validity of the family's undertaking in a long treatise, *On the Oblation of Children.* However, the Synod of Mainz in 829 granted the request of the young man who later made a name for himself by composing an unorthodox treatise on predestination.[30]

The children who lived in a monastery were brought up by aged monks who had to watch them night and day. Were their pedagogical methods as harsh as has commonly been believed? Certainly the master had his rod in hand and knew how to use it to constrain the recalcitrant and stimulate the indolent: "Neither child nor youth shall be spared. The cruel rod shall fall on lazy children," cried a poet in the preface of his book. In the liberal arts fresco in Theodulf's palace, Grammar was a woman with a whip in her left hand. That was a literary and artistic commonplace which must be carefully interpreted. From the beginning of their order, we know that Benedictine monks had been hostile to the brutal methods of ancient pedagogy, preferring to trust the innate virtues of the infantile nature. Benedict counseled respect for the judgment of the young monk, "since Samuel and Daniel were placed in judgment over the elders from their youth." He also wanted the young to be included in the chapter meetings, "for often the Lord reveals better ways of proceeding to the young." The Venerable Bede loved to recall the four qualities of the child: "He does not persist in anger; he does not carry a grudge; he is not delighted with the beauty of women; and he says what he thinks." Commenting on the proverb, "Madness is rooted in the heart of a child," he explained that "child" was meant in a figurative sense. "For we know many children to whom wisdom has been given."[31] It was therefore necessary to respect children and not brutalize them, for, as Chrodegang of Metz said: "One who wants to snatch away the wheel risks breaking the vase. We must uproot vices prudently and charitably, following the maxim, 'Nothing too much.' " In his commentary on the Rule of Saint Benedict, Paul the Deacon advised masters:

> Act with moderation and do not birch them, or they will return to their beastliness after correction. A master who, in his anger, reprimands a child beyond measure should be pacified and corrected. Strong-arm methods may render a child naughtier than ever.

Paul envisaged that children would be supervised by a group of three or four masters. He advised that they should not be expected to live in overly harsh material conditions but should be provided comfortable clothing, abundant nourishment, and heat in winter.[32]

Regarding adolescents, the masters were less trusting. Young men had to be put on guard against their awakening sexual appetites and taught to remain chaste. They feared what an Irish penitential modestly termed "children's games" and the troubled friendships of older men for younger ones. Monastic authorities prescribed punishments of forty to a hundred days of fasting.[33] Moreover, Paul the Deacon wrote:

> Adolescents should be guarded and supervised until they are old enough to pass out from under their masters. A young man of fifteen who seems sufficiently reasonable should be freed from tutelage, and the abbot may trust him to an honest and pious monk who can supervise him and keep him near while he studies.

Alcuin also wrote counsels of moderation to the masters and pupils of his Abbey of Saint-Martin of Tours:

> You elders, raise the young folk in a spirit of sweetness. . . . Consider adolescents as your sons. . . . Instruct them through good example. . . . You adolescents, be submissive to your elders as to your fathers. . . .[34]

But could anyone keep a child or an adolescent from playing, even if he were a ninth-century shaveling monk? The masters were supposed to plan some moments of relaxation for them between religious offices and periods of intellectual or manual labor. The designer of the plan of Saint-Gall did not forget a recreation room (*vacatio*). Paul the Deacon suggested that "to strengthen the children and satisfy their natural needs, they should, at the discretion of the masters, be sent each week or month into a field or some other place where they can play for an hour under the supervision of their masters." One hour a month, or even a week, seems very short to us! The young must have had other relaxations. Certainly the scheduling of time was less strict on Sundays and feastdays. The arrival of an important guest was always an occasion for diversion. King Conrad granted in perpetuity three days' holiday for the shavelings in memory of his visit to a monastery on Christmas in the year 910. The young monks would then have the right to do whatever they liked, even to imprisoning the monastery guests. This is one of the most ancient witnesses to the Feast of the Innocents (December 28) which was ultimately to be celebrated by all the clerks and monks of the West.[35]

Professors

The instruction of children was confided to particular masters whom our texts indiscriminately name *magistri scholae, scholastici, capita scolae*, which becomes *capiscol* or, more rarely, *doctores* or *preceptores*. This distinction between spiritual and intellectual masters was a ninth-century innovation. "Children must be confided to the care of a well-tested elder, though another might instruct them," said the Council of 816.[36] However, it is probable that only the important schools could effectuate this separation of powers.

In the Carolingian world there were some great professors whose renown went beyond their own frontiers. Raised at Ferrières, Lupus went out to spend eight years with Hrabanus Maurus at Fulda. The latter, a Frank by birth, had gone to study with Alcuin at Tours. Alcuin, indeed, had shaped more than one of the future masters of the Empire. We can even establish genealogies of masters: Alcuin "engendered" Hrabanus Maurus, who "engendered"

Lupus, who educated Heric of Auxerre, who in turn was the master of Remi. The poorest monasteries sought great professors for at least temporary sojourns. Thus the Abbot of Grandfel, in the Diocese of Basel, persuaded Iso, master of Saint-Gall, to teach in his monastery on condition that he might return to Saint-Gall three times a year.[37]

The masters would divide the pupils among themselves. They might teach them, as at Utrecht, for one trimester each or, as at York, divide them according to subject: reading, writing, chant. In the great schools they had assistants, who often succeeded in turn. Some pupils were also confided to more advanced students, *seniores,* and asked, in their turn, to help those still younger. The veneration of these pupils, particularly the older pupils, for their masters is attested in several letters which have been preserved. The ties which bound them did not weaken over the years. Masters followed their pupils' careers, asked to see them again from time to time at the monastery, and occasionally requested verses recalling the happy hours of their intellectual communion.[38]

A true master was distinguished not only for his learning but also for his devotion and disinterest. Education was free. Alcuin, in a distych, warned travelers that one road led to a tavern where a man would have to purchase wine while the other led to the school where instruction in the understanding of holy books was free.[39] To be sure, abbatial and episcopal fortunes were sufficient to accommodate the masters. Families paid for the education of their children with donations of land to abbeys, as we have seen. And some pupils sought the means to give special gratuities to their masters. Young Rupert, the future Bishop of Metz, wrote to his parents from his school at Saint-Gall that he was pleased with the instruction he was being given and wished them to send some new clothes and something for the remuneration of his masters.[40]

Pupils at Work
Let us follow young Rupert into the school at Saint-Gall, since we are lucky enough to have a map from that period. The school (*domus communis scolae*) was north of the abbatial church, surrounded with a barrier which defined the

quarter within which were exercised "the ambitions of studious youth," according to the legend. The rectangular edifice comprehended two large recreation rooms, lighted from above, opening out to courts around which were a dozen small rooms, 4 by 4 meters, the *mansiunculae scolasticorum.* Facing the principal entry, a gutter ran to the latrines which accommodated fifteen places. On the side, the length of the church, was the master's house which had two rooms: a public room and a chamber and latrines. Benedict of Aniane's reforms of 817 decreed that this "extern" school be open to scholars who wished to benefit from the monks' teaching. Oblates and novices destined for the monastic life were instructed at an "intern" school joined to the novices' lodgings east of the church.[41]

School furniture was always the same, whether in the extern school, the intern school, or even a canonical school. As in antiquity, children were given wax tablets and writing pens or styluses. They reproduced what had been noted on parchment. Smaragdus' pupils took notes on their tablets before transcribing them on "membranes." Hrabanus Maurus, for fear of losing the essentials of Alcuin's lessons, kept a little notebook of glosses.[42] We have some manuscripts which appear to be scholars' notebooks or perhaps the masters' own notes. One, dated 813, contains a questionnaire on medical discoveries, on the noises made by various animals (*bos mugit, eques hinnit, asinus rudit, elefans barrit* . . .), the elements of computation and grammar, medical recipes, and a letter on baptism.[43] Books were too precious to be entrusted to pupils. They would have to attain a reasonable age before they could take part in the annual distribution reported by Hildemar of Civate. In Lent, the books which had been loaned to each monk during the year would be brought to the librarian in chapter. Each monk placed the book he had read on a carpet, and the prior questioned him to determine whether or not he had mastered the reading. Then each monk was asked to choose a new book whose title was marked on a register with the name of the borrower.[44] Most of the younger monks had not attained this status. When once they learned the alphabet, they practiced laboriously in class or in the refectory. A more learned brother stayed at their sides to correct them gently when they made a mistake. Knowledge of reading meant knowledge of Latin, which was the literary language. As we noted above, the study of Latin demanded much effort, especially from pupils of Germanic origin, and the results were sometimes deceiving. One day, when Boniface was visiting the great palace of Pfalzel, down river from Trier, where the aristocrat Addula lived, the lord's grandson, aged fifteen, was requested to read aloud during the meal. "Do you understand what you are reading?" Boniface asked him. "Yes," answered the young man. "Then explain it to us." The adolescent retrieved the book and read the Latin text once more. "No," interrupted Boniface, "I am asking you to explain it in your own tongue." Gregory admitted that he could not do it. Having listened to the commentary which the missionary supplied, he was overcome and begged to follow after Boniface.[45]

Pupils began learning Latin by reading the little texts which Roman schoolboys had read before them: Cato's distychs, fables by Phaedrus and Avian as well as Solomon's proverbs, Alcuin's *Precepta vivendi,* and monastic apothegms or sentences. They learned to shape ordinary vocabulary into short sentences in the form of dialogues with their master. A manuscript from Saint-Gall preserves such a conversation between a pupil and his master. It begins:

> What else besides the oil and mustard should I carry on the plate?
> I will give you beans and gourds, and I will look in the pot for something to relieve your stomach. In fact, you are very tired of writing, and I myself am weary of talking.
> Thank you. Your throat is hoarse, and I would like to rest a little. . . .[46]

Pupils had glossaries drawn according to the plan of Isidore of Seville's *Etymologies* which provided the names of beasts, utensils, rooms of the house, just as one sees in the glossary of Cassell. In other dictionaries, like the glossary of Reichenau, the student could find the explanation of Biblical words. But it was not enough to know vocabulary; the sentence had to be construed. The master worked from a manual of elementary grammar in use since the fourth century, the *Ars Minor* of Donatus which Alcuin said was recommended to beginning children. The instruction was often laid out as a dialogue between master and pupil or between two pupils. Alcuin confirmed that "instruction requires frequent interrogation," and he used the "catechetical" method to instruct monks or royal pupils in grammar and rhetoric. One of his pieces begins:

> There were two young persons, a Frank and a Saxon, at Master Alcuin's school who had just recently penetrated the thickets of the grammatical wilderness. For that reason, they were pleased to employ questions and answers to strengthen their memories and cull some of the rules of literary science.
>
> The Frank said to the Saxon: "All right, Saxon, since you are the elder, you should answer my questions. I am fourteen, and I believe that you are fifteen."
>
> "I accept," answered the Saxon, "if you don't make the questions too hard or ask things pertaining to the philosophical disciplines. . . ."[47]

The dialogue touched on letters, vowels, consonants, syllables, names, relieved by innocent pleasantries and pauses. In an oral civilization, memory played a capital role. School children could accumulate the most diverse knowledge, facilitating the operation by memorizing versified tracts on grammar and computation. They could be seen, repeatedly chanting these mnemonic poems in cloister or at recreation leavened with versified declensions such as that which Sedulius sent as a joke to a certain Robert:

> *Bonus vir est Robertus*
> *Laudes gliscunt Roberti*
> *Christo, fave Roberto*
> *Longaevum fac Robertum. . . .*[48]

Learning was transmitted orally as well. Masters and sometimes guests conducted interrogations in passing. Paul the Deacon tells us of a prior who profited from the presence of learned guests by designating a child to converse with him on grammar, chant, calculations, or some other discipline.[49] In order not to embarrass the student, he pretended that he was not listening very attentively. But when the guest was gone, he went over it with the child, pointing out his insufficiencies in interrogation or response.

As the pupil became more learned, he made use of his parchment notebooks to gloss the texts which were explained to him. But he still had to know how to write, which was not quickly or easily learned. Unlike our present methods, their apprenticeship did not link reading and writing. Charlemagne himself was perfectly well able to read and was quite learned; but he did not know how to write, for he had begun too late. Writing was a particular technique learned by specialists, scribes, in the scriptorium. Inversely, quite a good scribe might have no penchant for study. Some "pen tests" on the margins of manuscripts relay the impressions of masters or pupils: "I am an ass who does not know how to write." Or again, "Child, practice on your tablets so that you may be able to write on parchment."[50]

Arithmetic, also, could be done orally or with gestures. Digital computation began in antiquity and continued to be utilized through the high Middle Ages. No one surpassed the classical manual of Bede. The last three fingers of the left hand, folded on the palm, meant the units. Different positions of thumb and index finger indicated decimals. On the right hand, hundreds and thousands were indicated by folding the fingers in a certain manner. For tens and hundreds of thousands, first the left and then the right hand touched breast, navel, and thigh. Thus one arrives at a million.[51] Small arithmetic problems were posed as riddles to children. For example: three brothers each had a sister. The six travelers came to a river where a single boat would not hold more than two persons. Since morality required that each sister cross with her brother, how did they do it? Or else: Six workers were engaged in building a house. Five were experienced and one an apprentice. The five men divided a salary of 25 deniers a day among themselves, subtracting the apprentice's pay which represented half the salary of each of the masters. How much will each receive?

Still more classic was the problem of the child killed by the serpent: a boy chased a boar and killed him but stepped on a serpent who gave him a fatal bite. His mother said to him, "My son, had you lived as long as you did and yet as long again and then half as much plus a year, you would have been a hundred years old" (16½ years × 2 = 33; 33 × 2 = 66; 66 and 33 and 1 = 100). Dhuoda often used this sort of problem, writing to her son Guillaume: "You have completed four times four years. If you had that much, plus as much, plus the half of the half (16 plus 16 plus 4), I would speak otherwise to you."[52]

Beyond these small problems, pupils had to be initiated into ecclesiastical computations—that is, the calculation of the years since the Incarnation, the indiction (cycles of fifteen years), epacts and concurrents (number of days of the solar year exceeding the lunar year), age of the moon on a particular day, etc.* This education was carried out progressively, and it was a rare student who gained perfect mastery of all the tables and wheels of computation. Carolingian manuscripts abundantly contain mnemonic poems, didactic encyclopedias in catechetical form, demonstrating the interest and difficulty of studying computation in the schools.[53] With this discipline, we can approach the higher levels of the program of studies.

Secondary Schools

The clerk or monk who wanted to go further with his studies began the liberal arts cycle. A much admired painting of the seven liberal arts ornamented the palace of Theodulf of Orleans. The fresco has disappeared, but we may still imagine it from the bishop's description.[54] At the foot of a great tree stood Grammar, the root of all knowledge, with a scraper in her left hand to obliterate error. On either side were Good Sense and Renown. Rhetoric and Dialectic occupied the upper branches. The former carried a walled city, for she intervenes in civic affairs and lawsuits. Dialectic, which enables us to distinguish truth from falsehood, had a wily serpent as attribute. Leaving aside Morality and its four virtues on the left, we can look higher to the superior liberal arts which form the Quadrivium: Arithmetic, Music, Geometry, and Astrology—which was, in fact, astronomy—all furnished with instruments symbolizing their function. In commissioning this fresco, Theodulf supplied as model the

* The term *epacts* applies to intercalary days.

poem of evocation to the liberal arts which had been written by an obscure pagan rhetor, Martianus Capella of Carthage, at the beginning of the fifth century. The work was written in the form of a novel, *The Marriage of Mercury and Philology*, and had an astounding success in the Middle Ages. Carolingians multiplied the manuscripts—we have about twelve—which glossed and commented on this scholarly manual.[55]

The liberal arts were not studied as ends in themselves. They were intended as an introduction to the "art of arts": philosophy or Christian wisdom. In a letter to Charlemagne, Alcuin expressed the desire to see a new Athens born in Francia, not only based on the liberal arts but sustained by the seven gifts of the Holy Ghost. The learned would use secular disciplines to understand and comment on the ultimate text, the Bible. Alcuin wrote to his pupils:

> My dear sons, may your youth advance on the road of the Arts daily until, in riper age and more robust spirits, you may attain the summits of Holy Scripture. From this beginning, you will become the fully-armed defenders and invincible preachers of the true faith.[56]

The Scholars at Work

> I read, I write, I study Wisdom day and night; I pray to God, my Lord; I eat and drink willingly; I invoke the Muses in verse; I sleep deeply at night and pray to God during the day.[57]

Thus Sedulius described his use of his time. Another Irishman pictures himself working in the company of his cat:

> I love, better than all glory, to sit in diligent study over my little book. Pangur Ban has no envy of me, for he finds a mouse in his snares while only an arduous explication falls into mine. He bumps against the wall and I against the severity of science. . . . He rejoices when he has a mouse in his paw as I rejoice when I have understood a difficult question. . . . Each of us loves his art. . . .[58]

Picture these learned folk, peaceful men, disposing of a harmonious leisure, reluctantly responding to an invitation come from court but opening their arms joyfully to the friend or courier bringing a manuscript they lack. Their libraries are never rich enough. They are always searching for well-edited manuscripts to correct errors in their own copies. Praising a Ciceronian treatise on rhetoric, Lupus of Ferrières wrote to Einhard:

> I possess it, it is true, but it is full of errors and many gaps, which is why I was collating my manuscripts with one I have discovered here. I believed it would be better than my own, but find it was more faulty.[59]

The learned man employed a notary to whom he dictated his own remarks or wrote them on a wax tablet from which the scribe could put a clean copy on parchment. Hrabanus Maurus, whose means were apparently straitened, deplored the need to be both notary and copyist for himself. Generally teams were at work under the direction of a master. Florus, Deacon of Lyon, who owned a very rich library, marked passages for recopying in the manuscripts he studied. Though autographed manuscripts are very rare, personal notes by Alcuin, Lupus, or Heric of Auxerre appear here and there.[60] Carolingian savants were perpetual students, never ashamed to show their ignorance and ask for explanations from more learned men about them. Having failed to understand Boethius' works on arithmetic, Lupus appealed to Einhard for help. In the same letter, he queried him on the quantity of certain syllables. He interrogated another correspondent on irregular verbs.[61] On the other side, however, these savants never hesitated to pass the most severe judgments on the literary production of their colleagues. Hincmar of Reims, for example, considered his nephew, Hincmar of Laon, too prone to use an Irish style. He delivered the following critique:

> You are convicted of vaingloriousness by your abstruse language, your compositions of words ransacked from glossaries and pointlessly interpolated. Your literary compositions have reflected this habit from your tenderest youth; above all, do you strain yourself in your verse and figurative poems to sow

words of foreign origin, abstruse and improper vocables, terms stripped of all utility and meaning, which you do not comprehend yourself . . . simply to stupefy the ignorant or to flatter listeners with sensitive ears. . . .[62]

Learned Carolingians had facile pens, too facile. They indulged themselves with lengthy developments of profane and religious subjects alike which repels the modern reader. They drew a little from themselves and much from others without being careful to cite the authors from whom they borrowed. They seized upon religious controversies to display their qualities as rhetoricians or dialecticians. The discussions between Ratramnus of Corbie and Paschasius Radbertus on the subject of the Eucharist or the virgin birth, between Gottschalk and Hincmar of Reims on the subject of predestination, were tense and often lacking in courtesy. Having intervened in the quarrel over predestination, John Scotus was treated most inconsiderately by Bishop Prudentius of Troyes, who called his doctrine nothing but "imprudent blasphemy, vain and inflated science, sophistic insanity, wordy dispute. . . ."[63] Nevertheless, John Scotus was the author of one of the rare original works, and he had attempted to go beyond the commonplaces of Latin theology by reference to the Greek fathers.

Knowledge of Greek, in fact, was rare among Carolingians outside of certain circles at Rome and in southern Italy, in Francia at Corbie, Saint-Gall, Laon, and Saint-Denis. The monks at the latter monastery were interested in the work of Denys the Areopagite, having persuaded themselves that he and Denis the Martyr were one and the same person. In 827, ambassadors from the Byzantine Emperor, Michael the Stammerer, presented to the monastery a manuscript of the works of Denys which was translated by a team of three monks by order of Abbot Hilduin, a pupil of Alcuin. A reader read the text aloud while a translator enunciated the corresponding Latin words and a scribe put them on parchment. However, so literal a translation was not satisfactory and was corrected by John Scotus Erigena who had settled at the court of Charles the Bald. John himself undertook translations of Gregory of Nyssa, Gregory of Nazianzus, and a tract of Maximus the Confessor.[64] John kept in touch with the school of Laon and the pupils trained there. Martin of Laon, among others, used his famous glossary (manuscript of Laon, 444). This Graeco-Latin dictionary was enriched with citations from various authors, with translations, with Greek poems by John and Martin, and even some fragments of bilingual dialogue which enabled learned men to say in Greek: "Bring wine, put it on the table, and pour us something to drink. . . ." Nor did John Scotus confine himself to translating Greek theologians. He used their model of a dialogue between master and pupil in writing his own great five-volume work on the *Divisions of Nature.* This book, the first philosophic and theological synthesis of the Middle Ages, astounded his contemporaries with its audacity and novelty, and they condemned it in the end.[65]

In general, Carolingian authors compensated for the absence of a strong philosophical turn with their mastery of the Latin language, whose beauty they had rediscovered. Their poems, in the classical metric fashion or in the rhythmic manner, are the most beautiful legacies of the Carolingian Renaissance. If, in their youth, these poets were seduced by the charms of pagan poetry, their scruples against sacrificing on the altar of the Muses were expressed in old age. Theodulf wrote to the pupils of Orleans, "Young children, these games are fitting at your age." The aged Alcuin, who had so loved Virgil in his youth, advised his monks at Saint-Martin not to read him. Carried away with zeal, Ermenrich of Ellwangen wrote:

> Let us renounce that liar Virgil and leave him to bury himself with Apollo and the Muses at the bottom of the Styx. Let him embrace Proserpine and attend to Orpheus addressing songs to the infernal gods for the recovery of his Eurydice: how the King of Heaven must curse such vain imagination! Lord, what else shall we call this but excrement falling from your carriage horses! But sometimes, even in shit, gold can be found. As you know, fertilizer prepares the field for a more abundant grain harvest: thus, though the pagan poets speak impure words to the degree that they are untrue, yet they can be very useful in preparing us to understand the divine word.[66]

This diatribe is sufficient testimony to the dilemma of the Carolingian poets. Every Christian humanist knew or would come to know the same conflict.

The Learned Laymen

Among these clerks and learned monks we must not forget the existence of lay aristocrats for whom cultivation was one of the criteria of nobility. A hagiographical account of the youth of a saint born into the aristocracy does not neglect to mention: "He was sent to school; he was instructed in the liberal arts, 'as is the custom with sons of nobles,' or 'as befits a noble.'" Was that a formula describing a desirable ideal, or was it ever realized? We certainly have enough witnesses to affirm that there were learned aristocrats beyond the princes and their immediate families. When a child began to outgrow his toys, his parents, particularly his mother, taught him to read the psalter, a book of elementary pious readings which could be carried in the hand. Through learning the psalter, he was familiarized with grammar, chant, and the rudiments of ecclesiastical offices. Gerald of Aurillac's biographer, Odo, born about 880, was confided to a priest living in the paternal castle who gave him the first elements of his instruction. At nine years of age, he was sent to the court of Fulk of Anjou.

The athletic training which young people later received threatened to erode the foundations of their intellectual training. While mothers insisted that their sons give themselves over to reading like clerks, their fathers preferred to see them learn to mount a horse, draw the bow, and skillfully cast falcons.[67] But the young aristocrat never completely lost the memory of his early instruction. He could always sign his name, sometimes in a clumsy hand, at the bottom of an act. We have the autograph signatures of men and women beside crosses from several authentic documents from Italy and southern France.[68] But even signing with a cross does not mean that one did not know how to write. Princes, who generally did know how to write, still placed their monogram at the bottom of their acts.

When young people arrived at court, they found a favorable milieu for study. They shared the activities of princes and formed ties of friendship with clerks. Alcuin, who numbered many laymen among his correspondents, often reiterated that intellectual cultivation is not a clerical privilege. Einhard, after having received his initial instruction at Fulda, was sent to court at seventeen to pursue his studies.

Like clerks, laymen loved books, and their libraries were well stocked. Charlemagne collected not only gospels, sacramentaries, and luxurious psalters in his palace but also profane works. His successors, who were also bibliophiles, commissioned manuscripts from different scriptoria throughout the Empire and asked savants for books to deepen their learning. Lothair asked Hrabanus Maurus to give· him a commentary on the books of Jeremiah and Ezekiel. He asked Angelomus of Luxeuil for a commentary on the Song of Songs, whose reading could constitute a retreat from the tumults of political life and console him for the death of his the instruction of the young Charles the Bald. The latter, whose secular and religious culture equaled that of any of the clerks of his entourage, loved the two manuscripts and interested himself in all the productions of the intellect. About half a hundred books were dedicated to him. When he left for Italy, in 877, he destined the books of his "treasury" to be divided between the churches of Compiègne and Saint-Denis.[69]

Following the example of princes, lay aristocrats also collected books. Angilbert enriched the library of Saint-Riquier with a gift of two hundred manuscripts for which we have a catalogue. Count Gerward gave about twenty books to the Abbey of Lorsch. We have lists of the contents of the libraries of Marquis Ewrard and Count Eccard. The same titles were in each of them. There were numerous religious books: Latin or Germanic Gospels, psalters with commentaries, liturgical books, and works of exegesis. To cultivate their spirituality, these aristocrats also used booklets of private prayers, a sort of layman's breviary, saints' lives, the *Synonyms* or *Lamentations of a Sinful Soul*, by Isidore of Seville, in several forms, and the "mirrors" which Alcuin and Smaragdus composed. As was proper to men with political responsibilities, their libraries included historical and juridical books: the *City of God*, Orosius' *History*, Gregory of Tours's *History of the Franks*, and Paul the Deacon's

History of the Lombards. Along with collections of Roman and Barbarian laws, there were books on medicine and geography. Vegetius' treatise on military art and a treatise on agriculture, doubtless that of Columella, completed this diverse collection.

Collating the titles to which another layperson, Dhuoda, wife of Bernard of Septimania, made reference in her *Manual*, we can conclude that this cultivated woman possessed some exegetical books, or at least choice excerpts from them, *florilegia* from both spiritual and moral works. She is known to have consulted numerous works, citing Isidore, Augustine, Gregory, Prudentius, some saints' lives, and even the grammarian Donatus, whose poetry she discusses. She may have learned the versified paraphrase of the grammarian of which some examples have been preserved.[70] Dhuoda, who had probably been educated in Austrasia, wanted to be able to give her sons the benefit of her culture. In a letterbook composed over two years, 841 to 843, she compiled, in a language which aimed at elegance, an abridgment of all her theological and moral knowledge. In addition, as a "book of record," she recalled the principal moments in her life and gave the names of famous members of the family.[71]

We do not know of any other woman who wielded the pen in the ninth century. But we do know of other books written by lay aristocrats. Angilbert, the relative of Charlemagne, loved writing poetry which earned him the flattering nickname "Homer." His son, Nithard, inherited his literary talents. Growling all the while, he composed a history of the sons of Louis the Pious, at the request of his cousin, Charles the Bald, which remains one of the best chronicles of the age. Einhard, who was married after his stay at court, displayed undeniable literary qualities in his correspondence—nearly 69 letters which have descended to us—and in other works. There is a clear relationship between the works of lay and ecclesiastical authors. Layfolk were sent to school to the clerks and borrowed their habits of thought and expression.

But there were other lay aristocrats, the majority, who did not know Latin. Were they as illiterate as the common people? Was there no literary culture expressed in

Romance or Germanic languages? Were all the princes surrounded by magnates like Wigbod, who sneered on hearing the precious poems of Theodulf? And were they insensitive to all literature? There is indirect testimony to suggest that some of the lay aristocrats were interested in profane poetry which they sung among themselves. For them, Charlemagne ordered the collection of "the very ancient barbarous poems which sung of the histories and wars of bygone kings." These, unhappily, have disappeared. At the end of the century, a Saxon poet wrote that "poems in the vulgar tongue (*vulgaria carmina*) sang the praises of the ancestors of Charles and his relatives. They sang of the Pepins, the Charleses, the Clovises, the Theodorics, the Carlomans, and the Lothiars."[72] The *Hildebrandlied*, written at Fulda about 800, glorified war and single combat, providing a wealth of material from which the aristocratic ethic was defined. Other epic poems exalted the warlike virtues of the Franks. Orally transmitted from generation to generation, they were later put into writing. The eleventh-century and twelfth-century *chansons de geste*, the *Song of Roland*, the *Song of William of Orange*, the *Coronation of Louis*, *Floovant*, and more, all drew their material from Carolingian history.[73]

Aristocrats also loved to listen to persons whom the texts call *joculator* (from which we get *jongleur*), or *bardi*, who composed and sang humorous or erotic poems. Nor were they the only ones who had such tastes. Councils denounced bishops and clerks who wasted their time and risked the loss of their souls by listening to these "lusty songs."[74] About 850, Otfrid of Wissembourg paraphrased the Gospels in verse in the Germanic tongue to substitute for these "profane songs of the laity." For the same reason, Louis the Pious had a Saxon, reputed to be an excellent poet, compose the poem of Heliand (*The Redeemer*) which "surpassed in beauty all the poems of the Germanic language." In the six thousand verses which have come down to us, Christ was presented as a prince surrounded by his vassals; the shepherds as the guardians of a flock of horses; the palace of Herod and even the site of the wedding at Cana were described as the hall of a Germanic chief; Satan becomes invisible by using a *Tarnkappe*.* Peter's violent

* In German legend, the *Tarnkappe* is a cloak of invisibility.

reaction in striking off the ear of Malchus is praised while the invitation to love our enemies is passed over in silence. Even when he did follow the Gospels closely, the poet adapted them to his Germanic public. Similarly, the *Muspilli*, dedicated to the young Louis, son of Louis the Pious, described a curious combat between Elias and the Anti-Christ. Though he carried the day, Elias was wounded, and his blood running out on the ground caused the conflagration of the world and the destruction of the universe. In addition to these Christian epics, hagiographic poems provided idealized models to the nobility. Saint Gall was celebrated by Ratpert in a *carmen barbaricum*. The extraordinary adventures of Saint George were related in the *Georgslied*.[75]

The culture which expressed itself through writing and books was, as we have seen, reserved for an aristocratic minority. It remained foreign to the great mass of the population. For them, words and deeds provided means of expression.

The people manifested their joy or sorrow through singing and dancing which, though it appeared profane to some clerks, was charged with an incantatory religious power. Women glorified a victor by dancing and clapping their hands. Villagers celebrated an anniversary or wedding or simply a Sunday by making frenzied rounds about the church. They loudly honored their dead at the tombs in the cemetery. Some folk marked their adhesion to a particular group by participating in banquets and drinking parties.

The Church understood the importance of these fetes in the life of the people. Even while they fought against the apparent pagan survivals these popular expressions represented, clerics sought to bring this innate inclination into God's service through song and expressive gestures. They believed that incorporating mass participation into religious services contributed as much to their christianization as did moral preaching. Thus we must examine the origins of that astounding liturgical growth which characterized the Carolingian epoch.

Liturgical Revival

The Carolingian princes believed that they held their authority from God. Thus they considered the organization of worship and the guidance of the Christian people to salvation to be their primary mission. All people, from the Emperor down to the least of slaves, were expected to render perpetual acts of reverence toward God. Clerks and monks were to ensure prayers of adoration and praise in close liaison with the prince, supreme lord of the clergy.

Accordingly, royal legislation aimed to organize and unify the rituals of prayer. Charlemagne devoted numerous capitularies to liturgical life. He regulated Sunday rest, the assiduity of the faithful in attending to offices, the obligation of prayer, religious feasts, baptism, penitence, communion, and so on.[1] Pursuing the work of his father, Pepin, he attempted to replace Gallican liturgies with Roman liturgy. He had copies made of the Gregorian "sacramentary" which Pope Hadrian sent to him in 781. Six years later, he reminded all the clergy that the Roman chant should be used everywhere. We know that the reform was applied at Aix, Metz (thanks to Drogo), Lyon, and Saint-Riquier. But elsewhere? In 831, Louis the Pious sent Amalarius of Metz to Rome to secure a new antiphonary from Pope Gregory IV, "to restore the Gallican chant and offices to the Roman rite." Certainly, the incident seems to show that the Roman liturgy was not imposed without difficulty.[2]

The liturgical revival inspired many tracts and much discussion throughout the Empire. Alcuin and his pupil Amalarius, Agobard and Florus at Lyon, Hrabanus Maurus the German, and Walafrid Strabo studied the significance of liturgical acts. Amalarius sought allegories in the Mass to renew the sacred symbols by going beyond them. The episcopal throne was the throne of Christ; the censer represented the body of Christ from which rose the prayers of the saints; the seven candelabra carried by the acolytes signified the seven gifts of the Holy Ghost; the deacons gathered around the celebrant were the apostles, and the sub-deacons symbolized the women at the foot of the cross; the elevation of the host and chalice represented the raising of the body by Joseph of Arimathea, and so forth. Amalarius was attacked for this method of allegorical explication, but it was frequently revived during the Middle Ages.[3]

The Sacred Enclosure

If the allegorical exegesis of Amalarius was not followed by all, Carolingian liturgists unanimously insisted on the religious symbolism of sacred places and objects, following both Jewish and Germanic traditions of the sacred enclosure. Rituals were concentrated in a well-defined sacred space outside of which demonic forces swarmed. A church, regardless of size or whether it was built of wood or stone, was a sacred place. Christians were supposed to penetrate the enclosure with awe, desiring to glimpse the marvels of the other world. In the sacramentary of Drogo (825) the ceremony for dedicating a church emphasized aspersions, unctions, and prayers accompanying the consecration of the sacred space.[4] The clerks were put in possession of their own domain, the area enclosed by the chancel, where the unconsecrated, the laity, must not penetrate. In the center, rose the altar, a massive table of stone or marble surmounted by a *ciborium*, a baldaquin sustained by four columns lit with a crown of light.* Beyond the main altar, a number of secondary altars containing relics were placed in the choir and nave. Seventeen of these are indicated on the plan of Saint-Gall; Angilbert established forty of them at Saint-Riquier.

Sacred Objects

The clergy were responsible for the maintenance of the fabric and furnishings of a church. Regino of Prüm drew up a questionnaire for a bishop's pastoral visits. The visitor was to learn who had consecrated the church, to check that the roof was intact and that no doves or other birds were nesting in the eaves, causing filthiness and noise. Of what metal had the bells been made? Were the altar linens new or worn? Were the relics well guarded? Of what metal were the patten and chalice made? Was the corporal of good quality linen? Were there censer and pyxsis on the altar? How many clerks understood the arrangement of the altar?[5] Carolingian liturgy provided a special and novel role for three categories of objects. Bells not only summoned the faithful but were thought to have power to chase demons and the disorderly persons away. Lamps, arranged around the altars or carried in procession, triumphed over night, one of the most redoubtable enemies. Finally, standing or portable censers burned a perfume brought at great expense from the Orient. Rising like a prayer, incense enveloped the offerings disposed about the altar. During the ninth century this custom, borrowed from Oriental and Jewish rituals, spread throughout the Empire.

* A *baldaquin*, a canopy supported by four columns, is usually made of cloth, but it can be stationary and made from other materials as in the case of the famous Bernini baldaquin of Saint Peter's.

The Problem of Images

Amid the religious objects, images occupied a special place which had been the object of much discussion. The Caro-which was heatedly discussed. The Carolingians greeted the Council of Nicaea's rehabilitation of the cult of images in 787 coolly because they understood it badly. In preparation for the Council of Frankfurt in 794, Charlemagne had a dossier collected under the title *Libri Carolini.* One of the collaborators was Alcuin, who disapproved of the adoration of images as a cause of scandal to the humble or a cause of pagan idolatry. He called it a sacrilege to call an image holy or to cense it, because, he said jocularly, if one were to cense a picture representing the flight into Egypt, it might be either the Virgin or the ass who received the incense.[6] He allowed the image a non-religious decorative value. For that reason, he did not consider it necessary to call for the destruction of images like Claudius of Turin.[7] But he saw nothing but artistic or decorative value in them. But if images were to be used for the instruction of the faithful, an inscription (*titulus*) should provide explication of the painting:

> Picture a woman holding a child on her knees. If there were no inscription, how could you know whether it represented the Virgin with Christ, Venus with Aeneas, Alcmene with Hercules, or Andromache with Astyanax?

In any case:

> Men can understand things without seeing images but not without the knowledge of God. Moreover, it is a very unfortunate spirit which depends on the help of painters' pictures to remember the life of Christ and cannot draw inspiration from its own powers.[8]

Hrabanus Maurus answered Hatto of Fulda's claim that "painting was the most delectable of arts" by countering that the labor of the scribe, the effort of the chanter, or the application of reciters and readers were all superior to the work of painting. For the source of salvation is the Scripture.[9]

Paintings were, indeed, the only tolerable images;

statues were totally absent for they recalled idols too strongly. Only at the end of the century reliquary busts began to appear. This new stage of religious art, from which medieval sculpture developed, did not appear without scandal. Carolingian reticence regarding images can be readily explained by the ever-present fear of reviving pagan practices as well as by the influence of the Old Testament which we have already noted. In this area, Christians and Jews of the Empire found themselves in agreement.

Sacred Seasons

For the faithful, the sacred place was an anticipation of Paradise. Sacred times periodically permitted communion with eternity. The Church could not or would not suppress the antique fashion of counting time. The twelve months retained their pagan names. Einhard mentions that Charlemagne would have liked to give Germanic names to the months of the year, but he did not pursue the matter. The months were still divided into three periods: calends, nones, ides. The day was divided into twelve hours, shorter in winter than in summer, since the first hour corresponded to the rising of the sun and the last to its setting. In addition to the sun dial, water clocks were coming into use in aristocratic circles. The author of the Royal Annals marvelled at the sight of the clock which the Byzantine Emperor sent to Charlemagne:

> A mechanism moved by water marked the course of the twelve hours, and, at the moment when each hour was completed, an equal number of little brass balls fell on a bell placed below, making it chime to their falling. Then twelve knights came out of twelve windows.[10]

The peasants continued as they always had to mark time by the rhythm of days and seasons. The bell from church or monastery reminded them that there was another time, God's time. The priest reminded them that they must be aware of the feasts that punctuated the year: the beginning of winter was marked by Saint Martin's day; the return of spring means Easter time more than the renewal of vegetation; Saint John marks the beginning of summer and Saint Remi the vintage time. Every three hours the bell tolled, calling the monks to matins, lauds, prime, tierce, sext, nones, vespers, and compline. Christians were invited to follow the example of the monks and pray several times a day: "When you arise in the morning, repeat the name of God three times and the Lord's Prayer. Chant the canonical hours and say the prayers that pertain to the different moments of the day . . . ," Dhuoda counseled her son.[11] Booklets of private prayer, breviaries for the laity, and pocket psalters were written in the eighth and ninth centuries for those who desired to pray to God in unison with the monks.[12]

Sunday was the great religious climax of the week. Princes and bishops endlessly repeated that no work was to be done on that day. Even the most alienated swineherds and shepherds were invited to assist at the Mass. The faithful were urged to prepare themselves for celebration of this holy day, abstaining from sexual relations, dancing, and commercial transactions: "Honor the Sabbath, doing no servile work then, nor tending your own fields either, nor your meadow nor your vines if it is a question of hard labor. Do not engage in any legal affair on the Lord's Day. In the kitchen prepare only what is needed to nourish yourself," counseled Pirmin.[13]

If possible, the faithful were to arrive with lamps in hand to assist at Matins, fasting from Saturday night to Sunday. They would go home after Mass but return in the evening for vespers.[14] They took holy water at the entrance of the church, remaining always in the area reserved for them below the chancel, chanting or listening to chants.

Liturgical Chant

Though we do not lack tracts on musical theory, we know little of the performance of religious chant. We have been told that clerks and monks were supposed to learn chanting in school. The Council of 816 urged cantors to be alert in exalting the souls of the people not only by the sublimity of the text but also by the sweetness of the sound: "not with a voice too loud or disordered or unregulated but in an even and rounded voice so that the spirit of those who chant will be nourished by the sweet thought of the Psalms while the souls of the auditors will feed on their suave modulation." The Roman chant, called "Gregorian," was considered most apt to sustain the prayer of clergy and people. Though kings imposed it everywhere, Notker of Saint-Gall was astonished at the end of the ninth century by "the great dissimilarity, hardly to be believed, which existed between the chant of the Gauls and that of the Romans."[15]

Carolingian cantors created a musical notation, indicating the direction of the voice with an acute or grave accent as the melody mounted or descended. These notes, called *neums,* recaptured the principle of writing which had been forgotten at the end of antiquity. To retain the long vocalizations of the *Alleluia,* they had the idea of making words correspond to the notes, each movement of the melody being figured by a syllable. A monk of Jumièges, fleeing the invading Normans, transmitted this invention to the monks of Saint-Gall. The young Notker, who had a feeble memory, was quick to perfect the procedure. This *prosa,* as they called a sequence, was to spread everywhere. Then, by the end of the century, monks began to ornament their chant by adding a musical or vocal accompaniment to the melody, the first outline of what would become polyphony, the source of modern music.[16]

We can be sure that people accustomed to the more abrupt rhythms of profane music were not easily seduced by the monodic purity of Gregorian chant. Cantors did not hesitate to utilize varied instruments, and the organ was in use already. Notker says that Charlemagne took advantage of the arrival of Greeks at his court to have an organ built. It has been described to us: "This admirable instrument, with the aid of brass vats (*cuves*) and leather bellows, chases the air through brass tubes as if by magic, its roaring equaling the sound of thunder and its sweetness the light sounds of lyre or cymbal."[17] The naves of churches, like the rooms of a palace, were filled with the sounds of the lyre, zithers, harp, flute, horns, percussion instruments, cymbals, bone castanets, and hand bells (*campanae*). Such instruments commonly figure in manuscripts representing David singing the psalms.[18]

Cults and Cultures

The Mass

People loved the music and willingly sang in church. They even dared innovation, for they often preferred badly composed and rather unorthodox popular religious songs (*plebei psalmi*).[19] The faithful were asked to content themselves with the singing of the Gloria, Kyrie, and Sanctus, after which they should listen to the cantors and remain silent during the remainder of the ceremony.

This silence was difficult to secure. To people who could not understand the language or the gestures of the Mass, time seemed to drag. Some left before the Gospel and went out to chatter in the churchyard. In 859, Hincmar of Reims asked his priests to read an admonition after the Epistle because, he said, "I know there are men who leave before the Gospel and the sermon instead of waiting for the final benediction."[20] After the preaching, the faithful were invited to bring offerings to the altar, bread in baskets or on a piece of linen, as well as oil or wax for lighting, the first fruits of the harvest, and money. Since this procession of offerings risked disturbances to the ceremony and created a tumult round the altar (where women were forbidden access), it was advised that gifts be presented before the Gospel or after Mass.[21] The eucharistic bread, unleavened according to the Jewish custom, was prepared in advance. On great feasts, little blessed loaves were offered in eulogies to the participants. However, the Communion procession (given in both kinds) had lost its importance. The faithful communicated very rarely despite the recommendations of princes and bishops.[22] To be sure, the Eucharist was venerated and held in awe, and the laity were warned against the dangers of bad preparation. Under such conditions, weekly Communion could not be imposed, though bishops tried to exact at least three Communions a year, at Christmas, Easter, and Pentecost.[23]

The liturgical year was divided into the Christmas and Easter cycles. From the first Sunday of Advent, the faithful began their preparations for Christmas by sleeping apart, fasting, and making confession if possible. Christmas (with its three Masses) and Epiphany were celebrated ostentatiously. After Septuagesima*, the faithful were invited to

---

* 70 days ending with saturday of Easter week.

renew their life by vigils, fasting until evening, alms, and prayers. This was the moment for remitting the tithe, so difficult to pay, and preparing oneself for the annual confession on Ash Wednesday.

Penance

"Now the time has come when you must confess your sins to God and to the priest and efface them by fasting, prayer, tears, and alms." Thus began a sermon for the first Sunday of Lent.[24] To avow one's faults and do penance was one of the great preoccupations of Carolingian spirituality. A Christian could escape from the Devil's clutches only by recognizing his or her own sins. Though praiseworthy, a simple confession to God was considered insufficient by Alcuin and Jonas of Orleans.[25] They recommended that the laity might follow monastic examples, and confess everyday or venial sins to one another. But with capital sins, a list of which had been established by that time, it was necessary to have recourse to a priest, a spiritual doctor.

Private confession, introduced to the continent by monks from the British Isles, was practiced widely. Just as barbarian laws taxed each crime with a pecuniary composition, penitentials required a precise penance for each corporal sin—usually fasts or bodily mortifications. But the penitent could already relieve himself from certain very lengthy penances by prayer and fines. Thus a year of fasting was replaced by twelve three-day fasts or twenty-six sous, the recitation of three psalters, and three hundred strokes with a flog. Three days of fasting were equated with one hundred psalms recited at night and three hundred lashes or three deniers. The rich were quickly free of their penances. Some penitents could also ask for a third person to act in their place. "Those who do not know the psalms and, by reason of weakness, can neither fast nor do vigil, nor genuflect, nor hold their arms in a cross, nor throw themselves on the ground, may choose someone to undergo penance in their place and pay for it; for it is written: 'Bear the burden, one for the other.' "[26] Some clerks considered this system abusive and disqualified penitentials "whose errors are so evident that their authors are worthy of little confidence. These should be burned so that ignorant priests cannot use them to deceive people." Confessors "should not determine the duration and manner of doing penance according to the good pleasure of the penitent, or for motives of gain, friendship, fear, or complaisance."[27]

Bishops urged a return to the ancient practice of public penance, at least for grave faults. They invited priests and the faithful to denounce crimes they had witnessed themselves. This would restore public penance in all its vigor not only for princes but for all great sinners. (Louis the Pious was required to criticize himself and recognize his faults at Saint-Médard of Soissons in 833.) Regino of Prüm has left us a ritual for public penances to be performed on Ash Wednesday. The sinner, dressed in sackcloth, barefoot, and with downcast eyes, was to present himself to the bishop who would pour ashes on him, give him a hair shirt, and indicate the penance required of him before expelling him solemnly from the church.[28] Paulinus of Aquilea outlined a penance in a letter to a magnate guilty of having killed his wife for suspicion of adultery:

> You shall drink neither wine nor beer; you will eat no meat of any kind except at Easter and Christmas; you will fast on bread, water, and salt. Pass your time in fasting, vigil, prayers, and alms. Never carry arms or do any fighting. You are forbidden to remarry, have a concubine, or commit fornication. You shall never take another bath or participate in a banquet. At the church, separated from other faithful, you will keep yourself behind the porch, recommending yourself to the prayers of those who enter and leave. Throughout your life, you may receive Communion if you have the grace to find a priest willing to administer it to you. That is the only favor which we can accord you.[29]

The excommunicate resembled the criminal who, in Germanic law, was expelled from the familial or tribal community. He could no longer claim recognition from other Christians. In a period when the solitary individual was regarded as a wanderer, very nearly a dead man, this punishment was terrible indeed. The Church used and abused the weapon, even threatening to refuse the excommunicate burial in the cemetery. We can imagine the relief of the public penitent who, having satisfied his penance or benefited by a remission of the penalty, saw himself reintegrated into the Christian community on Holy Thursday.

But the rigorous and spectacular public penances did not succeed in replacing private penance, which the penitents favored. Instead, a distinction was developed which became classic in the later Middle Ages: for a grave public fault, public penance; for a grave secret fault, private and pro-rated penance. Dealing with the case of a guilty priest who had seduced a married woman, Theodulf indicated that "if the crime were notorious, he should be deposed and subjected to ten years of public penance, but if the act of fornication remained hidden from the eyes of the people, he should confess secretly and receive a private penance."[30]

Liturgical Feasts

The great week of Easter inspired grandiose ceremonies. We can follow the unfolding liturgy of Saint-Riquier from the *Institution of Divine Offices* laid out by Angilbert. On Palm Sunday, the monks made a procession to Saint Mary's Church, three hundred meters away. There they chanted tierce and received the palms.* Then, accompanied by the inhabitants of the bourg, they moved to the abbey atrium, mounting into the Church of Saint Sauveur to celebrate Mass. Three choirs sang the vigils for Thursday and Friday nights: one in the middle of the central nave and two others, composed of children, in the eastern part which was consecrated to Saint-Riquier. In the afternoon, three crosses were raised to be venerated by the monks, the people, and the children. On Holy Saturday after Mass, the baptismal fonts were blessed and the litanies of 135 names were recited. On Easter Sunday there was a solemn distribution of Communion for monks, clerks, and people. When the Mass ended, a great procession formed in Saint-Sauveur. It was headed by persons carrying holy water, three censers, seven crosses, followed by the great reliquary and six smaller reliquaries. Next came the seven deacons, seven subdeacons,

---

* *Tierce* is the office for the third hour of the day (computed from sunrise).

seven acolytes, seven exorcists, seven readers, seven porters followed by the monks seven by seven, the *schola cantorum* and the crosses representing the seven neighboring villages. The seven-part divisions on which the procession was formed symbolically paid respect to the seven gifts of the Holy Ghost. The procession followed the cloister gallery up to Saint Mary's, set out again for Saint Benedict's, the third church of the monastery, and then returned to the abbatial church for a new Mass.

At Metz, similar processions were organized during Holy Week between different churches of the episcopal cluster. The monks of Francia were doubtless ambitious to imitate the "stational liturgy" taking place in Rome during the same period in the great basilicas of the Lateran, Holy Cross, and Saint Mary Maggiore.[31]

Outside of the two cycles of Christmas and Easter, secular and religious authorities had established what might be called holy days of obligation: Ascension, the Feast of Peter and Paul, the Nativity of Saint John, the Feasts of Saint Michael, Saint Remi, Saint Martin, Saint Andrew, and four Feasts in honor of the Blessed Virgin (the Purification, the Annunciation, the Nativity, and the Assumption). This last was not honored everywhere. In 862, according to the *Annals of Saint-Bertin*, a miracle was required to oblige the inhabitants of Thérouanne to celebrate this feast.[32] The Marian cult, arriving from the East through Roman intermediacy, had not yet penetrated into the popular consciousness though it was beginning to attract the attention and fervor of the literate. Paschasius Radbertus wrote a homily on the Assumption, and Walafrid Strabo knew some beautiful verses in celebration of the Virgin, "mother, spouse, dove, house, queen, friend of all the faithful," whose floral symbols were roses and lilies.[33]

Every church celebrated the feasts of its local saints, feasts which became more numerous with a consequent augmentation of the number of holidays as they enriched themselves with relics. At Corbie, in 822, in addition to Sundays, the peasants had to stop working for thirty-six days a year. About 813, the Feast of All Saints, of Celtic origin, appeared and began to be observed generally on November 1.

Finally, there were certain days in the year consecrated to fasting and prayer: Rogation days, Mondays, Tuesdays, and Wednesdays preceding the Ascension, the minor litanies, and the major litany of April 25. "Four Periods" appeal for divine favors for the agricultural labors of the four seasons. Then exceptional fasts and prayers were established by kings in periods of difficulty and calamity. Thus, in 780, Charlemagne ordered that "the bishops were to chant three masses, recite three psalms for the king, the army, and the present tribulation; bishops, monks and nuns, canons and their men, as well as magnates would undertake two days of fasting."[34]

Prayer Associations

In addition to the official liturgical life, small groups formed here and there, of both clergy and laity meeting in confraternities of prayer. A Bern manuscript gives us the rules of a *societas* of clerks dedicated to Saint Peter. Twelve clerks met and elected a dean to pray and do penance together. On the Apostle's feast day they met in the church to chant the seven psalms of penance followed by a litany, prayers, confession, and attendance at Mass. Then they returned to the house of one of them for a silent lunch accompanied by a reading. Some of the provisions were to be reserved for the poor. They went back to church and, after a recitation of the psalms, returned to the house to end the day together. When a brother was ill, they undertook to go to his house, chant the penitential psalms, asperge the sick man with holy water while one of the clerks said a Mass for the sick. They would keep vigil day and night with the brother for twelve days, nourishing themselves on what they could find, down to bread and water, without protesting against the emptiness of the pantry. When death approached, they would all meet together and give Extreme Unction to the dying. For a month after the funeral, they would say the Mass for the dead. Then during the next year they would take turns in celebrating Mass for the same intention.[35]

Prayer associations for the dead were of Anglo-Saxon origin. In the eighth and ninth centuries they multiplied throughout the Carolingian church. Our first text on the subject comes from the Synod of Attigny in 762. Each of forty-four associates was entitled after his death to have a hundred masses and a hundred psalms said for him, in addition to the thirty masses celebrated by each bishop. Churches and monasteries exchanged parchment rolls listing the names of their dead and engaged themselves to pray for the defunct. In 842, Saint-Germain-des-Près, Saint-Denis, and Saint-Remi of Reims formed an association.[36] When a brother died, one of the monks would recite the psalter every day for a month. The priests would say Mass on the first, seventh, and thirteenth days after the death. The *liber memorialis* of Remiremont set down the rules for a prayer association among Remiremont, Inde (near Aix-la-Chapelle), Stavelot, Malmedy, Lobbes, Annegray, and Murbach. The brothers would intercede for each other, not only for the dead but for the living.[37]

Many craved the honor of reception into a confraternity of prayer. At the Council of Frankfurt in 794, the learned Alcuin was admitted into the association of council members. Like many Carolingians, Alcuin feared death, wept for his sins, and begged continual prayers from his correspondents. The approach of God's Judgment necessitated preparation with alms and offerings. Some men retired into a monastery to await death. Though burial within a church was formally forbidden to all but bishops and abbots, some people asked to be buried in the atrium, as near as possible to the church, "under the waterspout from the roof," to be refreshed with sanctified water. Parish cemeteries were often abandoned, and in these deserted places people and animals trampled over the graves. Hincmar was obliged to instruct priests to take measures against the opening of sepulchres and to prevent the stones of a sarcophagus and even bones from being used, as they often were, for paving roads.[38] That is why well-to-do families asked to be interred in the church yard. A husband and wife sought out the Abbot of Saint-Maxent in Brittany to request a place where their bodies could rest. They were shown the enclosure and then placed their offerings on the altar. The donation was confirmed by charter.[39]

Bishops, abbots, and even princes were privileged to be laid after death in the church near the relics. Pepin was buried at Saint-Denis, Carloman at Saint-Remi at Reims,

Charlemagne at Aix, Louis the Pious at Saint-Arnoul of Metz, Lothair at Prüm. Charles the Bald prepared his tomb at Saint-Denis, near the altar called the *Gazophylacium*. When he died while returning from Italy, his entrails were drawn out, his body perfumed with wine and aromatic spices, and the pieces put in a casket sealed with pitch and covered with leather. It was deposed provisionally at Nantua before being transported to the royal basilica.[40] Nithard, who died in the course of a warlike expedition, was sealed into a wooden casket covered with leather and filled with salt before being transported to his Abbey of Saint-Riquier.[41]

Christians used many means to assure prayers for themselves and their relatives. They had their names inscribed on diptychs placed on the altar, or engraved on the altar stones. The table of Minerva in Aude bears 93 graffiti from the Carolingian period.[42] In their wills, or in some other fashion, they were always asking not to be forgotten in the prayers of the living. Gisela, wife of Ewrard of Friuli, made arrangements to observe the anniversaries of her parents' deaths.[43] Before dying, literate people composed epitaphs for their tombs appealing for the prayers of the living. Here are some of the verses of the epitaph composed by Dhuoda:

> Let none pass by without reading. I call upon all passersby to pray thus: 'Good God, give her rest and ordain in your goodness that with the Saints she will share the eternal light.'[44]

All believers were fearful of the anguish of the next world. People sought to help the dead with chants (and sometimes with meals whose pagan character provoked clerical denunciation). Nor did the great escape fear of the Judgment. The Church did nothing to tranquilize them. Hincmar wrote to Louis the German, whose politics displeased him:

> Picture to yourself that hour which, you may be certain, no one can evade, when your soul will leave your body, when it will quit the world, the power, wealth, and the body itself, and appear naked and desolate without the help of spouse or children, without the intercourse or company of friends or vas-

Cults and Cultures

sals. . . . She will see all her sins and, seeing them, will feel the devils chain her and crush her while ever present to her eyes will be all that she thought, planned, and did against charity and her given faith which were not requited with sufficient penance. Then she will wish to flee but will not have the strength. For it is certain that the devils crowd around the deathbeds of all men as their souls leave their bodies, whether they be just or sinful.[45]

The dying were surrounded by ceremonies: final confession, numerous bodily anointments, prayers repeated before and after death.[46] It all contributed to the dramatization of the last seconds of human life and impressed the living. The Carolingian world was harsh and severe.

V

In
Search
of
Protectors

All the grandeur of the Empire, the prestige and wealth of the powerful, the renaissance of the intellect, and the beauty of religious ceremonies cannot disguise the hardship and misery of daily life. Granted that it is always difficult to judge of the happiness or unhappiness of other folk and other times by our own standards, our Carolingian ancestors had to bear evils which are objectively unbearable. To the natural hostility of their milieu, the cataclysms which we have noted in passing must be added. Even the clergy, however privileged, never failed to register these in their annals: climatic caprice, floods, plagues, epidemics among livestock, earthquakes, and famines. A table outlining these catastrophes year by year, despite the lacunae in documentation, is a sufficient demonstration in itself. (See Table I)

Begging and Brigandage

Beggars of all ages were found everywhere in the Empire. We can imagine them crowded near the church doors and massed under the portals, their numbers swelling on feast days and pilgrimages. Hagiographical texts depict genuine or fake paralytics, the lame, the blind, or simply miserable wretches hoping for a bit of silver or bread. One paralytic camped for five years at the door of Saint-Martin of Tours. A hunchback collected his sustenance every day near the tomb of Saint-Marcellin. The Abbess Leoba of Bischofheim provided food and clothing for the sick woman who lay at the entrance to the monastery. Some made their way into the church itself in search of shelter and the protection of the relics and stayed the night.[1]

Begging could be a profitable profession. A blind old man in Aix who was in the habit of begging from door to door with a crowd of the poor refused to pray for the restoration of his sight:

> Why do I need the vision I lost so long ago? It is worth more to me to be deprived of it than to have it. Blind, I can beg and none will repulse me. Rather, they hasten to attend to my needs. But if I had my sight back, it would seem wrong for me to beg alms even though I am old and weak and cannot work.[2]

249

A Century of Natural Disasters

Year	Drought	Hard Winters	Soft Winters	Plague
790				
800				
			808 R	808 R
810				
820			820 R	
		821 R		
				823 R
830				
		832 B		
				836 A
			838 X	
840				
		843 N		
			844 B	
		845 B		
		846 B		
850	850 X			
	852 X			
		856 B		856 B
				857 X
860		860 F B		
870				
	874 B	874 F		874 F
				877 F
				878 F
880		880 F		
	887 F			
				889 F

Sources:
Cap. = Capitularies

A = Astronome
R = Annales Royales
B = Annales de Saint-Bertin

Animal Epidemic	Floods	Earthquakes	Famine
			793 L
			805 Cap.
			807 Cap.
810 R			
	815 R	815 R	
820 R	820 R		820 R
		823 R	
		829 R	829 A
	834 A		
		838 X	
	839 B X		
	841 N		
		842 N	
843 N			843 F
		845 X	845 B
	846 B		
	850 X		850 F
			852 X
			853 X
	858 B	858 F B	
		859 F X	
	863 X		
		867 F	
			868 F X
		870 F	
	873 X		
			874 F
	875 F		
878 F			
880			880 F
881			
		886	
	887 V		

X = Annales de Xanten   F = Annales de Fulda
N = Nithard   L = Annales de Lorsch
    V = Annales de Saint-Vaast

The sight of beggars gathered in squares and at cross-roads was a cause of anxiety to the public power. In 806, Charlemagne took measures "to control the beggars who circulate around the country." Under Louis the Pious a supervisor was appointed to watch the conduct of these wretches at Aix. In effect, all sorts of vagabonds mixed in with these beggars: errant monks, clerks breaking the ban, shady merchants (*mangones*), pseudo-penitents, half-naked and weighed down with irons "pretending that a penance of wandering had been imposed on them."[3] Such people could become dangerous and turn to brigandage.

We have already seen that Carolingian roads were not very safe. Brigandage was rampant everywhere. Outlaws hid in the forests and posted themselves at the entrances of defiles to rob travelers of the few precious objects they might be carrying. They followed the army across the country in the hopes of pillaging the baggage.

Germanic laws imposed harsh penalties on all forms of brigandage, particularly arson and theft. In Italy, a thief of the servile class lost an eye the first time he was caught, had his nostrils slit the second time, and was put to death the third.[4] Equal punishments were visited on those who protected brigands. Charlemagne reinforced these measures and repeatedly denounced the packs of thieves, pillagers, and murderers afflicting Europe.

The difficulties which beset the end of the reign favored brigands. A capitulary of 804 was specifically devoted to this scourge. Counts were ordered to pursue brigands taking refuge in certain privileged domains.[5] (These were known as the lands with immunity.*) For a while, brigandage seemed less threatening under Louis the Pious, but by the middle of the century it was more menacing than ever. Bandits could profit from the fraternal dissensions rising out of the partition of the Empire by seeking refuge in another kingdom. Writing to a friend about 856, Lupus of Ferrières asked him to choose a safe road and seek "travel companions whose number and courage would facilitate their avoidance of brigand groups or their repulsion if

* Under the term "immunity," certain lords held royal grants protecting their lands from any intervention by royal officials.

necessary."[6] In the same period, Charles addressed the Capitulary of Servais to the repression of banditry. Italy had the same problems. Louis II declared that brigandage flourished everywhere with the complicity of counts and royal officers. Lay and ecclesiastical aristocrats as well as the more wealthy landed proprietors often connived with brigands to divide the loot.[7] The presence of the Normans favored the creation of such bands. Charles the Bald planned the organization of local resistance to outlaws. At the end of the century, Carloman promulgated a law against rapine at Compiègne.[8] But how could anyone struggle when, as Hincmar says, these brigands were not only protected by the great but paid to contract themselves out as assassins?

Routine Brutality

To add to this somber picture, we must remember the habitual brutality already apparent in Merovingian Europe and even Byzantium. Reading the Germanic laws which continued in force we are struck by the many forms of physical brutality that were anticipated, for the laws give precise details of the behavior for which financial compensation was to be expected. They speak of severed ears, with or without loss of hearing, the rape of poor women, eyes torn out, noses slit partially or totally, tongues cut out, teeth broken, beards torn, joints crushed, hands and feet cut off, testicles mangled. And the penalties ordained by the law were no less cruel. The classic punishment for rebellion was blinding, particularly for a member of the royal family. Judges did not recoil from punishing slaves with mutilation and castration, fire or drowning. Theodulf was one of the rare ones to protest these "barbarous" punishments. A bishop of Le Mans even castrated clerks who had displeased him. To be sure, that act provoked Charlemagne's intervention and the removal of the offending bishop.[9] The king tried vainly to prevent private wars, *faida* (feuds or vendettas), in which entire families were wiped out.[10] Civil war was no less terrible. The Aquitainians long remembered the devastation wrought by Charles Martel and Pepin III; nor did Bretons forget the campaigns of Louis the Pious in Armorica. Lothar's army, in the struggle with the king's brothers, behaved as though they were in an enemy country. And when combat was joined with pagans, the Frankish fury knew no limits. Chroniclers recounting the Saxon campaign coldly noted massacres of thousands of Saxons and the mass deportation of men, women, and children.

Norman Invasions

In their turn, the Carolingians suffered the ravages of pagans in the latter half of the ninth century. Even though clerks may have exaggerated the devastation wrought by the Northmen, we cannot make much of a case for the rehabilitation of the "good barbarians."[11] When fighting erupted, both sides were equally adept at slaughter. Even making allowances for the epic inspiration of the poets, Abbo's account of the siege of Paris in 885 demonstrates that the combatants were equally savage. While the Normans massacred everyone who had not gained a refuge on the island, the Franks "served the enemy with boiling oil, wax, and pitch," and "dealt death to innumerable assailants." The Abbot of Saint-Germain "succeeded in piercing seven men with a single arrow and, joking, ordered that they be carried to the kitchen." Though we may question the arithmetic, this trait of macabre humor was certainly part of the period's mentality.[12]

The mentality of the imperial population was marked as profoundly by the psychological disturbances to which the Normans gave birth as by the destruction they caused.[13] Norman tactics rested on incessant mobility and the shock of surprise, a ruse which was reputed to be demoniacal, paralyzing all resistance and provoking "waves of panic." A fugitive would recite in lurid detail the pillages and cruelties he had witnessed or heard of from others, and everyone would take flight. Men were sometimes seen on the roads running in both directions. Lay and religious leaders were the first to flee. Hincmar admitted that a count with a family to care for might be excused for fleeing a town but reproached ecclesiastics "not sustaining a wife and children" for doing so. But in 882, he did not hesitate himself to leave Reims in all haste carrying his treasures and the body of Saint Remi with him. Praises for those bishops and abbots

In Search of Protectors

who organized resistance were as high as they were rare. The monks applied Christ's words to the situation: "If they persecute you in one city, flee into another" (Matthew 10:20). They retired to their less exposed estates, packing their most precious objects into carts and boats, including manuscripts and saints' relics. Military chieftains and princes even took advantage of the Norman incursions to attack their own rivals, opposed Normans to one another when they could, or bought off the danger with heavy tribute without attempting to prevent the pillage of neighboring regions. The tributes raised from every people added up to enormous sums: 7000 pounds in 845, 5000 in 861, 6000 in 862, and 4000 in 866. Sometimes the king sought a sum superior to that exacted by the Normans in order to establish a reserve. In 877, Hincmar complained to the new king Louis the Stammerer against this practice which was onerous to everyone but especially to the Church:

> This unhappy people, already afflicted for several years with diverse and continual depradations and now beset with levies to buy the departure of the Normans, must have some amelioration of their state. Justice, which lies dead among us, must be restored to life before God can give us courage to face the pagans. For years the people of this realm have not defended themselves but have paid, have ransomed themselves; now not men alone are impoverished but the churches which once were rich are in ruins.[14]

But little by little resistance was organized. Charles the Bald had the great merit of raising his subjects "to the defense of the fatherland." "All men are to devote themselves to the defense of the country; counts are to build fortresses energetically, without defect and without delay, and keep the watch from these fortresses."[15]

Fortified bridges were rapidly built on the Seine, the Marne, and the Oise. Town walls which had gone to ruin or been quarried for the construction of churches and palaces were restored at Le Mans, Tours, and Orleans. At Chartres, the bishop abandoned the parts that were past repair and utilized an intact corner of the wall to build a fortress. Walls were put up around the abbeys of Saint-

Vaast, Saint-Omer, Corbie, and Déols. *Castra* and *castella* sprang up everywhere even without royal authorization to serve as refuges to the population whenever the alert was given. The people themselves organized resistance, taking initiatives which sometimes disquieted the great not so much for their efficacy, which was small, but because peasants might also seize the occasion to free themselves from their masters.

The Normans: Scourges of God

When the danger had passed, the ruins repaired and reconstituted, people meditated on the significance of the Norman raids. Paschasius Radbertus interrupted his commentary on the Lamentations of Jeremiah to draw the lesson of the siege of Paris in 845:

> Who would have believed what our eyes have seen, what made us tremble so? A troop of pirates, men gathered by chance, who came even to Paris and destroyed churches and monasteries on the banks of the Seine with impunity! Who would have believed that so famous, so vast, so populous a realm was destined to be humiliated by barbarians? Yes, all our sorrows are come because of the sins of priests and princes; there is the source of the calamities which overwhelm us. Long since, justice was banished from their courts and discord born which bathed the citizens of the same empire in blood. Everywhere fraud and trumpery are seen. The sword of the barbarians was drawn from its sheath, and it is God who has put it in their hands for our punishment.

The last phrase calls the words of Saint Jerome to mind: "It is our sins which give strength to the Barbarians."[16]

From the north came the terror and the scourge which must awaken Christians. "The aggressors are cruel, but this is only justice," said the bishops gathered at Meaux in 845, "for Christians did not obey the commandments of God and the Church." The time had come for the great examination of conscience. Warring princes must reconcile. Rapine and depredation must cease. The clamor of widows,

In Search of Protectors

children, and orphans must be heard, and the "poor" must be assisted. King Carloman addressed himself to the people in 884, declaring:

> How is it astonishing that pagans and strangers can dominate us and confiscate our temporal goods, that any one of us might be forcibly torn from his community, if indeed he is permitted to go on living? How can we possibly struggle with assurance against the enemies of the Church and ourselves when "in our own place we hold captive the spoils of the poor (Isaiah 33:1); when we go into battle with our bellies full of the fruit of our own rapine?"[17]

Definition of the "Poor"

Amidst the miseries and hardships of the Carolingian world, the powerful still saw the need to defend the "poor." What did they mean by the word? Recent studies have shown that the poor were not only "those who live in tears and submit to the anguish of hunger while the rich stuff themselves with food" but also those who suddenly found themselves in a state of weakness and dependence.[18] The Carolingians equated the poor with the oppressed: laymen exploited by the great, *coloni* victimized by the agents of the fisc, peasants in the clutches of usurpers. Charlemagne complained that "many known to be free men have forcibly been subjected to the great, that free men have been forced to give themselves over to the army or have been victimized by the arbitrary will of judges." Vain complaints! At his accession, Louis found "an incalculable number of people who had been oppressed by being despoiled of their hereditary lands and liberties."[19]

The "poor" also included those too young to defend themselves and those whom old age had overtaken, women bereft of husband or parents, those who fell into sickness and infirmity. A poor man is a man who has been driven from his familial milieu, voluntarily or not. Thus a pilgrim who left his homeland to venerate a sanctuary must be protected. The foreigner who had come to live in the Empire was also considered *pauper*. "Perhaps we paupers and pilgrims are a burden on you, disgusting by reason of our great numbers, our importunities and solicitations," wrote the Irishman Dungal to the Abbot of Jumièges, "but are you not the ones whom God appointed for our maintenance?"[20] But when a woman coming from Frisia arrived at Fulda, her hostess was prepared to sell her as a slave "because she had no country."[21]

Finally, refugees were included in the category of the poor. In 853 Charles the Bald asked his officers not to disturb those who had left their lands in flight from the oppression of the Bretons and Normans. He wanted them to be made welcome until they could return to their own homes. Some years later, he instructed his counts to register their names and the names of their lords so as better to regulate the marriages they made in their adopted country. Often these unhappy ones, wishing to find work, rented themselves as salaried employees to lords. But the masters, profiting from their misfortunes, reduced them to slavery or simply bound them over to some powerful person.[22]

What could these "paupers" do, these victims of injustice and cruelty inflicted on them by "Christian" society? Must they resign themselves to waiting for better days, or could they appeal to royal justice or the help of protectors?

Royal Justice

The Justiciar King

On his coronation day, a Carolingian king was charged with the maintenance of peace, concord, and equanimity among all Christians under his sway. He was to take Biblical princes for his model—to exercise justice and bring about the rule of equity—and he knew that God would demand an accounting from him. If the king were unfaithful to his task, anarchy and dissension would trouble his realm, and, what is more, the cosmic order itself would be disturbed. Even as their pagan ancestors believed in the magic power of kings, Carolingians were persuaded that a good king was a pledge of abundance and prosperity and that the very elements were beneficent to him. If he did not govern well, the world would be visited with natural catastrophes: earthquakes, epidemics, and famines; for, as Scripture says, "The universe will struggle against the insane" (Wisdom V.21). Thus Nithard ended his history of the sons of Louis the Pious, contrasting the order and harmony which reigned everywhere in Charlemagne's time to the troubles of his own time.[1]

A prince worthy of the name was expected to protect the weak and take widows, orphans, travelers, pilgrims, and strangers under his protection, *maimbour*. Or he might provide individuals with charters of protection to be invoked in case of arbitrary action against them.[2] As guardian of the public order, the king offered rewards of sixty sous apiece for punishing criminals attainted under the "royal ban": whose offenses included concealing fugitives, stealing pack animals, murdering pilgrims, forced requisitions for men of war, abusive collection of tolls and customs. Finally, the king aimed at protecting the non-free from the arbitrary actions of their masters. He commanded them to hand over *servi* accused of capital crimes to the public tribunals: thieves, brigands, assailants, were no longer to be at the mercy of expeditious and private justice.[3]

The Exercise of Justice

The king delegated his judicial functions to the count in the so-called *mallus publicus*. There, at least three times a year, the count presided over the tribunal and directed its proceedings. He had the help of assessors who "knew the law," *rachimbours* or *boni homines*. Toward 780, Charlemagne attached these men permanently to the tribunal under the title *scabini*, from which the French *échevin* is derived. The twelve *scabini* were reputable men trained to know the different laws and customs under which the accused lived. They opened the proceedings by asking him whether he would be tried by Salic, Ripuarian, Burgundian, Lombard, or Roman Law. If the man had been accused by his neighbors of some crime and accordingly had presented himself and his supporters to the tribunal to declare his innocence, the judge would give him a delay of several "nights" to prove his innocence. During that time, he could meet with witnesses for his acquittal. They swore with him (whence the name co-jurors) that he had not committed the crime of which he had been accused. The oath was administered in church on the Gospel or the relics stored there. If this method did not reveal the truth, the count might invoke the judgment of God. The practice of ordeals (*urtheil*, "proof" in German) was of Germanic origin, essentially a magical practice which spread throughout the Empire under various forms. The most popular was the ordeal of boiling water: the accused plunged his arm into the water to retrieve an object. If arm and hand were healed at the end of several days, he had proved himself right. Another ordeal was that of hot iron, which consisted of making the accused walk over nine white-hot cartwheel spokes spaced out on the ground. The proof of the Cross was introduced under Charlemagne. The accused and his accuser put their arms out in the shape of the Cross. The first to let his arms fall or to stumble was presumed guilty. Such proofs revolted some clerks. Agobard and Theodulf thought it impious to believe that God would reveal secret sins by such a procedure. Louis the Pious in 829 forbade the ordeal of the Cross "for the passion of the Lord must not be an object of derision." But Germanic custom was so strong that judges continued to employ ordeals for centuries with the blessings of the Church.[4]

The judicial duel, whose origins were very ancient, was another means of revealing guilt. It could be imposed on people of every social category. Ermold the Black gives us a lively story of two aristocratic Goths dueling in the palace park at Aix. They fought on horseback, a thing, he explained for which Franks have not the knack. The laws of the Alamans spelled out the fashion for regulating neighborly conflicts. When two neighbors disputed a piece of land, branches were to be placed on the planted earth in the center of the field. Touching them with their arms and praying that God would give the victory to him who deserved it, they then proceeded to fight it out. Among the Lombards, they fought with staff and buckler, and the defeated party had his right hand cut off as a perjuror while other false witnesses had to pay ransom for their hands.[5]

To control the conduct of comital justice, Charlemagne extended the institution of the *missi dominici*. In 802, their role and powers were outlined by a capitulary:

> . . . Do justice fairly, correctly, and equitably to churches, widows, orphans, and all others, without fraud, corruption, obstruction or abusive delay, and be vigilant that all your subordinates do likewise. . . . Above all, pay careful heed that you or your subordinates are not surprised into speaking to the parties with the idea of thwarting or retarding the exercise of justice: "Say nothing until the *missi* are gone; we will arrange it all amongst ourselves!" On the contrary, busy yourselves to facilitate judgment of cases pending in your court before our arrival. For if you make some bad turn of this type, or if you delay by negligence or malice the course of justice, be warned that we shall turn in a very severe report against you at our hearings. Read and re-read this letter and keep it well so that it may serve as a witness between you and us.[6]

The text was fair, the program ambitious, but all depended on the integrity of the *missi*. Describing his own discharge of the function, Theodulf speaks lightly of how he had to resist pressures and offers of gifts. Justice could miscarry. We have still a vivid picture of a local judge besieged by his cronies to secure a twist in the law:

> His wife hung on his neck, embraced him, and sought to bend him; for it is as habitual for women to employ artifice as for an archer to smear poison on

his arrow. Weeping, she said that he did not love her any more, that he listened to other women while she, she could obtain nothing. The servant, the nurse, even the maid, came to the rescue and sought to reconcile the spouses. Then came the judge, late to the tribunal, his knees wobbling, panting and heavy with the wine he had drunk. They wagged their fingers at him and laughed. . . .

In his turn, the *missus* was besieged by the litigants. Theodulf recalls:

One promised me a cup of crystal and pearls from the East if I would make him master of another's domains. Another offered me a great heap of coins, gold with Arab characters or silver with Latin inscriptions, if I would consent to turn over to him the farms, fields, and houses. Another secretly attracted the attention of my notary and whispered to him what he should pass on to me: "I possess a vase enriched with ancient carving of pure metal and notable weight. . . . If your master would permit me to falsify a charter, I will give him that antique vase, and when I have become the lord of these folk, I will not delay in compensating you for your good offices.[7]

Finally, the king might judge some important cases himself in his palace tribunal.[8] Hincmar, with his idealized memory of the court, boasted of the just functioning of the royal tribunal. He described the people without sustenance, in debt, or harassed by unjust accusations, of modest or noble condition, who had recourse to the king.[9] However, many examples show that courtiers succeeded in falsifying proceedings. Charlemagne's cousin Wala was charged with the defense of a widow who had come to Aix from Italy in winter to complain of her business agent's dealings. The agent had the widow murdered and then had two of the murderers killed by a third whom he trusted.

All the worthies of Italy, corrupted by gifts, went to work to ensure that one whom they knew to be a murderer should not be found guilty. . . . All the most influential people of the palace were trying to

In Search of Protectors

produce witnesses and all sorts of false evidence to obtain the acquittal of a guilty man.[10]

In his efforts to enforce respect for order and justice, Charlemagne determined to forge a personal link between himself and his subjects by means of the oath. From 789 on, he instructed his functionaries to extract an oath of fidelity from all. In 793, he repeated the order that the oath be taken by all the male inhabitants above the age of twelve in every county. Becoming Emperor, he imposed a new demand for oaths. Subjects were to swear on relics not only that they would be loyal but that they would respect the goods of the fisc, abstain from behaving shamefully to *miserabilae personae*, churches, widows, and orphans, and do nothing to falsify or frustrate justice. When one remembers the religious power represented by the relics, one must believe that many hesitated to perjure themselves. But could everyone in the Empire be reached? Those who escaped taking the oath could consider themselves dispensed from the duties it imposed. Moreover, the oath favored the development of a contractual conception of royalty, which ended by enfeebling monarchial power.[11] Finally, despite his own inclinations, the king encouraged the creation of groups and associations strongly united by mutual oath.

Mutual Help and Patronage

In Germanic society, an individual could not exist outside the community, and the isolated man was doomed to perish. The most fearful of punishments was to exclude a man from the familial or tribal group and make him a wanderer (*wargus*). But the strength of clan solidarity did not preclude seeking for support outside that traditional group as happens in many civilizations. Even as clerks collectively ensured the welfare of their members in prayer associations, so did the Carolingian laity seek to form groups and to assure themselves of moral and material aid from patrons. Popular associations which we can examine separately from several texts and the formation of links between man and man which multiplied in the aristocratic world seem to have proceeded from the same tendencies.

Collective Self-Help

To guard themselves against the brutality and injustice which the king could not suppress, common men and women naturally sought to form associations for self-help and prayer. In Germanic these were called *geldonias*, a word which appears later as "guilds." These associations are found early in Anglo-Saxon countries. In 779, they appear in the Capitulary of Herstal, where the king countenanced the formation of groups for material mutual assistance, to help victims of fire or those who had seen their goods perish in a shipwreck. However, he forbade such a group to form a *conjuratio* whose members joined in an oath which might lead them to conspire against royal authority. The capitulary of 789, which recorded the oath which was to be sworn to the king, prohibited *conjurationes* made on Saint Stephen's day. This feast fell on December 26, corresponding with the Germanic Yule, a time when special precautions had to be taken against the action of demonic spirits. Ritual drinking bouts were organized for that purpose, and since associations were wont to manifest their solidarity by participating in these common meals, religious authorities feared that these fraternal agapes would end in drunkenness and orgies.[12] Alcuin denounced "small gatherings which lead the people astray. They desert the churches and give themselves, not to prayers, but to intoxication." Hrabanus Maurus deplored the risks which grew out of orgies and drunkenness, words and gross games exchanged among the revellers. In 858, Archbishop Hincmar of Rheims thought it necessary to intervene "with regard to groups which people call guilds or confraternities" in which even priests mixed. He too pictured the feasts and carousing which ended in vomiting, financial extortion, and disputes leading to murder. He was willing to permit mutual assistance meetings only on the occasion of funerals, hoping that such gatherings would facilitate the reconciliation of embroiled neighbors who would all contribute bread and wine to be eaten together, with the surplus to go to the priest.[13] Despite warnings and threatened penalties (degradation of priests and imprisonment of laymen), it seems that all these recommendations were ignored. People needed to join in some activity beyond liturgical ceremonies and wanted some means other than the chanting of sacred

In Search of Protectors

hymns to celebrate their joy. Neither kings nor bishops could stem the spread of these collective self-help associations. The Capitulary of Worms, in 829, saw them as dangerous temptations to evil: associations (*collectae*) were interdicted because of their evil deeds. "We want to know if the negligence of the count has allowed their formation and left it unpunished. Those responsible are to be delivered up to us. The group who joined them, whether of free or servile origin, must submit to the punishment ordained by law."[14] But the general insecurity of the latter half of the century favored the extension of these groups. In 884, Carloman again denounced these *collectae* and guilds and required bishops and counts to have them all outlawed.[15] But could they really forbid men to use their right of mutual aid and legitimate defense?

Links of Man to Man: Making Friends

Aristocrats, too, had to form groups and create personal ties. Beyond the familial milieu and the conjugal union, they sought reliable friends in whom they could trust. Carolingian writers exalted friendship far above love: "When they find they are not enough in themselves and come to mistrust their own judgment, all men seek faithful friends in whom they can confide and open the secrets of their hearts," Abbess Eangyth wrote to Boniface.[16] Boniface, too, a man "who had a genius for friendship," wrote letters full of amicable effusions. His compatriot Alcuin was even more lyric when he wrote to a friend. He waited impatiently for the return of Arn of Salzburg and the moment when he might clasp his friend in the fingers of his desire:

> Oh, if only, like Habbakuk, I could be transported to your presence, how I would throw myself into your embraces. . . . How I would cover you with pressing kisses, not only on your eyes, but your ears and mouth and also your fingers, your feet—not once but time and time again.

We must take care not to place more significance on these declarations than they deserve. Alcuin often borrowed expressions from Jerome's letter to Rufinus (III.1) and from commonplaces in antique literature on friendship. Similarly, he says in a poem: "Sweet love mourns the absence of a friend. When will come the time that love desires? When will the day arrive?"[17] In his letters to Einhard, Waldo, or Odo of Corbie, Lupus of Ferrières was more sober but no less avid for affectionate thoughts. Aristocrats cemented their friendships with little gifts, caskets of wine, incense, or even combs. "I am sending you an ivory comb which I pray you to keep for your own use so that when you are combing you hair you will think more strongly of me," wrote Lupus of Ferrières to Bishop Ebroin.[18]

Taking a "Seigneur"

Friendship might take particular form in pouring out concrete demands for material aid. A Bavarian formula at the end of the eighth century poetically reflects the anguish of a man in trouble:

> Summer has gone, as well you know; warmth diminishes; autumn is here, and winter nears. The vegetables are giving out even as the swallows prepare for flight, and hay is lacking for the cattle. . . . I beg you for some subsistence.[19]

We still have a ninth-century contract between a powerful personage and a man in need of food and clothing:

> You should help and sustain me with nourishment as well as clothing, in measure as I can serve you and as I deserve from you. As long as I shall live, I will owe you service and obedience as a free man can offer it; and all the days of my life, I will have no power to loose myself from your power or *maimbour*, but I will owe you all the days of my life that I should remain under your power and protection.[20]

Historians have seen this text as an echo of the "recommendation" of the late Roman Empire as well as the beginning of the vassal tie. The contract was made between two free men for life. It carried reciprocal obligations and ordained penalties if either of the two parties should default.

During the political crisis which ended to the profit of the Carolingian family, the links of man to man had multiplied at every level. The Austrasian mayors of the palace owed part of their success to the clientele they recruited in this fashion. Pepin of Landen had already "attached the *leudes* (aristocrats) of Austrasia by ties of friendship." His successors pursued this practice, gathering round themselves *nourris* and *convives* (literally, those who are fed by or those who lived with a great man). These domestic warriors escorted their chief, and soon the word *vassus* appeared with the meaning which it later retained—that is, a free man under the command of a powerful one. Carolingian princes made vassalage one of the tools of their policy. Charlemagne sought to draw all parties around himself, binding to himself with ties of fidelity the aristocrats who served him. The *vassi dominici* engaged themselves with oaths on relics and by putting their joined hands, in sign of submission, into the hands of the one whom they would call *seigneur* (from the Latin *senior* or elder). When the king summoned the *ost*, he depended on his vassals to bring their troops. Other aristocrats, counts, dukes, bishops, had their own vassals, *pauperiores vassi*, as one chronicler ironically said.[21]

The seigneur made equivalent engagements for the submission and services of the vassal. Without that, the contract would have had little success. As we see in the Formula of Tours, at first dependents were actually fed and clothed by their patrons. As Marc Bloch so happily put it: "The earliest vassalage had an odor of household bread."[22] The master was the elder (*senior*); his men, his boys (*vassus*). Later, vassals began to receive presents, benefices (*beneficia*) usually in the form of landed property which must revert on their deaths or on the death of the lord. Vassals who were not thus *casati* to use an expression of the period, who had not received benefices, were increasingly rare. Charlemagne established safeguards against alienation by his vassals, the sale or exchange of lands donated as benefices. But in fact, how could he impede a man from confounding benefices which he had rendered fruitful as carefully as he could with his own goods and seeking to retain them after the death of the seigneur? We can sense this anxiety in two letters culled from Einhard's correspondence. In the first, Einhard intervened in favor of a count who possessed a small benefice in Burgundy conceded to his family by Charlemagne and then by Louis the Pious. The count, who was seriously ill and unable to go to recommend himself to Lothair, asked to keep his benefice until he was restored to health. In the other letter, Einhard spoke of a case where a man had received three manses and twelve slaves as a benefice from the Bishop of Wurzburg. The bishop had died, and the beneficiary wanted to keep the land until a new bishop was nominated.[23]

On the other side, how could a vassal, a good father of his family, fail to want to transmit the benefices he held for life to his heirs? If he could not, they were in danger of being reduced to want. On their side, the lords had some interest in allowing this inheritance to assure the fidelity of their vassals' descendants. Thus, in the ninth century, the inheritance of benefices became customary. Certain lands (like the Mâconnais) remained in the same family for generations. Charles the Bald's famous capitulary of Quierzy, affirming his own rights as king-lord, recognized that under certain conditions the sons of his vassals could expect to receive the paternal benefices.[24] Thus, partly through companionship and friendship, partly through agreements between a man and a powerful personage which were concretized by concessions of land, a new social and political organization took shape in the West. Men turned not only to the king and the public power but to their nearer lords. The center of gravity of political life shifted from the palace to the castle. The Empire fractured into small territorial units, and daily life took on new outlines. Feudalism was on the march.

When there was nothing to be hoped for from the justice of the king or his representatives, when there was no powerful man to take one under charge, when one was gnawed by hunger and laid low by sickness, then there was nowhere to turn but to the Church.

Protection by the Church

The Church as Protectress of the Weak . . .

All who knocked at a church door were to be received, even if they were criminals. The fleeing slave and the guilty free man could not be arrested once they had reached the limits of the atrium, for they could claim the right of asylum. Trying to prevent the abuse of this custom, Charlemagne in 779 reiterated that it had limits and commanded that a prisoner be dispatched to the tribunal once the order for his trial had been issued. Exercise of asylum rights also provoked conflicts between churches and monasteries. One affair was quite notorious. During Theodulf's episcopate a monk escaped from his prison in Orleans and took refuge in Saint-Martin of Tours. At the bishop's request, the king tried to have the prisoner seized, but the people of Tours protected him successfully. The bishop complained to Charlemagne, who commanded the remission of the monk to Theodulf's men. But, though Alcuin, the Abbot of Saint-Martin, submitted, the people of Tours intervened to stop the extradition. The bishop retaliated by sending his men to disrupt church services on Sunday. The city of Tours arose, and beggars invaded the church. The youngest monks attacked the Orleanais while the oldest tried to stop the brawl. The fugitive monk remained at Tours. Finally, the king sent a *missus* who seized him, returned him to the Orleans prison, and had the mutineers flogged.[1]

. . . and the Aged

For many, a monastery represented a safe haven from the cares of the world, and the fear of age. Charlemagne deplored the free men who consecrated themselves to God to avoid military service or other royal commands. He suspected that monks favored these "desertions" to accumulate new land for themselves.

To be sure, abbots did agree to accept and entertain layfolk, both men and women, in exchange for a remission of their goods. Some lived with the monks, and others were lodged near the monastery, receiving an alimentary pension. Rich nobles planned to pass their old age in monasteries: "If it should please me to enter a monastery and live there," wrote a woman to the Abbot of Saint-Gall, "I would give it the wherewithal to provide me with proper sustenance." Another benefactor of the same monastery stipulated a particular chamber, warmed, with a daily prebend equal to that of two monks and a new habit every year. A certain Willibald, anticipating old age and its consequent penury, made a still more favorable contract. He made a gift of land as a hospice for the poor in exchange for his own reception into the hospice. There he would have food and clothing, one linen robe and another of wool each year and a new mantle every three years, shoes and everything else to which a monk was entitled. If the contract were not honored, he would recover his land. The canons of Cysoing, near Lille, engaged themselves to lodge a layman, providing him with two loaves of bread daily, identical with their own, equal portions of stew, a full pint of beer, two litres of wine, and, every day, five sous for his pocket money.[2]

But those who had nothing could hope for disinterested assistance from the Church. For all Christians, lay, clerk, or monk, alms-giving was a duty, for alms were more efficacious than fasts in erasing sins. Great folk could never forget the poor who haunted the doors of their dining halls and packed themselves into church porticos. To assure themselves a welcome from the Great Judge, aristocrats prepared for distributions of alms at their deaths to individuals or establishments who could share them out more efficiently. Ansegisius, Abbot of Saint-Wandrille, left large sums of money to cathedral chapters, monasteries, and *xenodochia* (that is, houses for lodging the poor).[3]

Hospitality
Hospitality was also a form of alms-giving. As Charlemagne wrote in 789:

Let there be hospices in different places for travelers, places in monasteries and clerical communities to welcome the poor. For the Lord said, "Reward will come on the great day; I was a guest, and you gave me welcome."

In the ninth century, Hincmar wrote:

> Priests of the diocese ought to take care of guests, particularly the poor and infirm as well as orphans and travelers. They should admit as many as possible to table every day and provide them with a place to stay in a proper manner.[4]

Let us return to the plan of Saint-Gall. To the right of the abbey entrance lay the *domus peregrinorum et pauperum*, composed of a room lined with benches, two dorters, and outer rooms where there were an oven, kneading trough for bread, and a brewery. Symmetrically, the guest house at the left of the entrance was reserved for the rich and therefore more comfortable. Two warming rooms had been planned for them, as well as rooms for their servants and stables for their mounts. The duty of hospitality was to be extended to rich and poor alike. Aldric of Le Mans constructed a hostelry for the poor near the cathedral and another near the bridge over the Sarthe for the reception of bishops, counts, and abbots. These two categories of *hospitalia* can also be seen at Fleury-sur-Loire, Fulda, Jumièges, and Lobbes, reflecting the bipartite division of society which we studied above.[5]

The maintenance of hostelries was a heavy charge. Bishops and abbots budgeted regularly designated resources for that purpose. In 817, Louis the Pious reminded bishops that they were to reserve part of the Church's goods and the tithe from their domains for that purpose. Canons were often designated to look after guests. The same charge was confided to the porter and his assistants in the monasteries. At Corbie, the hosteller had to make daily provision of forty-five maslin loaves (a mixture of wheat and rye) and five of wheat bread, plus cheese, lard, and beans. The poor slept in beds covered with blankets and received used shoes and clothing which the monks no longer needed. The porter welcomed them on arrival and kept dishes and utensils for their use.[6] Thieves often crept among these nameless men, making it necessary to replenish the hostelry utensils frequently. Kings and bishops were also received there. The fathers at the Council of Meaux, however, mourned that the hostels which had flourished under their predecessors had been reduced to nothing and could not receive those who presented themselves there.[7]

A certain category of the poor could be called "privileged" and were inscribed in a register (*matricule*), under the ancient name of *matricularii*. According to Hincmar, *matricularii* were chosen from among aged men and women, the sick, those whom life had crushed, and the "poor." Young and able-bodied men, neatherds, swineherds, and the tenants who worked on the domains were not eligible. At Metz, the archdeacon was directed to distribute a quantity of foodstuffs to the *matricularii* and the remainder to the rest of the poor. In his chapter devoted to "The Hostelry of the Poor," Adalhard of Corbie provided that the twelve poor people who stayed the night should each receive a three-pound maslin loaf for the evening, a half-loaf the next morning, and two glasses of beer. Twelve were also accommodated at Saint-Paul of Lyon and at Saint-Gall. The symbolic number was chosen in memory of the twelve Apostles, but it could be surpassed elsewhere. Charles the Bald endowed the matriculated of Saint-Médard of Soissons with several dozen manses and four mills. The *matricularii* were to be chosen from particularly pitiable poor people or those whose visit to the sanctuary had resulted in a miraculous cure. In exchange they could render small entertainment or guard services. Those mendicants who appeared in defense of the right of asylum at Saint-Martin of Tours certainly represented the matriculated poor.[8]

Anyone who knocked at the door of the monastery was to be not only fed but nursed. The same word *hospitale*, as we know, has provided us our words hotel and hospital. The establishment of Aldric of Le Mans, near the cathedral, received blind men, drunkards, and other infirm. Abbey and chapter doctors could not refuse care to those who asked for it. But above all monks were spiritual doctors. They knew that maladies were caused by vice and sent as salutary chastisement. If human remedies failed to relieve the illness, they appealed to the bounty of God with prayer and visits to the tombs of saints to ask their intercession.

Protection by Saints and Relics

The Cult of the Saints

For the Carolingians, God was distant and severe. He was often represented as the lord of the divine castle, presiding like a powerful king over the celestial court of his vassals, the saints. He was the Divine Judge of the Apocalypse rather than the Lord of the Incarnation. On the mosaic of the chapel at Aix, Christ in majesty was enthroned among the twenty-four elders. Christ the judge was represented at Saint-Gall and at Mustair. Angilbert had an inscription painted at Saint-Riquier which began: "Powerful God, who governs heaven and earth, God, whose majesty reaches everywhere, look down from the height of your glorious throne. . . ." In their struggle against adoptianism, which saw Christ as God's adopted son, Carolingian clergy tended to accentuate the divine nature at the expense of the human.[9] Under such conditions, the faithful thought it best to seek God through the intermediacy of one of the saints:

> We, your very humble servants, pray that by him we may merit delivery from the darkness of our sins to bathe in the light of your celestial glory. With sturdy faith and all the strength of our devotion, we impatiently send prayers and sacrifices of praise through this intermediary to please you and help ourselves.[10]

A saint was a spiritual protector, patron of a town, an abbey, a prince, of all Christians. In him, everyone could be sure of support (*patrocinium*).

Traditionally, the Church had encouraged this devotion to the saints. Monks and clerks put the lives and miracles of God's heroes into writing. The texts were read in church on the vigils of feasts and pilgrimages. Moral examples were drawn from hagiography to reform the conduct of the faithful, who were more in need of personal examples than moral theology lessons. Finding few saints living among themselves, they turned affectionately and fervently to the martyrs of the first centuries or the saints who had borne Christianity to their own lands.

The faithful did not consider the observation of a feast day sufficient veneration for the saints of the Church.

To ensure protection, they sought physical contact; they needed to touch something which had belonged to the holy ones. There was a sacred tree under which Saint Riquier had loved to rest, and the woodman could not cut it down. The bed in which Gerald of Aurillac had slept and the table on which he took his meals became cult objects. The water served to Gerald or Conwoin*, the well water near the tomb of Saint Germain—which the monks sold at a high price, Abbo remarked—were credited with salutary virtues.[11] From the East, relics which represented nothing less than items which had pertained to Christ or the Apostles could be had. At Saint-Riquier, pieces of Christ's robe and sandals were kept, a little of the bread distributed to the Apostles, the milk of the Virgin, the hair of Saint John the Baptist, the strands of Saint Peter's beard, stones which had crushed Saint Stephen (still stained with his blood), and more.[12] But the most efficacious relics were the bones of the saints, maintained in their tombs, which everyone wished to possess, even if only a fragment.

The Relic Hunt

The emphasis laid on possessing relics explains the passion with which bishops, abbots, and laymen threw themselves into the quest for relics.[13] Everyone was alert for new discoveries of tombs or even of recent martyrs. In 858, the monks of Saint-Germain-des-Prés, disappointed in their search for the relics of Saint Vincent in Spain, were reluctant to go home with empty hands. Learning that some Christians had been martyred by the Moslems in Cordova, they hurried to that town and obtained the relics of Saints George and Aurelia.[14]

But such godsends were rare: the age of martyrs was long gone. The Carolingians had to extend the search for the relics of holy martyrs beyond the Mediterranean area. Bishops and princes sent emissaries to the distant East and even into Moslem Africa. Returning from Baghdad through North Africa, the ambassadors of Charlemagne visited the ruins of Carthage and went to worship at the church of

---

* St. Conwoin was Abbot of Redon in Brittany in the ninth century.

In Search of Protectors

Saint Cyprian. They succeeded in obtaining relics of the martyr and sent them on to Arles and Lyon where they were solemnly received by Bishop Leidrad.[15] When he built a new church to Saint Riquier, Angilbert wrote:

> Then (I appealed for relics) to the Roman Church, the generosity of Pope Adrian of good memory, and the venerable Leo after him. Through my master's envoys, I received some from Constantinople, Jerusalem, from Italy, Germany, Aquitaine, Burgundy, and Gaul; patriarchs, archbishops, bishops, and abbots have contributed others. Some were sent from the Sacred Palace from the great store assembled by earlier kings and above all by my master [Charlemagne] and, having merited grace from these alms, we have kept part of the whole and placed them in a sacred repository.[16]

Carolingians turned particularly to Rome because they wanted to possess the remains of the most famous martyrs and because of the fame of the abundant relics of the Eternal City. The cemetery churches had been empty since Paschal I had had two thousand bodies moved within the walls, but amateurs of relics still hoped to find some remaining in place. They were not, however, free simply to seize them without hindrance. When Abbot Hilduin of Saint-Denis sent Rodoin to look for the relics of Saint Sebastian, he had to employ prayers and gifts to sway several high personages. Even so, Pope Eugenius II hesitated for a long time before giving permission, because he feared the reaction of the Romans to the dispossession of their saint. The contradictory pressures exerted on the Pope can be clearly discerned in reading the account of the translation. The difficulties continued even when Rodoin opened the tomb. The Romans "with passionate sobs demanded that ignoble Gauls should not be allowed to carry the holy martyr from his mother land," and some of them blamed the "apostolic lord" for permitting the removal.[17]

The natural slow pace of negotiations was lengthened by such difficulties so that it is no wonder that many sought more expeditious action through the intermediacy of courtiers. Roman clerks were ready to cater to this wish. A deacon named Dieudonné, for example, who was in charge of the third cemeterial region, sought Einhard out at dinner and secretly offered him the relics of Peter and Marcellinus. During another trip, he offered Abbot Hilduin of Saint-Médard of Soissons the relics of Saint Tiburce. Then he went to Fulda with other propositions. Business prospered, and Dieudonné took his brother and a friend into partnership for a good price. No relic could be delivered without assurance of payment. When the monks of the Auvergne did not want to pay immediately, "the astute Romans insisted that they weigh out the money and show it to them if they wished to see their long-awaited martyr."[18]

An even more expeditious manner of procuring relics was simple theft. Such thievery was even regarded as a pious action inspired by God. When Rodoin stole the skull of Gregory the Great, "He was animated by pious devotion, the force of love, and impatient desire."[19] The thieves themselves "deserved praise for the pious fraud." Einhard's notary, whom the Roman courtier had abused, determined to steal the relics of Peter and Marcellinus. Inspired by a vision, he went to the church, prayed for God's help, and emptied the contents of the tomb into a silken bag. After sending the relics off with a courier, he remained in Rome himself for eight days to see whether the inhabitants would discover the theft. He caught up with the relics at Pavia, where he avoided meeting the deputies from the Pope to Louis the Pious. But Einhard was scandalized when part of the same relics were stolen in their turn.[20] Rodoin had far more difficulty stealing the skull of Gregory the Great from Saint Peter's crypt. He had to subdue the guards and make them swear eternal silence on the head of the Pope.

Rome was not the only scene of the theft of relics. Such robberies were perpetrated nearly everywhere. In 866, a monk of Conques successfully stole the head of Saint Foy and brought it back to his monastery. An aristocrat from Alet pretended to enter the service of the monastery of Saintes, the repository for the remains of Saint Malo, and made off with the relics of the Breton monk.[21]

Translations of Relics
The manner of securing relics was forgotten quickly enough. The essential thing was to get them. Then a solemn transla-

In Search of Protectors

tion scene could be played out. The waiting population ran out in a crowd to meet the approaching envoys, and their return took on the glamour of a triumphal procession. At each stop, the relics were displayed in a church or domainal chapel. Clerks organized prayer vigils, and the people held joyous feasts. Then the march began again the next day. Einhard described the coming of the relics of Saint Marcellinus conducted by a great crowd: "Another troop of the faithful came to meet us and accompanied us, singing the *Kyrie Eleison* without interruption until they were replaced by another crowd waiting at the second station."[22] At last the relics reached the sanctuary where they were to repose. When the bishop came out to meet the bearers of the relics of Saint Sebastian into Soissons, the crowd expressed overwhelming joy in applause and dancing:

> The choirs surrounded him on all sides singing psalms. Some carried standards shining in the midst of the hymns and the pleasant sound of musical instruments and the inexhaustible fumes of incense and diverse other perfumes. Others bore the emblem of the Cross, shining with yellow gold and resplendent with precious stones of different colors. Some carried perfume burners and caskets of incense, others candles which brightened the day with brilliant luminescence.[23]

Einhard complained that no words were sufficient to describe the popular joy at the approach of the relics of Saint Marcellinus, or, indeed, the dejection over his decision to transfer relics from Michelstadt to his new abbey of Seligenstadt where they would enjoy a more worthy setting. He tried to manage the translation discreetly at daybreak, but the news leaked out and Saint Marcellinus and Saint Peter went to their new sanctuary in the midst of sorrow and public mourning. Einhard himself felt regret at his separation from his celestial patrons when he went to court. He sent servants to get news of his treasury and even distributed some fragments to other abbeys so that he could meet his saints on his travels.

Conflicts between churches who claimed to have relics of the same saint were violent to the point of fanaticism. When the relics of Saint Helena arrived at Hautvilliers from Rome, the clergy of Reims maintained that the monastery was too small to command so great a treasure. When the monks refused to be dispossessed of them, the people of Reims claimed that the relics were false. A delegation was sent to Rome to secure proof of their authenticity by submitting those who had sent them to a "judgment by water." The Bishop of Laon, jealous of Soissons' possession of the relics of Saint Sebastian, cast doubt on their authenticity until the saint himself appeared to him in a dream.[24]

The "translation movement" continued throughout the ninth century, but around 840 it took on a more dramatic character. Monks were anxious to guard their treasures from the approach of the Normans, not only their furnishings and manuscripts but also the greatest of their treasures, the shrine containing the relics of their patron. The most unforgettable of these translations was that of the relics of Saint Philibert who had been venerated at Noirmoutier since the seventh century. The island was so dangerous after 819 that the monks settled at Deas on the shores of Lake Grandlieu where they constructed a church which still survives in part today. In 845, the increasingly numerous incursions of the Normans on the Continent forced the monks to retreat to Cunault and from there to Messay. But again the peril crept closer, and they had to leave again, this time into the Auvergne to Saint-Pourcain. Finally, the body of Saint Philibert reached his final resting place at Tournus on the Saône in 875.[25]

Saint Martin of Tours himself, the most venerated saint in Francia and all the West, was menaced by the Normans who turned up the Loire to seek out so rich a monastery for pillage. The monks carried the relics to Cormery and returned to Tours when the danger was over. Around 877, the monks interred their patron once again in a tomb that had been abandoned for far too long.[26] Popular manifestations and numerous miracles resulted from these forced translations. The saint's return generated enthusiasm in the restored monastery which contemplated his return but despair among those who had welcomed the relics provisionally. A triumphal procession swelled continuously as it neared home, with hymns and chants of joy rising up around the cortege. The bishop solemnly welcomed back the returning patron.

This translation movement deserves a separate study. It continued to the end of the ninth century and the beginning of the tenth while the Normans attacked Western France, especially Armorica. The relics of the Breton saints, Malo, Magloire, Brieuc, Samson, and even Guénolé venerated at Landévennec, joined the saints of Avranches and Coutances on the road to the French interior. They sought refuge in the Parisian region and the less exposed parts of Flanders, where some of them remained. Thus Malo, or Maclou, was venerated at Rouen, Pontoise, Montreuil-sur-Mer. Saint Maudé or Mandé gave his name to a village near Paris. Breton manuscripts which arrived with the relics can be found in the libraries of Boulogne, Lille, and Douai. Religious and cultural exchanges were thus initiated by the translations of relics between peoples who had often been ignorant of one another.[27]

Expectations from the Saints

The possession of relics constituted an assurance of efficacious protection against natural, human, or demonic afflictions. A newly conquered country in the process of Christianization, like Saxony, demanded relics to help their prosperity. The remains of Saint Guy were transferred from Rome to Saint-Denis and then to Corvey, carrying peace and prosperity to the land, as his hagiographer tells us. To this end the clergy of Paderborn sent clerks to Le Mans for the relics of Saint Liboire. Princes and aristocrats kept relics in their chapels and carried them along in their moves. When Charles the Bald founded a chapel in his palace of Compiègne, he had the relics of Saint Corneille translated from Rome to assure the protection of the sanctuary. When the nuns of Jouarre were suffering from penury and hunger, Abbess Ermentrude asked the Bishop of Sens for the body of Saint Potentian to reestablish the prosperity of the monastery.

The power of relics was displayed when enemies, particularly Normans, attacked Francia. Flodoard stated that the presence of Saint Remi saved the land of Epernay from pillage. During the terrible siege of Paris of 885, the remains of Saint Germain, which had been brought for safety to the island, were thought to have contributed more than the warriors to the repulse of the enemy. The monk Abbo wrote: "Tell us, O city of Paris, what princes will defend you?" Then the city responded: "Who else is my first defender but Saint Germain, all my strength and all my love. . . . He is to me a two-edged sword, a catapult, a buckler, a strong wall and agile bow." Endangered Parisians called Germain to their aid: "O Saint Germain, hasten to the aid of your children. Help, O holy Germain! Quickly, to our aid, or we are lost." "And where did Saint Germain come to the rescue? There, where the struggle was most heated."[28] If Paris, which was not the capital, had become one of the most important cities of the realm, if the Breton and other saints chose her as the land of refuge, it was surely because, saved by relics herself, she seemed to be marked by destiny.

Relics were thought to bestow health on the sickly body beyond the doctor's care. The records of translations and books of miracles drawn in part from the registers kept by monks are precise in their record of miraculous healings. Crowds moved over long distances in search of healing. Odilo of Soissons wrote:

> So great a number of people, from all the land of the Gauls and from Germania, and from provinces far from the sea, gathered that they filled every space, like grasshoppers, no matter how great it was. Among them, the blind, the lame, those with withered limbs, lepers, epileptics. . . .[29]

They came from Aquitaine, Berry, Champagne, Liège, and Helvetia to Seligenstadt where the remains of Saint Marcellinus reposed. Some came on foot; the blind and the paralyzed were carried by friends or rode in boats borrowed from merchants. Among the sick, there were children and young folk, grown men and women, and a few old people. Though the texts mention some clerks and monks, the bulk of the miracles benefited the common people, slaves, domestics of the great, and artisans. Some could walk only on all fours while others dragged themselves on their knees and others were so contracted that their knees touched their jaws. "A woman held up her hand, withered and parched of all liquid, and one of her feet had turned black from the same emaciation and dryness." Some men were so hunchbacked that they could never see the sky without lying on their backs. Einhard noted some who suffered from a trembling "malady which doctors call by the Greek name of *spasmon* and which is called *tremulosa* in Latin because of the continual agitation of the members which is its symptom." And we must distinguish the maladies of the "possessed," usually women and young girls, who cried out and struggled so violently that they had to be chained. Even more frightful were men stricken with ulcers, their bodies filled with pus and worms, their limbs swollen or so diseased that they fell away. This illness was probably elephantiasis or leprosy. There is certainly much material in these descriptions waiting to be exploited for the history of medicine.[30]

The sick boarded in sanctuary hostelries or spent the night at the church door, or even near the tomb. Praying, they waited for hours or days for some sign or vision that would announce their healing. They brought offerings, often modest like a piece of linen or a candle. Others promised to exchange a gift for the miracle. Healings most frequently occurred during the Mass or after a night of prayer. They were rapid and brutal. The sick person might fall face down on the ground, "as though he had been pushed" or "as though he had received a blow," and remain extended for a period as though dead. This period of lethargy could be immediately followed by a hemorrhage. Some rolled on the ground, vomited, and stood up healed.[31] The people who had been healed miraculously and the crowd around them all expressed their joy by crying and applauding and dancing. They would then have to fulfill the promises they had made if relapse was not to be inevitable, for the saints never loved the ungrateful.

Nor did the saints like to be mocked. If goods placed under their protection were interfered with, they might appear as justiciar. A man who had stolen some sheaves of wheat belonging to Saint Regnobert replied to the accusing monk: "If Saint Regnobert were a blade of rye, I would give him to my horse for feed." He fell dead on the spot. A peasant who ground his grain on the saint's feastday found that he could not stop his hand and foot from repeating the circular motion.[32] Saints knew how to respond to the appeals of victims of robbery and brutality and help those who were in distress. Innumerable reports of their intercession exist. Their chosen victims were unjust counts, extortionate land-lords, and brutal bishops.

Abuses

Inevitably the cult of relics gave rise to excesses. Bishops were obliged to intervene in swindles and scandals. Men and women at the tomb of Saint Firmin at Uzès were suddenly seized with epilepsy. The people panicked and tried to calm the anger of the saint by gifts of gold, silver, and cattle. Suspecting some sort of hoax financed by the clergy for the enrichment of the sanctuary, the bishop closed access to the tomb. The Bishop of Langres was similarly disquieted by the miracles provoked by the relics of an unknown saint at Dijon whose Roman origin had been taken as proof of authenticity. Women were falling into convulsions in the midst of their prayers. Soon the number of convulsed mar-ried women and young girls mounted to three or four hundred. Amolon of Lyon advised the bishop to remove the relics secretly to avoid a tumult and then to have them buried. He deplored the fact that the regularly ordained devotions to relics on specified days were being neglected while "the people throw themselves upon those which had been recommended by no one, of which nothing was taught, and which were sometimes even forbidden."[33] Carolingian bishops knew that the relic cult could degenerate into superstition and exploitation of popular credulity. They re-minded people that saints were only intercessors, and all religious manifestations should lead us to worship the true God. Princes and high clergymen denounced false martyrs and tested the authenticity of relics. Hearing that a vial con-taining Christ's blood had been found in Mantua, Charle-magne sent a *missus* to verify its origins.[34] An effort was generally made to establish some proof that what the people were venerating was indeed saintly. In 864, the Bishop of Constance submitted a dossier which he had compiled on the Abbot of Saint-Gall, Othmar, establishing his claims to sainthood to a diocesan synod. After a three-day fast, they authorized the translation of the relics.[35]

Pilgrimages

Carolingians did not hesitate to leave a comfortable palace or miserable cottage to take to the road to seek out the protection of the saints. There were many forms of pilgrimage.[36] Some visits to holy places were inspired by the search for relics, others to accomplish a vow, to expiate a hidden sin, or fulfill the obligation to do penance. Kings and high clergymen protected these "poor" on pilgrimage, exempted them from all taxes, provided stopping places where they could rest. In addition to hostelries which were open to all travelers, special houses of welcome for pilgrims had been created. Since the seventh century, the Irish knew that they would find *hospitalia* reserved for them at Auxerre, Honau (an island on the Rhine), Péronne, Pavia, Piacenza.[37] Debarking Anglo-Saxons were received at Saint-Josse, La Celle, a dependent of Ferriéres; Bretons, at Moutiers-en-Puisaye. In the ninth century, Murbach was called the "breeding ground of pilgrims." At the Alpine passes, Mont-Joux (the Great Saint Bernard) and Mont Cenis, or at the debouchements of the Alpine valleys at Aosta and Novalaise, and near Susa, monks waited to welcome pilgrims on the way to or from Rome.[38]

The Pilgrims

Pilgrims did not always hurry along. Adventurers and men of doubtful morality insinuated themselves into the crowds moving toward the holy places. Clerks and monks sometimes went without the permission of their superiors and used pilgrimages to escape the restrictions of the rule. Nuns particularly were in danger. Perhaps Boniface exaggerated when he said that all the religious women who came to Rome afterwards filled the brothels in French and Italian towns.[39] But the fathers of the Council of Aquilea feared the relationships which abbesses and nuns might form with men during the trip. They thus forbade all pilgrimage to Rome or elsewhere to them.[40] Some of the reasons given for a pilgrimage a pilgrimage were astonishing: laymen took the road not were astonishing: laymen took the road not only to obtain absolution for their sins but also for those which they would commit in the future. As Theodulf said: "It might be better to live honestly at home than to go to Rome. One does not get to heaven on foot but on good conduct." Another bishop, Claudius of Turin, was equally reserved in saying of the Roman pilgrimage: "I neither approve nor disapprove, for I know very well that if it does not do good to all, neither does it do evil to all."[41] But it would be more profitable to put goods aside for the poor than to pay for a pilgrimage. Many of the detractors of pilgrimages repeated the verse of a disillusioned Irishman: "To go to Rome, great fatigue, little profit. You will find the king you went there seeking only if you brought him with you."

Great Pilgrimage Centers

Any tomb containing relics might become a pilgrimage center. The maps which can be partially drawn from the history of the translation of Marcellinus and Peter show that the sick in search of a cure came over great distances to Seligenstadt, Ghent, Valenciennes, Maestricht. Certain monasteries with old reputations, renown, and, no doubt, an organization for welcoming pilgrims drew great crowds. Saint-Martin of Tours remained the most frequented tomb in Francia. Everyone from prince to pauper went there. Though, unhappily, we have no documentation for the ninth century, we are very rich in evidence for the sixth century, thanks to Gregory of Tours. The antique basilica, 53 meters long and 20 meters wide, was still standing. It burned at the beginning of the tenth century but was reconstructed very rapidly at great expense, for the monks were very rich. The pilgrims could approach at all hours and then collect powder from the tomb or oil from the lamps which burned continuously. They slept in the place or in hostelries near the monastery.

Pilgrims were also drawn to other saints' tombs: Saint Benedict at Fleury-sur-Loire, Saint Hilary at Poitiers, Saint Martial at Limoge, and Saint Germain at Auxerre. But a new center was already becoming well known: Saint Michel-aux-deux-Tombes, our Mont-Saint-Michel, was described by the monk Bernard about 870:

In Search of Protectors

At the summit of the mount there is a church in honor of Saint Michael, and twice a day, at morning and evening, the sea swells and encircles the mount, and men cannot go to the mount until the sea has retreated. However, on the feast of Saint Michael, the sea does not encircle the mount, and all who come to pray can reach the mount at every hour.[42]

The recently restored Carolingian church recalls the arrangement of the crypt of another sanctuary of Saint Michael of Monte Gargano.

Italian Pilgrimages

Again we rely on Bernard for a report on the important pilgrimage to southern Italy. In a grotto surmounted by an oak tree stood an image of the archangel. About fifty persons could worship there and leave their offerings. Bernard also visited Mons Aureus, which the latest works suggest was also a sanctuary dedicated to Saint Michael established near the village of Olevano sul Tusciano by the Bishop of Salerno. There we find the same arrangement: "a grotto comprised of seven altars, so dark that those who penetrate it must carry lights. Above it, there is a great forest." Certainly such shrines bear witness to a Christianized chthonic cult.[43]

From the Mons Aureus, Bernard gained Rome with its tombs of apostles and martyrs. From the seventh century on, the quest for Roman relics, the prestige of the Roman See, allied as it was to the Franks, favored the multiplication of pilgrimages to Rome. All Christians went to Rome as to a second motherland; they desired to go there at least once in their lives and even to die there.

When they arrived at Rome, pilgrims found lodging in the hostelries provided for each national group near Saint Peter's. The Anglo-Saxon *schola* included lodgings, a church, and a cemetery. Comparable ensembles on the same model existed for the Frisians, Franks, and Lombards.[44] Pilgrims used guidebooks to make their way through the labyrinth of Roman ruins and multiplicity of churches. The *Notitia ecclesiarum urbis Romae*, the *De locis sanctis martyrum quae sunt foris civitatis Romae*, and above all the "Itinerary" found in the Abbey of Einsiedeln were written or copied in Carolingian times. The "Itinerary," written in the eighth century, gives eleven succinct and precise itineraries, mentioning the principal antique and medieval edifices as do our "green" and "blue guides" today.[45] Pilgrims were supposed to visit the seven basilicas which had preserved their sumptuous adornments from late antiquity: Saint John Lateran (seat of the papacy and of the three basilicas of the Esquiline); Saint Mary Maggiore; Holy Cross of Jerusalem, where they venerated a piece of the true Cross; Saint Lawrence; Saint Paul outside the walls; and finally, also outside the walls, Saint Sebastian on the Appian Way and Saint Paul on the road to Ostia. The climax was a visit to Saint Peter's in the Vatican. We can imagine the pilgrims climbing the 35 steps leading to the atrium, making their ablutions in the great fountain and bowing before the bronze doors of the basilica. Entering the interior, they perceived the triumphal arch and the mosaic of Constantine and, below, the ciborium which protected the tomb. Passing the 96 columns of marble, admiring the silken stuffs displayed on either side, they came to kneel before the *confessio** under the grill which permitted them to see the sarcophagus lit by many lamps and decorated with golden bas-reliefs.

Pilgrimages to the East

Some of the richer and more daring pilgrims wished to push their trip beyond Rome to the places where Christ had lived. Palestine had been in the hands of the Moslems since the seventh century, but out of tolerance and self-interest they let pilgrims enter freely. The good relations which knit the Carolingian and Abassid princes together favored pilgrimages. If Charlemagne had not become protector of the holy places, he had obtained assurances of security for Christian travelers. He had also the power to aid the churches of Jerusalem materially. In general, Christians from the West could expect a warm welcome from the native Christian population.[46] If they respected the laws of the country and paid the travel taxes (13 deniers around 870), they could circulate freely everywhere. We have two accounts of pilgrimages: the travels of the Anglo-Saxon Willibald in the Holy Land from 724 to 729 and those of the

* See p. 30 above.

In Search of Protectors

monk Bernard who was in Palestine from 866 to 870. They both set out from southern Italy after getting passports in order. They sailed for two months on the sort of merchant ships which we have seen trafficking between the West and the East.[47] They prepared for the trip with descriptions of the holy places which had been copied since the sixth century. The most commonly used guide was the *De locis sanctis* written at the end of the seventh century and revised by the Venerable Bede.[48] The basilicas of Jerusalem were discovered to be as the guides described them: the Holy Sepulcher served by about 50 clerks, the church of the Mount of Olives where Frankish monks were installed, the Cenacle of Mount Zion where Christ had celebrated the Last Supper. From Jerusalem, they went to Bethlehem to worship in the grotto which protected the basilica restored by Justinian, and then they climbed north to Nazareth. At Cana they were invited to see wine preserved in the jugs which had served for the miracle. They bathed in the Jordan and were entertained by monks at the monastery of Saint John the Baptist. Pilgrims brought back a collection of *eulogies* from all these visits, most commonly consisting of phials of water, cloths which had touched the sanctuaries, powder and oils. To fool the watchful "customs officers," Willibald concealed his contraband balm in a gourd-shaped receptacle slipped into the opening of a hollow rod filled with naphtha.[49]

Neither Willibald nor Bernard pursued their travels farther. But the Sinai and the sanctuaries of Egypt still drew pilgrims. The *Deeds of the Abbots of Redon* recounts the great circuit in the middle of the eighth century completed by the aristocratic Fromund and his brother, Franks who had killed their uncle to get the inheritance. Condemned to visit the holy places with their arms weighed down with chains, they went to Rome, from there to Jerusalem, then to the Egyptian monasteries for two years. They took the road to Africa and prayed at the tomb of Saint Cyprian at Carthage. Their penance was judged still insufficient when they returned to Rome, and so they returned to the Holy Land, visiting the mountains of Armenia where Noah's ark had landed, back to Palestine and Mount Sinai. Back at Rome four years later, they still could not obtain remission for their sin. They crossed Italy, Burgundy, Neustria, finally arriving in Brittany. Though his brother died at Rennes, Fromund pursued his road to the tomb of Pope Marcellinus which the monks of Redon had translated from Rome some years before. There, following a vision, his chains fell away and he was healed of the wounds left by the iron. Despite the urgings of the monks who wished to keep him among them, he determined to go back to Rome to give thanks for his deliverance. But he had hardly begun his trip when he found at last the true end of all human wandering.[50]

In Search of Protectors

From the Mid-Eighth Century to the End of the Ninth Century

Chronology

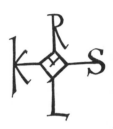

796 Submission of the Avars.
Alcuin Abbot of Saint-Martin of Tours.
Construction of Aix-la-Chapelle. Einhard at court

797 Submission of Saxony

800 Imperial coronation of Charlemagne.
Foundation of Conques. Capitulary *De villis*

801 Taking of Barcelona. Envoys from Baghdad to Aix

804 Death of Alcuin. Foundation of Gellone

812 Treaty between Charlemagne and
the Byzantine Emperor

814 Death of Charlemagne. Advent of Louis the Pious.
Death of Angilbert. Wala exiled to Corbie

816 Agobard succeeds Leidrad to bishopric of Lyon.
Benedict of Aniane Abbot of Inde. Council of Aix-la-
Chapelle. Stephen V crowns Louis at Reims.
Plan of Saint-Gall

817 *Ordinatio Imperii*. Affirmation of the unitary
principle of Empire. Revolt and submission of
Bernard of Italy

818 Expedition to Brittany

819 Marriage of Louis and Judith.
Redaction of *Vita Caroli* by Einhard.
Noirmoutier threatened by Normans

821 Deaths of Benedict of Aniane and Theodulf.
Normans on Atlantic coast

822 Adalhard of Corbie redacts his *Constitutiones*

823 Birth of Charles the Bald. Amalarius write *De officiis
ecclesiasticis;* Drogo Bishop of Metz

824 Marriage of Bernard of Septimania and Dhuoda at Aix

826 Harold of Denmark at Ingelheim.
Mission of Anscharius in Scandinavia.
Relics of Saint Sebastian at Soissons

827 Translation of the relics of Saint Marcellinus.
Byzantine embassy at court

829 Council of Paris. Bernard chamberlain.
Inheritance to Charles

830 Lothair's revolt and the imperialists

831 Jonas writes *De institutione regia.*
Conwoin Abbot of Redon. Amalarius at Rome

833 New revolt of Lothair. Penance of Saint-Médard of Soissons. Reconstruction of Saint-Wandrille by Ansegisus

835 Restoration of Louis; reprisals

836 Death of Wala, of Jesse of Amiens, Counts Hugues and Lambert

837 Revolt of Louis the German

839 Division of the Empire between Lothair and Charles

840 Death of Louis the Pious. Alliance between Charles and Louis the German. Death of Einhard

841 Attack on Quentovic by the Normans. Battle of Fontenay-en-Puisaye (June 25).
Dhuoda writes her Manual

842 Oaths of Strasbourg. The Saracens pillage Arles

843 Treaty of Verdun. Assembly of Coulaines.
Nithard writes his History.
Pillage of Nantes by the Normans

845 Hincmar Bishop of Reims.
Sack of Paris by the Normans

846 Sack of Rome by the Saracens.
Construction of the Leonine City

848 Condemnation of Gottschalk at Mainz.
Coronation of Charles at Orleans

849 Death of Walafrid Strabo. Defeat of Louis in Bohemia

850 Louis II associated in the Empire.
Normans on the Scheld

855 Death of Lothair. Normans on the Seine and the Loire

856 Death of Hrabanus Maurus

857 Rising in Aquitaine. Louis invades *Francia occidentalis.*
Death of Aldric of Le Mans

858 Nicholas I Pope. Charles the Bald attacks the Normans at Jeufosse. Trip of Usuard to Spain

860 Lothair II's divorce. Crypts of Auxerre

861 Normans sack Saint-Germain-des-Près

862   John Scotus writes *De divisione naturae*. Otfrid of Wissemburg writes his paraphrase of the Gospels in Germanic. Death of Lupus of Ferrières

864   Assembly of Pitres. Submission of Lothair II to the Pope. Normans on the Rhine

866   Death of Robert the Strong at Brissarthe. The relics of Saint Foy at Conques. Heric master at Auxerre

869   Death of Lothair II. Partition of Lotharingia between Charles and Louis the German.
Treaty between Bretons and Normans

871   Recapture of Bari from the Moslems

872   John VIII Pope

875   Death of Louis II. Charles the Bald crowned Emperor at Rome. Foundation of Tournus

876   Death of Louis the German

877   Capitulary of Quierzy. Death of Charles the Bald.
Louis the Stammerer becomes King of France.
Return of the relics of Saint Martin to Tours

878   John VIII in France

879   Death of Louis the Stammerer. Normans at Ghent.
Boso elected King of Provence

881   Charles the Fat Emperor.
Victory of Saucourt-en-Vimeu over the Normans

882   Death of Hincmar. Fortification of Soissons

885   Siege of Paris by the Normans.
Completion of the church of Corvey

887   Abdication of Charles the Fat.
Arnulf King of Germany

888   Eudes elected King of France

889   Guy of Spoleto King of Italy. Fortification of Corbie.
Hungarian raid in northern Italy

894   Foundation of the monastery of Aurillac

897   Abbo writes his poem on the siege of Paris

900   Hungarians in Bavaria

910   Foundation of Cluny

911   Normans installed in "Normandy"

A Preliminary Word on the Sources

For the convenience of the reader and to avoid repetition of bibliographic details, I present here a list of the main sources cited in the notes proper.

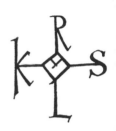

Notes

I. Collections of Sources

PL: *Patrologia Latina*, ed. J. P. Migne, Paris, 1844–1864.

MGH: *Monumenta Germaniae Historica.* Hanover-Leipzig, 1826 et seq.
    SS: *Scriptores.*
    SMR: *Scriptores rerum merovingicarum.*
    Capitul.: Capitularia regum Francorum, Vols. I and II.
    Conc.: Concilia, Vol. II.
    Formulae, ed. Zeumer.
    Epist: Epistolae Karolini aevi, Vols. III to VIII of the *Epistolae.*
    Poet.: Poetae latini aevi Carolini.

Liber Pontificalis, ed. L. Duchesne and C. Vogel, Paris, 1955–57.

AS: *Acta sanctorum*, published by the Bollandists, 1643.

ASOB: *Acta sanctorum ordinis benedictini*, ed. J. Mabillon and T. Ruinart, 9 vols., Paris, 1668–1701.

RH: *Revue historique.*

Corpus: Corpus Consuetudinum monasticarum, published under the direction of K. Hallinger, Vol. I, *Initia consuetudinis benedictinae*, Sieburg, 1963.

II. Editions of Authors Most Commonly Cited

ABBO of Saint-Germain-des-Près: *Le Siège de Paris par les Normands*, ed. and trans. (into French) H. Waquet, Paris, 1924 (2d ed., 1964).

Annales Royales, Annales de Saint-Bertin, Annales de Fulda, Annales de Saint-Vaast, Annales de Xanten, ed. R. Rau, in *Quellen zur Karolingischen Reichsgeschichte*, Darmstadt, 1968–1969. The *Annales Royales* have been translated into English by B. W. Scholz, *Carolingian Chronicles*, Ann Arbor, 1972.

ASTRONOMER: *Vita Ludovici*, ed. R. Rau, Darmstadt, 1968, Vol. I; English trans. A. Cabaniss, *Son of Charlemagne*, Syracuse, 1961.

DHUODA: *Manuel pour mon fils*, ed. and trans. P. Riché, *Sources Chrétiennes*, Vol. CCXXV, Paris, 1975.

EINHARD: *Vita Caroli*, ed. and trans. L. Halphen, Paris, 1938; English trans. L. Thorpe, London, 1970.

ERMOLD the Black: *Poème sur Louis le Pieux et épître au roi Pépin*, ed. and trans. E. Faral, Paris, 1932.

LUPUS of Ferrières: *Correspondance*, ed. and trans. L. Levillain, 2 vols., Paris, 1927 and 1935; English trans. G. W. Regenos, *The Letters of Lupus of Ferrières*, The Hague, 1966.

NITHARD: *Histoire des Fils de Louis le Pieux*, ed. and trans. P. Lauer, Paris, 1926; English trans. B. W. Scholz, *Carolingian Chronicles*, Ann Arbor, 1972.

NOTKER, *Gesta Caroli*, ed. R. Rau, Darmstadt, 1969 (2d ed., 1974). English trans. L. Thorpe, *Two Lives of Charlemagne*, London, 1971.

REGINO of Prüm: *Chronique*, ed. R. Rau, Darmstadt, 1969.

——, *De synodalibus causis*, PL 132, C 185–371, and Wasserschleben, Leipzig, 1840.

THEGAN: *Vita Ludovici imperatoris*, ed. R. Rau, Darmstadt, 1968.

III. Modern Authors

R. Boutruche, *Seigneurie et Féodalité*, Vol. I, Paris, 1959.

Catalogue de l'Exposition Charlemagne à Aix-la-Chapelle, French trans. Düsseldorf, 1965.

R. Doehaerd, *Le Haut Moyen Age occidental, Economies et Sociétés*, Paris, 1971.

G. Duby, *L'Economie rurale et la Vie des Campagnes dans l'Occident médiéval*, Vol. I, Paris, 1962; English trans. C. Postan, *Rural Economy and Country Life in the Medieval West*, London, 1968.

L. Halphen, *Charlemagne et l'Empire carolingien*, Paris, 1947 (2d ed., 1968).

J. Hubert, J. Porcher, and W. F. Volbach, *L'Empire Carolingien*, Collection Univers des Formes, Paris, 1968; English trans. J. Emmons, S. Gilbert, and R. Allen, *The Carolingian Renaissance*, New York, 1970.

Karl der Grosse: Lebenswerk und Nachleben, 4 vols., Düsseldorf, 1965.

R. Latouche, *Les Origines de l'Economie occidentale*, Paris, 1956; English trans. E. M. Wilkinson, *The Birth of the Western Economy*, New York, 1961.

E. Lesne, *Histoire de la Propriété ecclésiastique en France*, Vol. III, *Eglises et Trésors des Eglises du commencement du VIIIᵉ à la fin du XIᵉ siècle*, Lille, 1938.
Vol. IV, *Les Livres, Scriptoris et Bibliothèques du commencement du VIIIᵉ à la fin du XIᵉ siècle*, Lille, 1938.

Vol. V., *Les écoles de la fin du VIIIe siècle à la fin du XIIe siècle*, Lille, 1943.

Vol. VI, Les Eglises et les monastères, centres d'accueil, d'exploitation et de peuplement, Lille, 1943.

Settimana: Settimane di Studio del centro italiano di studi sull'alto medioevo, Spoleto, 1954 et seq.

Introduction

1. S. Dufrenne, "Les Illustrations du Psautier d'Utrecht," thèse dactylographiée, Strasbourg, 1972.

2. The following works especially deserve attention. J. Boussard, *Charlemagne et son temps*, Paris, 1968; English trans. F. Partridge, *The Civilization of Charlemagne*, New York, 1968. H. Fichtenau, *Das karolingische Imperium*, Zurich, 1949; English trans. P. Munz, *The Carolingian Empire*, Oxford, 1957. R. Folz, *Le Couronnement impérial de Charlemagne*, Paris, 1964; English trans. J. E. Anderson, *The Coronation of Charlemagne*, London, 1974. L. Halphen, *Charlemagne et l'Empire carolingien*, Paris, 1947 (2d ed., 1970). F. Lot, *Naissance de la France*, Paris, 1948 (2d ed., 1970). G. Tessier, *Charlemagne*, Paris, 1967.

At the time of writing, J. Devisse, *Hincmar, archevêque de Reims (845–882)*, Geneva, 1975–76, had not yet been published.

Chapter 1

1. Dicuil, *Liber de mensura orbis terrae*, Editions L. Bieler, Dublin, 1967. On Aethicus, cf. F. Brunhölzl, *Zur Kosmographie des Aethicus*, in Fest. M. Spender, Munich, 1969, pp. 75–89. A restatement on "the geography and conception of the world in the Carolingian period" has been made by S. Haquet (maîtrise d'histoire), Université de Paris X, 1972.

2. M. Destombes, *Mappae Mundi*, Amsterdam, 1964. *Liber Pontificalis*, I, 432. Micon de Saint-Riquier, *Poet.*, III, 297. Theodulf, *Poet.*, I, 547. On this poem, see A. Vidier, "La Mappemonde de Ripoll," *Bulletin de Géographie historique et descriptive*, Paris, 1911.

3. K. Miller, *Mappae Mundi, Die ältesten Weltkarten*, Stuttgart, 1895.

4. *Vita Faroni*, 9, MGH, SRM, IV, 184.

5. M. Hellman, "Karl und die slawische Welt," in *Karl der Grosse*, I, p. 708.

6. Notker, II, 12.

7. Notker, II, 1.

8. *Conc.*, II, 1, p. 173. *Epist.*, IV, pp. 143, 154. See also J. Deer, "Karl der Grosse und der Untergang des Awarenreiches," in *Karl der Grosse*, I, p. 719.

9. *Annales Fulda*, 900; Regino, *Chronique*, 889.

10. Ermold, p. 102.

11. *Annales Royales*, 813. Cf. H. Jankuhn, "Karl der Grosse und der Norden," in *Karl der Grosse*, I, p. 699.

12. E. Ewig, "Descriptio Franciae," in *Karl der Grosse*, I, p. 143. K-F. Werner, "Les Nations et le sentiment national dans l'Europe médiévale," RH, 1970, pp. 285–304, and, by the same author, "Les Principautés périphériques dans l'Occident au VIIIe siècle," *Settimana*, XX (1973), pp. 483–532.

13. K. Reindel, "Bayern im Karolingerreich," in *Karl der Grosse*, I, p. 220.

14. Nithard, IV, 2 and 6. On the customs of the Saxons, cf. *Translatio S. Alexandri*, MGH, SS, II, 674.

15. P. Wolff, "L'Aquitaine et ses marges," in *Karl der Grosse*, I, p. 269.

16. Astronomer, 4.

17. Notker, I, 32.

18. *Gesta Berengarii, Poet.*, IV, pp. 360 and 380.

19. Cf. P. Wolff, *Les Origines linguistiques de l'Europe occidentale*, Paris, 1970.

20. *Vita Caroli*, 29.

21. Nithard, III, 5.

22. Lupus, *Epist.* 35.

23. *Glossaire de Reichenau*, ed. Labhardt, Munich, 1968. *Glossaire de Cassel*, P. Marchot, Fribourg, 1895.

24. D. Norberg, *Manuel pratique du Latin médiéval*, Paris, 1950, p. 50.

25. *Conc.*, II, 1, 288.

26. W. Betz, "Karl der Grosse und die lingua theodosca," in *Karl der Grosse*, II, p. 300.

27. *Vita Caroli*, 29. See also F. L. Ganshof, "Charlemagne et l'administration de la justice," in *Karl der Grosse*, I, p. 394.

28. P. Riché, "Les Bibliothèques de trois aristocrates laïcs carolingiens," *Le Moyen Age* (1963), p. 99.

29. Agobard, *Epist.*, V, 158–59.

30. Cf. E. Amann, *L'Epoque carolingienne*, Paris, 1947, p. 247. H. Buttner, "Mission und Kircheorganization des Frankenreiches," in *Karl der Grosse*, I, p. 454.

31. Florus, *Poet.* II, p. 561, *Querela de divisione imperii.*

Chapter 2

1. Astronomer, 7.

2. Cf. K. R. Brülh, *Fodrum, gistum, servitium regis*, Cologne, 1968.

3. A. Gauert, "Zum Itinerar Karls des Grossen," in *Karl der Grosse*, I, pp. 307–321. Also see the maps established by K. R. Brülh, *op. cit.*, Vol. II.

4. See the old work of Lesne, *La Propriété ecclésiastique et les droits régaliens à l'époque carolingienne*, Lille, 1926, p. 392, and the essential work of K. R. Brülh, already cited.

5. Notker, I, 14. Leirade, *Epist.*, IV, 542.

6. Lupus, *Epist.* 115; *Capit.* II, 405.

7. Theodulf, *Poet.* I, pp. 493–520.

8. F. L. Ganshof, "La tractoria, Contribution à l'étude des origines du droit de gîte, *Revue Historique du Droit* (1927), pp. 69–91.

9. *Formulae*, ed. Zeumer, p. 292.

10. Lupus, *Epist.* 41, 8, 61.

11. Einhard, *Epist.* 56.

12. Nithard, II, 8.

13. Lupus, *Epist.* 101.

14. Cf. infra, p. 270–272.

15. Doehaerd, p. 265; J. Hubert, "Les Routes au Moyen Age," in *Les Routes en France*, Paris, 1959.

16. Usuard, *De translatione sanctorum*, PL 115, 939–960.

17. *Translatio S. Helenae*, 55–56. *Formulae*, ed. Zeumer, p. 429.

18. *Liber Pontificalis*, I, p. 445.

19. *Annales Royales*, 801.

20. Odo, *Vita Geraldi*, II, 17.

21. Regino, *Chronique*, 866.

22. P. Duparc, "Les Cluses et la frontière des Alpes," *Bibl. de l'Ecole des Chartes*, 1951.

23. *Annales Bertin*, 878.

24. Ermold, p. 60; Nithard, III, 12; Einhard, *Transl.*, 56.

25. *Vita Geraldi*, I, 29.

26. *Vita Caroli*, 17.

27. *Annales Bertin*, 865.

28. *Nithard*, II, 6.

29. *Poet.*, II, 423.

30. *De villis*, 64. Astronomer, 15.

31. *Translatio S. Liborii*, ed. Archives Historiques du Maine, XIV, 1967.

32. J. Lestocquoy, "La navigation fluviale au IXe siècle, les flotilles monastiques," in *Congrès de Jumièges*, Rouen, 1954, pp. 247–252; Doehaerd, p. 244; *Formulae*, ed. Zeumer, p. 313.

33. Lupus, *Epist.* 111.

34. *Inquisitio de theloneis Raffelstettensis, Capit.* II, 249. See, on the text, F. L. Ganshof, "Note," *Le Moyen Age* (1966), pp. 197–223; *Vita Bonifacii*, 8; *Vita Anscharii*, 11.

35. *Annales Royales,* 793; cf. H. Hofmann, "Fossa Carolina," in *Karl der Grosse*, I, pp. 437–453.

36. F. L. Ganshof, "Eginhard à Gand," in *Bullet. de la Soc. d'Histoire et d'Archéol. de Gand* (1926).

37. *Annales Bertin*, 875 and 876. Einhard, *Translatio S. Marcellini* 13; Nithard III, 4. *Translatio S. Liborii*, op. cit.

38. *Vita Caroli*, 1.

39. L. White, *Technology and Social Change in the Middle Ages*, Fig. 3, Oxford, 1962.

Chapter 3

1. On the forest, cf. C. Higounet, "Les forêts dans l'Europe occidentale du Ve au XIe siècle," *Settimana*, XIII (1966), pp. 343–398.

2. *Vita Sturmi*, PL 105, 425.

3. Ermold, p. 96; Notker, II, 8; *Annales Bertin*, 846, 858.

4. *De villis*, 69, *Capit.* I.

5. *De villis*, 46, *Dipl.* I, 256.

6. *De villis*, 47 and 58; Hincmar, *De Ordine palatii, Capit.* II, p. 523. Notker, I, 20, and II, 9.

7. Jonas, *De Institutione laicali*, II, 23. Cf. texts cited in the article "Chasse" of the *Dictionnaire d'Archéologie chrétienne et de Liturgie*, II, I, 1090–1091.

8. Ermold, pp. 22, 96.

9. Cf. the table, infra, p. 250–251.

10. Nithard, III, 3; *Annales Bertin*, 861; *Annales Royales,* 797.

11. Sedulius, *Poet.*, III.

12. Alcuin, *Poet.*, I, pp. 369, 270.

13. Walafrid Strabo, *Poet.*, II, 335.

14. Hrabanus Maurus, *De Universo*, PL 107, 680.

15. Lupus, *Epist.* 70.

Chapter 4

1. J. Hubert, "Evolution de la topographie et de l'aspect des villes de Gaule du Ve au Xe siècle," *Settimana*, VI (1959), p. 529–558. E. Latouche, *Origines*, p. 201.

2. E. Ewig, "Résidence et capitale dans le Haut Moyen Age," in RH, 1963, pp. 25–70. Partial Eng. trans. in S. Thrupp, *Early Medieval Society*, New York, 1967.

3. C. P. Bognetti, *Storia di Milano*, Vol. III, Milan, 1954. The poem on Milan is in *Poet.*, I, 34.

4. There is no study of the whole of Carolingian Rome, but L. Homo, *Rome Médiévale*, Paris, 1956, may be consulted.

5. M. Fleury, "Paris du Bas Empire au XIIIᵉ siècle," in *Paris, Croissance d'une capitale*, Paris, 1961, pp. 73 ff. M. Vieillard-Troiekouroff, "Les anciennes églises suburbaines de Paris, IVᵉ–Xᵉ siècles," in *Paris et Ile de France, Mémoires*, XI, 1960.

6. J. Hubert, "La Renaissance Carolingienne et la topographie des cités épiscopales," *Settimana*, I (1954), pp. 219–225.

7. *Epist.*, IV, 542.

8. Flodoard, *Hist. eccl. Remens.*, III, 5; Alcuin, *Poet.*, I.

9. *Gesta episc. Autissor*, PL 138, 265; Sedulius, *Carm.* II, 4.

10. Doehaerd, pp. 242–243. See the poem of Milo on Tournai, *Poet.*, III, p. 589.

11. *Gesta sanctor. Rotonensium*, I, 10. The author designates a prostitute by the curious word *apodix*.

12. On the *portus*, see F. L. Ganshof, *La Belgique carolingienne*, Brussels, 1958, pp. 121 ff.; G. Despy, "Note sur le 'portus' de Dinant au IXᵉ et Xᵉ siècle," in *Mélanges Niermeyer*, Groningen, 1967, pp. 61–69. By the same author, see also "Villes et campagnes au IXᵉ et Xᵉ siècle, l'exemple du pays mosan, in *Revue du Nord*, L (1968), pp. 145–168.

Chapter 5

1. Plan preserved in the Bibliothèque de Saint-Gall, published in facsimile by the Société d'Histoire du Canton de Saint-Gall, 1952. Reduced reproduction and commentary in *Catalogue de l'Exposition Charlemagne*, Aix-la-Chapelle, 1965, p. 391.

2. *Gesta Fontanellensis*, 17, ed. Lohier, Paris, 1936.

3. Statutes of Adalhard, *Corpus*, I, p. 365.

4. *Vita Willelmi*, 8, AS mai, VI, 811.

5. Hariulf: *Chron. Centulensis*, ed. Lot, p. 302.

6. E. Lesne, *Les Eglises*, pp. 391, 414.

7. Ibid., p. 48.

8. For Ferrières, Lupus: *Epist.* 49. For Aniane, *Vita Benedicti*, 22. For Saint-Riquier, Hariulf, ed. Lot, p. 70. For Charroux, O. G. Oexle, "Le monastère de Charroux au IXᵉ siècle," *Le Moyen Age* (1970), p. 193. For Saint-Germain-des-Près, diploma of 13 January 829.

Chapter 6

1. E. Ewig, "Résidence et capitale," R.H. (1963), pp. 29–71. The Actes du Colloque de Compiègne-Paris, April 1973, on *Les palais impériaux, royaux et princiers (IIIᵉ–XIIᵉ siècles)*, *Francia*, IV (1976).

2. Astronomer, 7.

3. W. Schiesinger and Gauert: *Deutsche Königspfalzen*, 1955–1963. W. Sage, "Zur archäelogischen Untersuchung Karolingischer Pfalzen in Deutschland," in *Karl der Grosse*, III, p. 323. On the excavation of Doué-la-Fontaine, cf. *Archéologie Médiévale*, III–IV (1973–74), pp. 5–110.

4. *Capit.*, I, pp. 250, 254.

5. S. Martinet, "Un palais décrit dans un manuscrit carolingien," *Mémoires de la Fédération des Sociétés savantes de l'Aisne*, XII (1966), pp. 1–13.

6. L. Hugot, "Die Pfalz Karls des Grossen in Aachen," in *Karl der Grosse*, III, pp. 534–572.

7. Ermold, p. 159.

8. *Capit.*, I, p. 298. *Capitul. De disciplina palatii* (820).

9. M. Vieillard-Troiekouroff, "La Chapelle de Charles le Chauve à Compiègne," *Cahiers Archéologiques* (1971), pp. 89–108.

Chapter 7

1. Abbo, p. 24; *Annales Fulda*, 782; Ermold, p. 212.

2. F. Lot, "Conjectures démographiques sur la France au IXᵉ siècle," *Le Moyen Age* (1921), p. 21, and *Naissance de la France*, Paris, 1948, p. 698.

3. R. Fossier, *La terre et les hommes en Picardie jusqu'à la fin du XIIIᵉ siècle*, Paris, 1968, v.1, p. 225. H. van Werreke, *La densité de la population du IXe siecle; Essai d'estimation in Annales du XXXᵉ Congrès de la Féd. archéol. et hist. de Begique*, 1936.

4. *Vita Caroli*, 30.

5. *Annales Bertin*, 869.

6. Regino, *De synodalibus causis*, II, 61.

7. *Annales de Lorsch*, 793; *Annales Fulda*, 868. Cf. Doehaerd, pp. 58–59, and the table, infra, pp. 250–251. On famines, see F. Curshmann, *Hungersnote im Mittelalter, VIII–XIII*, Leipzig, 1900, and M. Rouche, "Le problème de la faim à l'époque carolingienne, RH (1973), pp. 295–320.

8. Astronomer, 56.

9. See the work collected by J. T. Noonan, *Contraception: A History of Its Treatment by Theologians and Canonists*,

Cambridge, Mass., 1966.

10. Theodulf, *Statuta*, ed. de Clercq, in *La législation religieuse franque*, I, 338.

11. *Pénitential du Ps. Bede* II, 4, PL 94, 571; Regino, *De Synodalibus causis*, II, 66.

12. Gerbald de Liège, ed. de Clercq, in *La législation religieuse franque*, p. 360; Regino, *De Synodalibus causis*, II, 89.

13. Regino: *De synodalibus*, II, 82: *paupercula pro difficultate nutriendi.*

14. *Vita Leobae*, MGH SS XV, p. 127; Eng. trans., C. H. Talbot, *The Anglo-Saxon Missionaries in Germany*, New York, 1954.

15. Regino, *De synodalibus*, II, 60–69.

16. Diploma, ed. Muratori, *Antiquitates Italiae*, III, p. 587.

17. Jonas, *De institutione laicali*, II, *passim*. PL, 106, 121 ff. Cf. J. Chelini, *Les laïcs dans la société ecclésiastique carolingienne*, in *I laici nella società cristiana dei secoli XIe–XIIe*, *Acta della terza Settimana internazionale di studio Mendola, 1965*, Milan, 1968, p. 45. Also "La vie religieuse des laïcs dans l'Europe carolingien," thèse dactylographiée, Paris, 1974.

18. *Penitential of Pseudo-Bede*, PL 94, c. 573; English trans., J. McNeill and H. Gamer, *Medieval Handbooks of Penance*, New York, 1938.

19. *Vita Geraldi*, I, 2, PL 133, 643.

20. Jonas, *De Institutione laicali*, II, 4.

21. *Vita Caroli*, 18–20; *Annales Bertin.* 869; Thegan, *Vita Ludovici*, II, 4.

22. *Vita Geraldi*, I, 9.

23. Cf. supra, p. 34. Hariulf, *Chronique Saint-Riquier*, ed. Lot, p. 99; Astronomer, 23.

24. *Capit.*, I, p. 298.

25. *Lex Alem.*, 58; *Leges*, V, 1, p. 115. English trans., T. J. Rivers, *Laws of the Alamans and Bavarians*, Philadelphia, 1977.

26. Cf. C. Vogel, *Le pécheur et la pénitence au Moyen Age*, Paris, 1969, pp. 74–75.

27. Theodulf, *Statuta*, PL 105, 219.

28. Hincmar, *De nuptiis Stephani*, PL 136, 133. Cf. K. Ritzer, *Le mariage dans les églises chrétiennes du Ier au XIe siècle*, Paris, 1970, p. 270.

29. *Capit.*, I, 36.

30. P. Daudet, *Etudes sur l'histoire de la juridiction matrimoniale*, Paris, 1941.

31. On this affair, see E. Amman, *L'époque carolingienne*, pp. 370ff.

32. Cf. infra, p. 260.

33. Hincmar, *De nuptiis Stephani*, PL 136.

34. Boniface, *Epist.*, III, p. 276.

35. *Dicta Pirmini*, PL 89, 1037.

Chapter 8

1. G. Tellenbach, *Studien und Vorarbeiten zur Geschichte des Grossfränkischen und Frühdeutschen Adels*, Fribourg-en-Brisgau, 1957. K. F. Werner, "Bedeutende Adelsfamilien im Reich Karls des Grossen," in *Karl der Grosse*, I, pp. 83–142; L. Genicot, "La noblesse dans la société médiévale," in *Le Moyen Age* (1965), pp. 539–560. Also, "The Nobility in Medieval Francia," in F. Cheyette, *Lordship and Community in Medieval Europe*, New York, 1967, pp. 128–136.

2. Dhuoda, *Manuel pour mon fils*, p. 354.

3. Cf. infra, p. 242.

4. Hrabanus Maurus, *Liber de reverentia filiorum erga patres et erga reges*, *Epist.*, V, p. 403.

5. *Lex Bavar.* II, 9 MGH Leges V, 2, p. 302.

6. *Vita Caroli*, 19.

7. *Vita Caroli*, 20; Regino, *Chron.* 879.

8. Nithard, IV, 6.

9. *Annales Bertin*, 846; *Annales Fulda*, 887.

10. Lupus, *Epist.* 3 and 4.

11. Regino, *Chron.*, 876.

12. Ed. 887.

13. Dhuoda, *Manuel*, p. 352.

14. Cf. A. R. Lewis, *The Development of Southern French and Catalan Society, 718–1050*, Austin, 1965, pp. 123–124; J. Verdon, "Etude sur la femme en France du IX⁰ au XI⁰ siècle, thèse dactyliographée, Paris 1974.

15. Dhuoda, *Manuel*, p. 167.

16. Nithard, II, 7.

17. *Capit.*, II, p. 354. Cf. L. Halphen, *Charlemagne et l'empire carolingien*, Paris, 1947, p. 321.

18. E. Delaruelle, "En relisant le 'De institutione regia' de Jonas d'Orléans, l'entrée en scène de l'épiscopat carolingien," in *Mélanges Halphen*, Paris, 1951, pp. 185–192.

19. L. Halphen, *op. cit.*, pp. 247, 264, 291, 322ff.

20. *Capit.*, II, p. 447.

21. Nithard, II, 3.

22. Astronomer, 48. *Annales Bertin*, 858.

23. Nithard, IV, 7.

Chapter 9

1. W. Metz, *Das Karolingische Reichgut*, Berlin, 1960, and the studies of Tellenbach and his pupils cited above.

2. *Concilia* II, p. 401; *Notitia*, ed. Corpus I, pp. 485–499.

3. Cf. E. Lesne, *Les Trésors*, pp. 1ff. An original fragment of the accounts of a domain of Laon or Ghent has been studied by P. Gasnault, in *Bulletin de la Société Nationale des Antiquaires de France* (1970), pp. 310–318.

4. *Capit.*, I, p. 117.

5. Ibid., p. 254 (translated in Duby, I, p. 281).

6. Ibid., p. 83 (and Duby, p. 278). One may always use the edition of the *Polyptyque de Saint-Germain-des-Près* by B. Guérard, Paris, 1836, reedited by Longnon, Paris, 1886.

7. C. E. Perrin, "Le manse dans le Polyptyque de l'abbaye de Prüm à la fin du IXe siècle," in *Etudes historiques Noël Didier*, Paris, 1960, pp. 245–258.

8. *Les Statuta* are edited by J. Semmler, in Corpus, I, pp. 355–420.

9. *Gesta patrum Fontanellensis*, ed. Lohier, p. 117.

10. Einhard, *Epist.*, V, p. 105 (trans. in Duby, I, p. 304).

11. Lupus, *Epist.* 24, 30, 42, 45, 61.

12. On the usurpations of the laity, cf. E. Lesne, *La propriété ecclésiastique et les droits régaliens*, Lille, 1922, I, 1.

13. Flodoard, *Hist. eccl. Remensis*, I, 20, and III, 13.

14. *Capit.*, I, pp. 161, 163.

15. E. Lesne, *Les Trésors*, passim, and *Mittelalterliche Schatzenverzeichnisse, I, Von der Zeit Karls des Grossen bis zur Mitte des 13. Jahrhunderts (herausgegeben vom Zentralinstitut für Kunstgeschichte in Zusammenarbeit mit Bernard Bischoff)* Munich, 1967.

16. Hariulf, *Chronique*, ed. Lot, pp. 87ff.

17. Lupus, *Epist.* 32; *Annales Bertin*, 858.

18. *Annales Bertin*, 841, 877.

19. *Capit.*, I, p. 131.

20. Hincmar, PL 136, 32.

21. Council of Douzy, ed. Mansi, XVI, p. 663.

22. *Vita Geraldi*, I, 15 and 16.

23. P. Riché, "Les Bibliothèques de trois aristocrates laïcs carolingiens," *Le Moyen Age* (1964), pp. 87–104.

24. P. Riché, "Trésors et Collections d'aristocrates laïcs carolingiens, *Cahiers archeologiques,* XXII (1972), pp. 39–46.

25. Ermold, pp. 86–88.

Chapter 10

1. J. F. Verbruggen, "L'armée et la stratégie de Charlemagne," in *Karl der Grosse,* I, pp. 420–436.

2. Hrabanus Maurus, *De procinctu militiae romanae* 13, ed. Dummler, *Zeitschrift f. Deutsches Altertum,* XV (1872), p. 444.

3. See the descriptions of Alamanian and Bavarian tombs of the eighth century in *Catalogue de l'Exposition Charlemagne,* nn. 34ff.

4. J. Hubert, *L' Empire Carolingien,* p. 22.

5. Ermold, p. 26.

6. *Vita Geraldi,* I, 5.

7. Nithard, III, 6.

8. Ermold, pp. 220, 236.

9. Abbo, p. 56.

10. *Capit.,* I, p. 168, trans. in R. Boutruche, *Seigneurie,* I, p. 366.

11. *Capit.,* I, p. 116.

12. K. F. Werner, *L'art de la guerre en Occident, VIIIᵉ–Xᵉ siècles: Un essai d'appréciation,* forthcoming in *Annales.*

13. Cf. Verbruggen, op. cit., p. 421.

14. *Capit.,* I, p. 167.

15. Ermold, pp. 15, 122.

16. Nithard, II, 10. *Annales Fulda,* 841.

17. *Poet.,* II, p. 138; French trans. in D. Norberg, *Manuel pratique de latin médieval,* Paris, 1968, p. 166.

18. Ermold, p. 35. Regino, *Chronique,* 873, *nova et exquisita machinamentorum applicantur.*

19. Regino, ibid., 891.

20. Ermold, p. 45.

21. *Vita Caroli,* 13.

22. *Diplom.,* I, p. 241. Cf. P. Riché, *Trésors et collections.*

23. Sedulius, *Poet.,* III, p. 208.

24. *Poet.,* II, p. 138; *Laude pugna non est digna nec cantatur melode,* II.

25. *Poet.,* I, p. 116. On the *Ludwigsleid,* see R. R. Bezzola, *Les origines,* p. 216. On the origins of the chansons de gestes, see R. Louis, "L'épopée française est carolingienne," in *Coloquios de Roncesvalles, 1955,* Saragoza, 1956.

26. *Capit.*, I, p. 52; *Annales Royales*, 791.

27. *Annales Fulda*, 867.

28. *Ludwigslied*, trans. Willems, Ghent, 1845.

29. *Liber exhortationis*, 38 PL 99, 240.

30. Alcuin, *De virtutibus et vitiis*, PL 101, 638. Cf. P. Riché, *De l'Education antique á l'Education chevaleresque*, Paris, 1968, pp. 41ff.

31. *Manuel*, p. 77.

32. On the mirrors of princes, see H. Anton, *Fürstenspiegel und Herrscherethos im der Karolingerzeit*, Bonn, 1968.

33. J. Chelini, *Les laïcs dans la société ecclésiastique carolingienne*, pp. 24ff.; E. Delaruelle, "Jonas et le moralisme carolingien," *Bulletin de Littérature ecclésiastique* (1954), pp. 223ff.

Chapter 11

1. Lupus, *Epist.* 26.

2. Notker, I, 4–6.

3. Cf. the work of J. Semmler, "Karl der Grosse und das Fränkische Mönchtum," in *Karl der Grosse*, III, pp. 254–289.

4. Lupus, *Epist.* 106.

5. Ibid., 35.

6. Claudius, *Epist.*, IV, p. 601. Cf. F. Prinz, *Klerus und Krieg*, Stuttgart, 1971.

7. Alcuin, *Epist.*, IV, 2, p. 422.

8. *Gesta Aldrici*, ed. Ledru, p. 196. *Capit.*, II, p. 51.

9. Sedulius, *Poet.*, III, p. 199.

10. Notker, I, 18.

11. Jonas, cited by J. Chélini, *Histoire religieuse de l'Occident médiéval*, p. 150.

12. Alcuin, *Epist.*, IV, 1, p. 183.

13. *Capit.*, I, 63.

14. On the life of monastic women there are no complete studies. See Letter of Humbert, *Epist.*, V, p. 525; *De institutione sanctimonialum*, *Concilia*, II, p. 444.

15. *Capit.*, I, p. 163.

16. P. Schmitz, "Benedict d'Aniane," *Dictionnaire d'Historie et de Géographie ecclésiastique*, VIII, 177–188. See also J. Semmler, "Benedikt von Aniane," Ph.D. thesis, Mannheim, 1971.

17. *Vita Benedicti*, PL 103, 360.

18. *Vita Geraldi*, II, 6.

19. PL 132, 675.

20. E. Amman, *L'Eglise au pouvoir des laïcs*, Paris, 1940, p. 317.

Chapter 12

1. There is no comprehensive study except the article by J. Flekenstein, "Karl der Grosse und sein Hof" in *Karl der Grosse*, I, pp. 24–25, which advantageously replaces the old work of Haureau, *Charlemagne et sa cour*, Paris, 1854. Consult the monographs of Kleinklausz, *Alcuin*, Lyons, 1948, and *Einhard*, Lyons, 1942.

2. Hincmar, *De ordine palatii*, ed. *Capit.*, II, pp. 518ff. On the value of this text, see the article by Halphen in RH (1938), 169; Halphen, *Charlemagne*, pp. 155ff.

3. *Vita Caroli*, 33.

4. F. L. Ganshof, "Charlemagne et l'usage de l'écrit en matière administrative," *Le Moyen Age* (1951), pp. 1–25.

5. Giry, *Manuel de Diplomatique*, Paris, 1894, p. 519. Cf. the treatise on tironiennes notes described in *Catalogue de l'Exposition*, p. 433.

6. Theodulf, *Poet.*, I, p. 487.

7. *Vita Caroli*, 26. Notker, I, 5–8. On the chapel, cf. J. Flekenstein, *Die Hofkapelle der deutschen Könige*, Stuttgart, 1959. Ermold, p. 175, describes a ceremony in the chapel of Ingelheim.

8. F. L. Ganshof, "Charlemagne et les Institutions de la monarchie franque," in *Karl der Grosse*, I, pp. 349–394. Expanded version in Eng. trans. B. and M. Lyons, *Frankish Institutions under Charlemagne*, New York, 1968.

9. Hincmar, 29, ed. *Capit.*, II, p. 527. See Ganshof, ibid., p. 364.

10. Lupus, *Epist.* 67; Einhard, *Epist.*, V, pp. 113, 116, 118, 122.

11. Lupus, *Epist.* 16.

12. *Vita Caroli*, 24.

13. Ibid., 21.

14. Ibid., 22.

15. Poeta Saxo, *Poet.*, I., p. 366; Ermold, p. 181.

16. Ermold, p. 141; Notker, II, 9; *Annales Royales*, 802, 810. On this "park," see K. Hauck, "Thiergärten im Pfalzbereich," *Deutschen Königspfalzen I* (1963), p. 32.

17. *Vita Caroli*, 22, 24.

18. Milo, *Poet.*, III, p. 654.

19. Ermold, p. 179.

20. *Vita Hugonis,* ed. J. van der Straeten, in *Analecta Bollandiana,* 1969, p. 233.

21. Thegan, 19 *Mirac. Benedicti,* 18 PL, 124.

22. Theodulf, *Poet.,* I, p. 483.

23. Sedulius, *Poet.,* III, p. 186.

24. Alcuin, *Epist.,* IV, p. 392.

25. Astronomer, 21–23, *Capit.,* I, p. 298.

26. Radbert (Paschasius), *Vita Walae,* PL 120, 1615; Eng. trans. A. Cabaniss, *Charlemagne's Cousins,* Syracuse, 1967. Agobard, *Liber Apologeticus,* 2 PL, 104, 307.

27. Cf. the debatable thesis of S. Epperlein, *Herrschaft und Volk im Karolingischen Imperium,* Berlin, 1969.

28. Richer, *Histoire de France,* I, 15, ed. Latouche vol. I, p. 38.

29. Thegan, 44 *Mirac. Benedicti.*

30. Alcuin, *Epist.,* IV, p. 198.

31. Agobard: *De privilegio et jure sacerdotis,* PL 104, 138–139.

32. Theodulf, *Contra judices, Poet.,* I, p. 516.

33. Jonas, *De Institutione laicali,* II, 23.

Chapter 13

1. On slavery, see B. Guerard, *Polyptyque d'Irminon, Prolégomènes,* I, p. 277. C. Verlinden, *L'Esclavage dans l'Europe médiévale,* Bruges, 1955, Vol. I, *Péninsule Ibérique et France.* Doehaerd, pp. 184–189. R. Boutruche, *Seigneurie,* p. 307.

2. R. Latouche, *Les Origines,* pp. 75, 232. R. Fossier, *La Terre et les Hommes en Picardie,* I, 187.

3. Doehaerd, pp. 169–170.

4. Duby, I, p. 307.

5. H. Wopfner, *Urkunden z. Agrargeschichte,* p. 36.

6. *Cartulaire de Brioude,* n. 233.

7. A. Dupont, "L'Aprisio et le régime aprisionaire dans le Midi de la France," *Le Moyen Age* (1965), pp. 179–213, 375–397.

8. Duby, I, p. 298; Doehaerd, p. 167.

9. Doehaerd, pp. 188–89.

10. C. E. Perrin, "Observations sur le manse dans la région parisienne au début du IXe siècle," *Annales* (1945), pp. 39–52.

11. Duby, pp. 91ff.

12. Doehaerd, p. 187.

13. Ibid., p. 190, and Duby, I, pp. 103–107.

14. Duby, I, pp. 282–284.

15. F. L. Ganshof, *La Belgique Carolingienne,* p. 105; Doehaerd, pp. 194–195.

16. De Vaissette, *Histoire du Languedoc,* Vol. II, *Preuves,* n. 161. *Cartulaire de Brioude,* n. 192. Cf. G. Fournier, *Le Peuplement rural en Basse Auvergne durant le Haut Moyen Age,* Paris, 1962, p. 318.

17. *Lex Bavar.,* X, 7, 11.

18. W. Sage, "Frühmittelalterliches Holzbau," in *Karl der Grosse,* III, pp. 573–590.

19. *De villis,* 49. *Lex Salica,* I, 14, ed. Eckardt, 1969, p. 53.

20. *Vita Geraldi,* II, 21.

21. *Lex salica emendata,* 47.

22. Regino, *De synodalibus,* II, 64.

23. Texts on the creation of parishes in Duby, I, pp. 307–308. For the Auvergne, see G. Fournier, op. cit., pp. 427–428. One could also consult Imbart de la Tour, *Les Paroisses rurales du IVᵉ au XIᵉ siècle,* Paris, 1900.

24. Except for the Midi, see M. Durliat, "L'Eglise d'Argelliers; Une construction de l'époque de saint Benoît d'Aniane, *Revue Archéologique de Narbonaise,* I (1968), pp. 233–247.

25. Regino, *De synodalibus,* I, *interrogatio,* 39, 50, 70, 71.

26. Theodulf, *Statut synodal* 13, PL 105, 191.

27. *Capit. de Mantoue,* Capit., I, 93.

28. Regino, *De synodalibus,* I., *interrogatio,* 13–14.

29. *Formulae,* ed. Zeumer, p. 383.

30. Duby, I, p. 118.

31. Doehaerd, pp. 197–198.

32. *Capit.,* II, p. 323; trans. in Duby, I, p. 292.

33. *Cartulaire de Redon,* n. 260. Flodoard, *Hist. Eccl. Remensis,* II, 19.

34. *Vita Geraldi,* I, 24.

35. *Capit.,* I, 124, 301; II, 177, 209.

36. Ibid., II, 375.

37. *Annales Bertin,* 859; *Annales Fulda,* 873.

38. Regino, *Chronique,* 882.

39. *Capit.,* I, 123.

40. R. Latouche, *Les Origines,* pp. 179ff. M. Sabbé, "Quelques types de marchands au IXᵉ et Xᵉ siècles," *Revue Belge de Philologie et d'Histoire* (1934), pp. 176–187. F. Vercauteren, "La Circulation des marchands en Europe occidentale du VIᵉ au Xᵉ siècle," *Settimana,* XI (1964), p. 393.

41. *Capit.,* I, p. 30, and II, p. 317.

42. *Mirac. Sancti Germani,* AS mai, VI, p. 779.

43. Lupus, *Epist.* 122.

44. *Mirac. Sancti Philiberti*, I, 71. Cf. Lesne, *Les Eglises*, pp. 401ff.

45. *Mirac. Sancti Huberti*, AS, I, p. 819.

46. Ermold, p. 211.

47. Doehaerd, "Ce qu'on vendait et comment on le vendait dans le bassin parisien," *Annales* (1947).

48. Doehaerd, pp. 212, 228. *Capit.*, II, p. 251. Latouche, *Les Origines*, p. 185.

49. *Capit.*, I, p. 123.

50. *Formulae*, ed. Zeumer, p. 315. Cf. F. L. Ganshof, *Note sur le praeceptum negotiatorum in Studi A. Sapori*, Milan, 1957.

51. Halphen. *Charlemagne et l'Empire carolingien*, pp. 179–180. Ganshof, *A propos du tonlieu à l'époque carolingienne*, *Settimana*, VI (1959).

52. Alcuin, *Epist.* IV, p. 119. Cf. H. Laurent, "Marchands de palais et marchands d'abbayes, RH (1938), pp. 281–297.

53. Doehaerd, p. 283. H. Jankuhn, "Der fränkisch friesische Handel zur Ostsee in frühen Mittelalter," *Vierteljahrshrift f. Sozial-und Wirschaftsgeschichte*, XL (1953), pp. 193–243. On Anscharius' voyage, see *Vita Anscharii*, PL 118, 960.

54. A. Verhulst, "Origines et histoire ancienne de Bruges," *Le Moyen Age* (1960), p. 58.

55. Ed. and trans. Hadj Sadok, Algiers, 1949, p. 21.

56. Notker, I, 16.

57. *Capit.*, II, p. 130; *Annales Fulda*, 860. On Venice, see G. Luzzato, "Les Activités économiques du patriciat vénitien," *Annales* (1936), p. 26.

58. *Vita Geraldi*, I, 27. Cf. F. L. Ganshof, "Note sur un passage de la vie de Saint Gerauld," in *Mélanges Iorga*, Paris, 1953, pp. 295–307.

59. Theodulf, *Poet.*, I, p. 497.

60. Cf. Verlinden, op. cit.

61. *Itinerarium Bernardi*, PL 121, 569.

62. *Capit.*, I, pp. 51, 190. *Formulae*, ed. Zeumer, p. 325; *Capit.*, II, p. 41.

63. Agobard, *Epist.* V, p. 179. Cf. Verlinden, op. cit., p. 707.

64. Doehaerd, pp. 324–325.

65. Cf. the study by B. Guérard, in *Polégomènes de l'èdition du Polyptyque d'Irminon*, pp. 141ff., and Doehaerd, p. 326.

66. *Capit.*, I, p. 149.

67. Ibid., pp. 132, 187; II, pp. 87, 92. On "just price," see Vercauteren, "Monnaie et circulation monétaire en Belgique et

dans de Nord de la France du VIe au XIe siècle," *Settimana,* VIII (1961), p. 294.

68. *Annales Fulda,* 879.

69. *Capit.,* I, 74. Cf. Latouche, *Origines,* p. 182.

70. *Capit.,* I, p. 172.

71. There is no study on medieval weights and measures. See suggestions given by B. Guérard, *Prolégomènes,* pp. 159–196, and the article by Guilhermoz cited n. 73. For the *bonnier,* see L. Musset, "Observations historiques sur un mesure agraire, le bonnier," in *Mélanges Halphen,* Paris, 1951, pp. 535–542.

72. Notker, II, 1.

73. *De villis,* 9.

74. P. Guilhermoz, *Remarques diverses sur les poids et mesures du Moyen Age,* in *Bibliothèque de l'Ecole des Chartres,* 1919, pp. 5–100.

75. *Capit.,* II, pp. 44, 63, 318.

76. There are several studies on Carolingian coinage. See Doehaerd, pp. 306ff.; Grierson, "Money and Coinage under Charlemagne," in *Karl der Grosse,* I, pp. 501, 536; and the re-statement of J. Lefaurie, "Numismatique des Carolingiens aux Capétiens," in *Cahiers de Civilization médiévale,* 1970, pp. 117–137.

77. *Capit.,* I, p. 32.

78. *Capit.,* I, pp. 12, 140.

79. Ibid., p. 74.

80. Ibid., p. 152.

81. *Capit.,* II, p. 316.

82. *Capit.,* I, p. 140.

83. Cf. Lefaurie, op. cit., p. 120.

84. *Capit.,* II, p. 316.

85. Vercauteren, op. cit., p. 290.

86. Lupus, *Epist.* 75.

87. Doehaerd, p. 314.

88. *Capit.,* II, p. 310.

89. Doehaerd, pp. 334ff.

90. *Capit.,* I, p. 216.

91. Regino, *De synodalibus,* I, 221–228.

92. On the Jews, see B. Blumenkranz, *Juifs et Chrétiens dans le monde occidental, 430–1096,* Paris, 1960; and S. W. Baron, *A Social and Religious History of the Jews,* Philadelphia, 1957, Vol. IV, 48.

93. Letter of Stephen to Aribert, PL 129, 857. Cartulary of Saint-André le-Bas de Vienne, p. 211. Cf. R. Latouche, "Le Bourg des juifs de Vienne au Xe siècle,' in *Etudes N. Didier,* Paris, 1960, pp. 189–194.

94. *Formulae*, ed. Zeumer, pp. 309, 325, Agobard, *Epist.*
V, p. 182. Amolon, *Liber contra judaeos*, PL 116, 180.

95. *Annales Bertin*, 848, 852, 877.

96. Cf. Blumenkranz, op. cit., pp. 6–7.

97. On the alimentary customs of the *Judaisantes*, cf.
Epist., V, 200. On the prohibition of the Saturday rest, *Capit.*,
II, 417, *Exceptiones Egberti*, PL 89, 398; Agobard, *De judaeorum
superstitionibus*, *Epist.*, V, p. 185; Amolon, op. cit., PL, 116, 141.

98. *Annales Bertin*, 839.

99. *Alvari epist.*, ed. Madoz, pp. 211, 223, 241, 277. Cf.
B. Blumenkranz, *Des Auteurs chrétiens latin du Moyen Age sur
les Juifs et le judaïsme*, Paris, 1963, pp. 184–191.

100. *Epist. de baptizandis hebraeis*, *Epist.*, V., 229.

101. *Capit.*, II, p. 416.

102. *Capit.*, I, pp. 152, 259. *Formulae*, ed. Zeumer, p. 309.
Capit., II, p. 361.

103. Amalarius, *De ecclesiasticis officiis*, I, 19. Cf. Wilmart, "Un lecteur inconnu d'Amalaire," *Revue Bénédictine*
(1924), pp. 323, 329.

104. A. Graboïs, "Souvenir et légendes de Charlemagne
dans les textes hébraïques médiévaux," *Le Moyen Age* (1966),
pp. 22–23.

105. Alcuin, *Epist.*, IV, p. 285. Claudius of Turin, *In gen.*,
PL 104, 918. On the influence of Judaism, cf. De Lubac, *Exégèse
médiévale*, II (1959), pp. 147–148.

Chapter 14

1. J. Le Goff, "Travail technique et artisans dans le
système des valeurs du Haut Moyen Age (V^e–Xe siècles),"
Settimana, XVIII (1971), p. 329.

2. *Capit.*, I, p. 61.

3. H. Stern, "Poésies et représentations carolingiennes et
byzantines des mois," *Revue Archéologique* (1955), pp. 141ff.

4. *Vita Caroli*, 29.

5. Theodulf, *Carmina*, IV, 2.

6. Duby, *Economie*, I, p. 77.

7. Ermold, p. 178.

8. *Capit.*, II, p. 324; trans. Duby, I, p. 293.

9. Duby, *Economie*, I, p. 83.

10. *Gesta abb. Rotonensium*, II, Preface.

11. *Lex Salica*, XXXVI.

12. M. Bloch, "Avènement et conquête du moulin à eau,"
Annales (1935), p. 538; Eng. trans. J. E. Anderson, in *Land and*

Work in Medieval Europe: Selected Papers by Marc Bloch, New York, 1969. Duby, I, pp. 72–73.

13. Text translated in Duby, I, p. 300.

14. Duby, I, p. 85. *Contra* B. H. Slicher van Bath, "Le Climat et les récoltes au Haut Moyen Age," *Settimana*, XIII (1966), p. 414, and V. Fumagalli in *Rivista di Storia dell'sgricoltura italiana*, VI (1966).

15. M. Bloch, *Les Caractères originaux de l'histoire rurale française*, Paris, 1955, p. 7; Eng. trans. J. Sondheimer, *French Rural History*, London, 1966. Higounet, "Les Forêts," *Settimana*, XIII, p. 392.

16. *Capit.*, I, pp. 86, 172.

17. Doehaerd, pp. 103–105.

18. *Capit.*, II, p. 258. Cf. A. Dupont, "L'Aprisio et le régime aprisionnaire dans le Midi de la France," *Le Moyen Age* (1965), pp. 179–214, 375–399.

19. Regino, *Chronique*, 842. Ermold, p. 209. Dion, *Histoire de la vigne et du vin en France*, Paris, 1959.

20. *De villis*, 48. J. Durliat, "La Vigne et le vin dans la région parisienne au début du IXe siècle d'après le polyptyque d'Irminon," *Le Moyen Age* (1968), pp. 387–419.

21. Cf. Lesne, *Les Eglises*, p. 298.

22. *De villis*, 70. *De cultura hortorum*, ed. *Poet.*, II, 225, gesta.

23. *Consuetudines in Corpus*, I, p. 380.

24. *Formulae*, ed. Zeumer, p. 368.

25. *De villis*, 70.

26. *Lex Salica* VIII; Lesne, *Les Eglises*, p. 368.

27. Lupus, *Epist.* 106.

28. *Lex Bav.*, XIV; *Lex Alem.*, LXXIII–LXXV.

29. *De villis*, 13–14.

30. Ibid., 23, 66.

31. *Gesta Aldrici*, ed. Busson, p. 164. Cf. Lesne, *Les Eglises*, pp. 182ff.; Doehaerd, p. 78.

32. Lesne, *Les Eglises*, p. 277.

33. See "La Peinture du martyrologe de Wandalbert," in J. Hubert, *L'Empire carolingien*, p. 173; Duby, I, p. 296.

34. Einhard, *Epist.*, V., p. 105; trans. Duby, I, p. 304. *Formulae*, ed. Zeumer, p. 419.

35. Cf. infra, pp. 250–251.

Chapter 15

1. *De villis*, 62.

2. Cf. Halphen, *Etudes critiques*, p. 277.

3. P. Sternagle, *Die Artes Mechanicae im Mittelalter*, Munich, 1966 (cited by Le Goff, *Travail*, p. 260).

4. *Epist.*, VI, p. 184, *quid esset mechani, unde mechanica ars. Poet.*, III, 69.

5. *Chronique de Saint-Riquier*, ed. Lot, p. 307.

6. Lesne, *Les Eglises*, p. 262.

7. Doehaerd, p. 208. *Vita Geraldi*, II, 11.

8. Monneret de Villard, "L'Organizzazione industriale nell' Italia longobarda," *Archivio Storico Lombardo*, XLVI (1919).

9. Diploma of Louis the Pious, 829.

10. Hariulf, ed. Lot, p. 54; *Vita Geraldi*, II, 5.

11. Flodoard, *Hist. Eccl. Remens.*, II, 19.

12. Lupus, *Epist.* 25.

13. Hubert, *Europe des Invasions*, n. 278, and *L'Empire Carolingien*, n. 222.

14. *Lex Alem.*, LXXIV.

15. *Annales de Xanten*, 868.

16. *De villis*, 62.

17. Halphen, *Etudes critiques*, p. 278. Doehaerd, p. 212. R. Sprandel, *Das Eisengewerbe im Mittelalter*, Stuttgart, 1968, pp. 357–358.

18. Lupus, *Epist.* 106.

19. Notker, II, 17–18.

20. E. Salin, *La civilisation mérovingienne*, Vol. IV, *Les Techniques*, Paris, 1957, pp. 58ff.

21. Text cited by Salin, ibid., p. 275.

22. *Annales Bertin*, 869.

23. *Capit.*, I, p. 123, and II, p. 321.

24. Preserved at the museum at Bergsen and in the museum at Copenhagen. See Salin, op. cit., p. 106.

25. Notker, I, 29. Cf. Lesne, *Les Trésors*, p. 116.

26. *Vita Caroli*, 26. J. Hubert, *L'Empire carolingien*, p. 214.

27. Cf. supra, p. 122.

28. *Urkundenbuch des Landes ob der Enns*, II, p. 42; *Otfrid Evangelienbuch*, I, 1 verses 69–72, ed. Piper. Ermold, p. 212.

29. Doehaerd, p. 212.

30. *Manuel*, p. 153.

31. Salin, op. cit., pp. 211ff.

32. See Lesne, *Les Trésors*, pp. 186–187; Bischoff, "Die Uberlieferung der technischen Literatur," *Settimana*, XVIII (1971), p. 267.

Chapter 16

1. Cf. the charts of the *Catalogue de l'Exposition Charlemagne*, p. 384, and the texts relative to the construction collected by J. von Schlosser in *Quellenschriften f. Kunstgeschichte und Kunsttechnik des Mittelalters und der Neu Zeit*, series IV, Vienna, 1892.

2. *Epist.*, V, 548.

3. Ermold, p. 209. W. Zimmerman, "Ecclesia lignea und ligneis tabulis fabricata," *Bönner Jahrb. des Rhein. Landesmuseums in Bonn*, CLVIII (1958), pp. 415–454.

4. Sedulius, *Poet.*, III, p. 169.

5. *Vita Caroli*, 32; *Annales Royales*, 817; Regino, *Chronique*, 870.

6. *Vita Benedicti*, PL 103, 359.

7. On the utilization of Vitruvius, see E. de Bruyne, *Etudes d'esthétique médiévale*, Bruges, 1946, I, 243ff.; C. Heitz, "Vitruve et l'architecture du Haut Moyen Age," *Settimana*, XXII (1975), pp. 725–757.

8. See *Catalogue*, pp. 385, 391.

9. Heric, *Mirac. S. Germani*, 5.

10. Cf. J. Hubert, *L'Empire Carolingien*, pp. 1–67 and plates following p. 294.

11. Notker, I, 27. Cf. Lesne, *Les Eglises*, pp. 273–274.

12. *Vita S. Mauri*, 44, ed. Mabillon, ASOB, I, 275.

13. *Mirac. Dyonisii*, II, 38; *Gesta Sanct. Rodonensium*, II, 7.

14. *Leges Liutprandi, Leges*, IV, pp. 33, 178. Cf. Doehaerd, 239–240.

15. *Vita Pardulfi*, AS, oct. III, p. 437.

16. Flodoard, *Hist. Eccles. Remens*, III, 5. Notker, II, 11. *Gesta Wandregili*, 33; *Mirac. Maglorii*.

17. *Gesta Wandregili*, 17. *Lex Bav.*, 13. Cf. Duby, I, p. 292; C. Mathieu and G. Stoops, "Observations pétrographiques sur la paroi d'un four à chaux carolingien, in *Archéologie médiévale*, II (1972), pp. 347ff.

18. Einhard, *Epist.*, V, no. 59.

19. Einhard, *Epist.*, V, no. 61. Lupus, *Epist.* 84–85. Cf. Lesne, *Les Trésors*, p. 101.

20. *Capit.*, I, 119, 131, 136. Alcuin, *Epist.*, IV, 210; Hincmar, PL 125, 1087.

21. J. Hubert, *L'Empire Carolingien*, pp. 109, 111. A sketch for woodwork is shown on a manuscript from Sélestat (no. 104 [14], fol. 69r). Cf. B. Bischoff, op. cit., *Settimana*, XVIII (1971), p. 296, plate 5.

22. Cf. Lesne, *Les Trésors,* p. 104; *Formulae,* ed. Zeumer, p. 370. A piece of Carolingian stained glass has been discovered recently at Beauvais.

23. J. Hubert, *L'Europe des Invasions,* Paris, 1967, p. 253.

24. Heric, *Mirac. S. Germani,* 6. *Vita Caroli,* 26. Hariulf, *Chronique de Saint-Riquier,* ed. Lot, p. 54, recounts the difficult construction of the *ciborium* (*butico*).

25. Hubert, *L'Empire Carolingien,* p. 6.

26. Ermold, pp. 162–64. Agobard, PL 104, 225.

27. *Libri Carolini,* MGH; *Concilia* II, 2, pp. 151–152.

28. Ibid., p. 149.

29. See the Paris manuscript 11561 studied in *Revue Bénédictine,* 1930, p. 76.

30. Jean Diacre, *Vita Gregorii,* IV, 83, PL 75.

31. *Gesta Wandregisili,* 17; Frothaire, *Epist.,* V, 292.

32. Cf. S. Weyres, "Der Karolingische Dom zu Köln," in *Karl der Grosse,* III, 385–423.

33. *Mirac. S. Quentini,* MGH, SS, XV, p. 269.

34. *Mirac. S. Bertuini,* II, MGH, SS, XV, p. 516.

Chapter 17

1. J. Hubert, *L'Empire Carolingien,* pp. 71ff.

2. A. Peroni, *Oreficerie e metalli lavorati tardo antichi e alto medievali del territorio di Pavia,* Spoleto, 1967, p. 154.

3. G. Francastel, *Le Personnage trônant dans l'art chrétien d'Occident du IVe au XIIe siècle,* Paris, 1973.

4. M. Maccarone, A. Ferrua, *La Cattedra lignea di S. Pietro in Vaticano,* Vatican City, 1971.

5. Ermold, p. 180, verse 2354.

6. *Codex diplomaticus Alemaniae,* ed. Neugart, 1791, I, 549.

7. *De villis,* 42 (*lectaria, culcitas, plumaticas, baltlinias* . . . *drappos ad discum, bancales*).

8. *Capit.,* I, p. 254.

9. *Vita Benedicti,* 12, ed. Mabillon, ASOB, IV, I, p. 19.

10. *Vita Pardulfi,* AS, oct. III, p. 433, *agitatorium quod vulgo berciolum vocatur.*

11. *Vita Geraldi,* I, 26.

12. *De villis,* 42; Bref d'Annapes *Capitul.* I, p. 254, of Staffelsee, *ibid.,* p. 251. (*Vasa aena, plumbea, ferrea, lignea, abbedos, catenas, cramaculos. De huticis et coufinis id est scriniis.*)

13. Cf. H. Hinz, "Die Karolingische Keramik in Mittel europa," in *Karl der Grosse,* III, 262–287. M. E. Marieu, *La*

Céramique en Belgique, Brussels 1960. See also the remarks of J-M. Pesez in *Archéologie du village déserté,* Paris, 1970, p. 131.

14. Cf. *Archéologie médiévale,* I, 1971, pp. 272 and 279, and II, 1972, p. 192.

15. *Epist.,* IV, p. 116.

16. F. Rademacher, *Fränkische Gläser aus dem Rheinland in Bonn, Jahrbücher,* 1942, pp. 285–344. R. Chambon, *Histoire de la verrerie en Belgique,* Brussels 1955, and J. Barrelet, *La Verrerie en France de l'époque galloromaine à nos jours,* Paris, 1953.

17. P. Riché, *Trésors et collections d'aristocrates laïques,* p. 43–44. Lupus, *Epist.* 83, notes the wooden cups used on trips.

18. One might also consult the book of Enlart, *Manuel d'archéologie française* vol. III, Costume, Paris, 1916, p. 15–122.

19. Theodulf, *Carm.,* VI, 493.

20. Ed. J. Semmler, in *Corpus.,* I, p. 462.

21. Ibid., p. 371.

22. Ed. Hallinger, ibid., pp. 166–167.

23. *Capit.,* I, 256 and II, 248.

24. *Vita Geraldi,* I, 16 and II, 2.

25. Astronomer, 4.

26. *Vita Caroli,* 23.

27. Ermold, p. 172.

28. Cf. J. Hubert, *L'Empire Carolingien,* pp. 22, 139, 145, 152.

29. Cf. A. Boinet, *La Miniature carolingienne,* Paris, 1920, no. CLVIII and CLIX.

30. Judith offered her girdle to the church of Saint-Marcellin (Einhard, *Transl.,* 29.) See also the description of court costumes in Ermold, p. 174.

31. *Vita Hathumodae,* MGH, SS, IV, p. 167.

32. *Capit.* of 789. *Capit.* I, p. 61.

33. Cf. Lesne, *Eglises,* p. 258.

34. *De villis,* 43.

35. See the texts cited by Lesne, *Eglises,* pp. 256–261.

36. *Vita Caroli,* 19. Sedulius, *Poet.,* III, 533. Cf. texts cited by von Schlosser, *Quellenschriften,* nos. 1091–1098.

37. Cf. Lesne, *Eglises,* pp. 257–258.

38. H. Pirenne, "Draps de Frise ou draps de Flandre? in *Histoire économique de l'Occident médiéval,* Brussels, 1951, pp. 53–61. A. Geijer, Technical Viewpoints on Textile Design," *Settimana,* XVIII (1971), p. 711.

39. Cf. Wallace Hadrill, "Charlemagne and England," in *Karl der Grosse,* I, p. 693.

40. Notker, I, 34.

41. *Cartul. de Saint Bertin,* ed. Guérard, p. 66.

42. E. Sabbé, "L'importation des tissues orientaux en

Europe occidentale au Haut Moyen Age, IXe-X^e siecle," *Revue Belge de Phililogie et d'histoire*, XIV (1935), pp. 811, 1216.

43. Notker, II, 17.

44. Cf. Lesne, *Les Trésors*, pp. 241–250. P. Riché, *Collections et trésors*, pp. 42–43.

45. *Liber Pontificalis*, II, p. 76; Theodulf, *Poet.*, I, 499.

Chapter 18

1. Lesne, *Eglises*, pp. 151–152.

2. *Vita Geraldi*, I, 25. The *Vita Liudgeri* mentions that young Liudger wrote on bark (*pelliculas et cortices*) "usually employed for lighting" (*quibus ad luminaria uti solemus*), PL 99, 790.

3. References in Lesne, *Les Trésors*, pp. 218–220.

4. *Annales Fulda*, 874.

5. Lesne, *Eglises*, p. 63. At Doué-la-Fontaine a chimney has been dug up: see *Archéologie Médiévale*, I (1971), p. 273.

6. *Coutumes de Corbie*, ed. Semmler, in *Corpus*, I, p. 418.

7. *Vita Pardulfi*, AS, oct., III, 433–438.

8. Diploma, oct. 886.

9. Hincmar, *Epist.*, 9, *ad Egilonem*, PL 126.

10. Nithard, II, 8; Notker, II, 22. Saturday is called *Lourdagar* in Scandinavia. Concerning the Welsh, see *Vita Tathei*, ed. Wade-Evans, Cardiff, 1944, p. 272, *balneo parato, ut consuetudo erat in sabato*.

11. *Consuetudines*, in *Corpus*, I, pp. 436, 459, 518, 546.

12. Paulinus, *Epist.* IV, 516.

13. *Consuetudines*, in *Corpus*, I, pp. 436, 445, 459, 518, 546, 557.

14. *Capit.*, I, p. 63.

15. Ps. Bede, *De minutione sanguinis sive de phlebotomia*, PL 90, 959, recopied in 426 bis, medical advice, in MS Vat. Reg. 1625, fol. 662.

16. *Poet.*, II, 347. Poem translated by H. Leclerc, Paris, 1933. See also Lesne, *Eglises*, p. 304.

17. Laon manuscript 436 bis. Cf. E. Wickersheimer, *Manuscrits latins de médecine du Haut Moyen Age*, Paris, 1966, p. 41.

18. J. Lestocquoy, "Epices, médecine et abbayes," in *Etudes Mérovingiennes*, Paris, 1953, pp. 182ff. On this manuscript, cf. Wickersheimer idem, p. 112. The manuscript includes a recipe in Latin and Germanic (Bâle F III, 15 a), presented by G. Ets, *Altdeutsche Handschriften*, Munich, 1949, p. 26.

19. Manuscript of Poitiers 184, fol. 70. Cf. Wickersheimer, op. cit., p. 153.

20. *Pardulfi epist.* in Hincmar, ed. Sirmond, II, p. 838. Cf. the study by B. Merlette, "L'école de Laon et la médecine carolingienne," and one by H. Guillaume, "Les médecins laonnois et la science carolingienne: Questions de thérapeutique et de critique médicale," in *Actes de XCVI^e Congrès National des Sociétés savantes,* Toulouse, 1971.

21. See the Paris manuscripts analyzed by Wickersheimer, op. cit., pp. 54, 59, 61.

22. *Capit.,* I, p. 121. Hrabanus Maurus, *De institutione clericorum,* III, 1. *Poet.,* I, p. 408, and III, p. 197.

23. Manuscripts of Laon, nos. 420, 424, 444, 426 bis.

24. Wickersheimer, op. cit.; A. Beccaria, *I codici di medicina del periodo presalernitano,* Rome, 1956.

25. Manuscript of Paris 11219 and Florence. This latter is presented in *Catalogue,* no. 465.

26. Abbo, p. 64.

Chapter 19

1. *Vita Hugonis,* ed. *Analecta Bollandiana,* 1969, p. 254. *In aestivo tempore quo solent pauperibus alimenta deficere. . . .*

2. *Consuetudines,* ed. *Corpus,* I, pp. 163 (Monte Cassino), 382ff. (Corbie), 463 (legislation of 816).

3. *Würtembergische Urkundenbuch,* Stuttgart, 1849, I, 125.

4. Lesne, *Eglises,* p. 387.

5. *Vie de Saint Guénolé,* ed. Latouche, in *Mélanges d'histoire de Cornouaille,* p. 107.

6. *Vita Pardulfi,* AS, oct. III, p. 435.

7. *Vita Caroli,* 24.

8. *De villis,* 45. *Consuetudines Corbeiensis,* in *Corpus,* I, p. 376. *Casus S. Galli,* MGH, SS, II, p. 84. Cf. Lesne, *Eglises,* p. 360. Diploma of Charles the Bald for Saint Denis, 862, ed. Tardif, p. 117.

9. *Vita Geraldi,* II, 27.

10. *Consuetudines,* in *Corpus* I, p. 403. *De numero et divisione porcorum.*

11. *De villis,* 21 and 65v.

12. Notker, II, 6.

13. Cf. fishing scenes in *Vita Hugberti,* 8, MGH, SRM, VI, p. 487; *Miracula Remacli,* AS, sept., I, p. 701. A servitor of Gerald caught a *"capito"* in the Aveyron, *Vita Geraldi,* II, 29. This fish, mentioned in the Moselle poem of Ausonius, seems unknown elsewhere.

14. Cf. Lesne, *Eglises,* pp. 376–378.

15. Notker, I, 15. Alcuin, *Poet.* I, p. 220. Lesne, *Eglises,* p. 375.

16. Hrabanus Maurus, *De Universo,* PL 111, 505; *De villis,*

70; *Concil.,* I, 402; Lesne, *Eglises,* pp. 298ff., 368, 374. A sacramentary has recorded a prayer for beans, PL 121, 849.

17. *De villis,* 70 and 22; Walafrid Strabo, *Poet.,* II, 347.

18. Einhard, *Epist.,* 56. Lesne, *Eglises,* pp. 366–67.

19. The presence of a spice market at Cambrai is discussed. Cf. Sabbé, "L'importation des tissus orientaux," op. cit., p. 893.

20. On this manuscript, see Lestocquoy, op. cit., p. 185.

21. *Poet.,* IV, p. 591.

22. Theodulf, *Poet.,* I, 454; Alcuin, *Epist.,* III, p. 33; *Poet.,* I, 269.

23. Regino, *De synodalibus;* PL 132, 219.

24. *Poet.,* IV, 665.

25. On the parody of the Salic law, see d'Avalle, *Protostoria delle lingue romanze,* Turin, 1965.

26. Milon, *De sobrietate, Poet.,* III, 615; *carmina potatoria, Poet.,* IV, 350; Lupus, *Epist.* 65. Paul the Deacon, *Conjurationes convivarium pro potu,* I, p. 65. On *potationes,* cf. infra, p. 264.

27. *Casus S. Galli,* MGH, SS, II, p. 105. *Mirac. S. Germani,* 21.

28. *Conc.,* II, 401.

29. Sedulius, *Poet.,* III, 215.

30. Cf. Lesne, *Eglises,* pp. 346–348. J. Dekkers, "Recherches sur l'histoire des brasseries dans la region mosane au Moyen Age," *Le Moyen Age* (1970), pp. 446ff.

31. *De villis,* 45; Lupus, *Epist.* 30; *Cartulaire de Redon,* ed. Aurélien de Courson, p. 257. Letter of Theodomar to Charlemagne, ed. *Corpus,* I, 165.

32. Lupus, *Epist.* 30.

33. *Gesta Aldrici,* 69.

34. Lesne, *Eglises,* p. 46.

35. Verse written on the Laonnais manuscript *Vat. Reg.* 1625, studied by C. Leonardi, "Nuove voci poetiche tra secolo IXᵉ–Xᵉ s.," *Studi Medievali* (1961), p. 148.

Chapter 20

1. *Indiculus superstitionum et paganiarum,* ed. *Capit.,* I, p. 26. Council of Frankfurt, 43; de Tours, 42. Statutes of Gerbald of Liège, ed. De Clercq, *La Législation religieuse,* I, 360. One can find studies on pagan beliefs in Salin, *La Civilization mérovingienne,* Paris, 1959, Vol. IV, but the relative texts for the ninth century are not collected.

2. *Capit.,* I, p. 68.

3. Boniface, *Epist.,* III, p. 301.

4. Pirmin, *Scarapsus,* PL 89, 1036–1050.

5. *Indiculus: De sacrilegio ad sepulcra mortuorum, De sacrilegio super defunctos id est dadsicas . . . ,* Diocesan statute

of Besancon, ed. De Clercq, *La législation*, p. 372; Regino, *De synodalibus*, II, 55.

6. *Indiculus: De divinis vel sortilegis* . . . , Hrabanus Maurus, Penitential to Heribald, 30–31, PL 110, 471–494. *De magicis artibus*, PL 110, 1095. *Capit.*, II, p. 44. See P. Riché, *La Magie Carolingienne* in *Comptes Rendus de l'Académie des Inscriptions et Belles Lettres*, 1973.

7. Agobard, *Liber contra insulsam vulgi opinionem de grandine*, PL 104, 147.

8. *Capit.*, II, pp. 44–45.

9. Ibid., p. 345.

10. Regino: *De synodalibus*, II, 45, and 364; PL, 132, 352.

11. *Lex Salica*, 96. *Capitul. saxon.*, art. 6. *Lex Lomb.*, 379. Cf. J. C. Baroja, *Les sorcières et leur monde*, Paris, 1972, p. 75; Eng. trans., O. N. V. Glendinning, *The World of the Witches*, Chicago, 1973.

12. Nithard, I, 5; Paschasius Radbertus, *Vita Walae*, PL 120, 1617.

13. *Lex Bav.* 13, 8; *Lex Salica*, 32, p. 213.

14. Regino, II, 5ff., Statutes of Gerbald of Liège, 10, ed. de Clercq, *La législation* . . . , p. 360; Hincmar, PL 125, 716–717.

15. Cf. text in Jolivet-Mossé, *Manuel de l'allemand du Moyen Age*, Paris, 1959, pp. 310–313.

16. Regino, II, 367, PL 132, 353. *Concil.*, II, p. 292.

17. Boniface, Ep., 50, *Epist.*, III, p. 301.

18. *Indiculus: De ligneis pedibus vel manibus pagano ritu.* Pirmin, *Scarapus*, 5.

19. *Indiculus: De auguriis vel avium vel equorum vel bovum stercore vel sternutatione. De cerebro animalium. Admonitio Generalis*, 65. Capitulary of 802, 25. Statutes of Gerbald de Liège, 10, ed. De Clercq, p. 360.

20. Cf. E. Wickersheimer, "Figures médico-astrologiques des IXᵉ, Xᵉ, et XIᵉ siècles," *Janus* (1914), p. 157.

21. Regino, II, 367, PL 32, 353. MS of Paris 2773 and MS of Reims 73. Cf. Wickersheimer, pp. 56, 154.

22. *Indiculus: De eo quod credunt quia feminae lunam commendent. . . . De luna defectione quod dicunt Vince luna.* MS of Paris 11218. Cf. Wickersheimer, p. 110.

23. Hrabanus Maurus, *Homelia*, 42, PL 110.

24. Cf. Wickersheimer, pp. 40, 54.

25. *Vita Caroli*, 33; *Annales Bertin*, 842. Cf. Astronomical manuscripts presented in *Catalogue*, nos. 479, 480, 485.

26. Alcuin, *Epist.*, IV, pp. 185, 231, 249, 281; Dungal, p. 571.

27. *Vita Caroli*, 31. Einhard, *Epist.*, V, p. 129; Astronomer, 58–59, 62; Nithard, III, 5.

28. Lupus, *Epist.* 8.

29. *Poet.*, III, p. 321.

30. Einhard, *Translatio S. Marcellini*, 48; *Annales Fulda*, 874.

31. *Visio cuiusdam pauperculae mulieris*, ed. Wattenbach-Levison, *Deutschlands Geschichtsquellen im Mittelalter*, III, 317. *Visio Caroli* in Hariulf, *Chronique de Saint-Riquier*, ed. Lot, p. 144. *Visio Wettini*, *Poet.*, II, 303.

32. Paulinus of Aquilea, *Exhortatio*, 60.

33. Einhard, *Translatio S. Marcellini*, 49–50, 92.

34. *Annales Bertin*, 873; *Annales Fulda*, 858.

35. *Ecloga duorum sanctimonialum*, ed. Mabillon ASOB, IV, 1, p. 321. Abbo, p. 85.

Chapter 21

1. *Admonitio generalis* of 789, Preface.

2. P. Riché, *Education et Culture dans l'Occident barbare*, 3d ed., Paris, 1973, p. 550; Eng. trans. J. Contreni, *Education and Culture in the Barbarian West*, Columbia, South Carolina, 1976, p. 496.

3. *Capit.*, I, p. 60.

4. *Epistula de litteris colendis*, ibid., p. 79; *Concil.*, II, 169, p. 274. Cf. L. Wallach, *Alcuin and Charlemagne*, Ithaca, N. Y., 1959, pp. 198–226.

5. Chrodegang, *Regula*, PL 89, 1057.

6. *Concil.*, II, p. 318.

7. *Concil.*, II, pp. 471, 632; *Capit.*, II, p. 392.

8. *Capit.*, I, 32.

9. *Concil.*, II, p. 553.

10. *Capit.*, II, 37; *Concil.*, II, p. 669. Cf. Lesne, *Les Ecoles*, pp. 30–31.

11. Boniface, *Epist.*, III, 336.

12. Cf. Statutes of Theodulf, Hincmar, Rodolphe of Bourges, Riculf of Soissons.

13. Notker, I, 10.

14. Agobard, PL 104, 334. Leidrade, *Epist.*, IV. Cf. C. Vogel, "La réforme liturgique sous Charlemagne," in *Karl der Grosse*, II, pp. 217ff.

15. *Statuta Riculfi*, PL 99, 703.

16. Regino, *De synodalibus*, I, *Interrogatio*, 81, 93, 95.

17. Cf. C. Vykoukal, "Les examens du clergé paroissial à l'époque carolingienne," *Revue d'Histoire ecclésiastique*, XIV (1913), p. 94.

18. P. Sprockhoff, *Althochdeutsche Katechetik*, Berlin, 1912.

19. *Statuta Theodulfi*, PL 95, 191.

20. *Capit.*, II, 255.

21. *Statuta Walterii*, PL 119, 725.

22. Cf. *Concilia*, II, pp. 8–32; *Epist.* III, pp. 314, 316, 348.

23. Ratramnus of Corbie, *De nativitate Christi*, PL 21, 81.

24. Text edited by C. Vykoukal, op. cit., p. 94.

25. These texts have been gathered in a Diplôme d'Etudes Supérieures by J. M. Fauchon, "Enseignement, éducation et prédication d'après les capitulaires et les actes conciliaires carolingiens," dactylographiée, Bordeaux, 1963.

26. Leiradus, Amalarius, Theodulf, PL 99, 853, 893, 105, 223.

27. *Concilia*, I, p. 172. Alcuin, *Epist.*, 90. Text edited by E. von Steinmeyer, reproduced by M. Rouche in *L'Europe au Moyen Age*, Paris, 1969, I, 162.

28. For example, see the baptistery of Nevers in M. Vieillard-Troiekouroff, "L'architecture en France au temps de Charlemagne," in *Karl der Grosse*, III, p. 357. The plate of the binding of Drogo's Sacramentary shows a representation of a baptism.

29. Cf. the edition of Irminon's Polyptich by Longnon, Paris, 1895, and A. Rosellini, "Les noms de personnes du Polyptyque de Saint-Remi de Reims de 847," *Le Moyen Age* (1962), pp. 271–291.

30. *Concilia*, II, p. 240. Theodulf, PL 105, 196; Gauthier, PL 119, 733; Riculf, ed. Labbé, IX, 416.

31. *Concilia*, II, p. 357. Alcuin, *Epist.*, IV, p. 36.

32. Alcuin, *Epist.*, IV, p. 205. Hrabanus Maurus, *De Institutione clericorum*, III, 37.

33. Boniface, *Epist.*, III, p. 271. Ermold, p. 146.

34. Theodulf, PL 105, 191, *Capit.*, I, p. 110. Cf. "XIV homélies du IXᵉ siècle," in P. Mercier (ed.), *Sources Chrétiennes*, 161, Paris, 1970.

35. *Concile de Tours de 813*, 17. *Admonitio generalis*, 82.

36. Hrabanus Maurus, *Epist.*, V, p. 391. Pirmin, *Scarapsus*, PL 89, 1049.

37. *Vita Richarii*, AS, III, Nov., p. 425.

38. Jonas, *De Institutione laicali*, I, 18.

Chapter 22

1. See P. Riché, *De l'éducation antique à l'éducation chevaleresque*, Paris 1968, p. 114. Also P. Wolff, *L'Eveil intellectuel de l'Europe*, Paris, 1971; Eng. trans. A. Carter, *The Cultural Awakening*, New York, 1968.

2. Notker, I, 1. Cf. M. Capuyns, *Jean Scot Erigène*, Louvain, 1933; reprinted Brussells, 1969.

3. See the Mémoire d'Etudes supérieures of Mme. Rouaenet-Pilorget, "Les milieux intellectuels lyonnais de Sidoine

Apollinaire à Florus (430–869)," dactylographiée, Lyons, 1948. On Florus, see Dom Charlier, "Les manuscrits personnels de Florus," in *Mélanges Podechard*, Lyons, 1945.

4. E. Jeauneau, "Les Ecoles de Laon et d'Auxerre au IXe siècle," *Settimana*, XIX (1972), pp. 495–522; and J. Contreni, "The School of Laon from 850 to 930," dissertation, Michigan State University, 1971. P. Riché, "Les hagiographes bretons et la renaissance carolingienne," *Bull. Philol. et hist.* (1966), pp. 651–659.

5. P. Riché, "Le renouveau culturel à la cour de Pépin," *Francia*, II (1974), pp. 59–70.

6. Notker, I, 3, on the palace school. Cf. Lesne, *Les Ecoles*, pp. 34ff., and F. Brunholz, "Der Bildungsauftrag der Hofschule, in *Karl der Grosse*, II, pp. 28–31.

7. Alcuin, *Poet.*, I, p. 245.

8. *Vita Caroli*, 25.

9. Heric, *Poet.*, III, 429.

10. Alcuin, PL 101, 975.

11. Alcuin, *Epist.*, IV, p. 420.

12. *Poet.*, III, 561, and IV, 261.

13. Alcuin, *Poet.*, I, 320. On the scribal workshops and libraries, see Lesne, *Livres, Scriptoria*, passim.

14. Cf. Lesne, *Livres, Scriptoria*, passim, and the work of B. Bischoff, who is preparing a collection of Carolingian manuscripts.

15. Cf. *Catalogue*, p. 204.

16. Cf. Lesne, *Livres, Scriptoria*, pp. 319ff

17. Ibid., p. 349.

18. Ibid., p. 351; *Poet.*, III, 298.

19. Lesne, *Livres, Scriptoria*, pp. 375ff.

20. Ibid., pp. 404–421.

21. J. Hubert, *L'Empire Carolingien*, pp. 70ff. J. Porcher, "La peinture provinciale," and K. Hotler, "Der Buchschmuck," in *Karl der Grosse*, III, pp. 54–114. Lupus, *Epist.* 67.

22. Cf. Vezin, "Les reliures carolingiennes en cuir," in *Bibliothèque de l'Ecole des Chartes*, 1970, pp. 81–113. J. Hubert, *L'Empire Carolingien*, pp. 222, 234.

23. Lesne, *Livres*, pp. 790ff.

24. Ibid., p. 739.

25. Hildemar, Commentary on the *Regula*, PL 66, 733.

26. Lupus, *Epist.* 1, 5, 21, 35, 53, 69, 87.

27. Hrabanus Maurus, PL 108, 1000. Walafrid, *Poet.*, III, 394.

28. Lesne, *Livres*, pp. 793ff.

29. See W. Milde, *Der Bibliothekskatalog des Klosters Murbach aus dem 9 Jahr*, Heidelberg, 1968.

30. Cf. D. Illmer, *Formen der Erziehung und Wissensvermittlung im frühen Mittelalter*, Munich, 1971, pp. 19, 25.

31. P. Riché, *Education and Culture*, p. 452; J. Leclercq, "Pédagogie et formation spirituelle du VIᵉ au XIᵉ siècle," *Settimana*, XIX (1972), p. 255.

32. Paul the Deacon, *Commentaire de la Règle*, 37, 38, 53, ed. *Bibliotheca Cassinensis*, IV, 1880.

33. Penitential of Pseudo-Bede, II, 30–32; Eng. trans. in J. McNeill and H. Gamer, *Medieval Handbooks of Penance*, New York, 1938.

34. Paul the Deacon, op. cit., 63; Alcuin, *Epist.*, IV, 95.

35. *Casus S. Galli*, 1, MGH, SS, II, 84–85. Cf. Lesne, *Ecoles*, p. 402.

36. *Capit.*, I, p. 413.

37. *Casus*, p. 93.

38. *Formulae*, ed. Zeumer, pp. 423–429.

39. *Poet.*, III, 343.

40. PL 132, 534.

41. Lesne, *Ecoles*, p. 554.

42. Smaragdus, *Grammatica*, ed. Keil, p. 20; Hrabanus Maurus, *Poet.*, II, 186.

43. Manuscript, Paris, BN, no. 2796.

44. Hildemar, Commentary, PL 66, 733.

45. *Vita Gregorii*, 2, MGH, SS, XV, 1, p. 67.

46. Ed. J. Schwalm, in *Neues Archiv.*, 1902, p. 742.

47. Alcuin, *De grammatica*, PL 101, 853.

48. Sedulius, *Poet.*, III, p. 215.

49. Paul the Deacon, op. cit., 38.

50. Cf. Bischoff, in *Mittelalterliche Studien*, Munich, 1966, I, 86–87.

51. *Manuel*, pp. 295 and 333. On digital computation, cf. A. Quacquarelli, "Ai margini dell'actio: La Loquela digitorum," *Vetera Christianorum* (1970), pp. 199ff., and the work of A. Cordiolani.

52. *Propositiones ad erudiendos juvenes*, PL 101, 1155. *Poet.*, IV, 2, p. 573. *Manuel*, p. 339.

53. A. Cordiolani, "Une encyclopédie carolingienne de Comput," in *Bibliothèque de l'Ecole des Chartes*, 1943, and "Contribution à la littérature de Comput ecclésiastique," *Studi Medievali* (1960), pp. 107–208. G. C. Meersseman, "Manuali di computo con ritmo mnemotecnico dell'archidiacono Pacifico di Verona," *Italia Sacra*, VI (Padua, 1966).

54. Theodulf, *Poet.*, I, p. 547.

55. C. Leonardi, *I Codici di Marziano Capella*, Milan, 1960.

56. Alcuin, PL 101, 854.

57. Sedulius, *Poet.*, III, p. 225.

58. Cf. L. Gougaud, *Chrétientés celtiques*, Paris, 1911,

p. 246; Eng. trans. M. Joynt, *Christianity in Celtic Lands*, London, 1932.

59. Lupus, *Epist.* 1.

60. Hrabanus Maurus, PL 107, 729. Cf. Lesne, *Livres*, p. 355.

61. Lupus, *Epist.* 5 and 21.

62. Hincmar de Reims, *Epist. ad Hincmarum*, PL 126, 448.

63. *Epist.*, V, p. 632.

64. See P. Lemerle, *Le premier humanisme byzantin*, Paris, 1971, pp. 13ff.

65. M. Cappuyns, *Jean Scot Erigène*.

66. Theodulf, *Poet.*, II, 590. *Vita Alcuini*, MGH SS, XV, p. 193. Ermenric, *Epist.*, V, 356.

67. *Vita Odonis*, PL 133, 4; *Vita Geraldi*, PL 133, 644.

68. A. De Bouard, *Manuel de Diplomatique*, Vol. II, *Acte privé*, Paris, 1948, pp. 130ff.; P. Gasnault, "Les Actes privés de l'abbaye de St-Martin de Tours, VIII–XIIe siècles," in *Bibliotheque de l'Ecole des Chartes*, 1954, p. 33.

69. See Lesne, *Livres*, pp. 446–452, and B. Bischoff, "Die Hofbibliothek Karls des Grossen," in *Karl der Grosse*, II, pp. 42–62.

70. P. Riché, *Les Bibliothèques*, pp. 87–104.

71. See the Introduction to the new edition by P. Riché.

72. Poeta Saxo, in *Poet.*, III.

73. R. Menendez Pidal, *La Chanson de Roland et la tradition épique des Francs*, Paris, 1960. R. Louis, *L'épopée française est carolingienne*.

74. Alcuin, *Epist.*, IV, pp. 175, 250. *Concilia*, II, pp. 191, 264; *Capit.*, I, p. 94.

75. *Casus S. Galli*, MGH, SS, I, p. 57. On these poems, cf. A. Fuchs, *Les débuts de la littérature allemande VIIe–XIIe siècle*, Strasbourg, 1952, pp. 39–41.

Chapter 23

1. L. Halphen, *Charlemagne*, p. 213.

2. C. Vogel, "La réforme liturgique sous Charlemagne," in *Karl der Grosse*, II, pp. 217ff.

3. J. A. Jungmann, *Missarum Sollemnia*, Paris, 1950, I, 119.

4. M. Pelt, *Etude sur la cathédrale de Metz*, Metz, 1937.

5. Regino, *De synodalibus*, PL 132, 185.

6. Alcuin, PL 98, 1230. Cf. E. de Bruyne, *Etudes d'esthétique médiévale*, I, 261ff.; Eng. trans. E. B. Hennessy, *The Esthetics of the Middle Ages*, New York, 1969.

7. *Epist.*, IV, p. 610.

8. PL 98, 1182 and 1230.

9. Hrabanus Maurus, *Ad Bonosum*, 38, *Poet.*, II, p. 160.

10. *Annales Royales*, 807. Cf. the poem *De super clysidra.*, *Poet.*, III, p. 323.

11. *Manuel*, p. 129.

12. J. Chazelas, "Les livrets de prières privées du IXᵉ siècle," in *Positions de thèses de l'ecole des chartes*, Paris, 1959.

13. Regino, *De synodalibus*, II, 1; Pirmin, *Scarapsus*, PL 89, 1036.

14. Theodulf, *Statut.*, ed. de Clercq, p. 325.

15. *Concilia*, II, p. 414. Notker, I, 10.

16. J. Chailley, *Histoire musicale du Moyen Age*, Paris, 1950, pp. 61–79.

17. Notker, II, 7.

18. Notker, I, 18. Cf. J. Hubert, *L'Empire Carolingien*, p. 138.

19. Agobard, *De correctione antiphonarii*, PL, 104–333.

20. Hincmar, *Epist.*, VIII, p. 60.

21. Regino, *De synodalibus*, I, 72.

22. Council of Chalons (813), 46–47. Regino, II, 56. Theodulf, *Statut.*, 41 and 44.

23. For the eighth century, see J. Chelini, "La pratique dominicale des laics dans l'Eglise franque sous le règne de Pépin," *Revue d'Histoire de l'Eglise de France* (1956), pp. 161–174.

24. Ed. P. Mercier, *XIV Homélies du IXᵉ siècle*, Paris, 1970, p. 187.

25. Alcuin, PL 100, 337. Jonas, PL 106, 151. Texts collected and translated by C. Vogel, *Le pécheur et la pénitence au Moyen Age*, Paris, 1969, pp. 143ff.

26. Penitential of Pseudo Egbert, ed. Wasserschleben, p. 622; trans. Vogel, op. cit., p. 127; Eng. trans. in McNeill and Gamer, *Medieval Handbooks of Penance.*

27. See texts cited by Vogel, p. 196.

28. Regino, *De synodalibus*, PL 132, 245; trans. Vogel, p. 208.

29. *Epist.*, IV, 516.

30. Theodulf, PL 105, 215.

31. *Institutio de diversitate officiorum* in Hariulf, ed. Lot, p. 296; text studied by C. Heitz, *Recherches sur les rapports entre architecture et liturgie à l'époque carolingienne*, Paris, 1963, pp. 77ff.

32. List of feasts in *Concile de Mayence de 813*, c. 36. *Annales Bertin*, 862.

33. J. Leclercq, *La spiritualité médiévale*, Paris, 1961, pp. 115–116.

34. *Capit.*, I, p. 74.

35. Ed. A. Wilmart, "Le règlement ecclésiastique de Berne," *Revue Bénédictine* (1939), pp. 37–52.

36. K. Schmid, "Die Gemeinschaft der Lebenden und

Verstorbenen in Zeugnissen des Mittelalters," *Frühmittelalterliche Studien,* I (1967), p. 365.

37. Ed. MGH, *Libri memoriales,* I, 1970.

38. Hincmar, PL 125, 794. On cemeteries, see Lesne, *Eglises,* p. 137.

39. Cartulary of Redon, p. 184.

40. *Annales Bertin,* 877.

41. Hariulf, *Chronique,* ed. Lot, p. 265.

42. Le Blant, *Inscriptions chrétiennes de la Gaule,* II, 428.

43. Cartulary of Cisoing, p. 11. Cf. Molinier, *Les obituaires français au Moyen Age,* Paris, 1890.

44. *Manuel,* p. 357. See the epitaph of Alcuin and comments of Wallach, *Alcuin and Charlemagne,* pp. 256–265.

45. *Capit.,* II, p. 429.

46. Theodulf, *Statut.,* ed. de Clercq, pp. 347ff.

Chapter 24

1. *Vita Pardulfi,* 12. Einhard, *Transl.,* 14 and 42. *Vitae Liobae,* MGH, SS XV, p. 127. Cf. Lesne, *Eglises,* p. 157.

2. *Transl.,* 64.

3. *Capit.,* I, pp. 60, 125, 132, 146, 289.

4. Ibid., I, 49.

5. Ibid., I, p. 156, 181.

6. Lupus, *Epist.* 101.

7. *Capit.,* II, p. 86.

8. Ibid., pp. 344 and 370.

9. It would be impossible to cite all the texts which show the brutality of custom. As examples, see *Vita Geraldi,* I, 19; *Gesta episc. Cenom.,* 20, ed. Busson, p. 269; *Annales Fulda,* 866; *Annales Bertin,* 846.

10. *Capit.,* I, pp. 201, 440, 443; II, 33, 344. Regino, *De synodalibus,* II, 23, PL 132, 290.

11. A. D'Haenens, *Les Invasions normandes: une catastrophe?* Paris, 1970.

12. Abbo, p. 23.

13. Marc Bloch, *La Société féodale,* Paris, 1939, I, 28ff.; Eng. trans. L. A. Manyon, *Feudal Society,* Chicago, 1961. L. Musset, *Les Invasions, VIIe–XIe siècles,* Paris, 1965.

14. Hincmar, PL 125, 983.

15. *Capit.,* II, p. 361.

16. Paschasius Radbertus, PL 120, 220; trans. in d'Haenens, *Les Invasions,* p. 84.

17. *Capit.,* II, p. 371.

18. J. Devisse, "Pauperes et paupertas dans le monde carolingien: Ce qu'en dit Hincmar de Reims," *Revue du Nord* (1966), pp. 273–287.

19. Thegan, *Vita Ludovici*, 13.

20. *Epist.*, IV, 581.

21. *Translatio S. Alexandri*, 13. Cf. F. L. Ganshof, "La protection des étrangers dans la monarchie franque," *L'Etranger* (*Recueil de la Société Jean Bodin*), IX (1958).

22. *Capit.*, II, p. 273. Regino: *De synodalibus*, II, *interrogatio*, 77, PL 132-286.

Chapter 25

1. Nithard, IV, 7. *Annales Bertin*, 832.

2. *Formulae*, ed. Zeumer, p. 174.

3. *Capit.*, I, pp. 83, 181; II, p. 343.

4. See F. L. Ganshof, "Charlemagne et l'administration de la justice," in *Karl der Grosse*, I, pp. 396ff.; expanded Eng. trans. B. and M. Lyon, *Frankish Institutions under Charlemagne*, New York, 1968.

5. Thegan, p. 139. *Lex Alam.*, 86.

6. *Capit.*, I, p. 183, trans. Halphen, *Charlemagne*, p. 152.

7. Theodulf, *Poet.*, I, p. 493; poem analyzed by G. Monod, *Les Moeurs judiciaires au VIIIᵉ siècle d'après le Paraenesis ad judices*, in RH (1887), pp. 1-20.

8. Ganshof, op. cit., p. 407.

9. Hincmar, *De Ordine palatii*, ed. *Capit.*, II, p. 526.

10. Paschasius Radbertus, *Vita Wala*, ch. 26, PL, 120.

11. F. L. Ganshof, "Charlemagne et le serment," in *Mélanges Halphen*, Paris, 1951, pp. 259, 270.

12. *Capit.*, I, pp. 51, 66. Cf. E. Coornaert, "Les Ghildes médiévales," RH (1948), pp. 33-34, and the bacchic poem of Saint Stephen published by B. Bischoff in *Mittelalterliche Studien*, II (1967), p. 69.

13. Hincmar, PL 125, 776.

14. *Capit.*, II, p. 16.

15. Ibid., p. 375.

16. Boniface, *Epist.*, III, 14.

17. Alcuin, *Epist.*, IV, 36. *Poet.*, I, 226. See the remarks of H. Fichtenau, *Das Karolingische Imperium*, Zurich, 1949, 313; French trans., Paris, 1958; English trans., New York, 1957.

18. Lupus, *Epist.* 23.

19. *Formulae*, ed. L. Rockinger, *Quellen z. Bay. Geschichte*, VII (1969), p. 138.

20. *Formulae*, ed. Zeumer, p. 158; French trans. R. Boutruche, *Seigneurie et Féodalité*, Paris, 1959, I, 331.

21. On vassalage, see Boutruche, op. cit. See also F. L. Ganshof, *Qu'est-ce que la Féodalité?* Paris-Bruxelles, 4th ed., 1968; Eng. trans. P. Grierson, *Feudalism*, New York, 1961.

22. M. Bloch, *La Société féodale*, Paris, 1939, p. 361.

23. Einhard, *Epist.*, V., pp. 105, 145; translated in R. Boutruche, op. cit., pp. 340–351.

24. *Capit.*, II, p. 358, trans. in Boutruche, I, 357.

Chapter 26

1. *Epist.*, IV, pp. 393, 399–400. Cf. L. Wallach, *Alcuin and Charlemagne*, pp. 99–140.

2. See texts cited by Lesne, *Eglises*, pp. 37ff.

3. Ibid., pp. 152–153.

4. *Admonitio generalis*, 75, Hincmar, PL 125, 77.

5. Lesne, *Eglises*, p. 113.

6. *Constitutiones Corbeienses*, II, ed. Semmler, in *Corpus*, I, pp. 372–374.

7. *Concilia*, II, p. 408.

8. Cf. Lesne, *Eglises*, pp. 152ff.

9. Hariulf, ed. Lot, p. 55. Cf. C. Heitz, op. cit., pp. 137ff.

10. *Translatio S. Sebastiani*, 19, PL 132, 579–622.

11. Hariulf, ed. Lot, p. 83. *Vita Geraldi* II, 20, and IV, 19; *Gesta sanct. Rotonensium*, II, 1; Abbo, p. 93.

12. Hariulf, ed. Lot, pp. 63–64.

13. No studies on Carolingian translations exist outside of the master's theses of C. Thiellet, "Le Culte des reliques d'après les translations carolingiennes," and N. de Baron, "La Piété populaire d'après les translations carolingiennes," dactyliographiée, University of Paris, 1971.

14. Usuard, *De translatione ss. martyrum*, PL 115, 939–960.

15. Florus, *Poet.*, II, 544, PL 104, 349.

16. Angilbert, cited by Hariulf, ed. Lot, pp. 61–62.

17. *Translatio S. Sebastiani*, 9.

18. Ibid., 39. Cf. Guiraud, "Le Commerce des reliques au IXᵉ siècle," *Mélanges de Rossi, Mélanges de l'Ecole Française de Rome*, XII (1892), and H. Silvestre, "Le Commerce et le vol des reliques," *Revue Belge de Philol. et d'Histoire*, XXX (1952), pp. 721–739. P. J. Geary, *Furta sacra*, Princeton, 1977.

19. *Translatio S. Sebastiani*, 15.

20. *Translatio S. Marcellini*, 22.

21. Cf. Lot, *Mélanges d'histoire bretonne*, Paris, 1967, pp. 137–138, and P. Riché, "Translations de reliques á l'époque Carolingienne: Histoire des reliques de S. Malo," *Le Moyen Âge* (1976), pp. 201–218.

22. *Translatio S. Marcellini*, 21.

23. *Translatio S. Sebastiani*, 23.

24. *Translatio S. Helenae*, 14, 73. *Translatio S. Sebastiani*, 37.

25. Ermentaire, *Mirac. Philiberti*, ed. Poupardin, Paris, 1905, pp. 60ff.

26. P. Gasnault, "Le Tombeau de saint Martin et les Invasions Normandes," *Revue de l'Eglise de France* (1961), pp. 51–66. L. Musset, *Les Invasions*, Paris, 1965, pp. 220–221.

27. P. Riché, "Conséquences des Invasions normandes sur la culture monastique in l'Occident franc," *Settimana*, XVI (1969).

28. Abbo, pp. 85–87.

29. *Translatio S. Sebastiani*, 36.

30. Ibid., 30. *Translatio S. Marcellini*, 20, 39, 40, 86. *Translatio S. Helenae*, 64.

31. *Translatio S. Marcellini*, 39, 41, 61, 52, 39, 46.

32. *Translatio S. Regnoberti*, 16.

33. *Epist.*, V, pp. 206, 366.

34. *Annales Royales*, 804.

35. Iso, *Mirac. Othmari*, PL 121, 779–796.

36. There is no book on early medieval pilgrimages. H. Venece presented a thesis to the Gregorian University of Rome in 1955, but it is still unpublished. One might consult E. R. Labande, "Pélerinages et cultes des saints en Europe jusqu'à la première croisade," *Actes du Congrès de Todi* (1961); "Pélerinages" in the *Dictionnaire d'Archéologie chrétienne et de Liturgie*, XIV, 168–184; and P. A. Sigal, *Les Marcheurs de Dieu*, Paris, 1974.

37. L. Gougaud, "Sur les routes de Rome avec les pèlerins irlandais," *Revue d'Histoire ecclésiastique* (1935), pp. 257–271.

38. Lesne, *Eglises*, pp. 103ff.

39. *Epist.*, III, p. 354.

40. *Concilia*, II, p. 140.

41. *Poet.*, I, 557; Claudius, *Epist.*, IV, 612.

42. Bernard, PL 121, 579–574.

43. See F. Avril, and J. R. Gaborit, "L'Itinerarium Bernardi monachi et les pèlerinages d'Italie du Sud pendant le Haut Moyen Age," in *Mélanges d'archéologie et d'histoire de l'Ecole française de Rome*, 1967, pp. 269–298.

44. J. W. Moore, *The Saxon Pilgrim to Rome and the Schola Saxonum*, Fribourg, 1937.

45. See "Itinèraires" in *Dictionnaire d'Archéologie*, Vol. VII, and R. Lanciani, *Monumenti antichi pubblicati per cura della Reale Accademia del Lincei*, I (1890).

46. L. Brehier, "La situation des chrétiens de Palestine à la fin du VIIIᵉ siècle," *Le Moyen Age* (1919), pp. 65–75.

47. *Vita Willibaldi*, MGH, SS, XV, pp. 87ff.

48. *De locis sanctis*, ed. Meehan, Dublin, 1958.

49. *Vita Willibaldi*, p. 101.

50. *Gesta sanct. Redonensium*, III, 8.

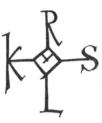

Index

Ingelheim, palace of, 14, 41, 42,
46, 76, 95, 156, 162
Irmentrude (Empress), 62, 164
Irminon, Polyptich of, 68, 137,
141, 199

Jeremy (chancellor), 93
Iso of Saint-Gall, 215
John VIII (Pope), 20, 159
John the Deacon, 157
John Scotus Erigena, 46, 145, 204,
206, 223, 224–225
Jonas (Bishop of Orleans), 26, 51,
52, 64, 82, 87, 93, 100, 238
Judith of Bavaria, 19, 62, 76, 98,
150, 165, 226
Julius Honorius, 3
Jumièges, 40, 115, 236, 271

Lambert (Count), 6
Leidrad (Bishop of Lyon), 15, 33,
194, 203
Leo III (Pope), 30, 92
Leo IV (Pope), 30, 31
Leoba (Abbess of Bischofheim),
50, 249
Liudolf (Duke), 7
Lombard Law, 11, 53, 154, 184,
260
Lothair I, 6, 13, 21, 63, 65, 72, 94,
95, 97, 98, 116, 185, 192, 226, 267
Lothair II, 46, 55, 62
Louis (Abbot of Saint-Denis),
146
Louis of Aquitaine, 21, 68, 88
Louis the German, 6, 10, 46, 62,
97, 115, 140, 147, 188, 189, 244
Louis the Pious, *passim*
Louis II, 81, 120, 229, 253
Louis III, 61, 120
Ludwigslied, 80–81
Lull of Mainz, 160
Lullus the Jew, 130
Lupus of Ferrières, 6, 10, 15, 16,
17, 21, 28, 70, 71, 84, 86, 94, 125,
142, 146, 147, 155, 176, 187, 209,
210, 214, 222, 252, 266

Mainz, Council of, 199, 212
Matfrid (Count), 82
Meaux, Council of, 15, 192, 256,
277
Meerssen, Assembly of, 64
Megenfrid (chamberlain), 97
Milo of Saint-Amand, 96

Nicholas I (Pope), 55
Nithard, 20, 61, 65, 75, 78, 187,
227, 244, 259
Normans, 6, 14, 27, 47, 68, 71, 72,
80, 81, 110, 111, 115, 128, 148,
176, 190, 205, 236, 253, 254, 256,
278, 279
Notitia de servicio monasteriorum,
67
Notker of Saint-Gall, 5, 15, 84, 92,
147, 149, 164, 205, 236

Odilo of Bavaria, 61
Odilo of Soissons, 280
Odo of Cluny, 19
Odo (Abbot of Corbie), 86, 142,
225, 266
Otfrid of Wissemburg, 149, 228

Pardoux (Saint), 155, 167, 171
Pardulf of Laon, 169, 170
Paris, Council of, 120, 183, 192,
256; siege of, 47, 76, 170, 255, 279
Partecipazio family, 116
Paschal I (Pope), 31, 275
Paschasius Radbertus, 223, 241,
256
Paul I (Pope), 165
Paul the Deacon, 201, 203, 213,
214, 218, 226
Paulinus (Bishop of Aquilea), 5,
81, 82, 189, 198, 203, 239
Pepin I, 14, 41, 42, 59, 80, 92, 112,
113, 117, 121, 122, 194, 205, 230
Pepin II, 7, 75, 82
Pepin of Herstal, 59
Pepin the Hunchbacked, 61, 206
Peter of Pisa, 130, 203
Pitres, Edict of, 110, 124
Prudentius (Bishop of Troyes),
203, 223
Prüm, 21, 68, 103, 104, 111, 118,
124, 147, 172, 210

Quierzy, Capitulary of, 268
Quininus, 42

Ratgar (Abbot of Fulda), 152
Ratramnus of Corbie, 197, 223
Regino of Prüm, 62, 126, 184, 195,
196, 227, 232, 239
Reichenau, Glossary, of, 161, 217
Richarde (wife of Charles the
Fat), 62

Index 333

University of Pennsylvania Press

Middle Ages Series

Edward Peters, General Editor

Edward Peters, ed. *Christian Society and the Crusades, 1198–1229*. Sources in Translation, including The Capture of Damietta by Oliver of Paderborn. 1971 1971

Edward Peters, ed. *The First Crusade: The Chronicle of Fulcher of Chartres and Other Source Materials.* 1971

Katherine Fischer Drew, trans. *The Burgundian Code: The Book of Constitutions or Law of Gundobad and Additional Enactments.* 1972

G. G. Coulton. *From St. Francis to Dante: Translations from the Chronicle of the Franciscan Salimbene (1221–1288).* 1972

Alan C. Kors and Edward Peters, eds. *Witchcraft in Europe, 1110–1700: A Documentary History.* 1972

Richard C. Dales *The Scientific Achievement of the Middle Ages.* 1973

Katherine Fischer Drew, trans. *The Lombard Laws.* 1973

Henry Charles Lea. *The Ordeal.* Part III of Superstition and Force. 1973

Henry Charles Lea. *Torture.* Part IV of Superstition and Force. 1973

Henry Charles Lea (Edward Peters, ed.). *The Duel and the Oath.* Parts I and II of Superstition and Force. 1974

Edward Peters, ed. *Monks, Bishops, and Pagans: Christian Culture in Gaul and Italy, 500–700.* 1975

Jeanne Krochalis and Edward Peters, ed. and trans. *The World of Piers Plowman.* 1975

Julius Goebel, Jr. *Felony and Misdemeanor: A Study in the History of Criminal Law.* 1976

Susan Mosher Stuard, ed. *Women in Medieval Society.* 1976

James Muldoon, ed. *The Expansion of Europe: The First Phase.* 1977

Clifford Peterson. *Saint Erkenwald.* 1977

Robert Somerville and Kenneth Pennington, eds. *Law, Church, and Society: Essays in Honor of Stephan Kuttner.* 1977

Donald E. Queller. *The Fourth Crusade: The Conquest of Constantinople, 1201–1204.* 1977

Pierre Riché (Jo Ann McNamara, trans.). *Daily Life in the World of Charlemagne.* 1978

Charles R. Young. *The Royal Forests of Medieval England.* 1979

Edward Peters, ed. *Heresy and Authority in Medieval Europe.* 1980

Suzanne Fonay Wemple. *Women in Frankish Society: Marriage and the Cloister, 500–900.* 1981

R. G. Davies and J. H. Denton, eds. *The English Parliament in the Middle Ages.* 1981

Edward Peters. *The Magician, the Witch, and the Law.* 1982

Barbara H. Rosenwein. *Rhinoceros Bound: Cluny in the Tenth Century.* 1982

Steven D. Sargent, ed. and trans. *On the Threshold of Exact Science: Selected Writings of Anneliese Maier on Late Medieval Natural Philosophy.* 1982

Benedicta Ward. *Miracles and the Medieval Mind: Theory, Record, and Event, 1000–1215.* 1982

Harry Turtledove, trans. *The Chronicle of Theophanes: An English Translation of* anni mundi *6095–6305 (A.D. 602–813).* 1982

Leonard Cantor, ed. *The English Medieval Landscape.* 1982

Charles T. Davis. *Dante's Italy and Other Essays.* 1984

George T. Dennis, trans. *Maurice's Strategikon: Handbook of Byzantine Military Strategy.* 1984

Thomas F. X. Noble. *The Republic of St. Peter: The Birth of the Papal State, 680–825.* 1984

Kenneth Pennington. *Pope and Bishops: The Papal Monarchy in the Twelfth and Thirteenth Centuries.* 1984

Patrick J. Geary. *Aristocracy in Provence: The Rhône Basin at the Dawn of the Carolingian Age.* 1985

C. Stephen Jaeger. *The Origins of Courtliness: Civilizing Trends and the Formation of Courtly Ideals, 939–1210.* 1985

J. N. Hillgarth, ed. *Christianity and Paganism, 350–750: The Conversion of Western Europe.* 1986

William Chester Jordan. *From Servitude to Freedom: Manumission in the Sénonais in the Thirteenth Century.* 1986

James William Brodman. *Ransoming Captives in Crusader Spain: The Order of Merced on the Christian-Islamic Frontier.* 1986

Frank Tobin. *Meister Eckhart: Thought and Language.* 1986

Daniel Bornstein, trans. Dino *Compagni's Chronicle of Florence.* 1986

James M. Powell. *Anatomy of a Crusade, 1213–1221.* 1986

Jonathan Riley-Smith. *The First Crusade and the Idea of Crusading.* 1986

Susan Mosher Stuard, ed. *Women in Medieval History and Historiography.* 1987

Avril Henry, ed. *The Mirour of Mans Saluacioune.* 1987

Marìa Menocal. *The Arabic Role in Medieval Literary History.* 1987

Margaret J. Ehrhart. *The Judgment of the Trojan Prince Paris in Medieval Literature.* 1987

Betsy Bowden. *Chaucer Aloud: The Varieties of Textual Interpretation.* 1987

Felipe Fernández-Armesto. *Before Columbus: Exploration and Colonization from the Mediterranean to the Atlantic, 1229–1492.* 1987

Michael Resler, trans. *EREC by Hartmann von Aue.* 1987

A. J. Minnis. *Medieval Theory of Authorship.* 1987